START
take 1

HDV
Filmmaking

SONY

Chad Fahs

HDV Filmmaking

Publisher and General Manager, Thomson Course Technology PTR: Stacy L. Hiquet
Associate Director of Marketing: Sarah O'Donnell
Manager of Editorial Services: Heather Talbot
Marketing Manager: Cathleen Snyder
Executive Editor: Kevin Harreld
Marketing Coordinator: Jordan Casey
Project and Copy Editor: Marta Justak
Technical Reviewer: Graeme Nattress
Thomson Course Technology PTR Editorial Services Coordinator: Elizabeth Furbish
Interior Layout Tech: Susan Honeywell
Cover Designer: Mike Tanamachi
Indexer: Kelly Talbot
Proofreader: Sara Gullion

ISBN: 1-59200-828-3
Library of Congress Catalog Card Number: 2005924929
Printed in the United States
06 07 08 09 10 PH 10 9 8 7 6 5 4 3 2 1

THOMSON

COURSE TECHNOLOGY
Professional ■ Technical ■ Reference

25 Thomson Place
Boston, MA 02210
www.courseptr.com

To my niece Kara, who was born while I was writing this book,
and the rest of my family for their love and support.

Acknowledgments

Thanks to the publishing team at Thomson, especially Kevin Harreld, Marta Justak, and Graeme Nattress.

Thanks to my agent David Fugate.

Thanks to all the filmmakers and artists who contributed interviews for this book, including Garrett Brown, Don Bluth and Gary Goldman, Brian Dressel, Jody Eldred, Steven Gonzales, Robert Hill, Paul Hirsch, and David Pfluger.

Thanks to Meghann Matwichuk for all your help and support writing this book.

Thanks to Concrete Pictures and everyone on the "MOOV" team who gave me encouragement and inspiration while writing this book.

About the Author

Chad Fahs is an author, editor, and digital filmmaker. His work as author and co-author include *Final Cut Pro 4 for Dummies, MacWorld DVD Studio Pro Bible, Mac OS X Panther in Ten Simple Steps or Less, Apple Pro Training Series: DVD Studio Pro 2, Flash MX Design for TV and Video,* and the *iPod and iTunes Digital Field Guide,* in addition to a variety of other courseware and training materials for Mac and PC users. In 1998, Chad started an Avid studio in Chicago, working with clients on commercial projects, electronic press kits, and experimental film and video projects. Chad is also an Apple Certified Trainer and has taught classes for Future Media Concepts in Philadelphia and Washington, D.C., training individual users and government employees on editing and DVD creation. He has also taught animation in the Multimedia Arts department at the College of DuPage, outside of Chicago. Currently, Chad works at Concrete Pictures in Philadelphia, creating HD content for an experimental, high-definition arts channel called *Lab HD* (formerly MOOV) on the VOOM and DISH satellite services. He also shoots and produces his own projects, which you can read about on his Web site, www.chadfahs.com.

Contents

Introduction...xiv

PART I   **INTRODUCTION TO HDV** **1**

Chapter 1   **Understanding High-Definition Video Formats.. 3**

What Is High-Definition Video?..........................5
>   The HDV Production and Post-Production Process.....12

Choosing a High-Definition Video Format.................16
>   HDV 16
>   D-VHS 21
>   DVCPRO HD/DV100 23
>   HDCAM and HDCAM SR........................24
>   D5-HD 26

Review of HD Formats 26

Chapter 2   **Choosing an HDV Camcorder.............29**

The Design of an HDV Camcorder.......................30
>   HDV Camcorder Types.............................30
>   Evaluating Image Quality 31
>   Viewscreens and Viewfinders.......................37
>   Audio Recording Options 38

HDV Tape Stock 44
>   Ergonomics 46

HDV Camcorder Comparisons 48
>   Sony HDR-FX1 and HVR-Z1U 48

Sony HDR-HC1 and HVR-A1U 54

Sony HVR-M10U 58
JVC JY-HD10U and GR-HD1 59
JVC GY-HD100U 60

Chapter 3 **Installing and Configuring an HDV Editing System 67**

Working with HDV 68
HDV Editing Systems 69
Graphic Cards 74
HDV System Recommendations 76
Setting Up a RAID Configuration 80
Connecting a Deck or Camera 89
FireWire 90
HD-SDI 92
Monitoring HD Video 93
Hardware Capture Cards 95
Blackmagic Design Decklink HD 95
AJA Kona 2 97

PART II **ACQUIRING HDV VIDEO AND AUDIO 99**

Chapter 4 **Operating an HDV Camcorder 101**

Basic Camcorder Operation 103
Using Zoom Controls 106
Using Focus Controls 110
Automatic Focus 110
Manual Focus 111
Adjusting Exposure Settings 115
Shutter Speed 117
Aperture (Iris) 120
Combining Shutter Speed and Aperture 121
Using Gain Controls 122

Back Light and Spot Light 124

Edge Sharpening 125

Skin-Tone Detail 125

Color Phase 125

Gamma Controls 125

Black Stretch 126

CinemaTone 126

CineFrame 126

Picture Profiles 127

Shot Transition 129

Setting the White Balance 130

Working with Lenses 131

Wide-Angle Lenses 132

Telephoto or Zoom Lenses 134

Macro or Close-up Lenses 135

Using Internal and External Microphones 137

Boom Microphones 138

Wireless Microphones 139

Recording Room Tone 141

Chapter 5 **Lighting for HDV** **143**

Basic Lighting Principles 145

Color Temperatures 145

Qualities of Light 148

Choosing a Lighting Setup 152

Selecting Lighting Equipment 158

Types of Light 158

Light Stands and Barn Doors 160

Special Lighting Techniques 161

Bouncing Lights 162

Creating Depth with Color 162

Lighting a Blue Screen or Green Screen 162

Safety Considerations 164

Chapter 6   Designing Effective Compositions. 165

Storyboarding 166
Composing for Widescreen Format 173
The Rule of Thirds 175
The 180 Degree Rule 176
Camera Placement and Shot Size 178
    Wide Shot 178
    Medium Shot 179
    Close-up 179
Selecting a Camera Angle 181
    Low Angles and High Angles 181
    Dutch (Oblique) Angles 182
Choosing a Camera Height 182
Using a Tripod 182
Moving a Camera 184
    Dolly Shots 184
    Panning and Tilting 185
    Stabilizing Devices 187
    Image Stabilization 196
Shooting People and Places 196
    Reverse Shots 198
    Point-of-View (POV) Shots 199
    Recording Time-Lapse Sequences 199
Shooting Like an Editor 201

PART III   EDITING AND EFFECTS FOR HDV 203

Chapter 7   Editing HDV 205

HDV Editing Software 207
    Final Cut Pro 5 207
    Lumiere HD 208
    iMovie HD and Final Cut Express HD 210

Avid Xpress Pro 211

Adobe Premiere Pro 1.5. 214

Sony Vegas 6 216

Ulead MediaStudio Pro 7 219

Canopus Edius. 222

Matrox 224

Pinnacle Liquid Edition 6 228

MPEG-2 Primer 228

Interframe (Spatial) and Intraframe (Temporal) Compression. . . 229

Group of Pictures (GOP) Structure 230

I-frames 231

P-frames. 231

B-frames. 231

Editing MPEG-2 and HDV 231

Logging Footage. 233

HDV Timecode 235

Drop Frame and Nondrop Frame Timecode. 235

Record Run and Free Run Timecode 236

Capturing Footage 237

Troubleshooting Video Capture 238

Online and Offline Editing 239

Common Editing Techniques. 244

Basic Editing 245

Working with Layers 248

Timeline Tools and Trimming Techniques. 250

Transitions 256

Chapter 8 **Color Correcting Video** **259**

Color Correction Workflow 262

Principles of Color Correction 266

Luma 267

Chroma 270

Additive and Subtractive Color 271

Color Space. 272
    ITU-R BT.709 versus ITU-R BT.601. 273
    RGB versus Y'CbCr 273
    Color Sampling 274
Calibrating an External Monitor 274
Using Video Scopes 277
    Waveform Monitor 277
    Vectorscope 279
Secondary Color Correction. 282
Simulating a Film Look 282
    Magic Bullet Suite and Magic Bullet Editors 283
    CineLook 2 285
    Nattress Film Effects. 286

Chapter 9   Editing and Mixing Audio. 287

Capturing Audio. 288
Sample Rate Considerations. 289
Editing Multitrack Audio. 290
Choosing an Audio Mixer 296
Adding Sound Effects 297
    Reverb 299
    Echo. 300
    Other Audio Filters and Effects 301
Composing a Score. 311
Removing Unwanted Noise 318
    Eliminating Hums. 318
Audio Editing Tips. 320

Chapter 10 Creating Graphics and Effects for HDV 323

Interlaced and Progressive Scan Video. 324
    De-interlacing Footage 327

HDV Pixel Aspect Ratios. 330
Working with Text and Graphics 332
Compositing 336
    Keying with Blue and Green Screens 338
    Composite Modes 344
Working with 2D Animations and Effects. 352
    Keyframes and Motion Control. 352
    Speeding Up and Slowing Down Video 354
    Using Plug-ins 355

Chapter 11 Working with 3D Animation and Effects 359

Introduction to 3D 360
    Modeling 362
    Creating Textures and Materials 364
    Lighting. 365
    Animation 367
    Rendering. 367
Advanced 3D Compositing Tips and Techniques 369
    Combining Video with 3D Animations and
        Environments 369
    Using 2D and 3D Particles 372
Creating Backdrops and Digital Matte Paintings. 374

Chapter 12 Delivering HDV Content 379

Outputting HDV 380
    Standards for Output. 381
    DVD-ROM Presentations. 383
    Windows Media Video 9. 384
HD-DVD. 390
Blu-ray Disc 395
Overview of DVD Authoring 400
    Preparing Your DVD Assets 400
    Still Menu or Motion Menu Creation. 401

Tracks and Slideshows 403
Using Scripts for Advanced Interactivity 404
Finishing and Burning a Disc 404
Encoding Video for DVD 407
Software Encoding. 409
Hardware Encoding. 410
Set-top DVD Recorders 411
Bit-Budgeting. 412
Encoding Clips and Sequences. 413
Creating Chapter Points with Markers 421
Additional Output Options 424
HDTV Displays 428
Projecting HDV 430
Transferring HDV to Film. 437

Index 443

Introduction

The intention of this book is to provide a resource for filmmakers who want to learn about the new HDV format, as well as those who are starting out in the world of digital films. It should appeal to working professionals, as well as film students who are interested in the latest tools and techniques. HDV is positioned to be the next DV, improving old standards, while taking advantage of the resolution and flexibility offered by the impressive HDTV formats we see today. As one of the first books on the subject of HDV, I felt it was important to cover as many HDV-related topics as possible, yet I wanted to do so without neglecting the creative process. While new high-definition formats like HDV bring greater production value to low-budget filmmakers, the ultimate goal is to make great films, regardless of the format you have chosen.

In this book, the main goal is to introduce you to the entire spectrum of HDV production and post-production processes. For those readers who are just making the transition to HDV, we begin by explaining the properties of the medium, including the high-definition formats that are available and what to look for when buying a new camera or setting up a computer system to handle your footage. Following this introduction, techniques for improving an image, such as the proper lighting of a scene and adjustment of camera settings, are considered. We then explore how to manipulate the images and audio that you've acquired, using a wide range of tools that are available on the market, many of which are in use at major studios and post-production companies. In general, intermediate level techniques are discussed, although you will find advanced topics as well, in addition to reviews of introductory film principles. For aspiring filmmakers and others interested in the craft of making movies, interviews with professional filmmakers and other artists are included. These interviews, with industry veterans like Garrett Brown, Paul Hirsch, Don Bluth, Gary Goldman, and Brian Emrich, provide inspiration and insight into the ultimate goal of this book—filmmaking.

Rather than focusing on software tutorials that you can find in numerous other publications, this book provides an overview of the tools and techniques that are most pertinent to making HDV movies and points you to other resources for more software-specific tasks. This was done to keep the subject of filmmaking as the primary focus and to appeal to the widest range of users possible. Overall, a knowledge of computers and filmmaking terminology is assumed, although information is also provided for readers who may be technically inclined but new to the field of filmmaking. Hopefully, by reading this book you will gain a better understanding of the potential that the HDV format offers you as a filmmaker and digital video professional.

How This Book Is Organized

This book is divided into three parts. Part I is an "Introduction to HDV"; Part II is about "Acquiring HDV Video and Audio"; and Part III covers "Editing and Effects for HDV." In retrospect, Part III could have been broken into two parts, to separate the post-production process from the finishing aspect of delivering on formats like DVD and film. Although the target audience of the book is intermediate to advanced users, there is plenty here for new users as well. Each chapter contains a mix of introductory material and advanced content, and many chapters contain interviews with professionals, for reading that is both instructional and entertaining in nature.

Chapter 1, "Understanding High-Definition Video Formats," provides an introduction to the topic of HDV and high-definition formats in general. Although many filmmakers will rely on HDV as their sole acquisition medium, there are other HD formats that may be utilized in further aspects of the post-production process, which (when used together with HDV) can help you achieve the best results.

Chapter 2, "Choosing an HDV Camcorder," covers the majority of current HDV camcorder models and discusses those features that will be most pertinent for the choice of device. While unable to cover every facet of each model on the market, this chapter provides a look at many of the most commonly utilized and sought after features of those camcorders that new buyers should consider.

Chapter 3, "Installing and Configuring an HDV Editing System," provides suggestions for putting together an HDV editing setup for both Mac and PC users, whether assembling a system for home or office.

Chapter 4, "Operating an HDV Camcorder," is for new camcorder operators, as well as seasoned professionals who may have questions about the methods for working with these new devices, particularly in regards to the Sony HDV camcorders.

Chapter 5, "Lighting for HDV," is an introduction to a few lighting principles, which will be most useful to new filmmakers, and a review for others. An interview with Jody Eldred sheds more light on the process of working with the Sony HVR-Z1U.

Chapter 6, "Designing Effective Compositions," discusses some of the key elements to producing a visually effective and interesting film or video project. In addition to coverage of basic filmmaking principles, it includes more advanced tips and techniques, as well as interviews with film professionals like Steadicam inventor and camera operator Garrett Brown, and animators/directors/producers Don Bluth and Gary Goldman.

Chapter 7, "Editing HDV," includes coverage of the software that is available for editing HDV, including questions directed toward several software companies that describe the advantages of their products in more detail. Editing tips and techniques are discussed, in addition to interviews with Oscar-winning editor Paul Hirsch and editor Steven Gonzales.

Chapter 8, "Color Correcting Video," covers the often overlooked topic of color correction and applies it to digital formats like HDV.

Chapter 9, "Editing and Mixing Audio," provides an overview of the post-production processes for working with audio in a video or film project. This chapter includes interviews with sound designer Brian Emrich and producer/engineer Robert Hill.

Chapter 10, "Creating Graphics and Effects for HDV," covers methods for using graphics and effects in your next HDV production, whether by simply working with text or shooting with a blue or green screen.

Chapter 11, "Working with 3D Animation and Effects," is a general overview of the ways that you can use 3D images and animations in your work, which is an important topic even for non-3D artists.

Chapter 12, "Delivering HDV Content," provides details on the formats and methods for delivering your finished HDV project. In addition to information on traditional mediums like DVD, this chapter includes information on new HD disc-based media such as HD-DVD and Blu-ray, as well as information on how to transfer your HDV project to film, courtesy of David Pfluger at Swiss Effects. Information on displaying and projecting your HDV footage is also discussed, with additional information provided by Brian Dressel.

HDVFilmmaking.com, the Web Site

In order to continue the dialogue begun in this book, a Web site has been set up, www.hdvfilmmaking.com. This should provide a source for new and emerging information on the topic of HDV and a source for "errata" from this book that will inevitably come up. Over time, I will publish tutorials and reviews of specific software products, as well as interviews with professionals working in the field.

Part I

Introduction to HDV

Chapter 1

Understanding High-Definition Video Formats

In the past few years, digital video has evolved from a professional medium to one that is widely used by almost everyone, including the average consumer. Much of this success is due to the DV format (MiniDV, DVCAM, DVCPro), which made working with high-quality video simple and fun. The ability that DV gives you to input video through a single FireWire or i.Link (as Sony refers to it) cable and the proliferation of intuitive software packages like iMovie cemented its adoption as the format of choice for aspiring filmmakers, regardless of experience. As we begin to preserve more of our images on DVDs, digital video cassettes, and hard disc recorders (such as TiVo), digital video gains greater significance, proving that these devices have an important role to play in many aspects of professional and private life.

As the availability and acceptance of digital video software and hardware increases, in addition to the increase of digital broadcasting, so does the demand for better quality video. The inevitable results are improved means of acquisition, display, and storage becoming available, leading (as we have now seen) to the widespread acceptance of high-definition televisions (HDTV) and, most recently, "consumer" HDV camcorders. High-definition video formats have become available to meet our growing expectations for better images (see Figure 1.1). Images surround us wherever we go, and the demand for brighter, sharper, clearer, and more colorful pictures increases by the day. This is also evident in popular entertainment, such as in the new action and adventure films whose creators turn to digital technology to make each film look better and more exciting than the last.

The initial success of digital video formats may be attributed to the pristine images they produce, but their continuing success is most certainly a result of their ease of use—particularly when capturing and editing video on a home computer without an expensive setup (including the need for capture cards and fast hard drives). However, high-definition video (referred to here as *HD, which includes HDV among its many formats*) presents something of a "two steps forward and one step back" scenario. While the overall quality has greatly improved, some of the advantages in working with digital video have been negated—at least for the moment. Capturing, editing, and outputting HDV in particular has become especially confusing, due to the recent lack of support in many software applications and the increase in the number of input and output options that are available. Fortunately, we are seeing these inconveniences start to fade as more companies realize the demand for HDV products and services.

I hope that this book can help answer some of your questions concerning this new format. This book should at least provide a launching point for those who are new to working in high-definition. Even for beginners, the more advanced portions of the discussion should act as a springboard for further exploration. Feel free to use this text as a reference and skip around as necessary, or (better yet) read each chapter in order to better understand the entire process of working with this exciting new high-definition format called HDV. For updates, additional information on HDV and HD in general, as well as tutorials, errata, and other topics related to film and video, visit www.hdvfilmmaking.com or access the site through a link on the author's homepage at www.chadfahs.com.

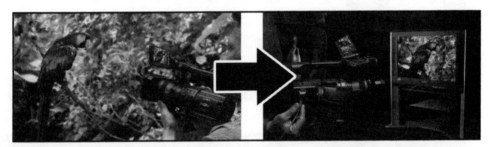

Figure 1.1 *High-definition video is revolutionizing the way we create and share images (Courtesy of Sony).*

What Is High-Definition Video?

High-definition (HD) is the general name given to the next generation of digital video formats for acquiring and distributing motion images that surpass the resolution and complexity of traditional standard definition (SD) formats. Anyone shopping for a new television set lately has seen this term used, and frequently abused, in new-product advertising. It is often used generically to mean "better than standard definition," but this could technically refer to any video with an image size larger than conventional video—480 horizontal lines (active display lines) for NTSC and 576 horizontal lines for PAL.

The term HDTV (High-definition Television) is correctly used to refer to the broadcast and viewing of high-definition video on a television set or other suitably equipped monitor and receiver. In this book I use the term high-definition, or simply HD, to refer to the general properties of high-definition video formats, including HDV, as well as those HDTV formats approved by a standards organization called the ATSC, or Advanced Television Systems Committee (special PAL frame rates were defined by the DVB, or Digital Video Broadcasting, group in Europe). The ATSC (see Figure 1.2) approved HDTV standards for video with a 16:9 aspect ratio, varying frame rates, and resolutions of 720 or 1080 horizontal lines. These and other specifications for HD video are discussed later in this chapter and throughout the book. See Figure 1.3.

Figure 1.2 *The ATSC (Advanced Television Systems Committee) approved the HDTV standards for the United States. Visit www.atsc.org for more information on the latest HDTV standards.*

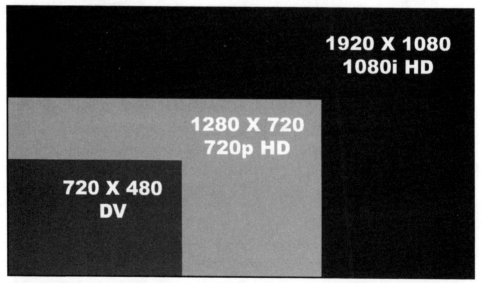

Figure 1.3 *At 1920×1080 pixels, high-definition images are six times the size of DV video (NTSC, 720×480 pixels) and 2.25 times the size of 720 p HD video (1280×720).*

Although an earlier, analog form of HDTV was created in Japan during the 1980s and broadcast in the early 1990s, high-definition video has only recently reached widespread acceptance as a form of digital television (DTV). Since Congress has mandated that all broadcasts in the United States convert to DTV by the end of 2006, you should hear even more about HDTV and related HD formats in the coming year (however, since HDTV is only one type of DTV broadcast—and is not a requirement of DTV—standard definition broadcasts will still be around for quite some time).

Out of the overall specifications for HDTV arose the possibility for future consumer HD formats that make use of the same broadcast specifications, such as HDV, to which this book is primarily dedicated. HDV was brought about as a means for consumers to take advantage of the same specs used for HDTV broadcasts (and HD-DVD), including its high-resolution images, variety of frame rates, and widescreen images.

Although the HDV format will be the focus of discussion in this book, HD, in general, is the larger category of video that it fits into. All HDV formats are part of a wider HD standard, while not all HD standards fall under the rubric of HDV. It is important to understand where HDV fits into the larger world of HD, since HD technology influences the choices we make in the process of producing and distributing HDV content.

Following are a few benefits of high-definition video:

- Unprecedented sharpness, resolution, and image detail.
- Wider screens and images that more closely match the aspect ratio of projected films.
- A variety of image sizes and frame rates to match the needs of a production.
- The ability to transmit video as data, which can be viewed on a television or computer and recorded without loss to digital recording devices, such as DVR, D-VHS, and, eventually, HD-DVD.
- Clear, digital images with quality that is maintained throughout the post-production process.

Among the 18 formats of digital television assigned by the ATSC are six specifically for HDTV (the broadcast and viewing of HD signals). Each of these HDTV formats includes an aspect ratio of 16:9 (for widescreen images) and consists of either 720 or 1080 vertical lines of resolution at varying frame rates and scan modes (interlaced and progressive scan modes are discussed in Chapter 10, "Creating Graphics and Effects for HDV"). Table 1.1 illustrates the main differences between these various formats.

Table 1.1 ATSC Standards for HDTV (NTSC)

Format	Resolution	Scan Mode	Frame Rate
1080i (or 1080 60i)	1920×1080	Interlaced	30 (60 fields)
1080p	1920×1080	Progressive	30
1080p	1920×1080	Progressive	24
720p	1280×720	Progressive	60
720p	1280×720	Progressive	30
720p	1280×720	Progressive	24

DROP FRAME AND NON-DROP FRAME COMPARISONS

When discussing frame rates, non-drop frame rates are often mentioned here for simplicity in comparisons, such as 30 fps instead of 29.97 (except where indicated). However, drop frame rates are more accurate when describing actual frame rates for broadcast. HDV for NTSC (whether 1080i60 or 720p30) is 29.97, which simply indicates that frames are counted differently over time to maintain sync with a real clock (although no frames are actually lost, and they still appear as 30 frames per second for editing and other practical purposes). Chapter 7, "Editing HDV," discusses the difference between drop frame and non-drop frame timecode and frame rates.

HDV arose recently as a variation on the HD formats shown in Table 1.1, and was designed with consumers and prosumers (those that blur the line between professionals and consumers) in mind. By introducing HDV to the marketplace, more users may now create content to be viewed (and manipulated) on a variety of devices, including computers, televisions, and video disc players (HD-DVD and Blu-Ray being the biggest).

As a portable, affordable, high-definition format, HDV looks like it is in a position to bring the means of HD production into the hands of more consumers and serious professionals. In order to understand how you can benefit from the latest crop of HDV tools and to find out whether HDV is a good match for your next production, it is important to first understand the basic HDV process, from shooting to final delivery.

The HDV Production and Post-Production Process

Creating a digital video project of any kind, whether HDV or DV, involves a basic three-step process (the number of steps actually depends on how you break the process down) that all videographers and filmmakers must follow. The first step in the process involves the acquisition of video (the act of shooting), the second step is the capture and editing on your computer, and the third step is the output of your finished program.

Step 1: Acquiring HDV

HDV video cameras offer improved image quality (based on resolution) and features that are a direct result of the digital medium and the high-definition format. Even so, the acquisition of digital video is essentially the same as with any other video format (or film, in many cases), beginning with the proper operation of a camera and the careful use of lighting to achieve good images. Shooting HDV means sharper pictures, more vivid colors, and cleaner audio (as compared with most analog devices, although the quality of audio compression may be debated), all of which can be packed into a device that is comparable in size and style to earlier DV cameras. The recent introduction of prosumer HDV camcorders from Sony has raised the bar on the quality of HDV devices, improving on the color and resolution of earlier cameras from JVC (although JVC now has new and improved HDV cameras on the market). In the months ahead, several more cameras will be announced and made available, increasing the number of options for a suitable HDV acquisition device. Harnessing the full potential of your HDV camera is covered in Chapter 4, "Operating an HDV Camcorder."

Step 2: Capturing and Editing HDV

The speed and simplicity with which video can be edited is one of the greatest benefits of the digital video revolution. In general, editing and manipulating HDV is easy once the video is captured onto hard drives using your computer. Unfortunately, in the beginning there were few industry standards for editing HDV—at least, few methods that were as easy to use and understand as those created for DV. Currently, working with HDV is becoming simpler by the day, since the standardization of methods for working with HDV (compared with the adoption of DV and other early forms of digital video) should be very quick. In fact, significant progress has been made already, and soon anyone who is familiar with DV will be able to edit HDV content with ease on a home computer.

WHAT IS NATIVE HDV SUPPORT?

The term "native" is used to describe an NLE's ability to capture and edit a video format, like HDV, in its original form, without having to convert the files to an intermediate format (this term is also discussed in Chapter 7 "Editing HDV"). With native editing, no quality is lost from your original video, at least until effects or transitions are applied, which requires recompressing the video before outputting to HDV tape or another format. In addition, working natively simplifies the process of capturing and editing clips into a timeline. Final Cut Pro 5 and Vegas 6 are two examples of software that provides native HDV editing. By comparison, the DV format is much easier to work with, since it requires relatively little assistance from the CPU—unlike HDV, which relies on the processor to decode and playback its complex, "Long-GOP" MPEG-2 video. Some manufacturers incorrectly claim that their software offers native HDV support. The ability to edit MPEG-2 in a timeline is not the same as true support for native HDV formats. Software that supports HDV is specially designed to handle the transport streams without sacrificing quality or adding additional steps to the editing process.

Getting HDV into your computer can be a relatively simple task, depending on the method you choose. Usually, a single cable (such as a FireWire or i.Link cable, technically referred to as IEEE-1394) will suffice to capture video and control your camera at the same time from your computer's desktop (see Figure 1.4). You may also use a special capture card installed on your computer (in addition to a converter device) to capture HDV through a serial digital interface (HD-SDI) or through the component analog connection on a professional deck. The benefits and drawbacks of various capture methods are discussed in Chapter 3, "Installing and Configuring an HDV Editing System," which also includes more information on setting up a system to capture and edit HDV (including the difference between 4 pin and 6 pin FireWire, or i.Link, cables). Adding effects and transitions, adjusting colors, and replacing a solid background with a different scene are just a few of the ways you can improve your video once it is in the digital realm.

Figure 1.4 *FireWire connections make capturing HDV easy.*

FIREWIRE CONNECTIVITY

Using a FireWire cable (also called *i.Link* by Sony) connected to your HDV camera gives you complete playback and recording control from your computer's desktop without the need to manually start, stop, fast-forward, or rewind a tape. In addition, all video and audio information is transmitted simultaneously, making FireWire connections the simplest method for native HDV capture and device control (something DV format users have experienced for a long time).

The ability to use FireWire with an HDV camera connected to a laptop computer makes the mobile high-definition studio an exciting option. In fact, by shrinking the size of devices and expanding the capacity for high-quality video storage, you can shoot your next HDV project in Tibet and edit it on the plane trip back!

Step 3: Outputting HDV

After your video has been captured and edited and effects have been added, you have a large number of output options for HDV at high-definition resolutions. Currently, the most popular methods for distributing HDV content include

D-VHS, Windows Media 9 on DVD-ROM, HD-DVD and Blu-Ray discs (developing and as yet untested delivery methods), or standard definition delivery on a DVD. HDV can also be compressed as low-resolution files for the Web and even sent to mobile devices, such as cell phones and personal digital assistants (PDAs). The number of practical uses for HDV and other digital video formats continues to grow, especially since the advent of broadband Internet service, better wireless communications, and the widespread usage of DVD players in the home. For more information on delivering HDV—including the creation of your own DVDs and the future of HD-DVD technology—see Chapter 12, "Delivering HDV Content."

Digital Video versus Analog Video

Although the term *digital video* can be broadly applied to any video that is acquired or distributed digitally, it is most often associated with the popular DV format—particularly MiniDV tapes and camcorders used by consumers and budget-conscious professionals. In recent years, digital video formats have become the standard for most video professionals, thanks to their high quality, low cost, and ability to easily edit and transmit images for the Web and DVD.

Analog video formats, such as VHS, 8mm, Hi8, and Betacam SP, are different from digital video in that analog video registers information in physical waveforms as opposed to in a series of digital bits (ones and zeros). The difference between analog and digital video is most noticeable when copying one tape to another several times. This chain of analog copies results in a progressive decrease in quality from one generation to the next, known as *generation loss*. If you were to copy one VHS tape to another and repeat the process several times, you would notice a dramatic reduction in quality between the first generation tape and its later generation copies.

With digital video, virtually no information is lost (barring drop-outs or damage to the recording medium) when transferring video back and forth to other tapes, a hard drive, or an optical disc, as all of the data remains intact within the digital domain—just like when you're transferring a file from one computer to another. However, with the frequent usage of techniques to recompress a particular digital video file for use in editing, applying effects, and delivering on DVD or the Web, a new, digital form of picture degradation is created. The results of recompressing digital video over and over are digital artifacts and image loss resulting from the type of codec (compression/decompression scheme) that is used.

Digital Video versus Analog Video

In order to maintain the best possible quality for your digital video throughout the production pipeline (whether HD, HDV, or DV), it is important to apply compression as infrequently as possible. Only when you are in the final stages of a project (such as when outputting to a DVD) should you consider using additional compression. In later chapters in this book, standard practices for maintaining the best image quality through all stages of post-production and subsequent forms of delivery are discussed in more detail.

Choosing a High-Definition Video Format

As I've just discussed, high-definition video comes in many forms that are not limited to the new HDV specifications. It's important for any filmmaker or producer investigating the options for his next project to carefully consider the differences (benefits and advantages) of working with a particular format. In terms of cost, reliability, and compatibility, these formats can vary greatly. Some of them are better for acquisition purposes, while others may be best suited for playback, archiving, or delivering a finished product. Choosing an HD format should be one of the first decisions you make when planning a new project, as the budget and other aspects of the production and post-production process are affected by the format you choose. In this section, I'll start by discussing HDV, the focus of this book, and then continue on to other HD formats, including D-VHS and other professional formats such as HDCAM and DVCPRO HD, which are more firmly entrenched in the broadcast and film worlds.

HDV

HDV is a "consumer" high-definition video format developed in 2003 by a consortium of manufacturers, whose primary members include JVC, Sony, Canon, and Sharp (see Figure 1.5). The goal of these companies was to create an affordable, high-definition format for acquisition and playback that could take advantage of the new high-definition televisions, video recorders, and other devices that had been coming to market over the previous few years. As a format, HDV delivers a larger, more detailed image than is possible with conventional, standard definition video (such as DV), along with a widescreen image and a variety of potential frame rates.

Figure 1.5 *The official members of the HDV consortium include JVC, Sony, Canon, and Sharp. You can find information on other companies that support the HDV format at the official HDV Web site, www.hdv-info.org.*

HDV Image Sizes and Scan Modes

Like most HDTV formats, HDV can be broken into two basic categories: 720p or 1080i. However, there are differences between the way HDV and ordinary HD formats handle their images, including differences between 1080i frame sizes, for example (see Figure 1.6). A single frame of 1080i HDV measures 1440×1080 pixels, or 1280×720 pixels for the 720p variety. By comparison, the size of a standard definition frame of video is 720×480 pixels for NTSC DV (or 720×576 pixels for PAL DV). The actual resolution of 1080i HDV, when played back on an HDTV set with the highest specifications, is 1920×1080 pixels, the same as you would expect from the most common HDTV standards. This is due to the non-square pixel dimensions that make up HDV images. Basically, 1080i HDV formats originate at 1440×1080 pixels and are stretched to fill a 1920×1080 frame on playback. Pixel aspect ratios, and the implications for working with still frames and graphics, are discussed in Chapter 10 "Creating Graphics and Effects for HDV."

Similar to standard definition formats, such as DV, HDV has both NTSC and PAL counterparts. Although both NTSC and PAL high-definition video standards use similar resolutions (1080i and 720p), each one has its own set of frame rates and scan modes (720 30p, 720 60p, and 1080 60i for NTSC; 720 25p, 720 50p, and 1080 50i for PAL). For an in-depth discussion of frame rates, see the timecode discussion in Chapter 7 "Editing HDV."

The 720p variety of HDV has a frame size of 1280×720 pixels and is scanned progressively, which means that frames are not interlaced and are captured and played back without a separation of video "fields". Conversely, the 1080i specification is a 1440×1080 picture with an interlaced scan mode, which means that each frame of video is divided into two fields (even and odd) that are captured and displayed one after the other, resulting in video that appears to contain more motion (essentially, 60 separate pictures per second versus 30). The benefit to using progressive modes is that you achieve a more film-like image and motion; interlaced video has a look that is associated more with home video recordings. There are benefits and drawbacks to each type of scan mode; these are discussed throughout this book, with in-depth coverage in Chapter 10 "Creating Graphics and Effects for HDV."

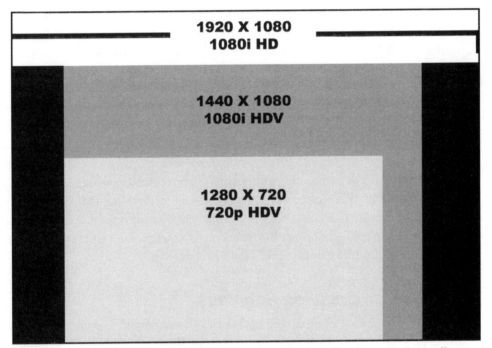

Figure 1.6 *The resolution of 1080i HDV is 1440×1080 pixels, although it is usually viewed at 1920×1080 pixels (non-square pixel dimensions are used to maximize storage space on a tape).*

HDV Frame Rates

In addition to its resolution and pixel properties, video (or any moving images, for that matter) is also affected by the rate at which it moves. The United States and Japan use video with a frame rate of approximately 30 (or 29.97) frames per second, or fps (part of the NTSC standard), while the majority of Europe and other parts of the world use 25 fps (curiously, the PAL standard is usually listed at 25 fps, although it technically describes the way color is encoded, and does not define frame rate or dimensions as commonly believed. PAL-M in Brazil is 29.97 fps and 525 lines, like NTSC; in general, it is alright to assume PAL refers to the most common European standard with 25 fps and 625 lines. In the early days of film, some cameras captured images at a slower rate of about 18 fps; today, films are usually photographed and projected at 24 fps.

However, even the rate at which film cameras record can vary greatly, depending on the needs of the shoot. For example, a scene that requires the use of miniatures, such as a model of a ship floating in a tank, would be shot at a much higher frame rate, such as 60 fps. When played back at 24 fps, the scene would appear to move much more slowly, creating the illusion of a larger object, with greater weight and mass. Explosions, fire, and other elements that are intended for compositing into a scene will usually be shot at a different frame rate for the same reason. The rate at which video cameras record has remained steady over the years—at approximately 30 fps for NTSC and 25 fps for PAL and SECAM (another SD broadcast standard that is similar to PAL, although not a tape format). With new 720p HD cameras (such as Panasonic's professional Varicam series), images can be captured at a rate of 60 full (progressive) frames per second, doubling the number of frames that are captured each second. For filmmakers who need the flexibility to "dial in" a frame rate while shooting, this increase of frames remains the primary advantage of using 720p HD cameras over 1080i HD devices.

HDV Compression Schemes

HDV is recorded using a type of MPEG-2 compression similar to that used by DVDs and broadcast by television stations that provide HDTV programming. (HDTV stations also utilize MPEG-4 compression for broadcasts; this is discussed in Chapter 12.) Once HDV video is captured as MPEG-2, it is stored in a transport stream file, or TS file, which wraps the MPEG-2 video and its related audio information together in a form that can be reliably transmitted.

ELEMENTARY STREAMS, TRANSPORT STREAMS, AND PROGRAM STREAMS

The data streams for MPEG-2 video and its associated audio files can be stored and transmitted in different ways. When dealt with separately, video and audio data (in addition to other data streams, such as subtitles on a DVD) are considered elementary streams. Elementary streams for HDV consist of a separate video file and a separate audio file, which can be seen most readily when editing video with non-linear editing software (or an "NLE", such as Final Cut Pro). Access to elementary streams is particularly important if you need to manipulate or edit the video and audio content. In order to transmit this data more easily, the separate streams are often wrapped together, or encapsulated, inside a transport stream. A transport stream (or "TS" file) is a single file containing (in the case of HDV) video and audio information that is more easily handled for distribution and broadcast. HDTV broadcasts, for example, transmit a transport stream that is decoded by your receiver. Video and audio information for HDV, as it is stored on a tape and transmitted to your computer, is also encapsulated inside a transport stream. You may capture and transmit transport streams to and from your computer, such as when copying files back and forth between your computer and a D-VHS deck. In addition to elementary streams and transport streams, a program stream (like a transport stream) also wraps video and audio information together, although it is better suited to storage on DVDs and other computer media. VOB files on a DVD are considered program streams, although you might think of a TS file in the same way. Both types of streams use a form of muxing, or wrapping together, to combine video, audio, and other information into a single file.

Utilizing widely available MiniDV (and soon, full-size DV) tapes, an HDV camcorder or deck records video with either a 19Mbps (720p) or 25Mbps (1080i) data stream, which is the same as or less than the data rate for DV. HDV is able to deliver greater resolution in the same amount of space as DV by relying on a form of MPEG-2 compression (the same type of compression used to create video for a DVD), which shrinks the data to a manageable size that can fit on a one-hour MiniDV cassette. At first look, these numbers appear to indicate that HDV presents a reduction in quality over DV, rather than an improvement. However, data rates don't necessarily tell the whole story. Considering the relatively small amount of data that is necessary for HDV, the HDV format actually has a larger data rate than what is broadcast by most high-definition terrestrial and satellite stations. (Most HD broadcasts share a considerable portion of their bandwidth with other channels—even alternate SD broadcasts of the same programs; this is called *multicasting*.) In practice HDTV broadcasts use about 13 to 19Mbps of data to transmit video and audio information (although they are capable of more), which can be almost half of what HDV provides. The main difference is that HDV can offer better data rates without the signal interference and inconsistent quality (fluctuating data rates) that is expected from most DTV and HDTV broadcasts.

HDV BIT RATE ENCODING

HDV uses MPEG-2 with constant bit rate encoding (25Mbps for 1080i and 19Mbps for 720p). Refer to Chapter 12, "Delivering HDV Content," for more discussion of bit rates, including the difference between constant bit rate (CBR) and variable bit rate (VBR) encoding.

HDV ERROR CORRECTION

As more visual information is represented by a smaller amount of data (a higher compression ratio), more information is at risk of being lost when a tape is damaged, particularly as a result of repeated use. For this reason, the improved error-correction capabilities of HDV (compared with DV) are a virtual necessity. Using greater redundancy than DV and error correction across a wider range of tracks, HDV ensures that even if some data is lost, the picture can still be displayed with little, if any, noticeable difference. However, when dropouts do occur with HDV, the loss of picture information can be catastrophic. Up to ½ of a second (15 or 12 frames, depending on NTSC or PAL shooting modes) may be lost, due to the nature of the MPEG-2 "GOP" structure (see Chapter 7 "Editing HDV" and later in this chapter for more information on the structure of MPEG-2).

HDV Audio

The audio format for HDV is a 48kHz, 16 bit format, which records to a compressed MPEG-1 Audio Layer II format at a data rate of 384kbps. This would seem to be a step down from the comparatively uncompressed audio recorded with DV cameras and decks. However, it is necessary to sacrifice the quality of audio to make room for more HD image information, which is already pushing up against the limit of what constitutes acceptable data rates for HD video. Using what is similar to a very high bit rate MP3 format, this audio should be acceptable for most casual recording situations (albeit, HDV audio uses a different MPEG-1 Audio Layer II specification, rather than MP3's MPEG-2 Layer 3 specification and at a higher sample rate than most MP3s—48kHz versus 44.1kHz). If you require a better, professional quality recording, you can choose to record to a separate MiniDisc, DAT (digital audio tape), or hard disk recorder and sync the sound up later (using a clapboard, timecode, or other cue to match picture with sound).

HDV Benefits

Apart from the technical specifications mentioned in the sections above, HDV has some general benefits that should be of interest to filmmakers who are seriously considering the format.

A few of HDV's benefits include the following:

◆ Widescreen images and a variety of frame rates to choose from.

◆ Shoot HDV and deliver DV today (in-camera down-conversion is common), while still being able to deliver HD in the future.

◆ The ability to edit high-definition video on a desktop computer without special hardware.

◆ Small, portable high-definition cameras and easily accessible recording media.

◆ Files that can be transferred and viewed on a variety of devices, including televisions, computers, and mobile devices.

◆ Quality that is preserved when the video is captured or copied.

◆ Improved error correction capabilities when recording and playing back from tape.

This list is only a sample of the benefits that HDV provides. As you progress through this book, you should begin to build a more complete appreciation for the technical and creative potential of HDV (as well as its limitations), in addition to other affordable high-definition formats.

HDV versus DV

Apart from their acronyms, what else do HDV and DV have in common? Less than you might think. Although they currently use the same tape mechanisms with equivalent recording times and nearly identical data rates (as well as non-square pixel dimensions), HDV and DV handle the recording of images in very different ways. DV compresses its images using a much less compressed format, at a compression ratio of about 5:1, while HDV compresses video to approximately 47:1. Although both formats use spatial compression methods, such as DCT (Discrete Cosine Transform) compression (which is similar to the compression used for JPEG files), HDV takes it one step further by adding temporal compression in the form of MPEG-2 (an in-depth discussion of MPEG-2 can be found in Chapter 7, "Editing HDV"). Temporal (or *interframe*) compression simply means that compression is applied over time and across frames, not just to individual frames. (Single frame compression is also referred to as *intraframe*.)

HDV uses a method that groups a series of frames together and only writes new data for information that has changed between frames. In MPEG-2 terminology, these frames are referred to as a *GOP*, or *group of pictures* (for HDV, as with most DVD-Video, a 15-frame or 12-frame GOP is used, as well as a 6 frame GOP for 720p HDV). While this type of compression is very efficient—recording HD resolution video in the same amount of space used for the DV format—it can also introduce compression artifacts, which are peculiar to MPEG-2 encoded video. It also means that HDV is harder for a computer to work with than DV because more computing power is required to decode a series of frames.

In many ways, HDV's compression methods are a step down from those utilized by the DV format, as much information is sacrificed to make HDV fit neatly onto a small cassette tape. However, the increased resolution offered by HDV overcomes its differences with DV, at least when viewed on an HDTV or high-definition monitor. Also, smaller file sizes and more compression do not always mean a perceptible difference in quality to a viewing audience. Consider the way that MP3 audio files can closely reproduce CD-quality sound at a fraction of the original size.

If HDV is to be a viable format for consumers at this point in time, it needs to be recorded, stored, played, and edited within the capabilities of most home computers. HDV's use of an efficient compression scheme—and the manageable file sizes it produces as a result—should allow this format to become a viable option for even casual users in the years to come.

D-VHS

The D-VHS format was developed by JVC as a way for consumers to watch pre-recorded HD material (movies delivered on tape; see Figure 1.7), as well as record their own HD programs from their HDTV receivers (ATSC formats supported). D-VHS is based on the existing ½" VHS cassette format, and it is backwards-compatible with VHS and S-VHS cassettes, which can be played and recorded in D-VHS machines. D-VHS uses a form of MPEG-2 compression to place video on a tape; this is very close to the compression scheme used for HDV. Video and audio information are captured and played back as a TS file and, for this reason, you are able to pass HDV files back and forth between a D-VHS deck, HDV camera, or computer with no loss in quality. D-VHS records all current HDTV standards, and it utilizes an audio bit rate of 576kbps, which is higher than the typical maximum of 448kbps bit rate for DVDs with a 5.1 channel Dolby Digital/AC-3 soundtrack.

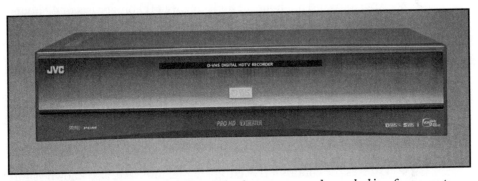

Figure 1.7 *The D-VHS format is one choice for consumers who are looking for a way to watch and record HD programming on their new HDTV, or for filmmakers who want to back up an HDV project so that they can watch it (at full HD quality) in their living room (although disc-based formats like HD-DVD and Blu-Ray are set to replace it). (Courtesy of JVC)*

In addition to its use by high-end consumers and other early adopters, D-VHS has become a very popular format for film directors, cinematographers, and producers to review film dailies shot on the set. Rather than spool a reel of film in a special screening room each day after a shoot, filmmakers can have their films transferred to a D-VHS tape (locked with a special encryption key to prevent theft), allowing them to watch material at their leisure with any HD or SD television set or projector.

HDV filmmakers are also finding D-VHS decks to be an excellent way to back up their HDV projects and media, as they can use a simple FireWire connection to pass an HDV transport stream directly from their camera or computer to D-VHS tape. Perhaps the only real drawback to using the D-VHS format to back up HD content is that the tape stock is not very sturdy and is susceptible to dropouts and other problems caused by stretching and frequent use. Still, as a means to watch HD content you have created, it is preferable to use a D-VHS copy than to subject the master tapes to rigorous use.

The following are a few advantages of using the D-VHS format:

◆ Affordable format for the recording and playback of HDV video and HDTV broadcasts.

◆ Achieves a data rate of 28.2Mbps, which is slightly higher than what is possible with the current HDV format.

◆ User-selectable data rates for recording ranging from 2Mbps to 28.2Mbps.

◆ Able to record 3.5 hours of high-quality HD broadcasts or 49 hours of low-quality material on a single tape.

◆ Lossless transfer of digital video information as data.

◆ A single, inexpensive cassette can hold approximately 44GB of video held as data.

◆ Compatibility with conventional VHS and S-VHS formats, allowing playback and recording of VHS media and a large library of analog material.

◆ Utilizes the common IEEE1394 digital interface, also known as FireWire or i.Link.

D-THEATER

The release of D-VHS format tapes and VTRs necessitated the development of special copy protection features to alleviate the anxieties of film studios and private copyright holders whose content would be needed to make the format viable in the consumer marketplace. As D-VHS offers a quality that is nearly identical (at least to the untrained eye) to the HD studio master that the movie originated on, it was important to develop a system capable of preventing illegal duplication and theft in the form of a perfect digital copy (similar fears arose when DVD was introduced). The digital copy protection format developed for D-VHS is called D-Theater; it is an encryption system for prerecorded films. Only D-Theater-capable players can play back D-Theater movies on D-VHS.

DVCPRO HD/DV100

DVCPRO HD (also called *DV100* and *D7-HD*) is a high-definition format developed by Panasonic; it is essentially an HD variant of the DVCPRO 50 standard definition format, with a maximum data rate of 100Mbps. It is also called DV100 for this reason, just as DV formats are sometimes referred to as DV25 or DV50, depending on the data rate that they use. This format utilizes 4:2:2 color sampling, which is (for practical purposes) the same as HDCAM, as well as the majority of professional SD formats such as DVCPRO 50 and Digital Betacam (color sampling is discussed in Chapter 8 "Color Correcting Video"). The typical frame sizes for DVCPRO HD are 1280×1080 or 960×720, depending on which variety of the HD specification that is chosen, and using non-square pixel dimensions to store images that are stretched on playback, similar to HDV (and, interestingly, HDCAM).

Apart from its excellent image quality (see Figure 1.8), which is on par with the HDCAM format, the main advantage of DVCPRO HD is that it can be transferred via FireWire to a computer or other device and edited in its native camera format without loss, much like DV (although HDCAM can be edited natively over HD-SDI using HD-SDTI on Sony's Xpri system, for instance; in the future, HDCAM may be edited natively on other systems as well). The low bandwidth required to edit DVCPRO HD makes this process possible, as transferring, editing, and storing DVCPRO HD is not significantly different from working with DV.

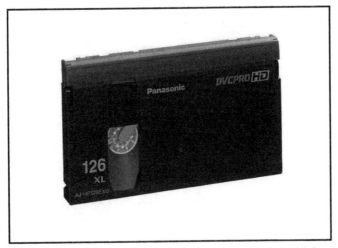

Figure 1.8 *DVCPRO HD makes it possible to capture high-quality HD video and audio over a single FireWire cable.*

Although DVCPRO HD shares similarities with HDV, particularly in the way non-square pixel dimensions are used to resemble a full HD image size, its method of compression differs significantly, as it does not rely on the same temporal, interframe compression methods used by MPEG-2 video. DVCPRO HD uses intraframe compression methods, which encode each frame independent of adjacent frames (intraframe and interframe compression are discussed in Chapter 7, "Editing HDV," along with MPEG-2). This method is similar to most other digital video formats, such as Digital Betacam, DV, DVCPRO 50, HDCAM, and others.

HDCAM and HDCAM SR

HDCAM is a tape format developed by Sony for its line of professional HD cameras and VTRs (see Figure 1.9). It is currently the most popular format for acquiring and finishing HD, and is also widely used as a camera master in Sony's line of ENG (Electronic News Gathering) and Cine Alta cameras. Even if your program does not originate on HDCAM (since many budgets do not permit shooting with HDCAM cameras and stock), it is an excellent format for outputting a finished program or movie onto when you're completing the online process (the difference between online and offline processes are discussed in Chapter 7, "Editing HDV"). You may also choose to copy your HDV footage directly to HDCAM tape prior to editing (through component outputs, if you have a capable deck, or into HD-SDI with a special HDV to HD-SDI convertor box), in order to work from a more robust tape stock, which works better in many post-production pipelines (if currently editing with HDCAM material).

You might think of HDCAM as the big brother to Sony's HDV format, with better color (4:2:2 sampling for practical capture and editing purposes, although technically, it is undersampled at 3:1:1 upon acquisition—its true color sampling specification), much less compression (between 7:1 and 10:1), and larger, more reliable tape stock. Like the HDV format, HDCAM stores its images at 1440×1080 pixels; they are resized back to 1920×1080 when you view them. HDCAM is able to record and play different varieties of 1080 line HD, including 24p, 25p, 50i, and 60i frame rates. In addition, HDCAM is capable of working with four 20-bit audio channels.

Next to D5, HDCAM is an industry standard format for delivering HD programs for broadcast or transfer to film, and it can be a good format for preserving your completed HDV movie as widespread use of HDCAM for broadcast purposes virtually future-proofs your investment (although D5 HD would be ideal for archiving and transfer, as discussed later, since it records the full raster image, which is particularly nice for HD to film transfers). Seeing as this format is found in the majority of HD facilities, it is safe to say that HDCAM decks and stock should be available for some time to come.

Figure 1.9 *HDCAM tapes are based on the same cassette style as Digital Betacam, and available in a variety of sizes and capacities.*

Figure 1.10 *HDCAM SR is an advanced tape format with better color, less compression, and greater resolution (full raster HD) than standard HDCAM, which is used with the Sony HDC-950 CineAlta camera pictured here (Courtesy of Sony).*

In 2004, Sony unveiled an update to HDCAM for high-end professional applications; this format is particularly suited for work that is intended for printing to film. The format is called HDCAM SR (the SR stands for *superior resolution*), and among its improvements on the standard HDCAM format are better color—closer to the quality of film (the option for 4:4:4 color sampling, in addition to 4:2:2)—, a full HD raster image, similar to the D5-HD format (1920×1080, versus HDCAM's 1440× 1880 that is resized upon playback), and a higher bit rate with less compression applied to the image. See Figure 1.10. It is also able to record and play back dual streams of HD, which makes it the perfect choice for 3D specialty programs (James Cameron's *Ghost of the Abyss* and Robert Rodriguez's *The Adventures of Shark Boy and Lava Girl in 3-D* are examples of projects that used this feature).

D5-HD

The top-of-the-line HD mastering format is D5-HD. This format, developed by Panasonic, originated as an uncompressed master format for SD material and was upgraded for use with HD material. This format can handle a wide array of HD material, including 1080 24p, 1080 60i, 1080 30p, 1080 50i (for PAL), 720 60p, and 1035 59.94i. At a ratio of 5:1 (in 10 bit mode) and 4:1 (in 8 bit mode), compression for this tape format is better than the HDCAM. In addition, D5-HD maintains a true 1920×1080 image size—as opposed to HDV, DVCPRO HD, and even DVCAM, which store their images at a smaller size and increase the resolution on playback (HDCAM SR shares many of D5-HD's features, while improving color sampling at 4:4:4).

Like the majority of professional HD decks (with the exception of some DVCPRO HD VTRs, which can use FireWire connections), D5-HD decks interface through an HD-SDI link. The longest available recording time for D5-HD tape stock is 155 minutes when used with 1080 24p material, although some low-end D5-HD decks are unable to play back and record 1080 24p. The majority of movie companies and high-end post-production facilities working in HD use D5-HD as their master format, as it is an excellent format for digital intermediates and other applications where the highest quality is required. D5-HD also supports the use of eight channels of audio.

Review of HD Formats

For most independent filmmakers and even budget-conscious producers, the choice of HD format is more a matter of cost than relative quality. Whichever HD format you choose, a marked improvement in quality is virtually guaranteed over the alternate SD format options that are available. It is likely that you have already decided in favor of HDV over higher-end formats like HDCAM or even DVCPRO HD. Still, you may be surprised to learn that these formats can be used for HDV projects with even the most modest of budgets. For example, DVCPRO

HD is an excellent intermediate format for editing and finishing an HDV-origi-nated project (particularly for users of Final Cut Pro HD editing software). Use of DVCPRO HD, and other HD formats, does not necessarily require the purchase of any additional hardware, apart from more or faster storage to meet your editing requirements, particularly when working with uncompressed HD formats. As more software and hardware manufacturers jump on the prosumer HD band-wagon, you may notice that formats that were previously out of reach due to bud-get constraints are actually a reasonable option for your production.

Table 1.2 reviews the high-definition (HD) formats discussed in this chapter, along with a few popular standard definition (SD) formats for comparison.

Table 1.2 HD and SD Format Comparison (NTSC)

Standard	Format	Frame Size (Recorded)	Frame Size (Playback)	Color Sampling	Compression Ratio	Video Data Rate (Mbps)
HD	HDV 1080i	1440×1080	1920×1080	4:2:0	47:1	2 Mbps
	HDV 720p	1280×720	1280×720	4:2:0	27:1	19Mbps
	D-VHS	Determined by Source	1920×1080 1280×720 (in addition to 480 line SD frame sizes)	4:2:0	Pre-compressed	28.2Mbps (Max)
	DVCPRO HD 1080i	1280×1080	1920×1080	4:2:2	6.7:1	100Mbps
	DVCPRO HD 720p	960×720	1280×720	4:2:2	6.7:1	100Mbps
	HDCAM	1440×1080	1920×1080	4:2:2	7-10:1	143Mbps
	HDCAM SR	1920×1080	1920×1080	4:2:2: or 4:4:4	2.7:1 (4:2:2 mode); 4.2:1 (4:4:4 mode)	440Mbps
	D5-HD	1920×1080; 1280×720	1920×1080 1280×720	4:2:2	4:1 (8 bit); 5:1 (10 bit)	235Mbps

Table 1.2 HD and SD Format Comparison (NTSC)

Standard	Format	Frame Size (Playback)	Color Sampling	Compression Ratio	Video Data Rate (Mbps)
SD	DV / DVCAM / DVCPRO	720×480	4:1:1	5:1	3.6MBps 25Mbps
	DVCPRO 50	720×480	4:2:2	3.3:1	7.7MBps 50Mbps
	Digital Betacam	720×486	4:2:2	2:1	90Mbps

Chapter 2

Choosing an HDV Camcorder

At the moment, there are only a few HDV camcorder models to choose from on the market, although the announcement and availability of new HDV models is constantly changing. However, choosing a camcorder and deciding which features are most important for your needs is not always easy. In the near future, choosing a camcorder will be even more difficult, with the addition of several consumer devices in addition to the current crop of prosumer models. In this chapter, I'll discuss some of the most significant options to consider when purchasing a new HDV camera. Although these considerations are not all-inclusive (there isn't enough room to cover every feature or camcorder option), they should give you a good idea of what to look for when browsing online, in a showroom, or at your local rental house.

The Design of an HDV Camcorder

The majority of camcorders, whether DV or HDV, are designed with the same basic principles in mind. For example, a camcorder's lens is usually fixed (with a few cameras offering the ability to switch lenses), and the LCD viewscreen is usually located to the left side (most cameras are designed for right-handed use). In addition, the record button on most camcorders is located nearest to the thumb, which usually falls at the back of the camcorder due to the placement of the side handgrip or strap. There are minor differences (or improvements) with some models, such as an additional record button near the top handle on the camcorder (all of Sony's and JVC's HDV camcorders have one of these buttons on their handles). Having this additional record button makes stopping and starting the recording process easier when you are holding the camcorder in unusual positions (for example, low to the ground or to one side). Apart from design, other important elements of an HDV camcorder to consider include what lens it is equipped with and what type of CCDs or image sensors—which capture the images before they are recorded to tape—it has.

HDV Camcorder Types

HDV cameras currently come in two different configurations. The majority of consumer-oriented designs are handheld devices, which fit easily in the hand with a strap attached. For some professional applications, a shoulder-mounted, ENG (Electronic News Gathering)-style camcorder with the ability to swap lenses is the ideal choice (in the future, larger tape sizes with longer running times may also be supported by this type of camcorder, such as the larger DVCAM style cassettes, although there are currently no plans for this). This type of camera is most familiar to professional camera operators, particularly those who began their careers using Betacam SP or Digital Betacam cameras. These larger camcorders often provide more features and better quality than their smaller counterparts; however, transporting a large camera around is not always practical, particularly when traveling by plane. Try to find a camcorder that provides a good balance of the features and size you require.

Evaluating Image Quality

It may be difficult to evaluate minor differences between similar video cameras, but looking closely at the features that can significantly affect the quality of an image should help you decide which camera is right for you. Of course, the inclusion of these features is often reflected in the price you pay for a camera. Ultimately, it is a matter of determining your specific needs and matching them with your budget.

Image Sensors

Video cameras use special image sensors to acquire images. The most commonly used sensor is called a CCD, or *charge-coupled device*, although CMOS (Complementary Metal Oxide Semiconductor) image sensors are becoming increasingly popular. A CCD or CMOS sensor is the electronic eye of your camera. More precisely, it is the retina, which captures light after it passes through the lens before sending it to the brain for processing (or the camera's CPU, in computer terminology). This little chip, which measures anywhere from 1/6 of an inch to 1/2 of an inch in most cameras, is the device that captures light and converts it into digital information. The larger the CCD, the more light and detail it can capture, thus the better the image quality you can expect to achieve. A 1/3-inch CCD, like those found in the Sony HDV camcorders, is generally the upper end for most prosumer cameras (2/3-inch CCDs found in some professional devices are more expensive, not to mention the 35mm equivalent sensors in professional, "film" style, digital cinema cameras, such as the Panavision Genesis and DALSA's Origin cameras).

Also important is the number of pixels the CCD uses to capture information; this also affects image quality. It's hard to accurately evaluate image quality based solely on pixel counts, as each camera's CCD works differently (for example, Sony's HDV camera line uses a technology called *Advanced HAD*, which produces excellent results). It's best to evaluate image quality in real-world situations, which is why product reviews, sample images, and user feedback are important indicators of a camera's quality.

While most consumer cameras are equipped with a single CCD chip (or, in newer camcorders, a single CMOS chip—see Figure 2.1), three-chip cameras are generally preferred by professionals and are found in the majority of prosumer and professional devices (although the Genesis and Dalsa cinema cameras mentioned earlier, for example, use a single 35mm-sized image sensor that has amazing quality). Three CCDs can dramatically increase image quality, as they are better able to reproduce color and sharpness by using individual chips for red, green, and blue color information. If it is within your budget, a three-chip camera is an ideal device for reproducing more detailed and vibrant images. The most popular three-CCD HDV camcorders are Sony's HDR-FX1 and HVR-Z1U. Both of the older JVC HDV camcorders (JVC JY-HD10U and GR-HD1) use a single CCD, although the new JVC GY-HD100 is a three-CCD camcorder, which also has an excellent lens and many other professional features. The current lineup of HDV camcorders with a single CMOS sensor (such as the Sony HDR-HC1 and HVR-A1U) partially compensate for the lack of three separate sensors with additional signal processing technology.

Figure 2.1 *Sony's HDR–FX1 and HVR–Z1U use three CCDs, while the HDR–HC1 and HVR–A1U use a single CMOS sensor (the new CMOS sensor is shown here). (Courtesy of Sony)*

CCD VS. CMOS

CCD image sensors are traditionally used for capturing video images, although CMOS sensors are becoming more common, arriving first in digital still cameras and now in digital camcorders. The difference between the two types is of interest to new camcorder buyers, as well as professionals that follow trends in the industry. Until recently, CMOS sensors were not used very much for high-quality video production, due (in part) to their lackluster low-light performance and poor signal-to-noise ratio. However, the latest CMOS (Complementary Metal Oxide Semiconductor) sensors provide much better sensitivity and signal-to-noise ratio than previous iterations, as well as having the benefit of lower power consumption, resulting in longer battery life as compared with CCDs. Lower power consumption also means that smaller batteries and more compact devices can be built. An added benefit of the CMOS imager is no vertical smear, which is a line that stretches from the top to bottom of a screen when the camera is pointed at extremely bright light sources—a problem that can occur with CCDs. Additionally, CMOS sensors can be cheaper to manufacture, since they are made using ubiquitous semiconductor technology and processes (millions of CMOS chips are produced every year), although the degree of control necessary for high-quality HD imagers means that the difference in price is generally negligible.

The Sony HDR-HC1 and HVR-A1U camcorders utilize a single, 3-megapixel CMOS imager, along with Sony's "Enhanced Imaging Processor" (EIP) (see Figure 2.2) and other proprietary technology to improve the speed and quality of the sensor (as well as helping with the capture of better still images). According to Sony, EIP technology, which uses a special algorithm to separate image data from texture patterns and brightness components, is responsible for their sensor's wide dynamic range. Using a special type of DSP (digital signal processor) is one way that Sony managed to make CMOS sensors viable for high-quality video. In fact, moving subjects are rendered clearer (CMOS have faster response time) and with much richer colors than you might expect from a single-chip device. The professional bias against single chip camcorders (as opposed to three-chip models) is most often based on the results of single CCD devices (such as the early JVC HDV camcorders), which can be inferior when compared to modern, CMOS sensors. This is especially true of the sensors in Sony's new camcorders, which use additional image processing techniques to improve performance. Also, Sony's CMOS image sensors have a larger photosentive area that enables more light to be captured, as compared with conventional CMOS technology, which can greatly improve the low-light performance of the chip (in addition to using what Sony calls the Correlated Double Sampling circuits). Overall, current three-chip, CCD camcorders outperform devices with a single CMOS sensor, although the gap in quality is narrowing, especially when three-chip CMOS sensors are released.

Figure 2.2 *Sony Enhanced Imaging Processor (EIP) improves the performance of its CMOS sensors (included in the HDR-HC1 and HVR-A1U). (Courtesy of Sony)*

Sony's HDV camcorders have an interesting way of achieving their significant increase in resolution. The CCDs on the HDR-FX1 and HVR-Z1U are actually captured as a grid of 960×1080 pixels. The pixels on the green CCD are offset halfway between the red and blue sensors, increasing the horizontal line of 960 pixels by 1.5 times their original size, bringing them up to 1,440 non-square pixels that are actually rectangles with a 2:1 aspect ratio (which are later resized to 1,920 pixels for display on an HDTV monitor). This process is called *pixel shift*.

ADVANCED HAD TECHNOLOGY

Sony's Advanced HAD (Hole Accumulation Diode) technology used in its CCD imagers improves the detail in its video. These particular chips utilize 1,120,000 pixels, and a special dichroic prism (a prism that splits light into two beams of color), which separates color information and produces more accurate results with less "bleeding." The Advanced HAD CCDs also allow more light to reach the imager, resulting in a better signal-to-noise ratio, which in turn reduces the noise that can result from shooting in dark conditions.

Lenses

For the most part, there is a limited choice of lenses for HDV cameras, and the only model that currently allows you to replace lenses is the JVC GY-HD100U (see Figure 2.3). Although DV cameras like Canon's XL-2 offer a choice of lenses—including the entire EOS photo series with a special adapter— most, current HDV cameras are stuck with a single fixed lens. Fortunately, the lens that comes with your camera is suitable for the majority of shooting situations. If you require more lens options, such as a special lens for wide angles or extreme close-ups (see Chapter 4 for more information on using these types of lenses), consider one of the many lens attachments on the market that screw onto the front of your camera's fixed lens, such as those sold by Century Optics. You should also determine if the lens is "fast" enough for your needs, meaning that by allowing more light to enter the aperture, faster shutter speeds can be selected (put another way, the lens can be open for shorter periods of time while still capturing enough light—see Chapter 4, "Operating an HDV Camcorder," for more information on aperture, iris, and shutter speed). You can determine the speed of a lens by looking at the lowest F-stop (or largest aperture) it is capable of at its widest focal length (zoomed all the way out). For example, F1.6 (shared by the HDR-FX1 and HVR-Z1U) indicates a relatively fast lens, while the lens on an HDR-HC1 is slightly slower at F1.8. A faster lens costs more to produce than a slower lens. Also, you might want to consider the focal length of a lens (also related to zoom range, or the magnifying power of a lens), which indicates its widest and narrowest angle of view—smaller numbers (such as 32.5 mm) are wider angles, while larger numbers (such as 390 mm) are narrower angles (measurements can shift depending on shooting mode or when adapters are used). Technically, focal length is determined by measuring the distance between the center of the lens to the surface of the camera's image sensor (CCD or CMOS). Although focal lengths for video are measured differently than for film (the distance to an image sensor is shorter than the distance to film), you might prefer to look at measurements in relation to their 35 equivalent, such as 32.5 to 390 mm (for the HDR-FX1 and HVR-Z1U), as opposed to the true video measurement of 4.5 to 54 mm (coming from a still photography background, I prefer the former). Check the lens specifications on any new camera or camcorder before you buy to make sure it matches your needs.

Figure 2.3 *Some HDV camcorders, like JVC's GY-HD100, give you a choice of lenses— an option that is missing from most other HDV camcorders on the market. (Courtesy of JVC)*

Many inexpensive consumer cameras are hindered by plastic lenses or low-quality glass. Plastic lenses, which you do not find on HDV camcorders, produce a "foggier" image with less sharpness and more imperfections than a glass element. Also, plastic lenses are less resilient than glass and may scratch easier, especially while cleaning. Fortunately, most manufacturers realize that professionals, and even consumers, require better quality, so they provide sturdier glass lenses with special coatings and high-quality elements, even though these can significantly raise the cost and weight of a camera. For HDV, a high-quality lens is a necessity, due to the increased sharpness and resolution of the HDV format. When shopping for a camera, look for a camera with the best glass lens that you can afford. Sony offers Carl Zeiss optics, which are renowned for their superior quality in professional cameras. Whichever camera you choose, remember that a good lens is one of the most important elements.

IMAGE STABILIZATION

Image stabilization is a common feature on many camcorders that helps to reduce the shakiness of handheld operation by making virtually imperceptible shifts in the position of the image as it's captured on the CCD. There are two forms of image stabilization available—electronic or optical. The optical option (which was previously available on only professional cameras) is superior in quality to the electronic form because it does not use as many pixels on the CCD to accomplish the stabilization. Sony calls this feature *Super Steady Shot*. Typically, the use of electronic image stabilization results in a reduction of quality, since the image must be zoomed slightly to compensate for missing pixels on the sides of the frame, the result of reframing. This results in an image that contains lower resolution than if it were shot with optical stabilization or if the feature were turned off. There are some cameras, such as the Sony PDX10 (DV/DVCAM), that utilize an oversized CCD, which allows the electronic stabilization to move the image without losing resolution. If you are shooting on a tripod or other stable surface, make sure to turn off the image stabilization feature to maintain the best quality for your video.

Viewscreens and Viewfinders

An integral part of any video camera is the display device that lets you see what you are shooting. Just about every video camcorder comes equipped with a viewfinder, similar to that on an ordinary photo camera, with either a black-and-white or color screen. Also, most video cameras have a flip-out LCD (Liquid Crystal Display) viewscreen for easy previewing and menu navigation without gluing your eye to a tiny eyepiece.

Using the adjustable LCD screens built into the side (or top) of a camera helps you to compose shots, whether the camera is mounted to a tripod, held in your hand, or raised over your head for an extreme angle. When purchasing a camera with an LCD viewscreen, check out the size of the viewscreen and its pixel count to determine if it is big and bright enough for your needs. Generally, LCD viewscreens are usually between two to four inches in size, with a pixel count of between 123,000 and 250,000 pixels. With the advent of 1080i HDV camcorders, increased pixel counts are a necessity for previewing higher resolution images. The Sony HDR-FX1, for example, has a very sharp 3.5-inch viewscreen with 250,000 pixels. The increased resolution of this screen makes focusing much easier (especially in combination with the expanded focus feature covered in Chapter 4).

VIEWING LCD SCREENS OUTDOORS

The majority of LCD screens do not work well in direct sunlight or bright light conditions. In these situations, the viewfinder is often the best option, as it's not vulnerable to glare—your eye is preventing light from entering the eyepiece. If it's important for you to use your LCD screen outdoors, you should consider purchasing a sunshade, which reduces the glare and shades the screen, making it easier to see. (Hoodman sells a collapsible fabric hood that comes in a variety of sizes for different cameras; find it at www.hoodmanusa.com.)

Although most users prefer to use a camcorder's LCD monitor to compose their shots, professional videographers still swear by their viewfinders (at least when a suitable studio monitor is not available). Some professional users prefer a black-and-white viewfinder to a color viewfinder, as the black-and-white screens are usually sharper, making it easier to determine whether a camera is properly focused. This is due, in part, to the larger number of pixels used in many black-and-white viewfinders. Even though the majority of users prefer color monitors, a black-and-white viewfinder (or a sharp color viewfinder) can be a nice complement to a color LCD viewscreen. Sony's HVR-Z1U is capable of switching the viewfinder from color to black and white to assist in focusing. However, there is no difference in resolution between the color and black-and-white modes on the HVR-Z11U's viewfinder (no extra detail in black-and-white image, although it is a nice marketing feature).

LCD VIEWING ANGLE

Most LCD viewscreens can swivel to achieve an optimum viewing angle. In fact, you can often spin a screen 180 degrees in the opposite direction, so that the people you are recording can see themselves.

Audio Recording Options

While image quality may be the most noticeable aspect of any video camera, audio quality should not be ignored, especially if you are planning to record a lot of dialogue for movies or documentaries. Fortunately, all HDV cameras come standard with digital audio that equals the quality you might expect from CDs and DVDs.

However, the best quality audio is not usually realized, due to environmental conditions, noise generated by the camera's motors, or a low-quality microphone that's built into a camcorder. In this section, I'll point out a few considerations for when you're purchasing audio gear to complement the excellent image quality of your digital video camera.

Microphones

Nearly all camcorders come equipped with a built-in microphone. Unfortunately, a built-in microphone is one of those features that tends to perform poorly—it's an easy way for manufacturers to cut corners. Of course, many videographers use the built-in microphone exclusively. Although a built-in microphone may be sufficient for the average user's needs, professional productions (or those aspiring to be) can benefit from the use of external microphones. For example, a wireless microphone unit could be placed on an actor's clothing to capture muffled dialogue, or a shotgun microphone could be used to focus on someone in a crowded room. Beginning filmmakers and videographers frequently ignore audio quality, and this is a telltale sign of an amateur production. Consider budgeting for a decent microphone and a pair of headphones to monitor the sound as well.

ATTACHING MICROPHONES TO A CAMCORDER

Many digital video cameras (even small consumer models) are already equipped with a special accessory "shoe" on top for attaching an optional shotgun microphone. The professional models of both Sony's (see Figure 2.4) and JVC's HDV camcorders include a special mount for a separate microphone, although even their consumer models are capable of accepting a microphone attachment. Some shoes, however, are proprietary, especially on consumer models (such as the Sony HDR-HC1), and may not easily accept devices by another manufacturer.

Figure 2.4 *Sony's HVR-Z1U camcorder comes equipped with XLR connections and the ability to accept a separate shotgun microphone in addition to its built-in microphone. (Courtesy of Sony)*

If all else fails, try re-recording dialogue (known as ADR, additional dialogue recording), adding sound effects, or recording a voice-over to mask location audio. Consult a few microphone manufacturers to find out how your next video production can benefit from a good microphone setup. Also, try supplementing any on-board audio recorded to your camera by adding a MiniDisc, DAT, or CD recorder to a live situation, such as when you're taping a concert or theatrical production. Be warned, however, that any audio you record as dual system sound may not sync up easily with your picture, especially on longer takes, since each device has its own internal clock. Over time (anywhere from a few minutes to an hour), the audio may lose sync, so be warned.

XLR versus RCA Connections

Professional audio and consumer audio products are often distinguished by their inclusion of XLR connections (see Figure 2.5); they don't use the ordinary "red and white" RCA cables found with the majority of audio products on the market, such as CD and DVD players. Of course, XLR audio and extra microphones are probably overkill for most casual uses, such as recording vacations or home movies. However, as professional audio products strive for extremely solid and quiet connections, they most often use the superior XLR connections to connect microphones to cameras or other recording devices.

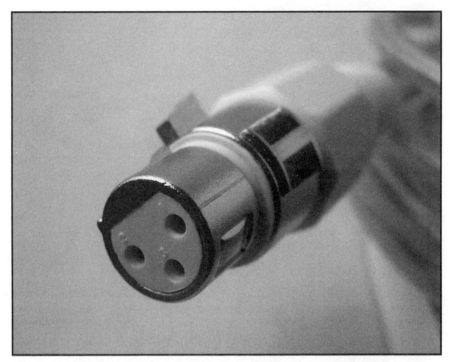

Figure 2.5 *XLR audio connections are larger and more secure than RCA connections (in addition to offering better performance).*

XLR cables are sturdy, provide excellent noise-canceling properties (due to the balanced connection) for transmitting sound information, and form solid connections by using larger, locking connectors. In contrast, RCA cables, which come packaged with most audio and video devices, are smaller and less sturdy, with only a single, unbalanced metal contact that connects with the camera or recorder.

If you are working with a consumer camera, you may want to consider purchasing a separate XLR adapter (BeachTek, at www.beachtek.com, makes some popular models, see Figure 2.6). These boxes connect to the back or underside of your camera for recording audio from wireless microphones, boom microphones, or even a better-equipped shotgun microphone. Most professional audio gear require XLR connections, so if you are planning to shoot clean dialogue for your next movie, you should seriously consider getting an adapter if your camera doesn't already come equipped with one.

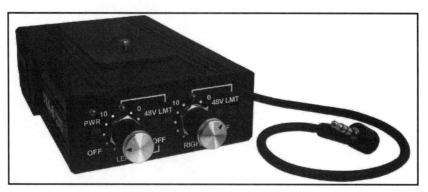

Figure 2.6 *An audio adapter with XLR inputs can be added to your existing camera, such as the DXA-8 sold by BeackTek.*

BALANCED VERSUS UNBALANCED AUDIO

Apart from the type of connector used to attach a microphone to a camcorder or other audio equipment in your recording or editing suite (XLR, RCA, mini stereo jack, and so on), there are two kinds of connections (or wiring setups) to be aware of when using audio inputs and outputs on any device—balanced or unbalanced. Balanced audio connections are ideal (such as the XLR connectors on a Sony HVR-Z1U) and important for achieving professional results, while unbalanced connections (such as those on the Sony HDR-FX1) are common in consumer audio devices.

To begin with, most audio cables are shielded (some better than others), yet even with proper shielding it is difficult to prevent hum and other interference from high-frequency noise produced by the electricity that surrounds us (the power that supplies lights, appliances, and wall outlets for example, which usually occupy the 60Hz frequency—in addition to other "harmonics" existing in various frequency bands of an audio circuit). In fact, the shielding itself can be the source of some hum, due to the nature of ground wires and the differences in reference points that determine voltage (electrical potential). A typical problem for audio setups is called a "ground loop," which is caused by connecting the ground wire from one source to the ground wire of another (differing ground connection potentials). This often occurs when multiple devices with mismatched electrical currents are connected together, which fails to measure voltage in the same way (the zero volts reference point can differ for each device, if it is not properly balanced). Varying reference points and multiple ground paths created by complex wiring setups (imagine a large audio facility or studio shoot with heavy cabling) are problematic to achieving clean, noise-free audio. This relates to the basic problem with "unbalanced" audio—the input and output have a single voltage relative to ground.

For professional audio gear, one way to eliminate problems with noise and hum caused by outside interference is to use "balanced" audio connections. Balanced connections use two wires, each with its own voltage running in the opposite direction from the other—two phases relative to ground (anti-phase). Both signals are equal in amplitude, but opposite in phase. For example, if they were added together, the result would be silence, although by combining and amplifying the difference between the two opposite signals, noise is suppressed (a transformer at the receiving end can cancel out the noise that is common in both signals). Also, using a ground wire that is independent of the signals (which is found in XLR connectors, for example), keeps the ground of multiple devices separate from each other, to avoid the ground loop effect mentioned earlier. The use of balanced audio connections is particularly important when using long cables, which are common in many production situations, such as when using a boom microphone or running lines to a mixer. Long cables act as antennas for outside interference, thus they should be kept as short as possible, properly shielded, and balanced to reduce noise. For camcorder operators, any microphone inputs' connections should be balanced to avoid noise.

In general, RCA connectors and the majority of home stereo connections (including the mini stereo jack or RCA connections on a camcorder) are unbalanced, while XLR connectors (which include three pins, two for audio and one ground wire) are usually balanced.

If your camcorder does not have XLR connectors built in, you can purchase a separate audio adapter (like those sold by BeachTek, see Figure 2.7) to add XLR inputs that connect to the line level inputs on your camera. Even unbalanced connections (particularly those close to the receiving device, such as the inputs on a camcorder like the HDR-FX1) may overcome much RF interference by using line level audio, which is amplified and thus stronger than most outside interference, particularly at short distances and when captured with a balanced input. This explains the ability of camcorders with unbalanced inputs to make use of balanced, XLR adapters, which pass a balanced signal over a very short distance into the camcorder's mini jack.

Figure 2.7 *XLR connectors, such as the inputs on the Beachtek DXA-8 adapter, offer balanced audio for professional results (professional model camcorders, like the Sony HVR-Z1U and JVC GY-HD100U offer built-in, balanced XLR connections, although the Sony HDR-FX1 requires an adapter for the best performance).*

HDV CAMCORDER INPUTS AND OUTPUTS

The majority of HDV camcorders are equipped with similar input and output options. These include a LANC jack (for remotely controlling operations of your camera, such as zoom and record), headphone jack, microphone line in, and (occasionally) XLR ports for superior audio. In addition, there may be video outputs that include S-Video and composite video connections for SD output (composite video connections are not found on current HDV camcorders, although they are common with DV camcorders and older, analog devices). Additionally, component connections, which separate a video signal into its basic color elements for improved quality (the only analog HD output available—see Figure 2.8), and RCA ports for audio are included. By default, HDV camcorders also include a FireWire connection (also called *i.Link* or *IEEE 1394*), which is used for transmitting video and audio information to a computer—a necessity for editing and storage. When shopping for a camcorder, make sure that the one you choose is equipped with all of the ports you need for suitable connections.

Figure 2.8 *A special component video cable (component outputs are shown here with the JVC CU-VH1U HDV deck) allows you to view HDV output from your camcorder on a monitor or HDTV with component inputs. (Courtesy of JVC)*

HDV Tape Stock

Although current HDV camcorders may use any type of MiniDV tape stock, companies like Sony have developed tapes that are especially formulated for HDV recording (see Figure 2.9). These tapes provide better performance and reliability with less error and fewer dropouts (signal loss, which is often due to missing magnetic material on the tape). In fact, Sony claims that its tapes offer 90 percent fewer errors, 50 percent fewer dropouts, 50 percent less shrinkage, and less noise compared to standard MiniDV cassettes (although noise levels in the context of digital tape stock does not affect the video quality that is recorded, unlike analog formats, such as Betacam SP).

Figure 2.9 *Sony's new HDV tape stock is sturdier and more reliable than standard DV cassettes.*

Sony's HD DVC media uses a new tape lubricant that improves stability under a variety of operating conditions and a new tape formulation called *Advanced Metal Evaporated* (AME II). AME II is a second-generation MiniDV tape technology that reduces the size of the metal particles through a process called *super oxidation.* This process creates a smoother tape surface, which improves the performance of the tape as it moves over the recording and playback heads. As a bonus, these new tapes offer three additional minutes of recording time (63 minutes instead of 60 minutes) over standard MiniDV cassettes. Initial reports indicate that these tapes work very well, and they seem to live up to the company's claims of stability. However, it's difficult to make an accurate comparison between the reliability of newer and older media—particularly where HDV is concerned—as HDV has improved error correction already and possesses other differences that make it not directly comparable to the DV format (for instance, the dropouts experienced as a result of the HDV MPEG-2 format differ from DV recordings, which utilize a different scheme altogether).

For some users, the choice to purchase the new media over standard MiniDV cassettes (particularly for casual recording) may be driven by price—Sony's DVM-63HD HD DVC tapes are currently listed at $18 per tape. Whenever possible, choose one brand of tape media and stick with it, as the type of lubricant in the tape mechanism differs from brand to brand. Some users report problems when switching to another type of tape; this is most likely a result of its effects on the camera's or deck's tape mechanism, which becomes accustomed to a particular type of lubricant.

MIXING HDV TAPE STOCKS

The use of different tape stocks, and (as a result) different tape lubricants, can be a serious problem for HDV camcorders and decks (this was also a problem with some DV tape stocks). Each manufacturer may use its own formulation of lubricant (including the new type by Sony, mentioned in this section), which does not always mix well when combined with the lubricant from another tape. The result may be clogged heads in your playback and recording mechanisms (the consequence of wet lubricant mixing with an older, dry lubricant from a previous tape stock). For example, the lubricant from a Sony HDV tape may not work well with an outwardly similar tape by Maxell. Although not everyone will experience problems, the safest solution is to pick one tape stock and stick with it indefinitely. However, this is often not practical, or possible, since you may be given tapes to edit that were shot by a different user.

Ergonomics

In the 1950s, the term *ergonomics* was coined to describe the interaction between people and their working environment, particularly the ways in which machines meet the needs and motion of the human body. The primary concerns with respect to ergonomics are efficiency and safety. Is your camcorder a good fit? Does it rest easily in the palm of your hand or balance softly on your shoulder? Where are the audio meters, menu buttons, and A/V connections located? These are important questions for anyone planning on spending more than a few hours with his or her camcorder. After all, it's difficult to enjoy using a device that is uncomfortable and whose operation is impractical.

ETYMOLOGY OF EROGOMICS

Ergonomics is a combination of two Greek words, *ergon* meaning work and *nomoi* meaning natural laws—simply defined as *the science of work.*

Before purchasing your next camcorder, consider going to a store or trade show where you can pick it up, shoot with it, play with the buttons, and move it around in your hand. This should help you determine whether its form factor meets your physical needs. Does it have a handle on top for performing low shots and another set of buttons for controlling the recording? Is it top heavy or does it lean to one side? While these questions may not affect your ultimate purchasing decision, they are factors that can make a difference when you're trying to choose between similarly equipped models.

Also, think about the situations in which you may be using the camera and how this may affect its operation. For example, if you are going to be taping a lot of video at an all-day event, such as a wedding, you probably want a camera that isn't too heavy and has an easily adjustable viewfinder, which won't cause discomfort after several hours of continuous shooting. Some camcorders, like Sony's HDR-FX1, require you to use the handgrip and hold the lens at the same time. This provides maximum control for shooting and operating the focus, zoom, and iris controls, while helping to steady the rather hefty camera body. Sony also sells an optional (and, at $400, expensive) shoulder brace to make holding the HDR-FX1 and HVR-Z1U easier. The original JVC HDV camcorders can also take advantage of a brace like this, as they are held in much the same way (although they are slightly smaller than the Sony cameras). The older JVC cameras also tend to feel less sturdy than the Sony models, although the new JVC GY-HD100 has a substantial form and is perfectly suited to resting on your shoulder. In fact, the new JVC HDV camcorder has a specially placed, cushioned earpiece that aligns with your ear when holding the camcorder on your shoulder.

In addition, consider the placement of basic camera operations on the device. The placement of manual controls on the camcorder body, rather than in electronic menus, makes shooting easier when you are trying to capture a shot quickly.

HDV Camcorder Comparisons

The following section outlines some of the basic specifications and features of a few of the most popular HDV cameras on the market today. While the new Sony HDV camcorders have more professional features than the original, JVC hand-held devices, there are other factors to consider when choosing a camcorder. For example, for some users, the 720p capabilities of the JVC cameras outweigh their lack of resolution, as it gives them progressive capture. However, for film output, shooting at 30p does not necessarily produce the best results. In fact, shooting at a standard rate of 60i (interlaced frames) provides more motion information for converting to other frame rates. In addition, the Sony cameras produce images with better color, as a result of their three CCDs and improved optics, and they operate better in low light situations than does the JVC (due to a superior lux rating). Take a look at some of the special features of each camera, as outlined below, for a technical comparison of each model.

Although most of the current HDV cameras do not produce a true 24 frame, progressive image (which is popular with filmmakers and those intending to transfer to film the JVC GY-HD100 is the first exception, since it offers real 24p recording), the Sony cameras do produce a "fake" version of the 24-frame effect that might be enough for users who simply want the look of film motion on their televisions—that is, if they don't mind the flickering effect it produces. Still, unless you can record true 24p images, it is usually best to save any frame rate conversions for post-production, where you have greater control over the process. In general, it is best to shoot 60i, no matter what camera you are using, unless your device has a true progressive frame mode.

Sony HDR-FX1 and HVR-Z1U

The first HDV camcorders from Sony marked a new beginning for the HDV format. These cameras, the HDR-FX1 and HVR-Z1U (see Figure 2.10), provide many of the same features found in prosumer DV camcorders (such as the Sony PD-170 or VX2000), while adding new features and improving on the resolution of all previous devices, including the first-generation HDV camcorders produced by JVC. Using 3 1/3 CCDs and recording at a resolution of 1,080 lines (the maximum number of lines in the HDTV specifications), these camcorders present an exciting option for today's low budget filmmakers.

Figure 2.10 *Sony's new first consumer/professional HDV camcorders, the HDR-FX1 (right) and HVR-Z1U (left). (Courtesy of Sony)*

The HDR-FX1 and HVR-Z1U share many features. In fact, the front end of each camcorder, including imagers and lens, are exactly the same. Both camcorders include an excellent Carl Zeiss Vario-Sonnar T lens with 12x optical zoom (the 35mm equivalent of a 32.5mm to 390mm lens). Full manual controls (in addition to automatic modes) are possible with each device, including a wide variety of shutter speeds, 24-step iris control, and a manual zoom ring with markings. Each camcorder is capable of shooting HDV or DV (with built-in down-conversion for prerecorded material as well), which makes them ideal for acquiring HD images, even if you only need SD today (shoot once, deliver twice). The ability to make the switch from HDV to DV should assuage the short-sighted skeptics who argue that shooting HDV is impractical, since most of their audience is only able to view SD formats at this time. Soon HD-DVD and Blu-Ray disc formats (in addition to current red laser options) will make HD material highly sought after. See Chapter 12, "Delivering HDV Content," for more information on output options.

Overall, the new Sony cameras feel comfortable, even with the larger-than-usual design. The viewfinder's unusual location on the handle grip makes it easily viewable, while keeping it out of the way of other controls on the body of the camera. All of the manual controls you need are easily accessible on the camera; there is no need to search through several menus. Even the specially designed lens hood and easy opening lens cover are nicely designed. A separate lens cap is not necessary, although additional lens attachments may require you to leave the hood off. The FireWire port toward the back of the camcorder is positioned at an odd, downward angle, which may require you to elevate the camcorder while capturing to avoid bending the cable or damaging the port. The recessed battery compartment leaves ample room for a large capacity battery, like the NP-F970. Overall, these camcorders are very solid and nicely designed, and they are a real improvement over Sony's previous DV camcorders.

Figure 2.11 *The Sony HDR-FX1 was the first 3-CCD HDV camcorder and the first low-cost HD device sold by Sony (initially sold as a "consumer" device and produced by its consumer division—notice the lack of XLR connections). (Courtesy of Sony)*

New features that are unique to these cameras include the ability to automatically create "scene transitions" by pressing one of two user-defined buttons that reproduce zoom, focus, iris, shutter, and other controls that move between predefined settings. (A "rack" focus effect—when an object in the foreground is brought into focus while the background is thrown out of focus—can be smoothly produced in this way.) Picture profiles can also be saved that define settings for particular shooting conditions. An example would be a preset for shooting sunsets and another for a concert hall environment.

Unique CinemaTone and CineFrame recording modes are also included with these camcorders, to help approximate the properties of film gamma and frame rates. The primary differences between the HDR-FX1 (see Figure 2.11) and HVR-Z1U are in the extra, professional touches. The HVR-Z1U's ability to switch between NTSC and PAL shooting modes (60i and 50i) for both HDV and DV formats is a plus, particularly for filmmakers that prefer the 50i (25 fps) shooting mode for transfer to film (a perceived benefit that can be disputed for film transfer, while still great for acquisition and delivery of broadcast material within PAL countries). Both camcorders can shoot DV and down-convert HDV to DV, although a true progressive mode for 480p standard definition images (DV format) is also included in the HVR-Z1U.

Built-in XLR audio inputs are another benefit of the HVR-Z1U (see Figure 2.12), as are professional SMPTE timecode features, such as a Free Run mode for syncing up multiple camcorders (see Chapter 4, "Operating an HDV Camcorder," and Chapter 7, "Editing HDV," for more information on timecode). Timecode can also be set manually on the HVR-Z1U, and user bit values may be added to the tape (information for date, time, scene, etc. may also be added). Additionally, the HVR-Z1U has a black stretch option (important for a more accurate film-look) and an extra CinemaTone mode (the HVR-Z1U has CinemaTone 1 and 2 presets, while the HDR-FX1 is limited to the equivalent of CinemaTone 2) and CineFrame modes (HVR-Z1U adds CineFrame 25, which is actually smoother and more film-like than the CineFrame 24 option on both camcorders). The HVR-Z1U also adds the ability to switch between a color or black-and-white viewfinder (although with no actual advantage in resolution). And you can operate both the viewfinder and viewscreen simultaneously (the HDR-FX1 limits you to using one at a time).

Hypergain (for shooting at less than 1 lux at night), six assignable buttons, additional picture markers (center, safety, and 4:3 markers—the HDR-FX1 only includes a center marker), crop (in addition to squeeze and letterbox) for HDV to DV down-conversion, a color correction function (an in-camera effect for changing the color of a target object while leaving other objects unaffected), and other menu options are available solely for the HVR-Z1U. Many of these features may not matter to the casual user or even to some professionals. XLR audio is one of the most obvious differences between the two camcorders, although a separate adapter can be purchased for the HDR-FX1. If XLR is not a deal breaker, options like black stretch and 50i shooting modes may be another reason to choose the HVR-Z1U, although if you are shooting for 60i formats and can handle audio separately (or not at all, if shooting visuals is your primary concern), the HDR-FX1 might be all you need.

Figure 2.12 *The Sony HVR–Z1U camcorder is shown here with a 16:9 viewscreen open and the optional shotgun microphone attached. (Courtesy of Sony)*

Table 2.1 lists a few of the differences and similarities between the Sony HDR-FX1 and HVR-Z1U camcorders.

Table 2.1 Sony HDR-FX1 and HVR-Z1U Comparison

Model	HDR-FX1	HVR-Z1U
CCDs	3–1/3 inch	3–1/3 inch
Lens Mount / Filter Size	72mm	72mm
Optical Zoom	12 X	12 X
Focal Length	4.5–54mm 32.5–390mm (35mm Equivalent)	4.5–54mm 32.5–390 mm (35mm Equivalent)
Image Resolution	1440×1080 pixels	1440×1080 pixels

Model	HDR-FX1	HVR-Z1U
LCD Viewscreen	3.5 inch color w/ 250,000 pixels	3.5 inch color w/250,000 pixels
LCD Viewfinder	Color Only	Black-and-White/Color Switchable
Recording Modes	Mini DV, HDV	Mini DV, DVCAM, HDV
Video System	1080 60i	1080 50i/1080 60i
Shutter Speed	1/4–1/10,000	1/4–1/10,000
Iris	F1.6–F11	F1.6–F11
Gain	0dB–18dB, by 3dB	0dB–18dB + Hyper, by 3dB
Minimum Illumination	3 Lux	3 Lux (Hyper Gain Supports Less Than 1 Lux)
Display Markers	Center Marker	4:3 Marker, Center Marker, Safety Marker
4:3 Output	Letterbox, Squeeze	Letterbox, Squeeze, Crop
All Scan Mode (Similar to Under Scan Mode on Other Camcorders)	No	Yes
Picture Profile Presets	6	6
Assignable Buttons	3	6
SMPTE Color Bars	1 (not true)	2 (full screen and partial)
Black Level (Setup)	No	0–7.5 (Only in NTSC Mode)
Black Stretch	No	Yes
Timecode	Drop Frame Record Run No Timecode Preset or Reset	Drop Frame/Non-Drop Frame (Selectable) Record Run or Free Run Preset or Reset Timecode
Audio	12 Bit, 32kHz/16 Bit, 48kHz; Dual Channel	12 Bit, 32kHz/16 Bit, 48kHz; Individually Adjustable
Audio Input	Stereo Mini Plug	2-XLR w/Phantom Power (48 Volt), Mono or Stereo
Component Output	480i/1080i	480i/480p/575i/576p/1080i

Sony HDR-HC1 and HVR-A1U

Not long after the availability of their first, professional HDV camcorders (the HDR-FX1 and HVR-Z1U), Sony announced two new camcorders—the HDR-HC1 and HVR-A1U—intended for consumers and professionals, which nicely complement their larger siblings. The HDR-HC1 (see Figure 2.13) is a consumer camcorder that breaks the HDV price barrier at under $2,000 (approximately $1,999 suggested list, although it is currently selling for closer to $1,800), while the HVR-A1U (see Figure 2.14) is a professional camcorder, similar in size and operation to the consumer model, but with features associated with the HVR-Z1U (approximately $3,500 suggested list). The primary difference between these new camcorders and the original HDV models is size (the new camcorders are much more compact) and the addition of a single CMOS image sensor in place of 3 CCD imagers. Both the HDR-HC1 and HVR-A1U have a single, 1/3-inch 3-megapixel CMOS image sensor, which can record still images in addition to video. Stills can be recorded at 2.8 Megapixels (1920×1440) onto Memory Stick or at 1.2 Megapixels (1440×810) onto tape. Although these are the first HDV camcorders to use a CMOS sensor, other camcorders with CMOS have been available in the past, such as the Sony DCR-PC1000 DV camcorder. At under two pounds (the HDR-HC1 weighs between 1 and 1.5 pounds), and significantly more compact than their larger HDV counterparts, these camcorders are ideal for travel and other situations that require mobility.

Figure 2.13 *Sony's HDR-HC1 is the most inexpensive, consumer HDV camcorder currently available. (Courtesy of Sony)*

In addition to the use of a CMOS sensor, the size and resolution of the chip in the HDR-HC1 and HVR-A1U differ from the HDR-FX1 and HVR-Z1U. In order to capture the greater than HD resolution pictures in its still mode, the camcorder uses a chip that has a 1920×1440 pixel resolution (1440 vertical lines instead of the usual 1080), which is then chopped off on the top and bottom to produce the 16:9 aspect ratio of HD recordings. Although the sensors have an effective 1920×1080 resolution for video, these pixels are only pertinent for the capture, not the recording of HDV. The signal that is recorded to tape is still 1440×1080 non-square pixels, which conforms to the HDV specifications. Additional photo features (at least on the HDR-HC1) include a pop-up flash, which has low, normal, and high settings, and a "burst shot mode" that can record images 3 to 25 images at a time in 25-second intervals. Both camcorders have a 10x optical zoom (a 120x digital zoom is included as well, although digital zoom should always be avoided) and use a Carl Zeiss Vario-Sonar T lens (excellent coated optics, shared by Sony's other HDV camcorders). In addition, each camcorder is equipped with an expanded focus (essential for critical focusing of HD images), shot transitions (although no curves on the HDR-HC1), guide frames, and a plethora of other features, many of which can be found on the larger camcorders (of course, features vary by model).

Figure 2.14 *Sony's HVR-A1U is a smaller counterpart to the HVR-Z1U and shares many of its professional features, such as XLR audio inputs, DV/DVCAM operation, and 50i or 60i shooting modes. (Courtesy of Sony)*

Another unique feature of the HDR-HC1 (and as expected in the HVR-A1U) is the use of a touchscreen that offers access to menu items and playback controls (Sony has been using touchscreen viewfinders for a while now, such as the screen on a PDX10, the DV counterpart to an HVR-A1U). The 2.7-inch widescreen LCD on the HDR-HC1 (and HVR-A1U, although pixel count is to be determined) has a resolution of 123,000 pixels (or about half the pixels of the viewscreen on the HDR-FX1—see Figure 2.15). The viewfinder on the HDR-HC1 is actually sharper than its viewscreen, with a resolution of 250,000 pixels, which is the same as the viewfinder on the HDR-FX1. A sharp viewfinder with plenty of pixels makes focusing much easier, which is especially important with HD formats, since it is very easy to obtain soft, unfocused images as a result of the difficulty to discern fine detail without a good monitor (expanded focus is important for this purpose as well, in addition to features such as peaking). Another consumer-type feature of the HDR-HC1, common with other Sony consumer camcorders on the market, is called NightShot (or "Super NightShot Plus Infrared System," in this case), which allows you to see short distances in darkness, while casting a green glow over your subjects.

The design of these camcorders is unique for a consumer-style device. Most critical camcorder controls, such as focus and zoom rings, as well as an "exposure" dial are located on the body, most on the lens barrel, which provides easy access while shooting. Probably the least appreciated feature would be the bottom loading tape mechanism, an unfortunate design decision which requires you to remove the camcorder from a tripod or mounting plate in order to load a new tape (a real problem when shooting events). Apart from the professional features already mentioned, one of the HVR-A1U's new features, which is not included in any other Sony HDV camcorder, is a Histogram Indicator, which displays the brightness, or exposure (also referred to as latitude), of areas in your image. The Tele Macro mode is also unique to both the HDR-HC1 and HVR-A1U, which records macro (small, or close-up) images at a distance. The Tele Macro mode may help you to achieve a more film-like picture when shooting a subject at a distance, by separating them more easily from the background, keeping them in focus while the background is thrown out of focus.

Figure 2.15 *The Sony HDR-HC1 includes a 2.7 inch, touch-sensitive viewscreen. (Courtesy of Sony)*

As should be expected, the HDR-HC1 and HVR-A1U do not perform as well as the higher-end HDV camcorders, especially when comparing low-light performance (for example, the HDR-FX1 has a lux rating of 3, while the HDR-HC1 is rated at 7). In general, CCD sensors perform better in lower light, which partially explains the superior results of the HDR-FX1 and HVR-Z1U when compared with current, consumer camcorders using a CMOS sensor. However, the images in both devices can be remarkably good, and under controlled lighting the results are very similar to the larger units. In fact, CMOS sensors offer advantages to CCDs, such as eliminating the vertical "smearing" that can occur on video images when pointed at an extremely bright light source. Together with advances in CMOS technology and Sony's proprietary tools, one can glimpse a bright future for more CMOS usage in video acquisition devices. If you are a consumer looking for a higher-end camcorder, or if you are new to HDV and do not need as many professional controls, then the HDR-HC1 is an excellent choice. Although its features do not match up with the HDR-FX1, it is one of the best camcorders in its price range, HDV or otherwise. If you are a professional who needs a compact second camera with features that nearly match your HVR-Z1U (such as XLR audio or more flexible SMPTE timecode options), then the HVR-A1U (see

Figure 2.16) could be the camcorder for you. In addition to being great for general-purpose recording, both the HDR-HC1 and HVR-A1U are useful as "B-cameras" (second unit photography or alternate angles) or a "crash cam" (a camera intended for dangerous situations, where you would not want to send an expensive camera, such as skiing, skateboarding, skydiving, or hanging out the window of a moving car).

Figure 2.16 *The Sony HVR-A1U shown here in profile. (Courtesy of Sony)*

Sony HVR-M10U

The first (and currently) only dedicated HDV deck from Sony is the HVR-M10U (see Figure 2.17). This deck provides the same recording and playback options as the HVR-Z1U camcorder (same frame rates), including 1080i and 720p formats (only playback of 720p formats are possible on the HVR-Z1U and HVR-M10U), although it is more compact and better suited to a desktop editing session (a standard camcorder battery may also be attached for portable operation). On the front of the device is a 3.5-inch LCD monitor and a flip-down panel that reveals additional controls. Tapes are inserted behind the front display and controls by flipping down the entire facade to reveal a mini-DV size tape deck (both DVCAM and DV tapes in HD or SD formats are accepted, although it does not support large-style DVCAM cassettes). Like the HDV camcorders, this deck can easily down-convert HD to SD (HDV to DV), and it provides professional SMPTE timecode features that match the HVR-Z1U (Record Run/Free Run, Regeneration, Preset, User Bit preset, User Bit time). In fact, the HVR-M10U is essentially an HVR-Z1U without the lens. Unfortunately, the HVR-M10U is lacking some of the features that might better justify purchasing it, such as a device instead of a camcorder, apart from alleviating the wear and tear on the slightly more expensive HVR-Z1U (it is approximately the same price as an HDR-FX1). For example, an HD-SDI output would help put it squarely in the realm of a professional studio, which often relies on HD-SDI for inputting video through a special capture card (in the case of HDV, it could be "upsampled" to an uncompressed format for editing, color correction, and effects work).

Figure 2.17 *The Sony HVR-M10U is a portable HDV deck with features that match the HVR-Z1U. (Courtesy of Sony)*

JVC JY-HD10U and GR-HD1

Released in June of 2003, the JVC JY-GR-HD1U was the first HDV product to market and was quickly followed by its "professional" counterpart, the JVC JY-HD10U (see Figure 2.18). Both units record at 720 30p (no 720 24p mode) with a resolution of 1280×720 pixels. The JY-HD10U has a few minor improvements over the consumer-oriented GR-HD1, including XLR inputs and color bar generators, features that are targeted towards professional users.

Figure 2.18 *The JVC JY-HD10U was among the first HDV camcorders (a single CCD, 720 30p device). (Courtesy of JVC)*

Perhaps the biggest factor that prevented these JVC camcorders from achieving greater popularity was the use of a single-chip (CCD) instead of the three-chip configuration seen on the majority of professional camcorders (not to mention the initial fear and difficulty of working with an untested and little-supported format). In general, a single chip produces color that does not match up to the accuracy of a three-chip device, which uses separate sensors for red, green, and blue colors. If you are looking for a low cost, single chip HDV camcorder, consider the Sony HDR-HC1 or HVR-A1U over these early HDV camcorders, which lack the image quality, resolution, and features that have become synonymous with HDV in recent years. Of course, owners of these camcorders can utilize their HDV footage like they would any other HDV media. In fact, some producers still use their camcorders to shoot second unit "HD" for television and independent films.

JVC GY-HD100U

JVC's latest entry in the HDV market is a real success in terms of professional features and design. The JVC GY-HD100U (see Figure 2.19) is the first true 24p HDV camcorder and offers filmmakers many of the features that they seek in a camcorder built for film-type work. In fact, JVC says its "features and ergonomics are optimized for digital cinematographic use." It is also the first HDV camcorder to feature an interchangeable HD lens system. The GY-HD100 includes a 16x Servo Fujinon HD lens, although a 13x (3.5 mm focal length) wide zoom HD lens is also available from JVC, as well as standard 1/2-inch lenses that can be used with a special adapter.

Figure 2.19 *The JVC GY-HD100U is the first true 24p HDV camcorder (720 24p, in addition to 720 25p and 720 30p HDV modes), and the first in JVC's line of ProHD camcorders. (Courtesy of JVC)*

JVC refers to their HDV format as "ProHD" rather than HDV. Despite its unique name, it is just another way of saying that they offer "professional" HDV recording formats, all of which are not available on the Sony camcorders (true progressive shooting modes, although at 720 line resolutions). The GY HD-100U (see Figure 2.20) allows you to shoot HDV in 720 24p, 720 25p, and 720 30p modes at 1280×720 lines without scaling (each 1/3-inch CCD has an array of 1280×720 pixels. Other professional features include balanced XLR audio inputs, SMPTE timecode options, special gamma modes, a removable memory card for storing user presets, and the option of 2 channel or 4 channel audio for DV modes (4 channel audio is 12 bit, 32kHz PCM as opposed to 2 channel, 16 bit, 48kHz PCM audio for standard DV modes—HDV is always MPEG-1

Audio Layer II, not PCM) all at an initial list price of $6,295 (the inclusion of a professional, Fujinon lens also makes this a good deal). See Figure 2.21. If you intend to shoot 24p HDV in the near future, then this camcorder is for you. While its shoulder mounted style is not especially suited to packing in a bag for weekend vacations, its main purpose is as a serious, film-capable device, intended for independent films, documentaries, and broadcast video productions. As an additional note, look for the GY-HD7000U ENG/EFP style camcorder in 2006, which features 720p in addition to 1080i modes (as well as 2/3-inch CMOS image sensors and the ability to record onto larger-style DV cassettes).

Figure 2.20 *A front angle view of the JVC GY-HD100U with the viewscreen open. (Courtesy of JVC)*

Table 2.2 shows a brief comparison of the Sony HVR-Z1U and the new JVC GY-HD100U, two of the best professional HDV camcorders currently available (although the GY-HD100U was not available at the time of this writing, leaving some information absent for accuracy).

Table 2.2 Sony HVR-Z1U and JVC GY-HD100U HDV Camcorder Comparison

Model	Sony HVR-Z1U	JVC GY-HD100U
CCDs	3–1/3 inch	3–1/3 inch
HDV Recording Modes	1080 60i (1440×1080)	720 24p, 720 25p, 720 30p (1280×720)
Scan Mode	Interlaced	Progressive
Video Data Rate (HDV)	25Mbps	19.7Mbps
Cinema Modes	CineFrame 24, CineFrame 25, CineFrame 30	720 24p
Shutter Speed	1/4–1/10,000	1/6–1/10,000 (24p Mode), 1/7.5–1/10,000 (30p Mode)
Iris	F1.6–F11	NA
Gain	Auto or 0 dB–18 dB in 3 dB steps	Auto or 0 dB–18 dB in 3 dB steps
ND Filters	1/4 and 1/32	1/4 and 1/16
Optical Zoom	12 X	13 X
Image Stabilization	Optical	Optical
Weight	4 lbs, 4 oz.	6.9 lbs.

Figure 2.21 *Using the Mini35 image converter from P+S Technik (shown here with matte box and follow focus), the JVC GY-HD100U can utilize real 35mm film lenses. (Courtesy of JVC)*

Panasonic HVX-200 and P2 Cards

Although it is not an HDV camcorder, the new Panasonic HVX-200 DVCPRO HD camcorder poses a challenge to Sony and JVC. This camcorder uses a higher data rate format called DVCPRO HD (see Chapter 1, "Understanding High-Definition Video Formats," for more information), which offers fewer compressed images. (DVCPRO HD is also called DV100, since its data rate is 100Mbps, just as other DV formats are 25 Mbps—the standard, DV format we are already accustomed to—and DV50, for higher quality SD images.) Not only is it less compressed than HDV, but it is compressed differently—better, in fact (in terms of quality), since it uses all I-Frames just like other DV formats (no IBP, interframe compression, as discussed in Chapter 7, "Editing HDV") and offers 4:2:2 color sampling, which is an improvement over the 4:2:0 sampling of the HDV format.

Instead of using cassette tapes to record HD video (although the HVX is capable of recording DV to MiniDV cassettes), this camcorder records to a unique brand of non-movable media called P2 cards. A P2 card is basically a tiny solid state hard drive in the form of a PCMCIA card. Video data is written to these cards instead of tape, which makes it easy to quickly offload QuickTime clips to an editing workstation, without needing to log and capture using traditional, tape-based methods—a simple file transfer is all that is required. A special, portable P2 card reader is sold by Panasonic, for easily transferring file to a built-in hard drive, and many laptops will be able to access P2 data through a PCMCIA slot, although special drivers may need to be downloaded from Panasonic's Web site. This is ideal for news gathering purposes, which require quick turnaround, in addition to small film shoots that do not roll a lot of "film." Once these P2 cards increase in capacity and come down in price, they will be an even more attractive option to content producers. It is expected that a single 8GB P2 card (2GB and 4GB are also available, while much larger capacities are projected for the future) will cost around $2,500 when the HVX-200 is released, although you will be able to get 2 P2 cards as an option with the camcorder at a reduced price of about $2,000 apiece, or just under $10,000 for the camcorder and two cards). At 8GB per card, each card may fit approximately 8 to 20 minutes of HD video (8 minutes of 1080 60i and 720 60p, and 20 minutes of 720 24p). Until cheaper, higher capacity P2 cards are available, a separate hard disk recorder may be an option for budget-minded filmmakers who shoot a lot of video. However, one of the concerns with using P2 cards or hard drives is the lack of an easily archivable tape format, since all video exists solely in the digital realm and must be wiped from the cards in order to make room for more material. Perhaps recordable HD-DVD or Blu-Ray discs will be an option for backing up footage, or dedicated hard drives that can be stored (although they may fill up quickly).

In addition to its unique compression method, recording format, and storage considerations, the Panasonic HVX-200 offers an incredible range of frame rates and frame sizes. This is the first camcorder in its price range (in fact, anywhere NEAR its price range—the first under $100,000) that offers 1080 24p recording (for comparison, the JVC GY-HD100 HDV camcorder offers 720 24p, as well as 720 30p progressive scan rate modes). Also, the HVX-200 can record 720 24p, 720 30p, 720 60p, 1080 30p, and 1080 60i (in addition to 480i and 480p modes and the 1080 24p already mentioned). In terms of HD recording, the HVX-200 is a close match to the high-end VariCam series of HD cameras sold by Panasonic (with some features of a Sony CineAlta mixed in as well). In fact, the 720 60p mode offers the possibility of excellent slow motion video for the first time in an (relatively) inexpensive camcorder. Television and film productions that currently use the VariCam could easily see this unit becoming an ideal, secondary camera, especially on location shoots.

It will be interesting to see where these affordable HD formats lead. Will HDV be replaced by DVCPRO HD as the format of choice for independent filmmakers and discerning professionals? For the near future, that does not seem likely (at least on the lower end of the budget scale), although only time, equipment cost, format features (where DVCPRO HD seems to lead), and product availability will tell. Also, what does Canon have up its sleeve? It's signed on as part of the HDV consortium, although (as of this writing) nothing has been announced from the company about future HDV product launches. Visit this book's Web site, www.hdvfilmmaking.com for more information on current and future releases.

HDV FILMMAKING UPDATES

For more information on the latest HDV cameras and accessories (as well as tutorials and other video-related information), visit www.hdvfilmmaking.com, which is also linked to from the author's Web site, www.chadfahs.com. HDVFilmmaking.com is the official site for this book and will include errata, links to relevant resources, and other information that is added over time.

Chapter 3

Installing and Configuring an HDV Editing System

While your choice of high definition format and camera are important, equally important is the computer system that you choose to work with your video. In general, it is important to decide on the hardware and software you need before purchasing a camcorder or conducting a shoot, as each format may require its own setup for optimum performance. For example, some professional HD formats (such as HDCAM) require more hardware to do the job than HDV does.

Although HDV is touted as the successor to the consumer-friendly DV format, new users may be surprised by the system requirements that are necessary to edit or play videos. Fortunately, new solutions are arriving every day, including inexpensive options like iMovie HD, which allows HDV video to be simply captured, edited, and output from an iMac. As the popularity of the format grows, newer computer systems and software options should emerge to make the transition easier. For more advanced users and demanding professionals, a greater degree of control and quality is required. This is where third-party solutions for capturing and playback are necessary—such as the addition of specialized PCI cards and larger, faster hard drives for playback and storage of high-definition content. Regardless of your experience or immediate needs, it is important to be familiar with the many requirements and options available. Some of these options may improve your HDV editing experience in surprising ways.

Working with HDV

Although many HDV users (particularly consumers) will never need more than a simple computer setup to work with their footage, professionals and serious filmmakers often require better options to achieve optimal results. In order to achieve the best quality possible for applying color correction and effects, it is often necessary to work with uncompressed (or nearly uncompressed) HD formats as an intermediate step before outputting to your medium of choice. Uncompressed video of any kind, especially in HD resolutions, requires a computer that is fast enough and suitably equipped to handle the job. In addition, the files generated by these formats can take up a considerable amount of space on a hard drive.

For these reasons, a fast hard drive array with plenty of storage is required, along with sufficient RAM, processor speeds, hardware cards, and methods for monitoring your video. Specifically, uncompressed HD formats, such as material captured from HDCAM tape through HD-SDI inputs on a capture card require a wider bandwidth for data to travel through, while formats like DVCPRO HD require considerably less space and bandwidth and can be edited natively (although, at 100Mbps, its data rate is four times that of HDV's 25Mbps). If you are working with uncompressed video, even if your footage originated on HDV and you are "bumping it up" to another format, it is often necessary to use a hardware capture card, such as Blackmagic Design's Decklink HD or AJA's Kona 2. In this case, more capable hard drives, such as a suitably equipped RAID setup, are able to support the capture and playback that these cards and your computer rely on. Depending on your choice of HD format and hardware, these extras can add considerably to the budget for your editing system.

HDV Editing Systems

The majority of new multimedia-equipped computers on the market are suitable for basic HDV editing tasks, though many of these computers may require a little extra investment on your part to make the process smoother. Other HDV capture, editing, effects, and output options, as I will discuss in this book, can also benefit from better, faster machines with more dedicated hardware choices. HDV, like DV, is actually low bandwidth video, when compared with both uncompressed standard and high-definition formats. However, HDV does contain 4.5 times the number of pixels that DV contains; this is more demanding on system resources, requiring more processing speed, memory, and storage space. Also, the temporal (or *interframe*) form of compression used by HDV (similar to that used by DVDs) is more demanding than the strictly spatial (or *intraframe*) methods used by DV, which rely greatly on the computational skills of your machine (that is, faster CPUs are required). See Chapter 7, "Editing HDV," for more information on HDV compression schemes. Even the "intermediate" codecs that are intended to smooth over the process of working with HDV can require a lot of power (some more than others).

Purchasing an HDV Editing System

If you are in the market to buy a new machine for HDV editing, there are a few options you might consider. Turnkey video editing systems (see Figure 3.1) are available from several companies that specialize in finding the best combination of devices for working with HDV or other high-definition formats. Companies such as Digital Film Tree, which specializes in high-end film and broadcast Apple products, can put together a professional system for a client and train them on the proper usage and maintenance of the system. Other companies, such as ProMax and B & H, provide showroom and mail order services for buying a prebuilt editing system (some even include standard definition NTSC/PAL monitors, HDV cameras, and decks). However, with a little research, you can find a suitable computer on your own, Apple or PC, and the necessary software to work with your HDV footage at a price you can afford.

Assembling a computer yourself from the ground up requires advanced knowledge of motherboards, which handle all communications between hardware components, and an understanding of processors and other devices that affect performance. If you know enough to do this yourself (or trust someone to do it for you), you can potentially get the best fine-tuned results for editing on a PC. (Macs are not quite as customizable, but are already built with performance in mind.) If you aren't that technically savvy, it is best to go with a turnkey system or purchase a machine that you can easily configure yourself. Most users purchase a fast computer from companies like Apple, Sony, HP, or Dell and upgrade the necessary components with bigger, faster hard drives, additional RAM, and special video cards.

Figure 3.1 *Turnkey systems, such as those sold through Open HD (www.openhd.org), are an easy solution for putting together an HDV editing system. (Courtesy of Adobe)*

RAM (Random Access Memory)

Although it may seem like a lot of money and expertise is needed to work with HDV on a computer, there are actually several options currently available for making the editing of HDV content nearly as simple as working with DV. If you have purchased a computer in the last couple of years, chances are that it can be used "as is" or can be modified to meet the requirements of HDV.

The first place you can start improving your computer inexpensively is with the addition of more RAM. Your computer's ability to perform multiple tasks, or those that eat up resources quickly, is frequently a result of processor speed and RAM, or *random access memory*, which represents the amount of information that can be stored and retrieved instantaneously by the operating system and its applications. Popular editing software, such as Final Cut Pro, requires at least 1GB of RAM to work well with low-bandwidth HD formats like HDV and DVCPRO HD, which can function without special cards but require the host computer to take up the slack. Typically, the least amount of RAM any computer can use to edit HDV is 512MB, although 1–2GB is more realistic for working smoothly with HD. This is perhaps most important for HDV, which is a processor intensive format, rather than less compressed formats like the Apple Intermediate Codec. In general, it is a good idea to load up on as much RAM as you can afford, particularly for graphics and video work, as your system can always make use of it.

If you are attaching special video cards (as discussed later in this chapter) or multiple hard drives, such as in a RAID setup, extra RAM is even more important. Purchasing reliable, brand name RAM, such as that from Crucial and Corsair (to name only a couple examples), is important to maintaining the stability of your system (it has been tested and guaranteed not to be defective), so try *not* to cut corners too much on cost.

Hard Drive Storage

In addition to having sufficient RAM, adding more dedicated storage for video is often necessary, even if you do not plan on keeping material on your drives long-term (see Figure 3.2). A minimum of two hard drives is necessary for a good HDV editing system. The main system drive (or C drive on a PC) should contain all of the applications and operating system resources, while separate drives should hold any media you capture or edit. This method not only keeps media organized, but it also improves performance, as the editing application is not reading and writing to the same drive (project files are generally saved to the system drive) and the system drive is not becoming fragmented.

The storage requirements for HDV are actually greater than for DV in many instances because intermediate codes and render files can eat up those extra gigabytes in no time (intermediate codes are the temporary storage formats used for editing HDV, such as Apple's AIC codec; these are discussed in Chapter 7, "Editing HDV"). Many users find FireWire hard drives are a good solution for their video storage needs. Unfortunately, there is only so much you can do for the speed of an external FireWire or USB 2.0 drive. Most external hard drives, whether FireWire or USB, are limited by the amount of data that they can transmit each second. However, if you intend to work with HDV at its native data rates, you can achieve surprising results from most hard drive devices.

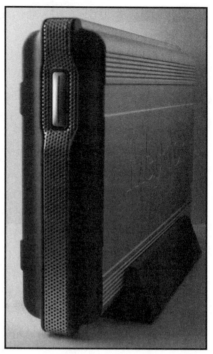

Figure 3.2 *External FireWire drives are suitable for HDV editing and the storage or transport of larger files.*

As the data rates for a particular HD format increase, so do the storage requirements. Not only do you need a suitable amount of space for the raw video files captured from a tape or hard disk recorder, you also need space for the intermediate formats and render files that are produced by your editing software when transitions, effects, and color correction are processed. In general, it is a good idea to account for at least twice or even triple the space for HD media as you have raw data. For example, if you are capturing an hour of HDV, you will need a little less than 14GB of hard drive space for the file in its native resolution. As an intermediate codec (whose data rate is nearly twice that) can triple that number, at least 42GB of space is necessary for every hour of HDV, depending on what software you are using to capture and edit your video. If you plan on applying color correction, transitions, and other effects, you need to account for even more space for the render files. Fortunately, hard drive space is relatively cheap these days and continues to drop in price.

Table 3.1 lists the estimated hard drive space necessary for popular HDV and HD formats. All numbers are rounded to the nearest GB and do not include space for intermediate files (except where indicated) or render files, which can differ depending on what system you are using (for example, Apple's AIC codec, with requirements mentioned below, versus CineForm's codec).

Table 3.1 Storage Requirements for High Definition Video (Approximate)

Format	Capture Rate (Mbps/MBps)	Capacity (GB/Hour)
HDV 720p 30	19Mbps/2.5MBps	9GB/Hr
HDV 1080i 60/50	25Mbps/3.3MBps	12GB/Hr
DVCPRO HD 720p 24 (when duplicate frames are removed during capture)	40Mbps/5MBps	18GB/Hr
DVCPRO HD 720p 30 (when duplicate frames are removed during capture)	50Mbps/6.25MBps	23GB/Hr
DVCPRO HD 1080i 60, 720p 60	100Mbps/12.5MBps	44GB/Hr
Apple Intermediate Codec (AIC), 720p 30	56Mbps/7MBps	25GB/Hr
Apple Intermediate Codec (AIC), 1080i 60	96Mbps/12MBps	42GB/Hr
Apple Intermediate Codec (AIC), 1080i 50	112Mbps/14MBps	49GB/Hr
Uncompressed 720p 24	368Mbps/46MBps	165GB/Hr
Uncompressed 720p 30	400Mbps/50MBps	180GB/Hr
Uncompressed 720p 60	800Mbps/100MBps	360GB/Hr
Uncompressed 1080p 24 (8 bit)	784Mbps/98MBps	353GB/Hr
Uncompressed 1080p 24 (10 bit)	880Mbps/110MBps	396GB/Hr
Uncompressed 1080i 60 HD (8 bit)	960Mbps/120MBps	432GB/Hr
Uncompressed 1080i HD (10 bit)	1,320Mbps/165MBps	594GB/Hr

In addition to capacity, the speed at which a hard drive spins is important, as higher data rates for video require the drives to spin faster. Typical rotation speeds include 5,400 rpm (revolutions per minute), which is a low speed suitable for simple editing and bus powered devices, to 7,200 rpm (most common and recommended speed) and even 10,000 rpm for more expensive, high performance drive setups. The formatting of hard drives as a RAID solution (as discussed in a later section) can improve the speed further, and is necessary for working with uncompressed or high bandwidth video formats.

SERIAL ATA (SATA) VERSUS ATA

Newer computers, like the Apple G5, use SATA (*Serial ATA*, or *Serial Advanced Technology Attachment*) internal hard drives instead of the older ATA drives (also referred to as PATA, or Parallel ATA, and IDE). Serial ATA drives transfer data in a single stream, using packets of information sent at about 30 times the speed of parallel systems. A Parallel ATA interface uses multiple streams, requiring more time to process and sync the incoming and outgoing information to ensure the integrity of the data. More streams equals longer process times. By sending data one bit at a time (very quickly), Serial ATA is much more streamlined and requires very little time to process data, since the data it is receiving is more reliable and always in sync. Also, it is easier to maintain sync on one fast stream, rather than multiple streams. This increase in performance means that current SATA drives are capable of achieving speeds of about 150MBps (MegaBytes per second), and up to 300MBps with the latest second-generation drives. Future SATA drives will have a data rate of 600MBps. In addition, the cables and setup required for a SATA drive are also simpler, more direct, and require less power than those of older ATA drives.

Graphic Cards

The video graphics card is another basic component of an HD editing system that has become more important as the graphic tasks once handled by the CPU are managed by more specialized components. This is partly a result of visually demanding operating systems like Windows XP and Mac OS X. The GPU (Graphic Processing Unit) or VPU (Visual Processing Unit)—the terms are often used interchangeably, although VPUs are a more flexible type—is the card that handles the display tasks for your computer system. These are not to be confused with other specialized video cards, such as the Blackmagic Decklink HD, which provides input and output (IO) for video and audio while enhancing some editing and effects capabilities.

Whether you are playing games or watching video, the card that runs your display may require more processing power and memory to accommodate the complexity of the video and graphics you are displaying. Newer operating systems, such as Apple's OS 10.4 Tiger, assign even more tasks to the graphics card, which can affect overall system performance and video previewing in QuickTime applications. ATI and NVIDIA are two companies that provide powerful graphic cards (see Figure 3.3). Some cards even include H.264 support for improved playback of HD video on HD-DVD and Blu-Ray discs.

Figure 3.3 *The ATI Radeon X800 XT is one example of an excellent video card that handles the display and rendering of complex graphics better and also allows for the use of larger monitors.*

In general, the card you are using to display your video currently has little effect on your system's video editing capabilities (although many future systems may be GPU powered). It does, however, have an effect on special effects applications (such as After Effects, Motion, or 3D software), which have already become a part of the post-production pipeline—particularly those that use Open GL (Open Graphics Library), a cross-platform language for creating 2D and 3D graphics, usually assisted by hardware. These cards also determine the size of the display you can use (for example, you would need a very high-end card to run a 30-inch monitor). Many cards also include the ability to connect more than one display, in order to achieve dual-monitor setups, which are common in most editing bays.

HDV System Recommendations

Although it is possible to assemble a system one piece at a time, it is often best to know beforehand what you might need, in order to avoid purchasing unnecessary equipment or components that do not work well with your system. Also, it is important to make certain that the system you choose is capable of performing all the tasks you require, even if you do not plan on upgrading right away.

The following recommendations are only a few of the configurations that are suitable for editing HDV at this time. By the time you read this, better options may exist and the high-end specifications will certainly change as faster processors and upgraded operating systems are released. It is the age-old predicament of the computer buyer. Should you buy now or wait six months for a faster system at the same price? Regardless of when you purchase a computer, hard drive, or video card, the next upgrade is only a few months away, so (unless you believe what you read on message boards or have some inside information on equipment releases) simply purchase a system as your needs dictate. Even Apple's switch to Intel processors is a couple years away (at the time of this writing) and even then your current system and its software will still be fully capable for most purposes, or with only minor upgrades.

A minimum setup for editing HDV on a Macintosh would include (see Figure 3.4):

◆ 17" 1.8GHz iMac G5 with Mac OS 10.4 or later

◆ 1GB RAM

◆ 160+GB internal hard drive, 200+GB external FireWire hard drive

◆ iMovie HD (part of the iLife suite of applications, which ships with new computers) or Final Cut Express HD. Final Cut Express HD is an inexpensive option for editing HDV on a Mac, while offering many more capabilities than iMovie HD, which is the minimum requirement.

Figure 3.4 *An inexpensive setup for editing HDV on a Macintosh computer would include a new iMac with iMovie HD or Final Cut Express HD. (Courtesy of Apple)*

A minimum setup for editing HDV on a PC would include (recommendations change by hardware/software manufacturer —see Figure 3.5):

◆ Pentium 4, 3GHz (or AMD equivalent) with Windows XP Home or XP Professional (Service Pack 2), including a suitable graphics card (see software requirements)

◆ 1GB RAM

◆ OHCI compatible FireWire (IEEE 1394) interface (if it is not already installed)

Figure 3.5 *A relatively inexpensive PC setup for editing HDV might include a prebuilt, Pentium 4, 3GHz computer such as this Dell Precision series. (Courtesy of Dell)*

◆ 100+GB internal hard drive, 200+GB external FireWire hard drive
◆ Sony Vegas 6 (also available in Vegas+DVD bundle), Adobe Premiere Pro 1.5 (also available in Adobe Video Collection bundle), or other software discussed in Chapter 7, "Editing HDV"

For filmmakers who require the fastest and highest quality systems for editing their features or television programs, the system requirements (and budget) may jump considerably. Productions requiring the best possible output (regardless of the format the video originates on, even HDV) need to be able to handle uncompressed HD, which may have very high data rates. Even formats with slightly greater compression than HDV, like DVCPRO HD, can make use of the increased speed. HDV can become part of the process as well, if you convert it to one of these higher quality formats. For example, you can shoot on HDV, capture the video to an uncompressed format (such as Blackmagic's 8 or 10 bit codecs), edit at full quality, apply effects, then output to HDCAM, film, or even back to HDV (in-depth coverage of the various workflows are covered in Chapter 7, "Editing HDV").

An ideal Macintosh-based HDV online editing system (see Figure 3.6) would include:

◆ Dual 2.7GHz G5 with Mac OS 10.4 or later (PCI-X slots, not just PCI, are required for capturing uncompressed HD with a capture card)
◆ 2-4GB of RAM (or as much RAM as you can afford)
◆ 800+GB SATA RAID (internal or external, including FireWire solutions) or a 5.6 TB Xserve RAID (for long-form, uncompressed HD editing)
◆ Blackmagic DeckLink HD Pro or AJA Kona 2
◆ Blackmagic Design HDLink or AJA HDP HD-SDI to DVI-D converter (for monitoring)
◆ Two 23" Apple Cinema displays (one for the computer desktop and the other for monitoring video)
◆ Final Cut Studio (includes Final Cut Pro 5, DVD Studio Pro 4, Motion 2, Soundtrack Pro, and Compressor 2)

An ideal PC based HDV editing system would include:

◆ Dual CPU 64-bit Xeon 3.6GHz Dual Processor with Windows XP Professional

Figure 3.6 *An ideal Macintosh setup for editing high quality HD video would include a new G5 with Cinema Display, plenty of RAM, a fast RAID array, and a special hardware card for capturing and playing back uncompressed video. (Courtesy of Apple)*

◆ 2GB RAM (or as much RAM as you can afford)

◆ 160+GB Boot Drive

◆ 800+GB RAID

◆ Blackmagic Decklink HD Pro or Bluefish 444 Catalyst, HD Lust, HD Fury, or HD Iridium XP I/O capture card (optional cards for uncompressed HD formats)

◆ Miranda HD-Bridge or similar converter (optional decoder/converter for capturing HDV output through IEEE-1394 FireWire into HD-SDI input on capture card for up-conversion to uncompressed or less compressed HD formats)

◆ Two 23" HP LCD monitors or two 24" Dell LCD monitors (or one HP monitor and a Sony LUMA LCD for professional video monitoring—extra monitor may require converter)

◆ Sony Vegas+DVD, Adobe Video Collection (Professional), or Avid Xpress Pro HD (current support for HD includes high-quality DNxHD intermediate codec)

For additional PC system recommendations, visit Open HD at www.openhd.org, where you can find systems for working with other compressed and uncompressed HD formats in a variety of price ranges. This is a new service offered by Adobe who has partnered with companies like HP, Dell, Intel, and Microsoft to build turnkey editing systems specifically for HD video formats.

Setting Up a RAID Configuration

In order to capture, play back, and edit uncompressed high-definition video, you need a very fast hard drive setup. The best solution for storing and working with video at these high data rates is a RAID, or *redundant array of independent disks*. A RAID is a series of hard drives that are connected together and treated as one large drive. Once a RAID has been set up, it is as easy to use as any other hard drive, as the computer only sees a single volume. If you intend to work with all of your video at HDV data rates, a RAID is not necessary but can still improve overall video performance or (in certain cases) integrity of data. In fact, even if your footage originated as HDV or DVCPRO HD, you might consider converting it to a less compressed format for color correction and effects (as will be discussed in Chapters 8, 10, and 11), especially if you will eventually master to a higher quality format like HDCAM or HDCAM SR, which might necessitate a fast RAID setup (see Figure 3.7 for a picture of an Apple Xserve RAID—a prime example of a professional RAID setup). Multiple layers of HDV and DVCPRO HD can also be used when stored and played back from a RAID.

WHEN TO CHOOSE A RAID

The following section is most pertinent to professional users or those that require optimum performance and speed, particularly when utilizing uncompressed HD formats (HD captured using HD-SDI inputs or up-converted from HDV to a less compressed form in an NLE) or when editing with multiple streams of HDV. RAIDs are equally useful for standard definition video and will allow you more flexibility in the types of formats you can capture and edit. Just be aware that, depending on the type of RAID setup that you choose, you may actually decrease the reliability of your data (some configurations lack redundancy). When setting up a RAID, you will also "lose" hard drive space, since space is shared across multiple drives. While this may add to the cost per gigabyte for usable storage, it often yields greater speed that is necessary to work with HD video. For casual users and those on a budget, a fast FireWire hard drive is all that is necessary for editing HDV.

RAIDs can improve the performance of hard drives by increasing speed and in some cases providing fault tolerance, which prevents the loss of important data (whether you see any gains in speed or fault tolerance depends on the raid setup chosen). Drives are "striped" together and data is accessed from multiple discs simultaneously. Data is sent to the appropriate drives using either a software or a hardware RAID controller, which allows data to be written or read from multiple drives at the same time, thereby increasing the speed of data transfers in many instances.

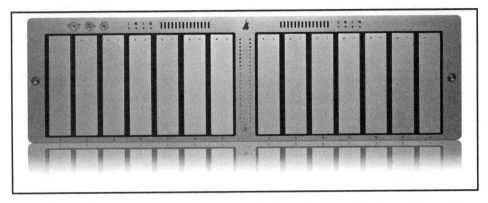

Figure 3.7 *The Xserve RAID from Apple is a high-performance RAID setup for working with uncompressed HD video on the Mac. (Courtesy of Apple)*

Some RAID setups also provide fault tolerance through "mirroring." Mirroring creates a duplicate of the data on one hard drive and applies it to another. This means that one or more drives in your array might be devoted to backing up information that exists on the other drives. The RAID controller can be used to send the same data to multiple drives, as long as the drives are the same size. Using this method means that it is easy to set up a RAID to create duplicates of your data. If a drive is lost, you can simply replace it with a new drive and rewrite the data to it from your backup disc (or vice versa). However, this security comes at a price, as you must have twice as much hard drive space, doubling the cost of the hard drives you need to purchase. For this reason, you might choose to use a basic RAID setup (such as RAID 0) for speed alone, without the added fault tolerance. In fact, RAID 0 not only lacks fault tolerance, but increases the instability of data—when any one drive fails in a RAID 0 setup, all data is lost.

Compromises between speed, storage, and security exist for virtually every user's needs. These are discussed in the descriptions of the available RAID solutions below. Although a few more RAID solutions are available than are listed here (including RAID 0+1, 10, and 30 setup, which are listed in Table 3.2, as well as others), the following options (particularly Raid 0, 3, 5, and 50 (5+0)) are often the most common and best suited to digital video applications.

SOFTWARE VERSUS HARDWARE RAID CONTROLLERS

The choice of RAID controller is often a decision of price versus performance. In general, software controllers are cheaper but less efficient than hardware controllers. Professional situations that require the greatest reliability and performance often rely on hardware controllers. Software controllers have become much better in recent years, with some solutions offering a great degree of control and the ability to better customize a setup to meet your specific needs. Also, hardware and software RAID controllers may be used together in certain situations. Hardware controllers are particularly useful for RAID 5.

RAID 0

Raid level 0 (see Figure 3.8) is one of the easiest RAID solutions to implement and requires a minimum of two drives to set up. Data is broken into blocks and distributed evenly among all the drives in the array (each block is written to a separate drive), without mirroring any drives (this is also known as a *non-redundant array*, as no information is written twice or backed up). The main advantage to using RAID 0 and not mirroring hard drives is that 100 percent of your storage is available for use, as data is not duplicated anywhere in the array. It also provides a very fast, if not totally reliable, set of drives. In fact, a RAID 0 setup is actually less reliable than a single drive, since when one drive fails, they all fail. The more drives you have in a RAID 0 setup, the less data security you have. Still, many people tempt fate and use RAID 0, since it is the fastest type of array at the cheapest price. If you have a backup of your data (on tape or another disc) and simply require the speed, RAID 0 is a good choice.

Although one controller is fine for this type of RAID (and typically found in lower-cost solutions, such as the G-Raid drives sold by Media and the FireMax sold by ProMax), the best results are achieved when multiple controllers are used, with one controller for each drive. In recent years, software controllers have become more capable and now offer a less expensive solution to hardware controllers. You can create one of these setups fairly easily using a disk utility (Mac

OS X comes with RAID software), or you can buy preconfigured drives that require no setup at all—just plug it in and your RAID is ready to use. Software controllers may ship with your drive or may be already installed as part of your operating system; applications like SoftRaid are another alternative.

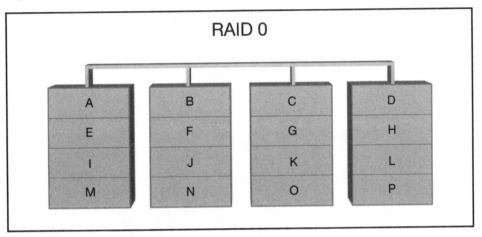

Figure 3.8 *RAID 0 drive setup without fault tolerance.*

The only drawback to using RAID 0 is its complete lack of fault tolerance, meaning that if one drive fails, all data in the array is lost. For noncritical applications, this may be perfectly fine. In fact, RAID 0 works great for digital video applications where a tape backup exists. This is the method that most users are familiar with, as it is the way in which the majority of small setups with two drives work (single-unit FireWire hard drive enclosures with two drives striped as one are popular RAID 0 solutions). However, post-production facilities or home users who are concerned with the reliability of their data should look at one of the other RAID options available.

RAID 1

Raid level 1 (see Figure 3.9) is also very easy to set up and requires a minimum of two drives (the total number of drives should be in multiples of two), although more are typical. Using mirrored pairs of drives (for redundancy of data), RAID Level 1 can potentially read data at twice the rate of a single disk (although the write time is the same as with a single disk), while providing protection in case of drive failures—even across multiple discs. This type of RAID setup is generally inefficient when compared to other RAID setups, and is perhaps best suited to situations in which multiple users need to access critical data simultaneously across a network. It is not recommended for demanding video applications, particularly involving capture of uncompressed HD. However, RAID 1 is suitable for working with HDV at native data rates and can provide the peace of mind that comes with data backup capabilities. For HD work at uncompressed or higher data rates, RAID 1 is not recommended.

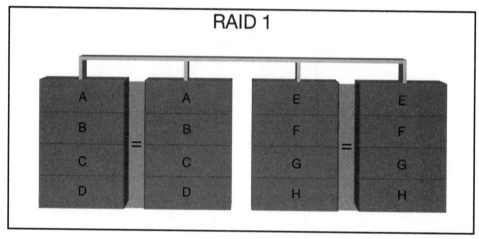

Figure 3.9 *RAID 1 drive setup.*

RAID 3

Raid level 3 (see Figure 3.10) configurations require a minimum of three drives and can be difficult to set up. Data is striped sequentially across multiple drives, with an additional drive reserved for parity, or the storage of numbers that indicate the sum of all data on the other discs (this allows for rebuilding of lost data when a drive fails). If any single drive fails, you can rebuild the RAID, although if more than one drive is lost, you lose all your data. Additionally, in a RAID 3 configuration, the equivalent of one drive of data is sacrificed in order to achieve parity. In this particular setup, software controllers are not recommended because they require more system resources and are thus unreliable. In general, the read and write rates for RAID 3 are fairly high, although the complexity of setting it up, and the lower speeds when compared with RAID 0 and RAID 5, make it suitable for video but not generally recommended.

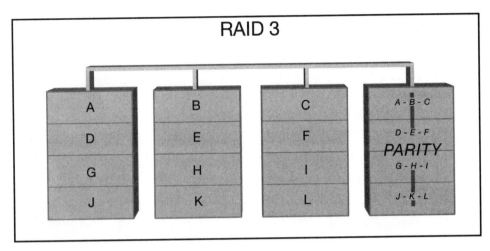

Figure 3.10 *RAID 3 drive setup.*

RAID 5

Raid level 5 (see Figure 3.11) is a popular option; it writes data and parity information across all of the drives in the array. It is capable of very high data rates, which make it a good choice for HD video. In case a drive is lost (a RAID 5 is able to rebuild if one drive is lost, although not as easily as with RAID 1), parity is written to a different drive than where the original data resides. As a separate drive is not used for parity information, data can be written faster and performance is improved, although the need to write parity can still slow things down. In a RAID 5 setup, parity information can be used to reconstruct data from a lost drive (using the rotating parity array that is spread across multiple drives), although if more than one drive goes down, you lose data for the entire array. A RAID 5 setup requires a minimum of three drives, although a combination of seven drives is more common, as in an Xserve RAID. A good hardware controller is also preferable.

The performance of a RAID 5 can be improved by adjusting the size of the stripes on the drives (a similar performance tweak can be performed on other RAID setups to some extent). Stripes are blocks of data that range in size, depending on the usage of the drives. Smaller stripes (as small as a single sector, or 512 bytes) are generally better for video; they spread data across all disks in the array, resulting in data transfers that occur in parallel, which in turn increases speed and performance. Larger stripes (as much as a few megabytes in size) write larger blocks of data that fit on fewer drives, decreasing the effective speed of an array. Next to RAID 0, a RAID 5 would be the recommended choice for a balance of speed, safety (lacking in RAID 0), and capacity.

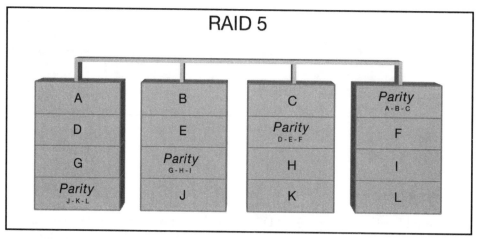

Figure 3.11 *RAID 5 drive setup.*

RAID 50 (5+0)

A RAID level 50 (see Figure 3.12) is essentially a group of RAID 5 arrays striped together as a RAID 0, with the same parity seen in RAID 5 and the block striping found in RAID 0. The use of RAID 0 makes the drives fast, particularly when writing data, while RAID 5 provides a limited amount of fault tolerance and safety due to the parity. RAID 50 (also called RAID 5 + 0), may not be as widely used as some other RAID setups discussed here (particularly in comparison to the most common RAID 0) because the installation is more involved and it requires more drives. A good hardware controller is generally required for this setup.

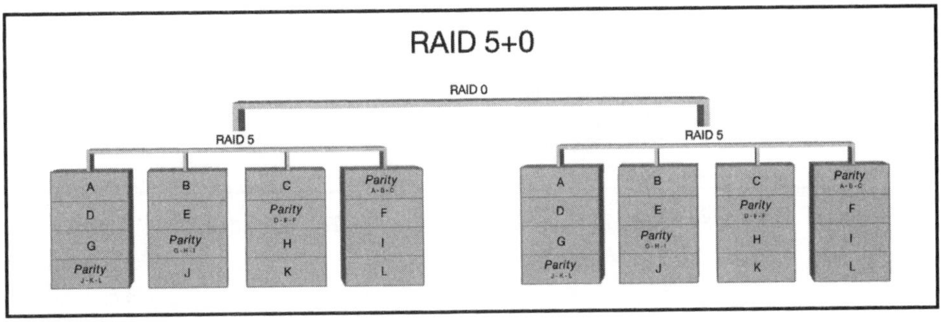

Figure 3.12 *RAID 50 (5+0) drive setup.*

JBOD (JUST A BUNCH OF DISCS)

JBOD (Just a Bunch Of Discs) is a collection of smaller drives that are combined into a single, larger volume. JBOD is not a RAID, and there is no real advantage in using one for video work. While a RAID uses "partitioning" to divide a drive up into smaller volumes, a JBOD uses "spanning" (not to be confused with striping) to combine multiple drives into a larger volume. A JBOD configuration with two, 100GB hard drives creates a single 200GB volume—a simple process of adding two or more drives together—although there is no speed gained by doing so (as opposed to RAID 0, for example). In fact, it does not matter whether you choose to use drives separately or combine them into a JBOD, since they lack fault tolerance and do not provide any performance advantages. If you have a lot of drives scattered about your office, you might consider combining them into a single JBOD, particularly if you are looking for a way to maximize hard drive space and store noncritical files. For video capture and playback purposes, use a RAID, which in the right setup may improve speed and (in some instances) redundancy of data.

Table 3.2 Summary of RAID Levels

RAID Level	Number of Disks	Storage Efficiency (Total % of original drive capacity, assuming drives of equal size are used)	Fault Tolerance	Read Speed	Write Speed	Notes
0	2, 4, 6, 8 …	100%; 1TB would yield 1TB of usable storage.	No	Very High	Highest	The failure of any drive results in the loss of the entire array (only suitable for noncritical data). Despite its lack of redundancy, RAID 0 is inexpensive, easy to set up, and relatively fast.
1	2, 4, 6, 8 …	50%; 1TB would yield 500GB of usable storage.	Yes (Loss of one drive in every set of two)	High	Medium	All data is duplicated on a second drive, which offers a high level of protection at the cost of space (capacity is cut in half, since you need a duplicate drive for every drive in set).
3	3 +	66% for 3 disks (or number of drives—1/ number of drives); 1TB would yield 750GB of usable storage.	Yes (Loss of one drive)	Medium	Medium	A good alternative to RAID 0, with redundancy of data on a separate parity drive.
5	3 +	66% (or number of drives—1/number of drives); 1TB would yield 750GB of usable storage.	Yes (Loss of one drive)	High	High	Reading and writing to all drives simultaneously affects performance.
0+1 (01)	4, 6, 8 …	50%	Yes	High	High	Striping and mirroring combined (without parity). Provides the speed of RAID 0 with the fault tolerance of RAID 1. Basically, a RAID 1 striped across RAID 0 arrays.

RAID Level	Number of Disks	Storage Efficiency (Total % of original drive capacity, assuming drives of equal size are used)	Fault Tolerance	Read Speed	Write Speed	Notes
10 (1+0)	4, 6, 8, …	50%	Yes	High	High	Provides the speed of RAID 0 with the fault tolerance of RAID 1. Basically, a RAID 0 striped across RAID 1 arrays.
30 (3+0)	6 +	(Number of Drives in each RAID 3 Set—1/ number of drives in each RAID 3 Set); two RAID 3 arrays, each with four 250GB drives and striped together as a RAID 0 would yield 750GB of usable storage, or a 75% efficiency.	Yes	High	High	Basically, a RAID 0 striped across RAID 3 arrays.
50 (5+0)	6 +	(Number of drives in each RAID 5 Set—1/number of drives in each RAID 5 set); two RAID 5 arrays, each with four 250GB drives and striped together as a RAID 0 would yield 750GB of usable storage, or a 75% efficiency.	Yes	Highest	Very High	Basically, a RAID 0 striped across RAID 5 arrays.

Connecting a Deck or Camera

In the digital video realm, most cameras, decks, and computers connect to each other using one of only a couple of interface types (for video capture and output), including FireWire and SDI (serial digital interface) or HD-SDI. Analog connections may also be used if you are equipped for them, although the signal needs to be converted to a digital form before it can be captured and manipulated by a computer or output to a digital tape. For most users, both novice and professional, FireWire is likely the connection you will use most often, particularly for HDV. However, with increasingly inexpensive HD capture cards and monitoring devices, the HD-SDI interface is also a popular choice, particularly in professional broadcast and film environments.

FireWire

The most ubiquitous data connection, or bus interface, for the input and output of video from digital devices is FireWire, or IEEE 1394, a technology developed by Apple and applied to a large variety of devices on both PCs and Macs (Sony refers to it as i.Link). HDV and DV camcorders, as well as some consumer set-top devices like D-VHS players, also use FireWire for transferring data. FireWire is unique in that it can provide all video, audio, device control, and power through a single cable. In fact, FireWire is partially responsible for the success of DV (and soon HDV), as it simplifies the capture and editing process for consumers. It is also widely used in hard drives, in addition to other peripherals, such as scanners, digital media players (like the iPod), and musical interface devices (including some mixers). The "plug-and-play" capability (when a computer instantly recognizes a connected device) it provides and the ability to daisy chain up to 63 devices through a single port add to its versatility. With FireWire, it is also easy to move a hard drive and share it with other systems.

FireWire is currently available in two basic varieties: FireWire 400 or FireWire 800. FireWire 400 is the oldest and most common type; at 400Mbps it still provides more than enough bandwidth for DV and HDV and most everyday data transfer speeds (a measure of the bus speed, not the speed of the hard drive mechanism). However, at twice the data rate (800Mbps), FireWire 800 bus speed is ideal for playback of multiple video streams and other video-intensive uses, particularly with FireWire RAID setups. Moving large files between drives is also easier with FireWire 800, which can cut transfer times in half.

When purchasing FireWire cables, make certain you pick the right ones. Unfortunately, FireWire 800 is not as backward-compatible with FireWire 400 as you might think, so you need to purchase the correct cables for both. Also, the number of pins (and size) of connectors at either end a cable can vary, especially for FireWire 400. For example, most video cameras and smaller devices (in addition to the majority of Sony hardware and computers) tend to use the four-pin variety (dropping the power connectors), while Apple and many computer manufacturers use the six-pin type on the front and back of their machines (see Figure 3.13). When capturing from a camera or some decks, you will most likely use a cable with four pins on one end and six on the other. However, for dubbing between cameras or decks you may need a different cable with small four-pin connections on both ends. Hard drives and other peripherals, on the other hand, are almost always equipped with six pins on both ends. As an additional note, the length of a FireWire cable is limited to 4.5 meters, or about 15 feet. You can daisy chain cables with other devices to extend the length, though you will need to purchase a cable extender/repeater device if you need to boost the signal for connection with machines in another room or when shooting on a large stage.

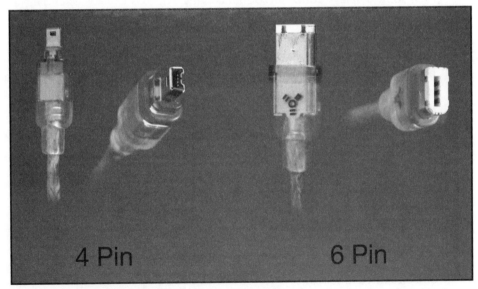

Figure 3.13 *FireWire cables come equipped with either four-pin (no power) or six-pin connectors, or both.*

Although FireWire is a widely recognized standard, there are some cards and devices on PCs with FireWire connections that do not properly recognize other FireWire devices. If you are working on a PC and intend to use your computer's FireWire or i.Link connection (particularly if it is included on a separate PCI card), you need to make certain that it is OHCI (Open Host Controller Interface) compliant. If your computer is having trouble recognizing your devices, this may be the problem, but also check to make sure the latest drivers and firmware are installed. Fortunately, as the use of FireWire for capturing and editing video is so widespread, the majority of FireWire controllers in computers are OHCI compliant. Check the documentation that came with your computer and capture card, or just make certain to look for OHCI-compliant devices when making your next computer purchase.

HD-SDI

SDI, or Serial Digital Interface, is a connection type that offers both standard and high-definition varieties (or HD-SDI). The majority of professional broadcast I/O devices (including converters and capture cards—see Figure 3.14), decks, and even some displays utilize these connections. An SDI cable is essentially a digital coaxial cable, with BNC connectors (bayonet-style connectors found on most broadcast equipment to hold a cable securely) at each end. However, make sure to use real SDI cables rather than composite video cables, which are not as likely to provide the data integrity necessary for HD work. SDI signals transmit uncompressed, digital component video information (typically, Y'CbCr for component digital, although dual-link HD-SDI for 4:4:4 film work with discrete red, green, and blue signals may be used), which maintains the purity of the image, as opposed to composite connections that combine this information into a single channel. In addition to video, an SDI signal can also incorporate up to four embedded channels of AES/EBU, 48kHz, 16 bit audio channels. SDI cables can be extended to around 300 meters, although this is more than is recommended. As a side note, Sony's Xpri systems use an "SDTI"

Figure 3.14 *HD-SDI connections are common on HD video I/O cards and converters, such as the Blackmagic HDLink.*

connection, which uses a "dub" signal over SDI, and allows for the native editing of HDCAM material, much as you might edit with DVCPRO HD over FireWire.

Monitoring HD Video

As with hard drives, video cards, and editing software, the number of HD monitoring options is growing with time. However, the enterprising indie must find creative and inexpensive alternatives among LCDs and other computer displays, unless they are able to afford a studio CRT (Cathode Ray Tube) HD monitor or professional LCD monitor. CRT HD monitors are ideal for color correction since they provide the most accurate color with the richest blacks and greatest contrast ratios. Unfortunately, they are also quite expensive and increasingly hard to find (no more CRTs are being produced and warehouse stockpiles are dwindling). In either case, an HD CRT is not capable of displaying an entire 1920×1080 picture; therefore, an LCD with enough resolution is best for pixel perfect images. A standard-definition CRT is still a good choice for many systems, as it provides an adequate preview of overall color and a gauge of how SD televisions may crop the image (with the overscan area of the television screen, as discussed in Chapter 10, "Creating Graphics and Effects for HDV"). This is important because the majority of households still own an SD television, which they may use to view the broadcast or DVD versions of your project. If you are purchasing a CRT, make sure it is truly professional with a Blue Only button for accurate calibration (see Chapter 8, "Color Correcting Video," for calibrating instructions). Sony makes some very reliable CRT monitors, as well as new LCD screens. Professional LUMA LCD monitors are being touted by Sony as ideal for monitoring HD, since they include component inputs and other professional features, like Blue-Only and In-scan modes, as well as area markers for judging title and action safe boundaries.

The most practical and least expensive option for monitoring true HD is to use an LCD computer monitor with the appropriate pixel dimensions adapted for video use and separate from your computer system's monitor (see Figure 3.15). For example, by installing a video card in your computer that is equipped with HD-SDI or component video outputs, you can connect an LCD monitor either directly to your computer's video capture card (which often includes an output/monitoring option), or through a box that converts the video into a signal the display can accept. This method is currently the most feasible for the majority of users and has been made easier by the sale of special devices that accomplish accurate, pixel-for-pixel display. Blackmagic Design makes an excellent device called the HDLink, which connects an HD-SDI output from a video card or deck to a monitor with DVI inputs (the majority of new LCD monitors are equipped with DVI, a digital replacement for VGA and older analog connections). Apple's 23" Cinema displays make a great HD monitor, particularly for users of Final Cut Pro, though PC users can use the same monitor. Hewlett Packard also makes an equivalent monitor, with nearly the same specifications. However, the HP monitor also offers component inputs built into the monitor, which is an excellent way to view analog signals sent from a video card or to watch true HD video from the component output on your HDV camcorder (Sony's HDR-FX1 and HVR-Z1U include component outputs). Additionally, Sony and Dell are two other companies that make inexpensive HD-capable computer monitors.

Figure 3.15 *Although broadcast HD monitors provide accurate monitoring, they are expensive and can be replaced by a less expensive LCD monitor, such as a high-resolution 23" display.*

Hardware Capture Cards

Professional video users who require the best performance and highest-quality formats have need of additional hardware. This is particularly true when working with HD formats, which may require additional input and output options, while putting a strain on even the fastest CPU. There are many types of video cards to assist with the capture and editing of HDV and other HD video formats. The following section contains information on a couple of the most popular capture cards available for use in your HDV editing system. Although the discussion here includes cards from Blackmagic Design and Kona, there are other manufacturers that produce similar devices, such as Bluefish 444, Digital Voodoo, and Aurora. Using one of these cards (along with a suitable CPU and hard drive setup) can greatly improve your HD capture and editing experience, particularly when utilizing HDV in combination with DVCPRO HD or an uncompressed HD format, elevating your next project to a higher level of professionalism—not to mention alleviating some of the frustration of monitoring HD and HDV video properly or playing back sequences in real time from your NLE software.

Blackmagic Design Decklink HD

Blackmagic Design currently creates some of the most popular cards for input, output, and monitoring of HD video (as well as handling SD formats) for both the Mac and PC platforms. Their present lineup of HD-capable capture cards are part of the DeckLink HD series, which includes the DeckLink HD, DeckLink HD Plus, DeckLink HD Pro 4:2:2, and DeckLink HD Pro 4:4:4 options (see Figure 3.16). Each of these cards has the ability to take in and play out HD video through HD-SDI connections, the most common digital video input/output option for high-end professional decks and converters. Audio capture and monitoring capabilities are also built-in, as well as the ability to use an external video monitor to preview video, broadcast designs, and animations in Final Cut Pro, Adobe After Effects, and Photoshop, as well as several other applications. Custom gamma tables may also be loaded into the DeckLink system preferences for instant setup of multiple workstation displays or when matching the color balance of a particular camera on set. (They currently include presets for professional HD cameras like the Panasonic VariCam and the Grass Valley Viper, although you can create your own settings to match the camera that you work with.) The DeckLink HD Pro 4:4:4 model is even compatible with the Sony HDCAM SR series of decks, and allows for the full range of colors for film work. The DeckLink series has several other useful features, such as the ability to accelerate real-time effects in Final Cut Pro, RS422 deck control ports for frame-accurate control of professional decks, and the ability to down-convert video for recording to SD format decks and viewing on SD monitors. When used together with an HDLink, the DeckLink HD series offers a total solution for uncompressed HD capture, output, and monitoring. For more information on the latest cards and the features they offer (many of which can be updated with firmware and free software add-ons from the company), visit www.blackmagic-design.com.

Figure 3.16 *Blackmagic Design's DeckLink HD cards are one choice for the capture and output of high-quality HD video over HD-SDI connections.*

While you are on the Blackmagic Design Web site, check out the other I/O options they offer, such as Multibridge Extreme and Multibridge Studio (see Figure 3.17). Both of the Multibridge devices offer bidirectional converters, converting HD to SD or digital to analog and back again. Both versions of the device can be used rackmounted and as a stand-alone converter. Additionally, Multibridge devices include a DVI output for monitoring HD on an inexpensive LCD, which eliminates the need for a separate HD Link converter as mentioned previously. Multibridge with PCI Express will even allow you to display 2K feature film resolution and 4:4:4 color sampling on a 30-inch display (2K film has a 2048×1536 pixel resolution—a 30-inch Apple LCD can display more than this at 2560×1600 pixels). In addition, the other capture, output, and effects acceleration of the DeckLink HD cards is included, all in a flexible external unit with plenty of connection possibilities.

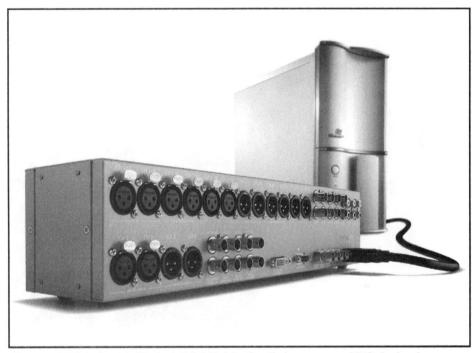

Figure 3.17 *Blackmagic Design's Multibridge Studio is an external I/O device that presents a complete solution for capturing, converting, outputting, and monitoring HD video. (Multibridge Extreme is also available with less ports and a cheaper price.)*

AJA Kona 2

Another company that makes excellent I/O devices for working with HD and SD formats is AJA. Their Kona 2 capture card for the Mac G5 (see Figure 3.18) is particularly popular with Final Cut Pro editors and includes acceleration of DVCPRO HD and HDV formats. (Blackmagic Design has added similar acceleration to their cards.) A separate breakout box (or "BOB") can be added to provide additional input and output options for the card. Like the Blackmagic Design DeckLink HD cards, the AJA Kona 2 requires a PCI-X slot to work with uncompressed HD. Up-conversion and down-conversion are also a part of the card, as well as RS-422 device control, support for several applications in addition to Final Cut Pro (such as Adobe After Effects and Photoshop), and dual link 4:4:4 sampling for film work, among other features. AJA also offers options for monitoring HD on an LCD using the HDP series of converters. (AJA offers several other converter options to meet your particular needs.) Check out their Web site at www.aja.com for up-to-date information on the Kona 2 and their other excellent products.

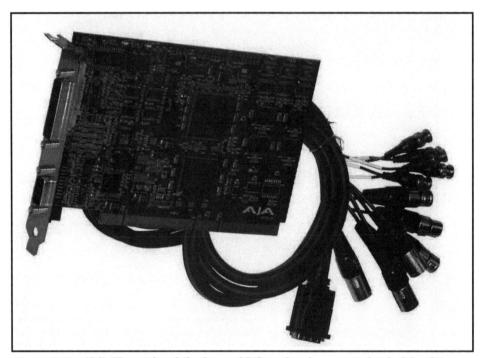

Figure 3.18 *AJA's Kona 2 is a fully-featured I/O card and converter for the Mac G5.*

Part II

Acquiring HDV Video and Audio

Chapter 4

Operating an HDV Camcorder

Once you have made a decision about which HDV camcorder to use on your next production, it is time to consider some guidelines for shooting. The principles are fundamentally the same for shooting most types of digital video, whether DV, HDV, or even HDCAM. Getting the best results requires an intimate knowledge of your camcorder, adherence to some basic principles of camcorder operation, and patience in trying to find the best settings when working under difficult conditions. HDV does possess some unique properties that can make getting the results you need a challenge, but your comfort with the format should grow through frequent use (see Figure 4.1). Shooting HDV is a good way to familiarize yourself with the format (although editing, which is discussed in Chapter 7 "Editing HDV," is the true test for HDV novices). After you learn to accept its limitations and explore its potential, HDV will no longer be so intimidating.

Figure 4.1 *The Sony HDR-FX1 represents the next generation of camcorder operation and design, and it is the first HDV camcorder with three CCDs. (Courtesy of Sony)*

Basic Camcorder Operation

It is important to familiarize yourself with your camcorder's features before you start shooting. As every device is slightly different, it is a good idea to consult the owner's manual to get a good idea of the layout of buttons, menus, and other features (some hidden) of your camcorder. Once you are confident with basic camcorder operations, you can begin to investigate the more advanced features of your camcorder. Although some of the instructions that follow might appear rudimentary, it is important for any camera operator, whether beginner or professional, to think seriously about basic operating procedures—some of which can have the greatest effect on the quality of your video.

- **Holding the camcorder.** A steady hand and a solid stance are very important. Rest your elbows on a table or another horizontal surface if possible. Keep your legs far enough apart (approximately shoulder-width) to provide a stable base and to prevent you from leaning in any one direction. Also, make sure to hold the camera with two hands while pressing your elbows into your sides to minimize shakiness. It is extremely difficult to keep a camera steady when moving it without a tripod. However, if you must move the camera by hand, keep your arms tucked into your sides with your feet firmly planted on the ground and rotate from the hips. Combined with your camera's image stabilization feature, this method may give you surprisingly good results.

- **Powering up the camcorder.** After you have taken your camera out of its case, make certain that you have inserted a fully charged battery before starting to use its recording functions. Most manufacturers provide an optional charger accessory that allows you to charge one or more batteries without attaching it to your camcorder. You may also choose to connect an AC power adapter to your camcorder for operating without batteries.

- **Loading recording media.** The majority of camcorders still use tape media, although a new generation of camcorders is beginning to use nonmovable media, such as Panasonic's P2 cards (the Panasonic HVX-200 is a DVCPRO HD camcorder that uses P2 cards, although it is not HDV), and you can already find hard disk recorders for HDV camcorders, such as the FireStore FS-4Pro from Focus Enhancements (www.focusinfo.com) and upcoming devices designed for JVC camcorders. Once a tape, or disc, is inserted, carefully close the media door. Make certain that you do not apply too much pressure to the doors when closing them and follow the guidelines that are listed on the camera itself or in the instruction manual to insure safe operation. The Sony HDR-HC1 and HVR-A1U use a bottom loading tape mechanism, which makes it difficult to change tapes quickly, especially when the camcorder is mounted on a tripod. (You must remove the camcorder from the tripod, and the separate mounting plate if you have one, in order to access the tape door.)

◆ **Navigating menus.** Every digital video camcorder has some type of electronic menu system that is activated from a menu button usually located on the side or back of the camcorder or near the viewscreen. A scroll wheel, or set of up-and-down arrow buttons, is also available for easily navigating the numerous menu options and submenus. Sony's HDR-FX1 and HVR-Z1U have done away with the LCD touchscreen navigation, which is seen as a "consumer" option that is especially suited to smaller devices, such as the HDR-HC1 (and possibly the HVR-A1U). A touchscreen can simplify the arrangement of shooting options for novices while maximizing the amount of available real estate on the camcorder body. Just remember that using a touchscreen to navigate menus shakes the camcorder while shooting, more so than typical button operation might.

◆ **Operating recording controls.** Every camcorder has at least one button for initiating (recording) and stopping (pausing) the shooting function. The Record/Pause or Start/Stop button, as it is usually called, is located near the hand grip, at the back of the camcorder, or in another location on the device that puts it within close proximity to your thumb or forefinger. Some camcorders put an extra Record button on the top of camera, so that it is within easy reach when holding a camcorder by a top handle for low shots or unique angles.

◆ **Operating playback controls.** Although the primary purpose of a camcorder is to record new material, each camera is also equipped with VCR-style playback controls (some of which are illuminated panels or located on an LCD touchscreen) so that you can watch material on the viewfinder, LCD viewscreen, or a separately attached television set or monitor. The ability to review material that was recently shot is an important feature, as is the ability to play back video for capturing onto your computer. Connections for sending video and audio to a television are either built into the camera itself, or they are part of a separate video *shoe* that connects to the bottom of the camera. Most of the current HDV camcorders, including the Sony and JVC models, do not require a separate shoe device. These devices are common for smaller camcorders, which do not usually have the space for large video and audio inputs and outputs on the camcorder itself. Although RCA connections for video (as well as a separate S-video connection for superior picture quality) and audio are a prerequisite for standard definition playback of HDV material (down converted from HD to SD), HDV camcorders may be equipped with a component output as well. The component output on the current Sony cameras, for example, is actually quite small, utilizing a single port with a special cable to break out the signal into three separate connectors (red, green, and blue), which otherwise would not have fit easily onto the body of the camera.

◆ **Monitoring Video.** As you record video using an HDV camcorder, it is necessary to check your shots and make certain that focus, exposure, and other settings have been properly accounted for. To do this, you need a video monitor—preferably with HD resolution—to judge accurately what you are seeing. In many instances, you may not have an HD monitor in the field (portable HD monitors are not within the budget of the average filmmaker, although slightly cheaper LCD models can be found), which means that you must rely on the camera's built-in LCD viewscreen or viewfinder, which can make checking focus difficult (Chapter 2 includes a discussion of what to look for in an on-camera screen). A separate SD monitor can help, but the focus is equally difficult to check on a screen without the requisite number of pixels, even if it is a good CRT (Cathode Ray Tube), such as the high-end CineAlta CRTs. However, CRTs can still be helpful for inspecting color during a shoot, while LCD monitors (which lack the CRTs' accuracy with black levels) are fine for checking composition, title safe areas, and focus. The resolution of LCD screens is generally superior to a CRT, which makes them a better choice for checking focus.

COMPONENT CONNECTIONS

Component inputs/outputs separate picture information into red, green, and blue elements (see Figure 4.2), the primary building blocks of a video image, in addition to luma (although, technically speaking, most "component" signals on HDV camcorders are actually encoded as Y'PbPr (Y'PbPr is used for analog component video signals, while Y'CbCr is used for digital component video signals), which adjusts RGB and luma information for the video color space, as discussed in Chapter 8, "Color Correcting Video." This separation helps to maintain the best possible analog signal by keeping each signal pure. Component outputs are necessary for viewing HD resolution material on many HDTVs (especially earlier models), unless an HDMI or DVI connector is available for a perfect digital connection (see Chapter 12, "Delivering HDV Content," for a comparison of HDMI and DVI connections).

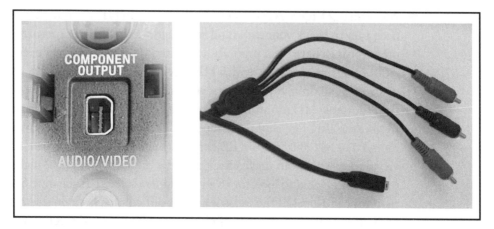

Figure 4.2 *Component connections have three separate connections for each color in your video image (often described as RGB, although "component" signals for analog video output on HDV camcorders are actually encoded as Y'PbPr).*

Using Zoom Controls

Camcorders are equipped with a zoom lever or "rocker" button, which rocks (or slides, in some cases) forward for zoom in and backward for zoom out. This button is labeled with a W for wide shots (zoom out) and a T for tight close-ups (zoom in). See Figure 4.3. Compositional terms like *wide shot* or *close-up* are reviewed in Chapter 6, "Designing Effective Compositions."

HDV camcorders also include a zoom ring on the front of the camera for manually adjusting the zoom with a twist. In fact, some of the newer cameras, such as Sony's HDR-FX1 and HVR-Z1U, include a non-perpetual zoom ring on the front of the lens (*non-perpetual* means there are physical start and stop points—from the widest shot to the tightest, telephoto zoom) that includes millimeter markings to indicate the actual amount of the zoom. As opposed to the zoom ring on a film camera or other "real" optical lens, this zoom ring is electronic and does not actually turn the lens directly. Instead, a servo motor in the camera turns the lens, creating the realistic feel when you're zooming in or out or when you're simply lining up a shot.

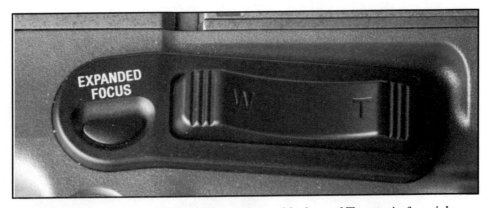

Figure 4.3 *On a zoom button, W zooms out for a wide shot and T zooms in for a tight close-up.*

In fact, zooming is a great way to help frame a shot (or reframe it), particularly from a distance. Zooms are great for shooting details that are otherwise unreachable by other means, such as a high window or a wild animal that is easily startled. It is usually best to use the zoom controls to line up a shot before you begin recording. The constant back and forth, zoom in and zoom out motion of many amateur videos can become tiring very quickly. Just remember that, as with any other technique, zooming should not be overused.

If you do choose to use zooms, try to zoom very slowly. A slow "crawl" into a shot is much more effective than a sudden zooming motion, which can induce motion sickness in viewers. It is particularly important for HDV that you try to minimize any unnecessary motion, as the MPEG-2 compression scheme used to record images onto tape is notoriously difficult at handling rapid changes (due to the temporal compression discussed in Chapter 7, "Editing HDV"). You may have noticed that many movies and television programs use a very subtle zooming motion into or out of a shot, one that is barely perceptible but which adds a psychological feeling of momentum to an otherwise static composition. Sony's HDR-FX1 (see Figure 4.4) and HVR-Z1U include a handle zoom button with a special switch to adjust the rate of zoom from High (H) to Low (L). In addition to using the levers for zooming, you can use the zoom ring on the front of the camera to quickly produce a zoom; this is especially useful when reframing a shot, as the zoom levers may be too slow to make quick adjustments. Zooms are also a part of the shot transition feature (discussed in a later part of this chapter), which can automatically adjust the rate of a zoom while shooting—a smooth "ramp up" and soft stop effect can be achieved with this feature.

Figure 4.4 *The zoom switch, located on the top handle of the Sony HDR-FX1.*

AVOIDING ZOOM NOISE

Zooming too quickly with the zoom ring may produce audible motor noise that is loud enough to be recorded by the camera. When doing a fast zoom, it would be best to use the zoom levers for making adjustments.

USING ZOOM CONTROLLERS

Zooming slowly and smoothly can be difficult on most cameras, particularly those with small zoom controls. This type of zooming requires extreme concentration and a deliberate hand. If you require perfect control over the speed of your zoom, you should consider purchasing a zoom controller (see Figure 4.5) that attaches to your camera through a Lanc connection (most prosumer camcorders are equipped with this connection). Using one of these controllers, you can set the speed of your zoom to a slow crawl without worrying about the amount of pressure you are applying to the zoom lever. Varizoom (www.varizoom.com) is one of several companies that manufacture these controllers.

Figure 4.5 *A special zoom controller, such as these models from Varizoom, helps you create smooth, crawling motions with your zoom, and in some cases allows you to adjust focus and other basic controls remotely.*

Once again, remember to limit the use of zooms in your video. Excessive zooming can be irritating for a viewer and is an obvious indication of amateur videography (think about how many times you have noticed zooms used in your favorite movies). Most of the time, physically moving a camera is preferable to zooming in on a subject. If you do decide to shoot with zooms, remember that slow, crawling zooms are much better than faster ones. Also, give your shots plenty of static time after you have reached the end of the zoom, so that viewers have time to settle their eyes and to make sure that you have enough material for editing later. In addition, zooming uses a lot of power and is a major drain on your battery. Use zooms sparingly to conserve power, or purchase a battery with longer life, such as the Sony NP-F970 (InfoLithium L Series).

DIGITAL VERSUS OPTICAL ZOOMS

Every video camera is equipped with zoom capabilities that magnify an image. Some cameras even have two types of zooming capabilities—optical and digital, which you may have noticed while shopping for a digital still or video camera. Optical zooms are as straightforward as they sound; they use your camera's lens as a telescopic device to physically enlarge the image you are observing. As a result, no loss of quality occurs—with the exception of some minor edge detail or distortion. Digital zooms, on the other hand, enlarge an image digitally and do not add any detail to the image. As a result, digital zooms severely degrade and pixelate (add blockiness to) an image, and they are not recommended for this reason. The results are nearly identical to zooming in on an image in Photoshop where individual pixels become visible the more you enlarge the picture. Digital zooms are especially noticeable with video, which uses relatively low image resolutions compared to digital still cameras. Digital zooms should be avoided whenever possible. In fact, most current HDV camcorders do not include a digital zoom capability (the Sony HDR-HC1 is at least one exception), as it is not an appropriate feature for professional use.

Using Focus Controls

Focus controls are an essential part of both film and video cameras. By adjusting the focus of a camera, you can shift the attention or interest given to a subject within the frame. Most importantly, proper focus keeps an image sharp and well defined, not soft and fuzzy. Whether automatic (adjusted by the camera) or manual (adjusted by the operator), focus is one of the most important ways of affecting your camera's picture quality.

Automatic Focus

Your camera uses automatic focus to adjust instantly to the changes in the subject that you are recording, particularly its distance from the camera and the brightness of its surroundings. Just as the other automatic functions of your camcorder attempt to compensate for new conditions, automatic focus does its best to find a pleasing average—though it is not always accurate. To improve the results that you get with automatic focus, make sure that you maintain a suitable distance from your subject, not too close and not too far, and avoid changing light conditions. Nighttime shoots with minimal light sources are particularly problematic, as are concert events with spotlights and shots that drift into and out of the shade on a sunny day. Avoid these situations or try to reduce the amount of change in your frame when possible—such as people walking by the lens, the headlights of passing cars, or other distracting motions. If you find that you still need help with maintaining image sharpness, you should think seriously about using manual focus, as described in the next section (see Figure 4.6).

The automatic focus on most HDV cameras does a decent job right out of the box. However, it is also susceptible to "hunting," or automatic focus adjustments that occur sporadically to account for changes in distance, light, and other properties that affect what is seen in front of the lens—the same effect that occurs with other types of video and digital still cameras. This phenomenon can be particularly annoying when the camera is sitting stationary on a tripod (where, ideally, it would produce predictable results), as dim lighting conditions or the presence of someone or some object passing within range of the lens can

Figure 4.6 *Switch your camera into manual mode to access better focus controls, or back to automatic when you want the camera to do all the work (on the HDR-FX1 and HVR-Z1U, this means turning the Auto switch on or off).*

start it searching for a new focus. For this reason and for those mentioned previously, manual focus is often the best choice, even for a simple shoot.

Manual Focus

While automatic focus can be a great feature for the majority of users, there are many situations in which adjusting the focus manually gives you greater artistic control. Switching your camera into manual mode allows you to use the focus ring on the front of your camera for making precise adjustments (see Figure 4.7). At any point when focusing manually you may choose to activate the auto focus button (usually labeled Push Auto or Push Focus), which temporarily activates the auto focusing capabilities of the camera to adjust the focus for you. This can be a good way to test your focusing skills—compare your results with those of the camera's automatic focusing feature.

Figure 4.7 *The manual focus ring on the Sony HDR-FX1 makes adjusting focus quick and precise.*

The following are a few scenarios for which using manual focus might be the best solution:

◆ Subjects that are placed at different distances from the camera, where they may confuse the automatic focus.

◆ People or objects moving through the frame, causing the camera to switch focus.

◆ Fast-moving objects that are difficult to lock focus on.

◆ Extremely bright light sources pointed at the camera (spotlights, lamps, or even the sun), which may confuse the automatic focus.

To obtain the best results in all shooting situations, it is important to understand how to work with manual focus controls. Most likely, the HDV camcorder you are using is fitted with a focus ring at the base of the lens for changing focus quickly, easily, and precisely. A slight twist of the focus ring brings objects into focus or blurs others, depending on their distance from the lens. You may adjust focus to selectively highlight only certain areas of the screen or to give equal attention to foreground and background elements. There are two commonly used techniques for adjusting focus—selective focus and deep focus—as described next.

USING EXPANDED FOCUS AND PEAKING

Some camcorders, like the Sony HDR-FX1 and HVR-Z1U include a special feature called Expanded Focus (see Figure 4.8). By pressing the Expanded Focus button, the center of the screen is magnified about four times, showing clearer edges (which are sometimes hard to see on a small viewfinder or viewscreen) on objects and allowing for easier focusing when you're making manual adjustments. This is particularly important for HD video, as the greater amount of detail can make accurate focusing difficult. Misjudgments in focus can be avoided by zooming into the image to check whether your focus is soft (magnification is only present on the display, and is not recorded to tape). Ideally, an HD resolution monitor would be set to check color and focus. However, the Expanded Focus feature eliminates the need for a separate monitor and uses the viewscreen built into the camcorder instead. After you release the focus ring, or when you press Record Start/Stop, the display returns to normal. In addition to using a decent monitor (and the expanded focus option), the "peaking" function on your camcorder may be used to aid in focusing, which creates edges around areas in your image when they are in sharp focus.

Figure 4.8 *The Expanded Focus button on the Sony HDR-FX1.*

USING BLACK-AND-WHITE VIEWFINDERS

Some professionals prefer the use of black-and-white viewfinders—such as those found on Sony's HVR-Z1U—for focusing, as they are usually sharper and reduce the image to only the critical luminance information, where edge detail is viewed more easily. Although the black-and-white viewfinders on many professional camcorders add extra pixels to increase sharpness, the number of pixels for the black-and-white mode on the HVR-Z1U is actually the same as its color viewfinder (an attempt to appeal to professionals, although no extra sharpness, or resolution, is gained).

Selective Focus

Selective focus lends a more professional look to any production, as it is a technique commonly associated with film cameras, where focus is directed to an object or a person and continually adjusted (or *pulled*) to maintain definition and sharpness (see Figure 4.9). For example, you can adjust your camera's focus to reveal only objects that appear close to the camera, such as a subject's face against a busy background.

ADJUSTING DEPTH OF FIELD WITH IRIS SETTINGS

You can alter a camera's aperture (or iris) settings (as described elsewhere in this chapter) to achieve an effect similar to selective focus, thereby altering an image's depth of field or the range of distance at which an image is sharply focused.

This is a technique that is often used for portraiture because it eliminates extraneous information from the back or sides of the screen—information that may detract attention from the subject you are shooting. A particularly impressive use of this feature is for pulling a person out of a crowd by adjusting the focus to a precise distance (a manual focus ring with lens markings and a special handle, like those on the Sony HDR-FX1 and HVR-Z1U, makes this task easier). Selective focus renders anyone passing through the background, in front of the camera or at any other distance, in soft focus (blurred), while keeping the subject sharp and defined. Selective focus also helps to reduce the clutter in a scene by directing the viewer's attention to only the important elements. In addition to making focus adjustments, you can open the iris up (with smaller aperture values, as discussed in the next section) to narrow the range of focus and make only close subjects sharp and in focus.

Figure 4.9 *Deep focus and selective focus are ways to direct the viewer's attention.*

Deep Focus

Deep focus—when subjects placed in the foreground and the background are equally sharp and in focus—allows viewers to follow the action that occurs at a wide range of distances within the same frame. Setting the focus controls on your camcorder to Infinity can do this for you automatically, effectively eliminating the need to focus the shot on both close and distant subjects. Closing the iris down, by using larger aperture values, decreases the volume of light and also widens your range of focus. However, eliminating selective focus is not always the best solution because deep focus is often associated with a video look, which many filmmakers try to avoid. How you adjust the *depth of field*, as it is called, depends on the type of story you are trying to tell, and like any other type of shot, deep focus should be used selectively. If you are trying to achieve a more cinematic result, then you should consider reducing the depth of field by using selective focus or special filters (other techniques for achieving a film look are discussed in Chapter 8, "Color Correcting Video," and Chapter 10, "Creating Graphics and Effects for HDV"). An example of a relatively recent movie that made good use of deep focus was Michael Mann's *Collateral* (shot primarily in HD), wherein the deep focus capabilities of HD video were used to reveal details in the outdoor night scenes.

Adjusting Exposure Settings

Every video camera uses a system of aperture—or *iris*, a camera's "pupil," which lets more or less light into a lens—and shutter settings—the length of time that a single frame is recorded onto a CCD—to adjust the exposure of an image. Fortunately, most video cameras include automatic exposure adjustments, which relieve users of the guesswork involved in getting acceptable results. Automatic settings are especially nice for on-the-go shots, such as shooting video while on vacation or in situations where you do not have a tripod and enough time to experiment. For the majority of camcorders, you do not need to select the automatic exposure setting, as it is the device's default function. From the moment you take it out of the box, your camcorder is ready to shoot without needing any special adjustments.

However, there will be times when you'll want more control over your camera's settings to get precise results. By manually adjusting exposure settings, you can often get better-looking shots than if you were to just use your camera's automatic features. This is especially true for movies or videos in which lighting is an important element. Unfortunately, users sometimes forget that their cameras possess this untapped potential. Flipping the M switch on the side of your camera or turning a dial or switch for making individual settings is usually how you select a manual mode to override the automatic functions. For some cameras, you may also need to access the main menu and choose manual controls from a list of menu options. The Sony HDR-FX1 and HVR-Z1U put most of the manual controls on the camera body— the way many more expensive, professional ENG-style cameras do— for when instant access to important settings is critical.

CHECKING EXPOSURE WITH ZEBRA STRIPES

Before you begin making adjustments to the exposure settings on your camera, you may choose to turn on zebra stripes if your camera has this feature. Zebra stripes indicate the exposure level of a picture (like a light meter); diagonal lines appear across areas of the image that are overexposed or are in danger of being too bright (see Figure 4.10). Depending on the settings your camera has available, you may be able to adjust the sensitivity of the zebra stripes that are displayed (100% is usually the default). Although zebra stripes appear in the viewfinder and viewscreen, they do not appear on the camera's output and are not recorded onto tape. Zebra stripes are a particularly useful guide when you're adjusting the aperture, or iris, setting on a camera. There are situations where a few zebra stripes, or "overexposed" areas of your images may be all right, such as bright light reflections on a sunny day.

Figure 4.10 *Zebra stripes help you to judge whether areas of an image are overexposed.*

Shutter Speed

Begin by accessing the menu system on your camcorder to locate shutter speed settings, or find the appropriate dials and buttons on the body of your camcorder. Depending on the model of camcorder you are using, you most likely need to put it into a manual mode before attempting to make any adjustments (check your camcorder's instruction manual for information that is specific to your device). Notice that there are several options to choose from, including 1/30, 1/60, 1/100, 1/500, and even 1/10,000. These are the shutter speeds for your camera (indicating fractions of a second), and in many instances, there are several additional options to choose from. A smaller number means a slower shutter speed. Slow speeds, like 1/60 or 1/100, are best for low light situations, while faster speeds, like 1/500 or 1/1,000, are designed for bright light—such as when shooting outdoors on a sunny day—and for action shots that require sharper pictures with less motion blur. A slower shutter speed can create "trails" or streaking in high motion shots, while faster shutter speeds decrease the amount of time the lens is open and limit the motion in a frame. Although the usual goal is to create natural looking motion with an appropriate shutter speed, you can decrease your shutter speed to create an other-worldly effect in high motion shots (typically, between 1/4 and 1/15 for the most dramatic results). For example, you can create streaks of light when shooting traffic at night or add style to a live concert performance shot under dark conditions (it works great for camera pans as well).

USING MANUAL CONTROLS

When using your camcorder in automatic mode (AUTO), exposure settings, such as shutter speed (in addition to iris, gain, and white balance), are made by the camcorder, sometimes with undesirable results. In order to maintain consistent, high-quality exposure settings, it is usually best to switch into the manual mode (MAN) by switching the Auto Lock button (on Sony HDV camcorders) to the middle position. After the automatic functions are turned off, you can press the buttons for shutter speed, iris, and gain to see their current values displayed in the viewscreen or viewfinder. For example, 60 fps is the usual shutter speed that you will shoot at (the most "normal" looking and natural speed that viewers expect to see), although it is likely that the auto settings will use other speeds as well, which can cause strobing or other effects where they were not intended. To begin a shoot, you might set your camcorder to manual (switch Auto Lock button to center position), with a shutter speed of 60 fps. With gain set to "0", you can open up your iris until the scene is exposed correctly (the zebra stripes' function can help you to avoid overexposing the image—just open the iris all the way up and then back down until the stripes go away). If the scene is still too dark, you might consider using gain, although it should be avoided in all other situations.

In general, the closer a moving subject is to the camera, the faster the shutter speed must be to avoid motion blur, although the angle and type of motion may have different affects. Additionally, as the subject's speed increases, the shutter speed should increase as well, at least if you need to maintain consistent image sharpness and avoid motion blur around the subject (particularly if the subject is moving straight across the field of view—a subject moving towards or away from the camera produces little effect). What this means, in practice, is that you may double the shutter speed when the subject's speed doubles, or when the distance between your subject and the camera is halved. Alternately, you may halve the shutter speed when the subject's speed is halved, or when the distance between the subject and the camera is doubled. If there is any confusion about the settings that are necessary to capture the sharpest image, a higher shutter speed is usually best. Of course, these are only suggestions for determining the correct shutter speed, since each shooting situation is different, particularly when the axis of motion (as mentioned earlier) or the focal length of the lens are taken into account (the amount of zoom also has an effect). Experience and a little experimentation are the best methods for finding a system that works for you. As an additional note, if you are making manual adjustments to shutter speed, you need to compensate by adjusting your aperture (discussed next), since they both control the amount of light that is captured by your camera—a change to one affects the other.

SHOOTING TELEVISION AND COMPUTER SCREENS

You can adjust your shutter speed to compensate for shooting computer monitors (specifically CRT) or television sets, whose refresh rates (the time it takes for a screen to display the lines in a picture) can cause your video display to pulsate or flicker (see Figure 4.11). Since most computer monitors and displays use a refresh rate of between 60Hz and 75Hz, a shutter speed of about 1/60 or slightly higher can sufficiently eliminate the annoying lines and flicker that occur. Ideally (as on many professional, broadcast camcorders), there is a "clear scan" button (or equivalent) specifically for shooting video screens, although the current HDV camcorders do not have this particular function. Otherwise, using a slightly slower shutter speed may effectively smooth out the image. If you have the need to shoot a computer display for your next production, try shooting an LCD screen, which should not flicker at all. In addition, when shooting under artificial lighting conditions (particularly when shooting in a 50Hz mode in a 60Hz country, and vice versa) using a shutter speed of 1/60 or 1/100 should prevent the slight flicker caused by a difference in electrical current that supplies the lights.

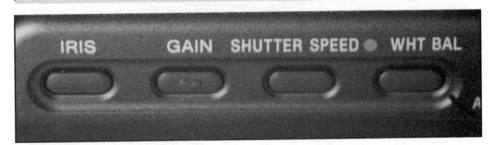

Figure 4.11 *Adjust your camcorder's shutter speed manually to eliminate jitter from computer monitors and televisions.*

Aperture (Iris)

The *aperture*, or *iris*, is the hole through which light passes into the lens. The size of this hole determines how much light is captured; thus, the more an iris is open, the more light passes through and the brighter the picture becomes. A smaller aperture (such as F22) creates a darker picture, while a larger aperture (such as F2) makes it brighter (see Figure 4.12). You can open or close the electronic iris on your camera to adjust aperture settings by placing your camera into its manual mode; otherwise, the aperture is adjusted for you automatically along with shutter speed. In general, adjusting the iris is the best way to control exposure with your camcorder, rather than changing shutter speed (most often, shutter speed remains constant, such as at 60 fps, while the iris is used to adjust exposure).

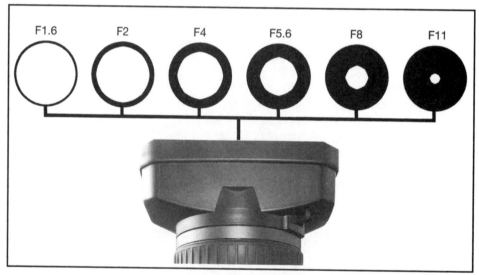

Figure 4.12 *Larger apertures (the opening in a lens that light passes through) have smaller F-stop numbers and smaller apertures have larger F-stop numbers.*

On the Sony HDV cameras, there is a real dial, labeled Iris (another name for aperture), on the front of the camera, just under the lens (see Figure 4.13). This dial provides you with direct control of the aperture without having to access it through an electronic menu. Select an *F-stop*, or iris level, in which your subject is properly exposed, even if other areas of the screen are too bright or too dark. Once the subject looks correct, you might adjust your shutter settings to compensate for underexposed areas of the frame. Check the zebra stripes mentioned earlier to make sure the image isn't overexposed (bright, white areas that are washed out, eliminating all detail from the image). Also, changes in focal length, such as zooming in and out, can change the available aperture values. The maximum apertures on the Sony HDR-FX1 and HVR-Z1U, for example, are F1.6 with the lens zoomed all the way out and F2.8 with it zoomed all the way in. To avoid incorrect exposure settings, make sure to zoom in or out before adjusting your iris.

Combining Shutter Speed and Aperture

As mentioned in the previous section, a change in aperture requires a change in shutter speed (and vice versa) if the amount of light hitting the sensor is to remain the same. For

Figure 4.13 *The Iris control dial on Sony's HDV camcorders (HDR-FX1 and HVR-Z1U).*

example, you might choose a lower F-stop (larger aperture), such as F2, to reduce depth of field for a portrait shot, although you will also need to adjust the shutter speed to avoid a change in exposure. As a general rule of thumb, you can keep an exposure level consistent by halving the aperture whenever you double the shutter speed. By using this formula, you can alter your depth of field with changes in aperture or change the way motion is recorded with adjustments in shutter speed, while keeping the exposure the same. For example, if the correct settings for a scene are set at 1/500 and F4, equivalent settings would be 1/1000 and F2 (for less depth of field and faster motion), or 1/250 and F8 (for more depth of field and slower motion)—additional settings are available in both directions, although maximum and minimum values may differ by camera model. When the aperture is fully open (to get the minimum depth of field), you can add a neutral density (ND) filter to eliminate overexposure in situations where a higher shutter speed is necessary.

UNDERSTANDING APERTURE NUMBERS

Adjusting your shutter speed usually requires a change in aperture (or F-stop) as well, in order to maintain consistent brightness. For example, as you increase the shutter speed, you need to open up the aperture to let more light in, and vice versa (a decrease in shutter speed requires you to close down the aperture). Paradoxically, a large F-stop number (such as F22) creates a smaller aperture (or hole) through which light passes through the lens, while a smaller F-stop number (such as F2) increases the amount of light allowed in (larger aperture). For example, a shutter speed of 1/250 might (under specific conditions) require an aperture of F4, while a change in speed to 1/500 would require an aperture of F2. In addition, large F-stop numbers (small apertures) create more depth of field (the range of distance at which an image is sharply focused), while smaller F-stop numbers (large apertures) create less depth of field (see Figure 4.14). You might keep in mind the difference between large F-stop numbers and small F-stop numbers by remembering that Ansel Adams founded a group called F64, which derived its name from the small apertures and large F-stops necessary to achieve the extreme depth of field he used for exceptionally sharp, landscape photography (an extremely large F-stop is even more necessary for large-format cameras).

Using Gain Controls

Gain controls can be used to brighten up dark scenes or bring more details out of the shadows. Presets for low (0dB), medium (9dB), and high (18dB) gain are common (these presets can be changed in the Gain Setup menu), and manually increasing the gain, for example, in intervals of 3dB from 0dB to 18dB is possible (the larger the number, the greater the gain). AGC, or automatic gain control, is used automatically, unless gain is turned off or a manual setting is selected. AGC—or any gain controls for that matter—should be used sparingly and turned off when shooting dark objects, where "noise" can be a problem.

When shooting in dark situations, use manual gain if you must use gain at all. In fact, the main reason not to use gain is that electronic noise, or artifacts, which look like television static or snow, are introduced by increasing exposure for areas that naturally appear dark. This is similar to the grain you might see on underexposed film that is color-corrected and made brighter. In general, it is best to use as little gain as possible, unless you really need to reveal more detail and can live with the extra noise in the image. Unfortunately, the Sony HDV camcorders have relatively poor low light performance, and the automatic gain is often activated without warning. Remember, if you want to avoid using gain (which degrades the quality of your pictures, particularly in low light situations), then you must switch to manual mode and turn it to "0."

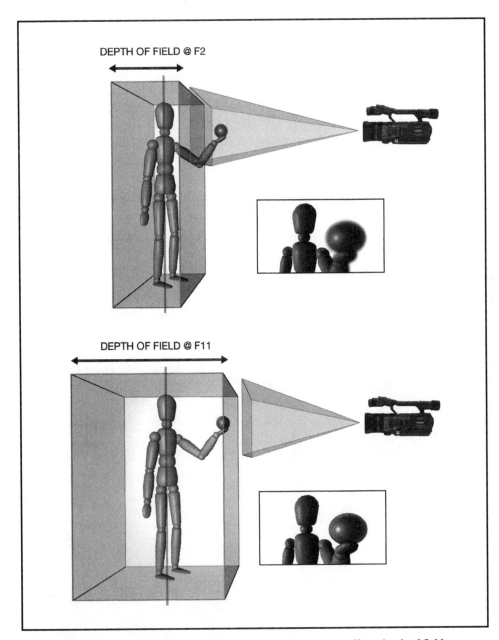

Figure 4.14 *In addition to influencing shutter speed, aperture affects depth of field—a closed aperture equals more depth of field (the amount of space in front of and in back of your subject is increased), while an open aperture equals less depth of field (the amount of space in front of and in back of your subject is decreased). In this example, notice how depth of field (or DOP) affects objects in front of the "plane of focus," not only behind your subject (a line is drawn through the subject to indicate the focus distance).*

Back Light and Spot Light

Some HDV cameras include special buttons that help adjust exposure when you're shooting under particularly challenging lighting conditions. One example is the Back Light button on the Sony HDR-FX1 and HVR-Z1U camcorders (located on the left side of the camcorder), which prevents a subject from falling into shadow when the sun or another bright light source is at its back (see Figure 4.15). For example, if you are shooting an interview subject whose back is to a window, you might consider pressing this button to balance out the exposure, so that the interviewee is made brighter and the windows are made less *blown out*—or when bright sources, like a window, become totally white through overexposure. Another useful feature is the Spot Light button, which prevents overexposure of skin and other reflective surfaces when lit by a strong light source (a light subject on a dark background). Shooting performers on a theater stage, where spotlights are used, would be an ideal situation in which to use this feature. Although not all cameras have these features, those that do may name them differently or hide them in an electronic menu of presets for various shooting conditions, rather than including them on the camera body itself.

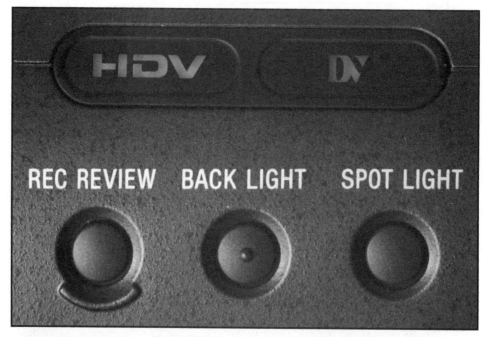

Figure 4.15 *The Back Light and Spot Light buttons can help compensate for difficult lighting conditions, such as when shooting toward windows or under theatrical lights.*

Edge Sharpening

Some cameras give you the ability to add sharpness to a recorded image by "enhancing" the edges surrounding objects in a scene, which is called "edge sharpening," "edge enhancement," or "aperture correction." This edge sharpening is used for separating bright and dark subjects in an image without increasing the overall contrast in the picture (it is similar to the Unsharp effect in Photoshop). Using this effect, the appearance of detail can be enhanced, making it more obvious (while not increasing the actual amount of detail), although some users find it a bit harsh for ordinary use. In fact, it can be a clear indicator of the "video look." It is usually best to leave this type of edge enhancement for post, rather than doing it in camera, where the effect cannot be removed later on.

Skin-Tone Detail

The skin-tone detail feature on some camcorders allows you to soften wrinkles by smoothing out lines on areas of the image that match a particular skin color (Caucasian skin tones are usually the default). You may have the option to specify a color range for a particular type of skin color, or you may simply have a range from narrow to wide. The skin-tone detail feature can be useful for reducing surface imperfections in interview subjects, especially those framed in close-to-medium shots.

Color Phase

Color phase controls affect the balance of color in an image. Although it is not an option that is regularly applied, you can use this control to shift the overall color of your video from a greenish color, for example, to a more reddish hue. In this way, you can make a picture warmer, by increasing the amount of red, or cooler, by increasing the amount of blue.

Gamma Controls

Gamma controls adjust contrast in a picture without affecting the black-and-white levels in the image. This is particularly useful for re-creating special film looks or enhancing colors without affecting the brightness of the picture. Special cinema-style controls (such as the CinemaTone option on the Sony HDV camcorders) can reproduce gamma curves with natural gradations that are similar to those in film. With this feature, you can often produce richer, more saturated colors that look less like video. However, it is often best to do major color-correction in post-production, where you have the most control over the image.

Black Stretch

Black Stretch (a feature of the Sony HVR-Z1U, not the HDR-FX1) provides more detail in shadow areas of the image by widening the gamma curve. The affect can be slight, although it is generally recommended when using CinemaTone settings or even for everyday shooting, since it helps to prevent underexposing an image.

CinemaTone

CinemaTone (a feature in Sony's HDV camcorders) adjusts gamma to decrease the brightness in mid-tone values, which can produce better reproduction of skin tones, as compared with ordinary video gamma. As a result, it can add a more "filmic" look to your video, which includes saturated colors and deeper blacks. While the CinemaTone look can be pleasing, there are drawbacks to using it. Since CinemaTone can remove details in the shadows, it is best avoided for general recording (particularly on the HDR-FX1) or used in combination with the Black Stretch feature on the HVR-Z1, in order to bring back more shadow detail. For use in low light situations, CinemaTone should be avoided all together, and Black Stretch used instead. Of course, if you are certain that CinemaTone provides the filmic look you are after (with crushed blacks), then by all means use it. You may also notice a decrease in latitude (range of available exposure) when the CinemaTone feature is engaged. The HVR-Z1U has two levels of CinemaTone settings, although the HVR-FX1 has just one. CinemaTone 1 (TYPE1) is only available on the HVR-Z1U, and it is a less aggressive version of CinemaTone 2 (TYPE2), which is the equivalent CinemaTone mode on the HDR-FX1. CinemaTone 2 creates the deepest blacks.

CineFrame

Although the Sony HDV camcorders do not provide the option for true, progressive scan images and adjustable frame rates, such as the 24p progressive frame recording preferred by many filmmakers (particularly those who intend to transfer to film), they do offer a special CineFrame feature on their camcorders to approx-imate the look of film motion. The CineFrame feature simulates the look and feel of progressive scan images, while still using interlaced recordings (see Chapter 10, "Creating Graphics and Effects for HDV" for a discussion of interlaced and pro-gressive video images). However, most users are disappointed with the results, especially filmmakers—for a true 24p HDV option consider the JVC GY-HD100. For those who do not intend to transfer their video to film and need a quick and easy way to approximate a film look, the CineFrame feature is still an option (although not recommended for general use). There are three different CineFrame options available—CF24, CF25, and CF30, each with its own feel and relative smoothness. In its manual, Sony refers to CineFrame 24 as having the "atmosphere of 24 frames per second adopted by film recording," while Cineframe 25 simply provides a "cinema-like atmosphere." None of these modes, unfortu-nately, is very smooth, although the stuttery look may have a limited usefulness and appeal for some productions. Additionally, the images suffer from degraded vertical resolution, as a result of the methods used to remove or double certain video fields (the removal and doubling of video fields is necessary to create the cadence of a different frame rate). If you want to use a CineFrame effect choose CF25. CineFrame 25 is smoother and actually closer to a true 24p look than CF24, particularly in high-motion shots (less motion stutter), as well as being more flexible. When using CineFrame 24, you are limited to a shutter speed of 1/60 and higher, while CineFrame 25 allows you to choose speeds ranging from 1/4 to 1/60 and up. However, when shooting CF25, use a shutter speed of 1/50 for best results (mimics the 180 degree shutter angle of film cameras). Fortunately, many users will not require true, 24p recordings, since 50i or 60i video can be transferred to film with excellent results, or special software applications (such as Magic Bullet) can create 24p video from their interlaced footage when it is needed.

Picture Profiles

Many camcorders are equipped with quick and easy presets to accommodate a variety of shooting situations. Sony's HDV camcorders, for example, include six "picture profiles" to quickly set up a shot. Although these profiles are provided with default settings, any one of the presets can be customized and saved for later use. If you frequently make use of the same settings (such as color, sharpness, or white balance), you can store them in one of these size profiles and call them up instantly each time you shoot. Tables 4.1 and 4.2 included here show the settings that can be customized in a picture profile, as well as the default settings that ship with each camcorder.

Table 4.1 HVR-Z1U Picture Profiles

	Profile 1 (PP1) HDV	Profile 2 (PP2) DVCAM	Profile 3 (PP3) PEOPLE	Profile 4 (PP4) FILM-LIKE	Profile 5 (PP5) SUNSET	Profile 6 (PP6) B&W
COLOR LEVEL	0	0	+1	0	+2	-8
COLOR PHASE	0	0	0	0	0	0
SHARPNESS	11	12	11	0	11	11
SKINTONE DETAIL	OFF	OFF	TYPE 3	OFF	OFF	OFF
SKINTONE LEVEL	MIDDLE	MIDDLE	MIDDLE	MIDDLE	MIDDLE	MIDDLE
AE SHIFT	0	0	0	0	-2	0
AGC LIMIT	OFF	OFF	12 dB	6 dB	12 dB	OFF
AT IRIS LIMIT	F11	F11	F4	F11	F6.8	F11
WB SHIFT	0	0	0	0	0	0
ATW SENS	HIGH	HIGH	HIGH	MIDDLE	LOW	LOW
BLACK STRETCH	OFF	OFF	OFF	OFF	OFF	OFF
CINEMATONE	OFF	OFF	OFF	TYPE 1	OFF	OFF
CINEFRAME	OFF	OFF	OFF	CF24	OFF	OFF

Table 4.2 HDR-FX1 Picture Profiles

	Profile 1 HDV	Profile 2 (PP2) DVCAM	Profile 3 (PP3) PEOPLE	Profile 4 (PP4) FILM-LIKE	Profile 5 (PP5) SUNSET	Profile 6 (PP6) B&W
COLOR LEVEL	0	0	+1	0	+2	-8
COLOR PHASE	0	0	0	0	0	0
SHARPNESS	11	12	11	0	11	11
SKINTONE DETAIL	OFF	OFF	TYPE 3	OFF	OFF	OFF
AE SHIFT	0	0	0	0	-2	0
AGC LIMIT	OFF	OFF	12 dB	6 dB	12 dB	OFF
AT IRIS LIMIT	F11	F11	F4	F11	F6.8	F11
WB SHIFT	0	0	0	0	0	0
ATW SENS	HIGH	HIGH	HIGH	MIDDLE	LOW	LOW
CINEMATONE	OFF	OFF	OFF	TYPE 1	OFF	OFF
CINEFRAME	OFF	OFF	OFF	CF24	OFF	OFF

Shot Transition

Sony's HDV camcorders include a new feature (lacking, even from the best DV camcorder on the market) called *shot transition*. With shot transition, you can register and then adjust a series of complex camera settings with the touch of a button, allowing you to perform smooth transitions from one type of shot to the next (see Figure 4.16). For example, you can use shot transition to automatically perform a precise rack focus (shifting the range of focus within a shot from near to far, or vice versa), or adjust your exposure settings to move effortlessly from an indoor to an outdoor shot. Shot transitions are created by adjusting camera settings (focus, zoom, iris, gain, shutter speed, and white balance) and then storing them in button "A" or button "B" on the body of your camcorder. While using the settings stored in button A, you can press button B to activate a seamless transition from shot A to shot B (a change in focus or zoom are common). Using the shot transition menu on your camcorder, you may also select settings for the transition's curve (linear, soft stop, or soft transition, which can ramp up or ramp down a transition), as well as duration (2 to 15 seconds) and timer settings.

Figure 4.16 *The shot transition feature, activated by settings stored in one of two buttons (A and B) is particularly useful for a "rack focus" effect.*

Setting the White Balance

Every camcorder is equipped with a white balance function, which controls the RGB color values that a camera records without the need for special filters. All camcorders offer automatic white balance, which attempts to arrive at a median value for, or best guess at, what constitutes accurate color. The problem that arises (as covered in Chapter 5, "Lighting for HDV") is when light sources of different temperatures are introduced into a scene, thereby inhibiting a camera's ability to accurately gauge what true color is. For example, many room interiors are a mix of lamps, windows, and other light sources of varying temperatures, each of which casts its own type of light. The automatic white balance feature generally records great, lifelike images when shooting outdoors in the sunlight. It does, however, have a difficult time with unnatural indoor light.

The best way to achieve precise results with color is to manually white-balance the camera yourself (see Figure 4.17). You can tell a camera what constitutes pure white by holding up a plain white sheet of paper in front of the lens (you may zoom into it as well) and pressing the manual white balance button on your camera. For some cameras, you may need to flip a switch or open a white balance menu to access this feature. Once you have balanced the camera, it should shift the colors of an image to correspond more accurately with the "real" world (see Chapter 5, "Lighting for HDV," for tips on creating color effects with the white balance feature).

Figure 4.17 *It is important to white-balance your camera before you begin shooting.*

Working with Lenses

Although most HDV cameras currently ship with a fixed lens that is not removable, there are companies that make special attachments to augment the capabilities of your existing lens. Century Optics (www.centuryoptics.com) is one company that makes these remarkable adapters, which fit over the end of your fixed lens (see Figure 4.18). Screwing an adapter into place opens up new possibilities, even for fixed-lens camcorder models. On higher-end HDV cameras, like JVC's GY-HD100 (and the forthcoming JVC HD-7000), a bayonet-style lens mount permits the exchange of entire lenses, leaving only the camera body in place—similar to what you can do with Canon's line of XL-2 DV camcorders. The ability to exchange lenses and attach a variety of special optics—even an entire series of photographic lenses—opens up more options for filmmakers when shooting scenes with specific requirements.

Regardless of what camera system you are using, understanding the different type of lenses that are available can help you to think of new ways to improve your own videography. In general, most commonly used lenses for videography can be broken into a few categories, such as wide angle, telephoto, or macro lenses.

Figure 4.18 *A variety of special lens attachments are available from companies like Century Optics. (Courtesy of Century Optics)*

Wide-Angle Lenses

A wide-angle lens increases a camera's angle of view and depth of field, expanding the amount of space that can be captured without moving the camera. This type of lens is particularly useful for shooting in tight places, such as the interior of a house, or for capturing wide vistas, such as a mountain landscape (see Figure 4.19). When you're shooting indoors, a wide-angle lens may capture the entire room instead of a single wall or corner. They are also useful for capturing multiple actors or subjects in a frame and can add intensity to close-ups on an actor's face.

Figure 4.19 *Wide-angle lenses are a good choice for panoramic shots or when shooting in tight spaces. (Courtesy of Century Optics)*

LENS ADAPTERS AND CONVERTERS

Although most consumer cameras do not offer a choice of lenses, wide-angle adapters (as well as macro and telephoto) can be purchased from companies like Century Optics, or sometimes directly from camera manufacturers like Sony. When purchasing a lens or lens adapter, make certain that the size of its threads match your camcorder; otherwise, it will not screw onto the front of your existing lens. For example, a lens adapter with a 58mm thread will not fit on a 72mm lens. You can sometimes buy a special step-up or step-down ring to use lenses (and filters) that do not match your camcorder's measurements. However, if you are using lenses that are too small for your existing lens (such as a 58mm lens or filter on a 72mm lens), you may notice vignetting, which is caused by the masking created at the edges of a frame (overlapping areas of black, caused by the smaller lens blocking the bigger lens, particularly when zoomed out at its widest setting).

One complication that is frequently encountered with wide-angle lenses is a distortion around the edges of a frame (often referred to as "barrel" distortion). The wider your lens, the more noticeable this distortion becomes, exhibiting the spherical properties of a lens and eventually producing a round image (like that of a "fish eye" lens, which turns an image into a circular picture similar in shape to a fish's eye). See Figure 4.20. In general, most camcorders offer a range that is roughly equivalent to a 28mm, 35mm, or 50mm photo lens, which should be adequate for most users and will not produce noticeable distortion at the edges. When looking for a wide-angle lens, remember that the smaller a lens' measurement in millimeters, the wider its angle of view. For example, a 28mm lens would give you a much wider image than would a 50 mm lens. Of course, the more options you have for framing, the better, which is why cameras with a wide spectrum of lens sizes are usually desirable. (JVC's GY-HD100 is an example of an HDV camcorder that offers the option of changing lenses, although you can purchase special wide-angle lens converters and attachments for Sony's HDV camcorders as well.) Many zoom lenses provide this sort of coverage. For example, you might find a lens that can be adjusted from a pleasantly wide 28mm to a tight 135mm.

Figure 4.20 *A fisheye lens is a wide-angle lens that can see in several directions at once (or, approximately, between 90 and 180 degrees) while distorting an image – an interesting effect for music videos, sports, and other stylized shoots. (Courtesy of Century Optics)*

Telephoto or Zoom Lenses

Telephoto lenses, which are essentially the same as the zoom lens on your camcorder, bring a subject closer to the camera while decreasing the depth of field in an image (see Figure 4.21). This means that faraway objects can be rendered in close-up, although a flattening effect occurs between the background and the foreground image. For most users, zoom lenses are most effective for reframing a shot. You should, however, be aware of the effect that a telephoto or zoom lens has on the relative sense of depth and space in your image. The flattening that occurs can be helpful when you are trying to make a background

Figure 4.21 *A telephoto lens (including teleconverters) can view objects at great distances, while "flattening" depth in an image. (Courtesy of Century Optics)*

more "graphic" by reducing perspective, an effect that can eliminate some distracting features located behind an actor, for example. Sometimes, even simple close-ups or medium shots are framed with a zoom lens, as it is often easier and quicker to use a zoom than it is to move the camera closer to your subject. By using zoom lenses, you can reduce the number of setups that are required to shoot a scene—essential for many documentary or ENG-type shoots, where you do not have the time to change lenses or move your camera location.

Macro or Close-up Lenses

If you need to shoot extreme close-ups on an object—such as an insect, flower, or an eye—you should consider using a special macro lens (also called a *close-up* lens or an *achromatic diopter*) that allows the camera to get within inches of an object without losing control of focus. The same companies that provide wide-angle adapters usually manufacture macro lenses (see Figure 4.22). You can purchase macro-zoom attachments (some macro lenses allow you to maintain zoom capabilities) in a variety of strengths, such as +2.0 and +3.5.

Figure 4.22 *Macro lenses (or achromatic diopters) help you focus at a very short distance from close objects, such as when shooting miniatures on a tabletop or details of objects in the field. (Courtesy of Century Optics)*

MULTIPLE CAMERA SHOOTS

Recording a live event, such as a concert, wedding, or another documentary subject, can be difficult when working with multiple cameras. Not only can the shooting be difficult, since you must track the positions of several cameras and camera operators, but the editing can be a challenge, particularly if you have a lot of material to sync up, or if cameras were not simply stationary on tripods, but actually moving around the scene. The use of special timecode features on a camcorder can simplify the process a bit (even if an external timecode generator, as used by some professionals, is not possible), as well as using a remote camera system, for those situations where you need to operate multiple, stationary cameras by yourself.

Using "free run" timecode can help you sync up cameras quickly in post, such as with the new multicam editing features in Final Cut Pro 5, even if camcorders were stopped and started again during a shoot (as opposed to the typical "record run" timecode used by the majority of consumer camcorders; see Chapter 7, "Editing HDV," for more information on timecodes). Only professional model camcorders, such as the Sony HVR-Z1U (unfortunately, not the HDR-FX1), include free run timecode as an option.

Follow the steps below to sync up three HVR-Z1U camcorders using free run timecode.

1. Position all of your camcorders next to each other (make certain that the time/date battery inside the camcorder is functioning).

2. Make certain that the IR (infra red) channels are set the same on all camcorders, in order to receive commands from a wireless controller.

3. Using the wireless remote control that came with your camcorder, set the free run timecode option for all cameras simultaneously.

Whether or not you decide to sync up your camcorders using free run timecode, a multiple camera shoot may also benefit from the use of a remote control camera system, such as a product by Grizzly Pro (www.grizzlypro.com) called the r-Three (see Figure 4.23). This type of system allows for live switching between cameras, as well as motorized operation of basic camera movement. For example, you can switch smoothly between three HVR-Z1U camcorders, see where each is pointed at any moment in time (using a couple of monitors), and then adjust pan, tilt, or zoom to reframe a shot or to follow action as it happens. This type of control can all be done from a single, video game style controller connected to an interface box that passes commands to a remote PTZ (pan/tilt/zoom) head attached to a tripod using a standard Cat5 networking cable. Whether you are using one camera or three, a remote control system can smooth out your camera moves, while allowing you to direct and shoot a live event like a big-budget TV production with several operators.

Figure 4.23 *Grizzly Pro (www.grizzlypro.com) provides affordable, portable, remote camera control systems, such as the r–Three, for recording live events or other multiple camera situations.*

Using Internal and External Microphones

For many amateur or documentary and event videographers, the decision to use an external microphone is usually based on budget and convenience (situations where you are moving very quickly or working solo make it impractical). However, for many professionals, the use of a separate microphone is considered a necessity. In many everyday situations—such as when you're shooting video on a vacation or simply capturing scenic backdrops—professional audio capabilities are not important. In fact, audio captured with a built-in microphone can be very good under the right conditions. Still, anyone shooting a movie or other project with professional aspirations should consider the benefits of using high-quality audio, particularly if there is dialogue involved. As discussed in Chapter 2, there are several different types of microphones and devices for capturing audio.

Whatever type of microphone you use, there are different techniques that you can use to get decent audio. Following are a few suggestions for improving the audio recorded with a microphone, particularly a built-in microphone that is a part of your camera:

◆ Place the camera close to your audio source and point it directly at your subject whenever possible (avoid any orientation at more than a 45-degree angle if you can).

◆ Do not point your camera into the wind. If it is a windy day, use a specially attached windscreen (a foam sock for your microphone) or make sure to activate the wind reduction feature on your camera (many cameras are equipped with this feature, which is usually accessed through the electronic menu).

◆ Turn off any electronic devices in the room that might cause humming or distracting audio interference. Air conditioners and computers are obvious offenders, and some fluorescent light fixtures can be problematic as well.

◆ Avoid recording in noisy locations, such as crowded malls or loud streets, unless you are interested in recording background sounds or crowd *walla*—the wall of noise created by many voices and sounds recorded together.

◆ Use headphones to monitor your audio and adjust recording levels when necessary. The volume of your audio cannot be raised after the shoot without affecting the quality. If the volume is too high, it might cause distortions that are irreversible later on. If you're uncertain about how to adjust the audio levels, use the automatic controls on your camcorder or adjust the loudest sound to a modest 12dB.

Boom Microphones

When recording dialogue or other point-specific audio, it is often a good idea to isolate the source of sound using a microphone that is placed in close proximity to the subject you are recording. In many instances, the best method to capture this type of audio—without getting a microphone into the frame while shooting—is with a boom microphone (see Figure 4.24), which is placed at the end of a long pole and tethered to the audio input on your camera or a separate field recorder. Boom microphones are used for recording interviews and for capturing the performances of actors on a movie set, whether shot on location or on a sound stage. Boom microphones work best when used with microphones that isolate the angle or range of space in which audio is captured, such as a short shotgun microphone. It is easier to get clean sound and remove extraneous background noise, while keeping voices close and distinct, with this type of setup (more on this later in the chapter). An on-camera microphone, even a shotgun style microphone that can focus on sound at a distance, cannot achieve the quality of sound that putting a microphone on a boom can achieve. A boom microphone can be reasonably "faked" using a vocal microphone tethered to a broomstick or other pole, although a professional boom pole includes the option of a mount for the microphone and an XLR cable that runs neatly from one end to the other. There are also many collapsible pole models that make transporting easy, such as those sold by K-Tek (including low cost, aluminum models in their Avalon series).

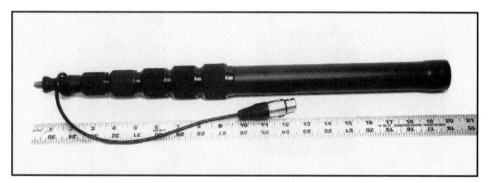

Figure 4.24 *K-Tek makes excellent boom poles for holding a microphone, including expandable models (such as the Avalon Traveler) that store neatly into a carry-on bag.*

Wireless Microphones

When recording audio for a subject that is located at a distance from your camera where boom microphones won't reach or are impractical, a wireless microphone is often the best answer (see Figure 4.25). Wireless microphones are great for recording interviews, particularly where a lavalier-style microphone can be attached to the clothing of the individual that is being recorded (lavalier, or lav mics, are tiny microphones that are easy to hide in discreet locations, such as a subject's clothing). Wireless microphones consist of two parts: a wireless microphone that can be attached to the talent, held in the hand, or placed on a boom; and a receiver attached to your camera or field recorder, which picks up the transmitted audio and records it to tape or disk. Wireless microphones are an essential part of many mobile video productions. Lectrosonics makes several, film-quality wireless mics, although they tend to be a bit pricey for the average user. If you cannot afford to purchase one of these professional systems, renting is often the best solution, particularly for shorter productions. Sony also makes their own wireless mic system, the UWP-C1/6264, advertised as an accessory for the HDR-FX1 and HVR-Z1U.

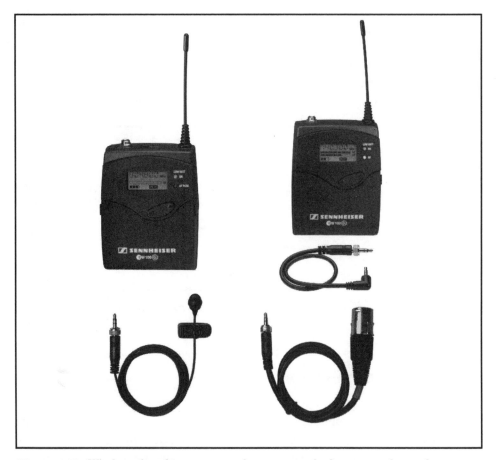

Figure 4.25 *Wireless microphones are a good way to record a human speaker, such as an interview subject, without the need for a boom. Shown here is a transmitter with cardoid lavalier and a portable receiver. (Courtesy of Sennheiser)*

AVOIDING BACKGROUND NOISE

The key to good audio, especially audio that is recorded outdoors or in other noisy situations, is being prepared. This means that you should scout a location before shooting to determine potentially problematic environmental sounds that might interfere with your shoot. A babbling brook might seem like a good place to shoot a nature video, but trying to record dialogue there would not be easy. A talking camera operator has ruined many good videos, making the audio unusable for editing. Locations within the flight pattern of a major airport are also problematic for a shoot. When scouting a location, listen with the ears of an audio engineer and think about environmental sounds that might cause a distraction or require an actor's lines to be looped (or dubbed) in post-production.

Wind, or even a slight breeze, is a particularly problematic noisemaker. Many camcorders are equipped with a special switch or menu option for reducing the noise caused by wind passing over the microphone. This feature only masks the worst sounds and does not completely remove extraneous noise. To do this, you need to purchase an inexpensive windscreen to place over the microphone. But camcorders with small, built-in microphones do not always benefit from wind blocking devices. Purchasing an inexpensive handheld microphone—which usually comes with its own windscreen—for your camcorder is a good solution to the wind problem.

Recording Room Tone

Regardless of location, it is important to record the natural sounds of a place; doing so can assist in the editing and sound mixing process. The ambient sound recording of a location is called *room tone*, and can include the reverberation of a large hall, the muffled sounds of a hotel room, or the constant hum of an air conditioner. When stitching together audio tracks from dialogue and other sound recordings, room tone can be used to fill in the gaps to smooth over cuts or areas that lack voices or other sound effects. Using room tone allows you to space out conversations or mix other elements together while maintaining continuity with your sound. After arriving on location, or before the end of a shoot, leave the camera or audio recorder running for a minute while you record room tone to document the space your video and its subjects inhabit. In Chapter 9, "Editing and Mixing Audio," the use of room tone is discussed along with editing audio and mixing sound.

Chapter 5

Lighting for HDV

We all experience, to some degree or another, the effects of light in our daily lives. Whether it is the play of shadows against our walls at night or the rays of sunshine that leak through the curtains after a misty morning, light can move us in surprisingly dramatic ways. After all, everything that we experience by sight, including color, is the result of light. The path to exceptional lighting for video and film is built on a foundation of time-tested principles and careful study. Professional cinematographers paint each scene with light, much like applying paint to a canvas, to create the environments and elicit the emotions that directors need to clearly tell their story. The best Directors of Photography (called D.P. or D.o.P.) have spent their entire careers creating emotions through the manipulation of light on a movie or television screen.

Lighting is the best way to improve the quality and overall impact of any video production. It is also a great way to achieve a distinctive mood or atmosphere that is lacking from a scene. By taking a look at some of the most relevant lighting principles and specific techniques, you should begin to understand the elements that contribute to effective lighting. Also, once you have familiarized yourself with some of the equipment and types of lights on the market, you can start to piece together a kit that is suited to your particular needs and budget. Even if you do not have the means to purchase special lighting gear, you can use many of the ideas in this chapter to work with inexpensive items from your garage or the hardware store. For additional lighting setups and ideas not discussed in this chapter (as well as links to other information on the subject), visit the book's Web site at www.hdvfilmmaking.com.

Armed with some basic lighting principles and a few good lights, you can greatly improve the quality of your next production. Just remember that lighting is an art, and is therefore subjective. Don't be afraid to be creative and experiment.

Basic Lighting Principles

In many ways, lighting is as much of a science as an art. Understanding both aspects of lighting can only improve your craft and help you to avoid many of the pitfalls you might encounter in working with lights.

Color Temperatures

Color temperature, a measurement that corresponds to the actual color that a light produces, is a concept that is often difficult to grasp for newcomers to cinematography. When dealing with the intangible, invisible element called *light* (what we see are actually reflections off of a surface), it can be challenging to visualize the effect it has until it has been captured and reviewed by a camera. Although our eyes adjust to make almost any light look white, cameras are much more sensitive to minor changes in light and have a particularly difficult time deciding what to do with color. For example, a white shirt under an ordinary light bulb should appear white to our eyes, although a video camera sees yellow. If the same shirt was viewed under a fluorescent lamp, it would appear blue-green to a camera, and in the sun it would look blue. The only way to account for variations in color is to tell the camera what should be white, so that it can adjust all other colors accordingly. The white balance feature on video cameras handles this task automatically, although when you are lighting a scene, it is best to set the white balance for each new shot manually in order to achieve the best color reproduction (setting the white balance is discussed in Chapter 4, "Operating an HDV Camcorder").

Different lighting situations produce different temperatures of light, which are most often measured in degrees. Kelvin indoor lighting tends to be about 3200K, while outdoor color balance is about 5600K. Some cameras include a dial or menu settings that correspond to one of these values, permitting the user to make basic manual adjustments, depending on the lighting conditions, although manually white-balancing is the best solution for video cameras. The type of lighting equipment that you choose has an effect on the temperature of a scene (this is discussed in more detail later in this chapter). Table 5.1 lists a few lighting situations and their corresponding color temperatures.

Table 5.1 Color Temperatures (Approximate)

Light Source	Degrees Kelvin
Sunrise or sunset	2,000K
Sunlight at noon	5,400K
Overcast sky	6,000K
Blue, summer sky	6,500–10,000K
Moonlight	4,100K
Candle flame	1,850K
Match flame	1,700K
100W household bulb	2,900K
Fluorescent lights	3,500–4,300K
HMI	5,600K

MONITORING COLOR

Even though the viewfinders and view screens on our camcorders allow us to monitor video while recording, it is easy to miss minor variations in color, especially if a monitor is not properly calibrated. Make certain that the color you see is the color you want; otherwise, you may have to use even more time in post-production color-correcting a scene. For critical shoots, a professional monitor is recommended, in addition to video scopes that can gauge the accuracy of your color and lighting. Serious Magic makes a version of their DV Rack software with an HDV add-on (PC only), which allows you to use video scopes to analyze your video on location, through the use of a laptop computer that is connected to your camera (see Figure 5.1).

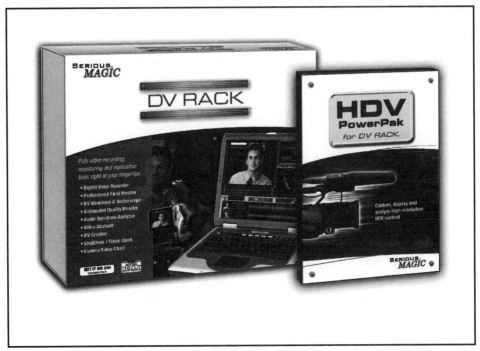

Figure 5.1 *It is important to monitor the accuracy of your color and lighting while shooting. Serious Magic's HDV add-on for its DV Rack software is one solution for PC users, which allows you to look at video scopes of footage from your HDV camera while on set.*

CREATING COLOR EFFECTS WITH THE WHITE BALANCE FEATURE

Although the purpose of the white balance feature is to accurately represent color, you can use it to create unnatural colors that reflect the mood or style of your production. By balancing a camera against a colored sheet of paper instead of a white card, you can shift the colors in a scene to create interesting effects. In order to achieve the look of a specific color, you need to use the color that is its opposite, as determined by a color wheel. For example, if you wanted to create a picture with a yellowish-green tint, you would need to use a blue sheet of paper to balance against. If you wanted to create a green look, you would need to balance against magenta, and so on. Try experimenting with different colors but make sure that you like the results—unless you think you can alter the results with color correction tools later on (see Chapter 7, "Editing HDV," for information on color correction techniques).

Qualities of Light

Apart from technical issues that are the result of light's interaction with the mechanical processes of a camera, light possesses a set of qualities that are most readily defined by broad categories, such as hard and soft. These are the dramatic, theatrical qualities that light brings to a subject, whether it is the human figure, a room, or another object. These classical qualities are the result of the direction and intensity of the light, and are often distinguished by the shadows that are created.

Hard Light

Hard light is an intense light that casts distinct shadows and creates clean, sharp edges on a subject (see Figure 5.2). An example of hard light is the sun on a clear, bright day. Spotlights are another example of hard light. As hard lights can be very harsh, it is best to balance them with a softer fill light.

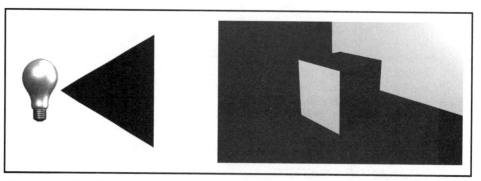

Figure 5.2 *Hard light produces sharp edges and distinct shadows.*

Soft Light

Soft light is much smoother and more flattering than hard light (see Figure 5.3). Examples of soft light include the sky on a cloudy day or fluorescent lights in a classroom. As soft lights are not directional (unlike hard lights), they are best for illuminating skin or for creating rounder edges on a subject. Examples of common soft lights for video and film are Kino Flo's (fluorescent lamps) or a diffused light, such as a Chimera. Hard lights can be turned into soft light by bouncing them with reflectors or adding diffusion in front of the light.

CASTING SHADOWS WITH LIGHT

The angle, quality, and intensity of your lights can have a significant affect on how shadows are cast. For example, a single key light that is placed directly in line with the camera and your subject should not cast a noticeable shadow. However, if the angle of your light is too high or too low, it can cast a shadow on the background (the degree to which it does that is also a result of the subject's distance from the background). Lighting faces can also be tricky. Many times, you do not want to eliminate shadows altogether, since that can yield a flat, uninteresting image. Traditionally, women are usually shot with a flat light that casts as few shadows as possible (softening facial features, to produce a more flattering, "feminine" image), while men are often shot with harder light that creates more shadows (to create a rugged, "masculine" look). Of course, the way you choose to light your talent is not limited by tradition, and should be made to suit needs of a scene or particular actor. It is important that you know where the shadows are cast on a face, which can be affected by both the quality and direction of your lights. For example, do your lights cast shadows around an actor's eyes? If so, this could be considered unflattering, producing a sinister look. You may also need an extra light to balance out the shadows from a nose or other facial feature. Use the shadows that light produces to your advantage, or find ways to cancel them out, usually by adding a fill light.

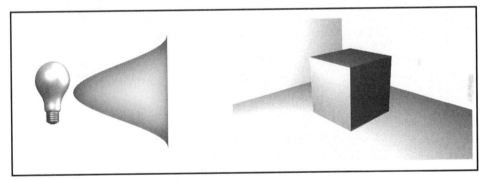

Figure 5.3 *Soft light produces smooth edges and gentle shadows .*

Interview:
Jody Eldred

Jody Eldred is a documentary filmmaker and cinematographer, as well as one of the earliest adopters of the HDV format (in particular, the Sony HVR-Z1U) for use on professional projects, including the TV series *JAG*. In addition, he has shot news for CBS and operated his own Sony HDCAM HDW-F900 on a variety of other projects.

Is lighting for HDV different than DV or other video formats?

Lighting theory is lighting theory, and those physics will never change. What lighting looks beautiful or ugly are the same with a home video camera and with IMAX. It's the subtleties that make all the difference. It's not so much the recording format (HDV vs. DVCam vs. HDCAM vs. Betacam...), but rather the camera and its ability to see into the darks and highlights, the way it reproduces color, and its resolution. With the Z1U, for example, in 1080i the resolution is 35mm film-like, so you need to be aware of how your subject looks to your eye, as that is pretty close to how it will look on camera. Things you would never notice in DV or even Betacam—like a piece of black gaffer's tape on a shiny black picture frame edge in the distance to take down glare—in HDV, 1080i mode with the Z1U, will look pretty much like a piece of black gaffer's tape on a shiny black picture frame edge. You see into the shadows and into the highlights, so you have to light for that and do set design for that, too.

What type of light sensitivity does HDV exhibit?

It depends entirely on the amount of ND, the gain setting, shutter speed. The Z1U must be close to 400 ASA but can shoot in very low light with terrific effect. With gain cranked up to give you two more stops (12 db.), the picture is not noisy at all and incredibly light sensitive.

How does shooting HDV compare with film?

Film has greater latitude, but the Z1U handles highlights like film, and you don't have to change film stocks to go from day to night shooting. 35mm film is amazing, but for $5,000 the Z1U can do an astounding job. I have intercut Z1U with 35mm film on two primetime network shows airing in HD, and you just can't tell the difference. (There is a difference, but it is really hard to discern unless you know in advance to look for certain shots.)

In terms of image quality and shooting, what are some of HDVs strengths and weaknesses?

Image-wise, I've gone over that in the above answers. In shooting, the Z1U is small, lightweight, and you can shoot in cramped places where larger HD cameras cannot go, or cannot go without a lot of time-consuming rigging. The Steadyshot feature makes it great for shooting in aircraft, boats and other moving vehicles, also making it excellent for camera mounts on motorcycles, cars, for skydiving, bicycles, you name it. Some of these we could never shoot in HD before. Due to the Z1U's small size and light weight, it will certainly become the standard for underwater photography, as its picture underwater is so close to the F900's, at 1/3 the weight and size. Also, because the Z1U is inexpensive, it is a better choice for dangerous locations where the camera might be damaged or stolen. And it can look like a home video camera, bringing less attention to the cameraman, which is very desirable in many shooting situations. Weaknesses are the small lens/imager on all cameras of this size, making shallow depth of field a challenge. And of course more expensive cameras like my F900 have a lot more color depth and resolution, which they should for 20x the cost.

Do you use any filtration or other accessories with your HDV camera?

I use the Chorale mattebox and follow-focus from Band Pro/16:9. It allows me to use filters, the eyebrow/French flag for glare control, and the follow-focus is essential for being able to critically control focus on that small lens. Being out of focus even a little bit in HD is not a good thing. I also put a Zoe zoom control on the handle, making it easy to do smooth zooms when holding it that way. I also bought the 16:9 wide angle lens, which I leave on all the time, and I bought a 1.6x telephoto converter from Century Precision to be able to reach out farther. Bracket1.com makes an L-shaped bracket that mounts to the bottom of Z1U and nicely snuggles up to the right side of the camera just in front of the handgrip, allowing the attachment of two wireless mic receivers. I have two Lectrosonic 201's on mine. So I can receive two channels of audio from my soundman with no cumbersome cables in the way. I love this.

What is your opinion of the CineFrame and Picture Profile modes on the Sony HDV cameras?

The Picture Profiles, especially PP4, are very useful. I dialed in the color a little more and took the sharpness down. I like shooting with Cinematone 2 and Blackstretch. Shooting in 50i, Cineframe 25 gives the closest look to film cadence.

(continued on next page)

(continued from previous page)

Do you have any special techniques or advice you'd like to share for operating a camera in the field, while shooting documentary footage?

Nothing different from how one would normally shoot good pictures. Use a tripod. Stop zooming and panning so much. Use a wide lens and get up close. Keep your eyes open and look for the drama unfolding around you. And for gosh sakes, use a good soundman and get perfect sound!

Do you have any other tips or suggestions for filmmakers shooting HDV?

You're dealing with 4–6 times the resolution of anything you've ever shot with before so you really need to pay attention to detail. It probably would make sense to rent a good HD monitor for a few shoots so you know exactly what you're getting. That's much cheaper and less painful than getting back to the editing bay and saying, "Oops," which I've done a few too many times in my career. Never again!

Choosing a Lighting Setup

Once you have chosen a person, object, or room that you want to light (see Figure 5.4), the next step is deciding which lighting setup you should use to best capture its features. The choice of setup depends a great deal on budget and the limits of your location, although even small, no-budget productions can benefit from the use of a few well-placed lights—even if they are only work lamps from Home Depot. Professional productions often require flexible and powerful lighting kits, like those provided by companies like Arri, Lowel (see Figure 5.5), or Kino Flo.

Whenever possible, before you begin a new lighting setup, it is best to start in complete darkness (or close to it). This is a good way to gauge exactly where your light sources are coming from, and it should help you control your setup more effectively. Of course, depending on your needs and experience, you may find it just as easy to start with the natural light in a room and work from there. For example, you might decide that leaving the window shades open produces a nice ambient light with which to begin a more detailed setup, such as three-point lighting.

Figure 5.4 *Kino Flo lights (4 Bank) on the set of a Hollywood movie. (Courtesy of Kino Flo)*

Figure 5.5 *Companies like Lowel provide lights that can be used in any type of setup, including the simplest, three-point setups. (Courtesy of Lowel)*

Three-Point Lighting

The most basic and commonly used lighting setup is referred to as *three-point lighting* (see Figure 5.6). The "points" referred to are three types of light sources—a key light, a fill light, and a back light—positioned at specific angles and distances from a subject. When put together, these lights create a neutral lighting effect that is effective for many scenes. Although three-point lighting is not necessarily the most exciting way to use lights, it is often the best choice for starting to light a scene. After you have mastered the three-point scheme, you can start to add, subtract, and adjust your lighting to achieve even more interesting lighting compositions.

SETTING UP LIGHTS IN ORDER

When lighting a set, remember to add lights in the correct order, beginning with the key light, then the fill light, and then the back light (in general, the easiest method, especially for beginners). Lighting in this way helps you to carefully balance and monitor the effects of additional lights in a scene.

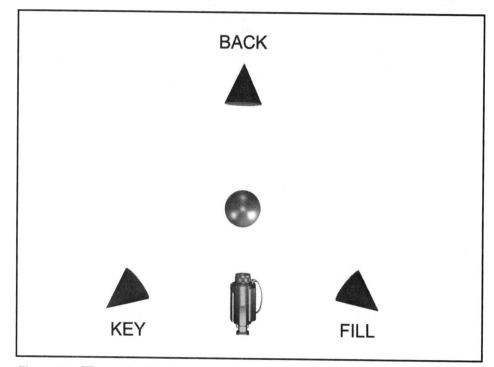

Figure 5.6 *Three-point lighting setups use key, fill, and back lights to provide neutral illumination.*

Key Light

A key light is placed close to the camera, usually to the side or above (see Figure 5.6). This is the primary light, which usually casts a hard light directly onto a subject. As a key light often produces a harsh light, it is important to be sure not to overexpose your subject. You should be able to tell when you have too much light on your subject, as the brightest portions of the image will appear unusually bright or "blown out"—an especially common problem with reflective surfaces, including skin.

If you do not want to lose detail on a person's face, for example, make sure that your key lights are adjusted to a manageable level or that your subject is moved to a satisfactory distance. Using the Zebra Stripes feature on your camera can help you to avoid overexposing areas by monitoring the brightness of the image.

As with any light, the height and angle at which the key light is positioned create different effects. In general, placing a key light at approximately 45 degrees or less to the right or left of a camera is desirable. It should also be positioned higher than a camera and at a level that produces the desired shadows on a subject. For example, when lighting a person, you usually want to cast shadows slightly downward (such as those produced by the nose) instead of across the face. Once you have tried lighting a few shots on your own, you will understand the results and difficulties of casting pleasing shadows.

Most camcorders have some sort of "shoe" on top for attaching a small video light or other device, such as a microphone. This can be a good place to attach a key light, particularly for smaller productions that cannot afford a separate lighting kit, or for quick, on-the-spot shooting that does not allow for extra setup time. The new LED Lite Panel is a great choice for a soft key light that attaches to a camera (see Figure 5.7).

Figure 5.7 *Key lights fixed to a camera, such as LED Lite Panels, are convenient and set up quickly .(Courtesy of Lite Panels)*

USING VIDEO LIGHTS

A couple of things to keep in mind when using a light that attaches to your camera are how much power the light requires (many video lights last less than 30 minutes on rechargeable batteries) and whether the light is too bright for your needs. The majority of video lights are glaring and harsh; such lighting is not particularly flattering to your subject. In fact, under this lighting, people look as though they were caught in head-lights. Using new, softer key lights that attach to a camera—such as LED Lite Panels or miniature Chimeras and Kino Flos—are better, if you can afford them; these lights work great for interviews.

REDUCING THE HARSHNESS OF VIDEO LIGHTS

If you choose to use a key light that attaches to your camera, make sure that it pro-vides enough diffused light to soften a subject. You might also try creating a makeshift filter for your light by clipping wax paper over the front—just be sure it is attached to the end of your "barn doors" and it doesn't get too hot. Ideally (and for safety), you should use a professional diffuser for your light. In addition, position yourself far enough away from your subject to reduce the intensity of light. For the most control, consider purchasing one of the on-camera lights sold by LitePanels, which consist of "cool," soft LEDs that can be easily dimmed.

Fill Light

Fill lights are softer light sources that are positioned to the side of a camera and the subject it is recording (see Figure 5.8). These lights are good for removing the shadows created by a key light or other lights in the surrounding environment. This is especially important for video, since its limited contrast range makes it nec-essary to control the high-lights and eliminate harsh areas of black (minimizing

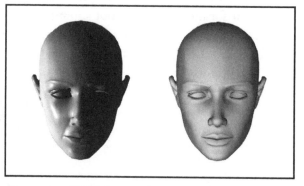

Figure 5.8 *Fill lights supply soft, non-directional light (image on the left has a single, hard key light, while the image on the right adds a soft fill light to evenly illumi-nate the face).*

the difference between light and dark, although in a studio you have more control over contrast, since you control all of the variables).

KEY LIGHTS AND FILL LIGHTS

A good rule of thumb is to make sure that your fill light is never brighter than your key light. You may even use several fill lights for a scene, as long as you make certain that their combined intensity does not exceed your key light. Too much fill light can wash out your image.

CHOOSING THE RIGHT SIZE FOR A FILL LIGHT

Try using fill lights that are as large as or slightly larger than the subject you are illuminating. For example, if you were lighting a face, you would want to make sure that the fill light was big enough to cover the entire surface. A standard light bulb, for example, would be too small, unless it was placed inside a soft "box" (such as those sold by Chimera and others) or umbrella for diffusing the light.

Back Light

Back lights are hard light sources that are positioned behind—and, in many cases, above—a subject. These lights help to separate a subject from its background by giving it an illuminated "edge" (separating foreground from background), which aids in creating a more three-dimensional image. For this reason, back lights are also called *rim lights*, since they are used to light the outer rim of objects in the foreground. Generally speaking, back lights are usually key light sources that provide a hard light, although they may be any type of light that helps to add illumination behind your image.

INTENSITY OF LIGHT

Try to make sure that your subject is not lit brighter than your background. While it might seem like a good idea to make a subject significantly brighter, doing so can add to the artificial look that is sometimes associated with video productions. If your intended effect is to have a more film-like appearance, then it is important to balance the intensity of light that is in the foreground and background. For instance, the foreground subject should not be much brighter than the background and vice versa.

Selecting Lighting Equipment

The lighting equipment you select depends greatly on your budget and how much you plan on shooting in controlled environments or sets, such as when interviewing a subject, shooting a movie, or creating a commercial. For anyone planning to shoot a movie or other commercial project, it is highly recommended that you consider investing in a small lighting kit, such as those offered by companies like Lowel (see Figure 5.9), Arri, Photoflex, Kino Flo, or another manufacturer. Many beginner sets (costing anywhere from $400 to $1,500) include everything you need to create a basic three-point lighting setup and are quite adequate for casual users. If you find yourself in a situation without proper lighting equipment—or if you just want to supplement the kit you already own—you can also purchase work lamps, fluorescent fixtures, and other lighting apparatus at your local hardware store. However, you should be aware of the issues concerning temperatures and the color casts they create for any light source you work with. Just remember that you should only mix sources when a camera is carefully white balanced and the results are monitored.

Types of Light

The type of light that you select greatly affects the color and quality of light that is captured, as well as the comfort and safety of a shoot. Before you choose a light, determine the best type to get the job done right.

Figure 5.9 *A professional lighting kit (available in many configurations) may include all of the equipment that you need for basic lighting setups. (Courtesy of Lowel)*

Incandescent Lights

The most common incandescent light is a standard light bulb, although many lightbulbs are now halogens. Incandescent lights are often harsh and use energy inefficiently, which means that it takes a lot of energy to produce relatively little light. These types of lights are fine for "practicals" (lamps and other fixtures that are present in a shot), but if you are looking for high wattage for shooting video (without blowing a circuit) you should probably choose a halogen light.

Halogen Lights

Halogen lights cast a purer light than do incandescent bulbs, and are more efficient with power. However, they do get very hot, which can pose a safety risk and make working on a heavily lit set very uncomfortable. Work lights that you can purchase at a hardware store are a good example of inexpensive halogen lights that

may provide adequate illumination for shooting video (although potentially uneven and unreliable). For the best results, purchase or rent a professional light. In addition to a variety of open-faced lights, fresnels are a commonly used incandescent light for professional video and film production (see Figure 5.10). Fresnels are lensed lights that produce an even, focused beam of light, and are often best for many hard light needs.

Figure 5.10 *Fresnels are often used as an even key light source, particularly when a hard light is required on a set. (Courtesy of Lowel)*

Fluorescent Lights

Fluorescent lights are very efficient and do not get hot (actors appreciate the lack of heat). However, they are generally not as bright as halogen bulbs, unless they are arranged in large arrays; they also may produce a slight green glow that some people find unpleasant, although professional daylight balanced lights eliminate this problem. As long as you white balance carefully, fluorescent sources are great to shoot with (see Figure 5.11). Keep a few of the small battery-powered fluorescent lamps in your bag for adding extra fill light to a set or for simply smoothing out harsh edges caused by high key lighting. Good fluorescent lights (like those produced by Kino Flo) are popular on film sets, as they provide a smooth, pleasing look when shooting faces and skin without generating heat that can make enduring such shots unpleasant.

Figure 5.11 *Ordinary fluorescent lights are good at filling in areas with a soft glow, although specially designed fluorescent lights for film and video have more natural color balance, such as Kino Flos, which are found on many film and television sets. (Courtesy of Kino Flo)*

Light Stands and Barn Doors

Light stands are anything that you can hang a light on, although professional stands (see Figure 5.12) are recommended. (They often come with a light kit.) If you do not have a traditional light stand (that is, if you are not using a professional lighting kit, and simply fashioning lights from fluorescent tubes and household bulbs), consider using microphone stands or makeshift broomsticks and large metal clips, which can be attached to shelves, frames, or pieces of wood. The ability to finely adjust the height and direction of your lights with a proper stand is nice (and often necessary), though you can just as easily fashion your own solutions for lighting, in case you are working with inexpensive lamps and other materials. However, using stands not intended for supporting lights may be a safety issue. This is particularly true when using lights that get very hot (anything that is not fluorescent), since an overturned stand can be extremely dangerous, causing severe burns or cuts from broken glass. Using sand bags can help with stability and should be used on a professional shoot to help anchor a light stand to the floor. In addition, make sure cables are secure and out of the way, as much as possible (securing power cables to the floor

Figure 5.12 *Companies like Lowel provide stands to support their lighting equipment. (Courtesy of Lowel)*

with gaffer's tape is a good idea). Also, many small lights that you would purchase in a kit come with "barn doors" built into them for controlling and directing the light. You may fashion your own barn doors or flags to control light using cardboard (as long as it is far enough away from the heat source), foam core, nonreflective metal, or anything that helps you limit the amount of light that escapes.

Special Lighting Techniques

Over time, you will encounter a seemingly infinite number of shooting conditions and lighting situations. In this section, several techniques are presented for dealing with challenging situations or for simply improving ordinary lighting. Finding new ways to light creatively is part of the challenge and reward of studying the art of lighting.

Bouncing Lights

One way to easily illuminate a room is to bounce a bright light off a white ceiling or wall. Pointing a bright work lamp at a white ceiling is a great technique for quickly and inexpensively lighting a small set, particularly when you only have one light to work with. Bouncing light is an equally effective technique for multilight shoots. By using a carefully positioned reflector, you can redirect unused key light for filling in the opposite side of a subject or for shining a spotlight. On a bright day, using a reflector (even if it is fashioned from a large sheet of aluminum foil fixed to a board) is a nice way to create a shimmering spotlight by redirecting the sun's rays. Reflectors are also a good way to get light into very specific areas of the frame, such as a thin ray of light cast across an actor's face or an illuminated statue in the back of a shot.

Creating Depth with Color

The many complexities of lighting are not limited to an understanding of brightness and darkness, blacks and whites, and shades of gray. Color is an oft-neglected element that provides an excellent way to establish depth or create complexity in a scene. In Chapter 8, "Color Correcting Video," color is discussed as it pertains to achieving a specific look; the discussion here is more concerned with the psychological effects that lights of varying colors have on a scene.

Colored lights in video productions each have their own peculiar properties, which lend themselves better to certain lighting effects. If you have colored cellophane or special gels for your lights, you can create interesting effects working with color, such as placing cool colors (like blue) or warm colors (like red) in either the foreground or background of a scene. Experimentation is the best way to decide what works best for your production. For example, you might try casting a red back light against a far wall when conducting an interview, or place a blue light on the right side of a frame and red on the other. Color is a great way to add separation and dimension to location shots.

Lighting a Blue Screen or Green Screen

The most important factor in creating a great composite (a combination of layers and elements creating a single image) from blue screen or green screen shots is the use of proper lighting to adequately illuminate and separate a subject from the backdrop. Most people do not use enough light or put the light they do use in the wrong locations, resulting in backgrounds that are difficult, if not impossible, to key properly (chroma keying, and other techniques for working with green and blue screen footage, are discussed in Chapter 10, "Creating Graphics and Effects for HDV").

When shooting a subject against a blue or green screen, it is extremely important that you illuminate the backdrop evenly and brightly (see Figure 5.13). The best way to do this is with a bright back light placed directly above the screen and pointing downward, or by having multiple large lights placed on both the left and right sides of the screen. Also make certain that there are no creases or wrinkles in the screen; these cause shadow lines that are difficult to remove later on. An adequate amount of fill light should also be used to more clearly separate your subject from the background. In addition, the subject should be far enough away from the screen so that light reflecting off of the colored backdrop does not spill onto it, causing a blue or green edge, which—depending on severity—can be difficult to fix with compositing software.

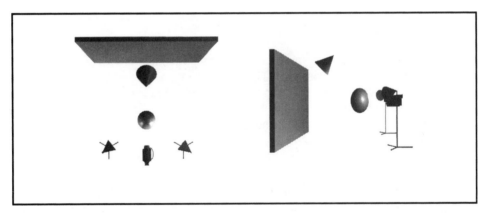

Figure 5.13 *Lighting a blue or green screen requires adequate illumination and carefully placed lights.*

Lastly, if you are planning to composite your subject into a scene, then you should consider the lighting that the new environment would use. After all, the idea behind compositing a subject with a blue or green screen shot is to create the convincing illusion that your subject is inhabiting a new environment. Make sure that the lighting you are using on a stage is motivated by the environment into which you want to place your subject. For example, make certain that you have a key light positioned where the "virtual" sun would be located. A poorly lit subject is a sure give-away that a scene was composited.

Safety Considerations

When operating any lighting equipment that is powered through an electrical outlet, it is important to anticipate potential safety risks. The most obvious step is to make sure that your cords are not frayed or otherwise damaged, as this could result in electrical shock or fires. If you do have frayed cords, make sure to replace them immediately or cover them thoroughly with electrical tape. Also, make sure that your cords are not easily tripped over by using gaffer's tape (duct tape or masking tape works fine also) to secure them to the ground. Furthermore, before plugging into a socket, it is best to ensure that the outlet is properly grounded by using a three-prong plug—failure to properly ground equipment could result in a shock.

TESTING POWER OUTLETS

Checking to make sure an outlet is safe not only protects you from potential shock and a blown fuse as a result of faulty wiring, but may also prevent the flickering that sometimes occurs as a result of intermittent current. You can purchase a small device to test an outlet for safety before plugging into it. A store like Radio Shack offers such devices for less than 10 dollars. They should be kept in your camera bag for use when shooting in new locations.

Any light that is not fluorescent can become hot very quickly and present a significant danger of burning anyone who touches it. When you are finished with your lights, turn them off and let them cool for several minutes before attempting to unscrew or move them. Sudden changes in temperature are also not recommended. For example, do not splash water on a hot light or leave it in the rain. Also, wait until a light has cooled before moving it into a new location. Getting a hot light wet or moving it from the warm interior of a house to the freezing temperatures of outdoors could result in shattered glass and bulbs. In addition, do not put anything flammable, such as a piece of paper, against a hot light. Paper may ignite when subjected to the temperatures produced by hot glass or metal.

Chapter 6

Designing Effective Compositions

While not every camera operator can become the next Gregg Toland, Haskell Wexler, or Janusz Kaminski, an understanding of shot composition and its related techniques will dramatically improve your camera work. In fact, even learning the few simple principles in this chapter can be useful when filming your next documentary, commercial, or narrative project. So pull out a few of your favorite movies and take a close look at the arrangement of elements within the frame. How can you apply these same techniques to your own pictures?

In general, the decision about how to compose a shot can be broken down into a few basic principles. Once these principles are adopted, placing a person or object in a picture can be accomplished without too much difficulty. For every rule there is an exception perhaps, but the approaches discussed in this chapter have been consistently applied (consciously or not) since the beginning of photographic history. Studying the principles of cinematography can answer important questions for a filmmaker, including "Did I get the right angle for this scene?" and "Do I have enough 'coverage' to make a good video from the footage I've shot?"

Of course, sometimes the most interesting outcome is the result of violating the rules. Knowing when to apply a principle and when to break the rules is the sign of a true artist. Remember, any systematic approach—whether in art or in life—is only a starting point that can be used or discarded as the situation requires. However, many photographic principles are based on consistently proven results, which means they can be trusted to produce satisfactory results under the widest variety of situations. In any case, it is usually best to understand the rules before you decide to break them. Even if you are familiar with the topics discussed below, consider how they might apply to the work you do with the widescreen, high-resolution HDV format.

Storyboarding

Filmmakers often create storyboards to aid them in the conceptualization and shooting of their films and television programs (see Figure 6.1). Usually, the creation of storyboards begins once a script is in place, although it may start even earlier in the process as a means to work through visual ideas for a scene. Apart from their use as creative tools, storyboards are helpful in keeping a picture on budget as they can speed up shooting and prevent unnecessary resources from being expended on set creation and crew allowances.

WS – Two figures walk towards each other...

MS – The first figure recognizes the other figure and says "Hi!"

MS – The second figure says "Hello!"

WS w/ foreground figures in focus

Figure 6.1 *Storyboards can assist any production in the planning of shots and sequences.*

Any video—whether a low budget movie, training video, or commercial project—can benefit from careful planning and storyboarding, even if shooting schedules and money for a proper crew is not required. Having enough video "in the can" that can be edited into a good movie is essential. Storyboards help to ensure that you have not missed important shots and that you have obtained the necessary coverage. Even if you are just shooting for fun, creating rough storyboards can generate ideas for interesting setups while shooting. The results are often better-composed pictures and lighting that are more satisfying for viewers and easier to edit into a logical sequence.

You might begin the storyboarding process by creating rough thumbnail sketches with a few notes about the type of shots you would like. For example, before shooting an instructional video for new employees at a corporation, try mapping out a few shots that you might require—such as close-ups of important tools, computer monitors, or signage in office hallways—in addition to any talking heads or exchanges between actors.

To be effective, storyboards should be economical, while communicating your ideas about the subject. In many instances, this means that a series of shots should be simplified, in order to communicate as much information as possible with the fewest number of setups. Knowing the number of shots you need before shooting a scene can reduce the number of times you move the camera, which helps maintain consistency from shot to shot and saves time on relighting a scene (another budget-saving measure).

A storyboard layout is most easily accomplished using pen and paper to draw rectangles, or *panels*, that represent the arrangement of a shot, and to make any notes about the composition, camera movement, and technical considerations that are required for that particular setup. In recent years, storyboards have evolved along with technology to include the use of *animatics* or animated storyboards. By editing together a series of storyboard images, you can get a better idea of how a scene plays as a movie (stills can be scanned from sketches created on paper or drawn directly in Illustrator, Photoshop, and other graphic applications). You might even record dialogue and other sound effects to help with the timing of your sequence; these can be cut together in any video editing application, such as Final Cut Pro or Premiere. Utilizing the built-in tools of your favorite NLE (nonlinear editor), you might include virtual camera moves by panning and zooming (scaling) to complete the illusion. You can find excellent examples of storyboards as special features on many of the DVDs you buy, including Pixar's *The Incredibles*, which illustrates this subject very clearly.

When still images are not enough to convey the depth and complexity necessary for planning the movements of actors and cameras, 3D animations can be used to model stages and environments where action takes place on virtual sets. This type of storyboarding is commonly referred to as *pre-vis* or *previsualization*, and is an area of growing popularity in the film industry (see Figure 6.2). The recent popularity of previsualization for films, and even some small scale projects, is made possible by faster and more sophisticated software tools, including applications built specifically to meet this need. One example of an inexpensive pre-vis software tool is Curios Labs Poser 5. Poser is a character animation application that uses detailed 3D puppets that can be animated to perform almost any type of action (you can also map a photograph of a real face onto a character's head). Although sets and environments cannot be created within the application, you can import Poser characters into other 3D applications to merge with a background.

Figure 6.2 *Previsualization is the process of creating storyboard sequences in three dimensions, often using specialized software, such as RealViz's StoryViz.*

For full featured pre-vis software that includes stages and environments, you might consider @Last Software's SketchUp 4 Film (basically, a CAD application with accurate set-construction tools), Antics (includes interesting scripting technology for automating animations), or a new tool from RealViz called StoryViz, which is intended for high-end professionals (this is reflected in its price and steep learning curve). Of course, you can also utilize any one of the standard 3D applications on the market, such as Maya, Cinema 4D, 3D Studio Max, and

Lightwave. Although none of these packages includes tools specifically for previsualization, they are capable of creating any type of prop or set design you might imagine. Once your pre-vis animations are rendered, you can edit them together as you would any other piece of footage.

Interview:
Don Bluth and Gary Goldman

One of the most important mediums for storyboarding is animation, where every shot counts. Two of the best animators around are **Don Bluth** and **Gary Goldman**, who both worked for Disney before creating their own studio (Don Bluth Films) with titles such as, *The Secret of Nihm, An American Tale, The Land Before Time,* and the classic *Dragon's Lair* animated arcade game. Don Bluth has also written a book called *The Art of Storyboard,* which is a highly useful and entertaining look at the art and practice of storyboarding. Many of these same techniques can be applied to live action films, as well as animated features.

How much detail is necessary for a good storyboard?

We like to include as much information as possible—the environment, good strong poses on the characters, suggested special effects, and some of the establishing sketches will usually be shaded for light source and colored for suggested mood.

Do animatics play an important role in your work?

Not always, but with good CG animatics, it can make a huge difference in communicating the action of the shot continuity. We used moving animatics for some of the sequences in *Titan AE.* It really helped expedite approvals and production of those complicated scenes (shots).

Apart from pen and paper, are any digital tools (such as Photoshop, etc.) used in the planning, storyboarding, and pre-production phases of your films?

Our usual approach is to draw with pencil, clean up and detail the sketch with pencil, then Xerox or copy the sketch in black, then shade or color with Magic Markers or Prisma-color markers. Up to now, we haven't taken the time to scan in the original story sketches and use Photoshop; however, with an efficient Photoshop operator, it would be a way to go. The original story sketches are always left in pencil for our archives.

How does creating storyboards for animation differ from live action?

It's pretty much the same. The idea is to flesh out the "direction" of the film, the continuity, the camera angles, close-ups, wide shots, eliminating unnecessary shots, adding shots that may or may not be directly necessary but bring additional entertainment to a sequence of scenes or shots, like off-screen character reactions. The better thought out the story sketches, the less hassle for the crew when the actual production begins. The more detail, the better the communication.

How is storyboarding for a game different than films?

It's really the same, except you must figure out resolves for the conflicts introduced in the continuity, plus "branching" of continuity, and alternate endings and failures or deaths to your key character. I refer, of course, to our original games, *Dragon's Lair I & II* and *Space Ace*. We haven't boarded a CG animated game in-house. In fact, we let the CG crew handle any storyboarding for the 3D version of *Dragon's Lair 3D: Return to the Lair*. It seemed to be more general with a lot of the action and conflict resolves being done on the fly, after story and action talk sessions, plus direct influences among the animators and sequence directors. However, there was much attention to the original backgrounds in dealing with 3D design of the environments. We did the boards for the movie portions of different games, *Dragon's Lair 3D*, and *I-Ninja* (for Namco), but not the game play. Being detailed in the story sketches with regard to the environment really helps the layout department, especially if you are concentrating on design and focusing the attention of the viewer with elements that point to where you want the audience to look, plus the way you light and color each sketch, which will also encourage where you want the audience to look.

What techniques do you commonly employ to help with the blocking and choreography of shots?

This would be your imagination. Visualizing in your mind what is happening, action wise, and how to break it into several shots of continuity, with interesting choreography and interesting and meaningful camera angles, that convey the drama or comedy of the sequence. Sometimes, we review other movies and see what those filmmakers did with a similar situation. Sometimes, we read other stories and look for inspiration. You never know where it will come from, but be prepared (with pencil and paper) to scribble down the idea when it comes. It could come in the middle of the night, waking you. Do not get caught without a way of putting the information down because you might forget your solution by dawn.

(continued on next page)

(continued from previous page)

Is there a key to figuring out the correct "beats" or timing for a scene, both in the storyboard stage and the actual film?

Sometimes, I board to the script and to a specific piece of music, from a film soundtrack, that I find appropriate for what I want the pacing of a sequence to be. Also, I always storyboard to an approved, final dialogue track, with the actors that will be voicing the character. This really helps to figure out what you are going to do with the camera. In the case of using a music cue, I time the actual beat with the editor. I've often asked the animators to use the same beat when they map out the poses of the character's actions. However, when we time out a sequence of story sketches, we again go to our imagination. Using a stop watch, think through the actions described on the story sketches, then cut off about a third of that time and apply the number of seconds or equivalent footage/frames to that sketch. If the scene or shot is described in more than one sketch, then divide up that quicker time and apply the appropriate number of seconds or film footage/frames to each sketch. I mentioned cutting the time down from what you imagine, because we generally apply more time than is necessary, and you want to keep your shots moving along. You can actually "open" up the length when you need to when editing with the computer; it is immediate, and you can see the results while viewing the timed story sketches in real time with the editor.

Your films Titan A.E. and Anastasia are two examples where 2D and 3D merge to achieve interesting results. What role do you see 2D and traditional animation techniques playing in the future? Also, how much do you foresee 3D becoming a part of your work?

Traditional animation is a great art form. It shouldn't be dismissed as passé or an archaic medium. When the Hollywood crowd has a few failures in 3D, they will be reminded that just because an animated film is done in CG, it isn't guaranteed success. Just as with traditional animation, it is all about story. You can have great imagery, but without a good story, it will fail. You can even have bad imagery and a great story, and you will still have success. But you must create endearing characters, characters that the audience can identify with. 2D will still be a major role in our animation careers, if nothing else than to help push 3D to new artistic heights. All the traditional animation principles apply to 3D/CG animation.

We cannot deny that 3D has been able to capture a larger audience for animation than ever before. We believe it may have something to do with the look of the video games being played by most teenagers today, and that similar look to these films. There is no stigmatism to 3D animation, whereas, with traditional animation, there is an unwritten rule that it is produced strictly for children or families with children as the target market. With this mindset firmly established, it is difficult to attract the 11 1/2-year-olds through the 19-year-olds to see a traditionally animated film. Not so with the 3D genre. But, again, you must still deliver a good story and believable character animation to entertain the audience. CG/3D isn't a fad. It is here to stay, and it is a great tool for animation.

Composing for Widescreen Format

Although some filmmakers are resisting the move to a widescreen format, most agree that the number of new compositional possibilities (the degree to which you can use the frame) outweigh the learning curve. The widescreen image better represents the human field of vision, providing extra space for wide-angle shots and attention-grabbing close-ups.

THE HUMAN FIELD OF VISION

The human field of vision is approximately 180 degrees in the horizontal direction and 90 degrees in the vertical direction (about 120 degrees per eye, with an overlap of about 60 degrees in front). For this reason, a widescreen image is better suited—at the proper dimensions—to reproduce natural vision. The standard 4:3 aspect ratio is closer to a square and places nearly as much emphasis on the vertical as the horizontal direction. When making the move to widescreen formats, you may need to think more about the horizontal plane than you have previously. Finding the best placement for images may require some new techniques, but you should soon learn to produce a natural, pleasing composition.

Even though HDV requires you to use the 16:9 aspect ratio, shooting for the 4:3 aspect ratio can still be important if you need to "protect" for 4:3 televisions (see Figure 6.3). Currently, the majority of TVs used in homes have 4:3 aspect ratios, making it necessary to consider a version of your program that is cropped for these screens (usually by taking out the center of the 16:9 image). An image with the 4:3 aspect ratio, which fills standard television screens, is often referred to (at least in DVD terminology) as *full frame video* as opposed to *widescreen video*. The term *full screen* can be misleading, though, as a significant portion of the original image is actually chopped off the sides during a process called *pan and scan*.

Figure 6.3 *The difference between shooting 4:3 and 16:9 is the extra space in the widescreen image.*

When you're shooting in 16:9 and protecting for 4:3 screens, it is often necessary to reframe shots that would have otherwise been done simply by filling the frame. For example, interview subjects are often shot "off axis" when protecting for 4:3 aspect ratios, as doing so makes it easier to crop to a smaller portion of the screen. This means that faces may actually look best in both aspect ratios when shot on the left or right side of the widescreen frame, as opposed to being placed directly in the center.

4:3 GUIDES ON VIEWSCREENS

Some HDV camcorders, such as the Sony HVR-Z1U, include 4:3 guides that can be overlaid on the viewscreen or viewfinder and turned on or off as needed. These guides make it easy to compose a shot that accounts for both standard and widescreen televisions. Many movie and television camera operators use similar guides on a field monitor to frame a shot in a way that facilitates the conversion between these various aspect ratios.

The Rule of Thirds

As you begin designing shots and composing images, it is important to consider a few basic principles and practical techniques for achieving good results. One of the first compositional techniques that any film student should learn is the "rule of thirds" (see Figure 6.4). The rule of thirds is a rough compositional technique that helps you to place a subject in the most interesting and effective areas of a frame. You begin by dividing a frame equally into three horizontal and three vertical sections by drawing four lines (two horizontal and two vertical). Placing a subject along one of the lines creates interest in a frame, while positioning a subject near any one of the four crosspoints creates even stronger interest. For example, placing someone's eye on a crosspoint is often the best way to film a face. Although the rule of thirds works best for video with a 4:3 aspect ratio, it does work well for widescreen images in many instances. In fact, the 16:9 aspect ratio builds on this principle and opens up more possibilities.

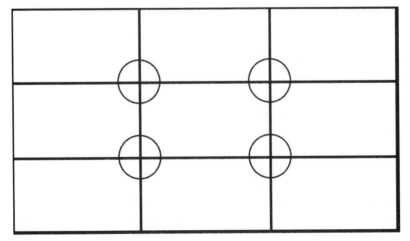

Figure 6.4 *The rule of thirds is a great device for achieving the best compositions.*

Using the rule of thirds, we can also surmise that any horizontal or vertical lines that do occur, such as an ocean horizon or row of palm trees, should be placed into an upper or lower third of the screen (as in the case of a horizon) or in a far left or right third (for a vertical object like a tree) to create a more interesting composition and avoid splitting a frame into two halves.

While composing a shot, you should also be aware of any objects in the background that might become a part of your shot. Try to avoid light poles or other vertical objects that might appear to stick out of a subject's head or otherwise interrupt the logic of your composition.

The 180 Degree Rule

An important guideline for the composition of film images is the 180 degree rule, which is essential for maintaining continuity, or logic, between shots. The 180 degree rule (see Figure 6.5) simply states that the relationship of two subjects must remain consistent, as determined by their positions along an imaginary line drawn between them (the line is usually perpendicular to the camera, although POVs and other shots may became a part of the sequence). As long as their positions remain the same, relative to each other (subject A on the left side of the frame, subject B on the right side of the frame), consistency can be maintained, and the audience knows how each subject relates to each other. If at any point you were to "cross the line" (breaking the 180 degree rule is referred to as "crossing the line"), then the relationship between your subjects is broken. By violating this rule, it becomes more difficult to discern the spatial relationship between subjects and their surroundings, resulting in disorientation for the viewer and difficulty when cutting shots together into a sequence.

For example, when cutting a dialogue scene between two actors, if an actor is facing left in one shot (camera 1 on one side of the line) and right in the next (camera 2 on the other side of the line), it is difficult to construct a logical sequence, since screen direction has been reversed. This would be the case in a two camera shoot if the cameras were on opposite sides of the line (as mentioned), or if a single camera were moved from one side of the line to the other.

The goal is to make the construction of a scene easy to grasp, while improving the transparency of edits through proper continuity. Minimizing the amount of unnecessary motion and complexity of spatial relationships in a scene allows a viewer time to concentrate on the dialogue and action, rather than analyzing a scene's geography and perspective. Of course, any rule may be broken, particularly if it is done properly. One way to cross the line is to move the camera across it during the course of a shot, which sets up a new relationship between your subjects (on opposite sides of the screen). As soon as a moving camera settles, a new line is established. In a dialogue scene with reverse shots (for example, a shot of actor A talking, followed by a reverse shot of actor B listening), most of the shots are framed similarly (close-ups, etc.) while maintaining the correct screen direction and not crossing the line (actor A is always on the left, while actor B is always on the right).

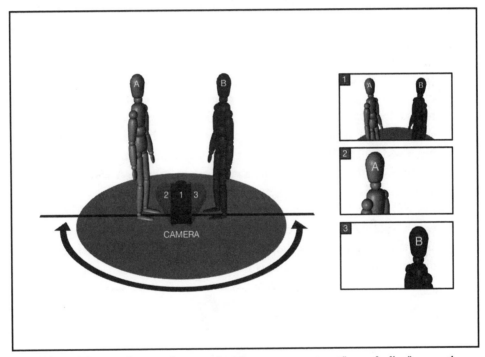

Figure 6.5 *The 180 degree rule states that the camera must not "cross the line" connecting two subjects.*

Camera Placement and Shot Size

The size and placement of your shots are the most important factors in communicating effectively with film or video. If your shots are composed carefully while you're shooting, it will be much easier to create a logical and dynamic sequence when it comes time to edit your video.

In this section, several of the most common types of shots are highlighted. These shots have been used in every movie and television show ever made, which demonstrates their importance and widespread acceptance as part of every filmmaker's vocabulary. No matter what type of project you are shooting, understanding these concepts should help to improve the look of your finished product.

Wide Shot

If you are shooting a beach, mountain, or other panoramic location, you should make sure to get a wide shot of the scene. A wide shot (WS), sometimes referred to as a *long shot* (LS) or a *full shot* (FS), is a frame in which the subject or scene is shown from a distance, so that it appears smaller in the frame. In the case of people, a wide shot allows you to see at least someone's head and feet, though most of the time a camera is even farther away from its subject. A wide shot is usually used as an "establishing shot" to set up a place or location (such as a beach or the exterior of a house) where the scenes that follow take place (see Figure 6.6). In this way, a wide shot provides context for the action. More generally, a wide shot is any shot that communicates the scope of a set or location by placing the viewer at a distance from the subject that is filmed.

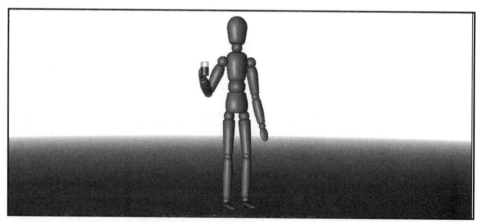

Figure 6.6 *Wide shots establish a location or setting, and may frame a subject from head to toe.*

Medium Shot

A medium shot (MS) is framed somewhere between a wide shot and a close-up, and is usually defined by the area from the waist up on a person (see Figure 6.7). Medium shots are perhaps the most common types of shot, as they provide a good balance of information about a subject and its surroundings. Details are relatively easy to discern in a medium shot, and it is also a good way to set up a scene, particularly one with dialogue between two people.

Figure 6.7 *Medium shots frame a person from the waist up.*

Close-up

Close-ups are the exact opposite of a wide shot and present a very large subject in the frame. These shots are often details on a subject, such as someone's face or eyes, or their hands holding an object (see Figure 6.8). The use of a close-up is a great way to direct a viewer's attention to details that might otherwise be missed or to place emphasis where there was none before. For example, you could use a close-up to show the ripples in a pool of water or to capture the expression on someone's face as they react to another actor's lines.

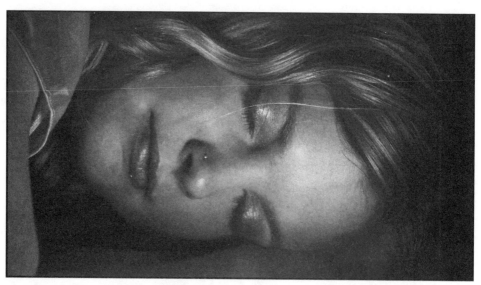

Figure 6.8 *Close-ups show details, such as features on a person's face (actress Liz MacDonald).*

Like the other shots mentioned, a close-up includes many variations, such as a medium close-up (MCU). A medium close-up provides more detail than a medium shot, although a subject is smaller in the frame than with a traditional close-up. An example would be a shot from the middle of the chest and up on a person. Extreme close-ups (ECU) are shots of very small details, such as a bead of water on a windowpane.

IDENTIFYING SHOTS

While there are a variety of shot sizes that can be used, it is not necessary to precisely identify every shot as one type or another, such as in the storyboard stage. In some instances, a wide shot might become a medium shot as an actor steps into a frame. Some shots are simply hard to define, although basic classifications can usually be drawn between wide, medium, and close shots. Knowing the use of each shot type and the way shots can be edited together into a sequence is more important than distinguishing between a medium close-up and an extreme close-up. It can be advantageous, however, to use precise classifications if you are trying to communicate your ideas to a director of photography or other crewmembers.

Selecting a Camera Angle

No matter how you decide to frame a shot, the angle that you choose to shoot it from is important. For example, if you want to make someone appear threatening, then you can try a low angle (looking up from below), which makes the subject appear large and gives him a looming presence. You might also use an unusual, oblique angle to achieve a disorienting effect. The following are a few angles typically used to create more interesting shots.

Low Angles and High Angles

Shots that are performed from near ground level are sometimes referred to as *low angles*, while a shot that is taken from above a subject is a *high angle*. These angles can be a great way to suggest the scale of a character or a shot. A low angle may be used to make someone appear taller and more menacing than they really are. This is also referred to as a *high hat* shot, as the hat on the subject's head is farther away from the camera (see Figure 6.9). When shot from a low angle, a subject may appear distorted and tapered, appearing larger at the bottom of the frame and thinner at the top (think of looking up at a tall building). A high angle, which is taken from above, achieves the reverse effect and is a good way to illustrate a giant's perspective or to take power away from a character. A subject appears to become larger at the top of the frame and smaller toward the bottom. Both low and high angles can be used to exceptional effect.

As with any of the compositional techniques discussed in this chapter, there are many uses for each type of shot, depending on the needs of your production. Looking for these shots in your favorite movies is often a good way to think about uses for your own productions.

Figure 6.9 *Low angles (or" high hats") make objects look taller (such as this building), while high angles make objects look shorter.*

Dutch (Oblique) Angles

Although most shots are performed from strictly horizontal and vertical directions, you can use your tripod—along with other attachments on special devices, like a jib—to tilt your camera in diagonal or oblique directions to capture unusual angles, sometimes referred to as *dutch angles*. Dutch angles may be effective for communicating paranoia or psychosis in a character, or for adding excitement to an otherwise uninteresting shot. Although they are not used very often in films, as they tend to be disorienting and distracting to most viewers, dutch angles are a fun way to experiment with the conventions of cinematography. Adventurous filmmakers have used these angles to great effect in martial arts themed films or horror movies, for example, where fast action and dynamic camera work are expected.

Choosing a Camera Height

Camera shots that are taken from eye height on the average person tend to be pretty boring. The next time you frame a shot, position the camera low to the ground or from a kneeling position. For example, if you are shooting a sunset at the beach, try shooting it with the camera low to the ground, instead of straight ahead, standing up. You can use this technique in a variety of positions and situations (kneeling, sitting, lying down). Also, try shooting the same scene from a slightly higher position, such as a stepladder or chair. The results can be subtle, but they add variety and interest to your shots. Perhaps you are shooting from a low height to reflect the viewpoint of a child. The Japanese director Yasuhiro Ozu frequently shot his films from about three feet off the ground to reflect the perspective of someone kneeling on a traditional Japanese tatami mat.

Using a Tripod

The first purchase for a new camera owner, after batteries and other necessities, should be a good tripod. Tripods are essential for capturing high-quality, stationary video (see Figure 6.10). Without a tripod, your shots will tend to look haphazard and uneven. Of course, if that is the effect you are trying to achieve (for example, in a video that replicates a TV news style or in footage shot in the heat of the moment), then hand-holding a camera is just fine.

Figure 6.10 *A sturdy tripod is essential to shooting good video, such as this professional tripod with fluid head by O'Connor (designed and priced for high-end HDTV cameras).*

A good tripod should provide adequate support for your camera and maintain its rigidity while pressure from the camera operator is applied to it. A thin, flimsy tripod is easily moved and does not provide the rock-solid base that is required for exceptional video. Manfrotto (www.manfrotto.com) makes a great line of relatively inexpensive yet solid tripods that are worth checking out. Other companies that produce professional quality tripods include Sachtler, Miller, O'Conner, and Davis & Sanford. You might also consider buying a spreader that keeps the legs of a tripod from moving, although this is strictly optional (some even come with spreaders built in).

The best tripods for video purposes also have fluid heads (the platform where a camera is attached, which includes a movable joint that fixes to the base), which allow you to turn a camera smoothly on its axis without any sudden, jarring motions. Many tripods that are built for still photography do not have fluid heads, making them unsuitable for video shoots that require movement. Another consideration when buying a tripod is how easily the camera can be attached or detached from its base. If shooting requires you to switch a lot between handheld shots and locked-off (tripod) shots, then you should consider a tripod equipped with a quick-release platform on its head.

KEEPING A TRIPOD STABLE

When shooting with a tripod, do not touch the camera or tripod unless it is absolutely necessary to do so (for example, when starting or stopping recording). This should help you avoid the shakiness and bumps that can ruin an otherwise good shot. If you need to start or stop the camera, consider using the buttons on a wireless remote control instead (many cameras come with one of these controllers). Also, whenever possible, do not extend a tripod's legs all the way or raise its center post too high. The higher a tripod is off the ground, the higher its center of gravity becomes; a high center of gravity significantly reduces the camera's stability. If you need to raise a tripod high off the ground, consider purchasing a special tripod riser or support platform, such as the Spider (the Spider Pod system consists of a tripod riser and standing platform for the camera operator). This type of platform is especially useful for filming concerts or other events where you need to raise the camera above the heads of a crowd.

Moving a Camera

It is almost always preferable to move a camera instead of relying on a zoom to get a shot. If you are able to change your position relative to your subject, then you should do so before attempting to adjust your framing with a zoom lens. In this section, I'll describe a few of the options for moving the camera that are available for adventurous filmmakers. Although most of these options require some sort of special apparatus (which may be cheaply constructed by industrious shooters) to realize a shot, the concepts that these tools introduce are an important element of any moviemaker's vocabulary. As the majority of movies that have been made in the past 100 years have utilized some of these cinematic devices to help tell their story, you can trust these devices to improve your video or film project.

Dolly Shots

Dolly shots are horizontal camera movements that move toward or away from a subject or even follow someone through a scene in a smooth, natural motion (see Figure 6.11). A simple—although rather rough—approximation is walking in a straight line while holding the camera in a fixed position. Casual users may find that walking with a camera in this way is enough to accomplish this type of shot. However, for true dolly shots, a camera is fixed to a truck (tripod fixed to a platform with wheels) that runs on a track for precise movement. This same sort of shot can be created by sitting with your camera in a wheelchair while someone pushes you, or by assembling a platform and tracks from boards, broom handles, and PVC pipe purchased at a hardware store. Dolly shots are an integral part of most professional films and are often the best way to follow a character through a scene while keeping a camera perfectly steady. However, be aware that the weight of your camera system and the dolly platform, as well as the straightness of the rails and the smoothness of the wheels, can greatly effect the quality of your shots. Heavier platforms are usually best, since they keep the apparatus firmly planted on the rails. Also, specially made dolly tracks, or even metal piping, are better than PVC pipe for use with a dolly.

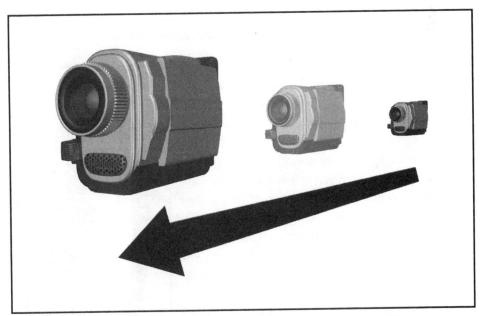

Figure 6.11 *Dolly shots move horizontally to follow the path of a subject (the camera may be positioned parallel or perpendicular to the path of motion).*

Panning and Tilting

Panning (or tracking) shots follow a subject from a fixed position, like a tripod, instead of a moving platform (see Figure 6.12). Panning shots usually move horizontally along a vertical axis (just like a head turning on a neck) and can be simply

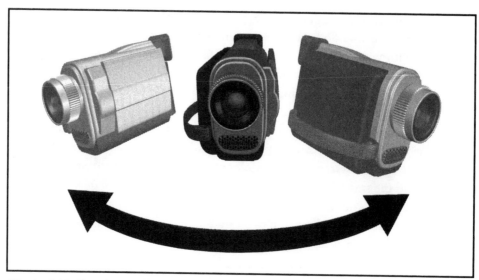

Figure 6.12 *Panning motions are easily performed from a tripod.*

performed by holding a camera steady in your hand and rotating your body to follow a subject's action or to create movement in a scene. As part of a sequence, panning is an excellent way to create an establishing shot (a shot that sets up a location or scene). You might, for example, decide to pan across a wide landscape or the interior of a building to capture the scale of the surroundings. At the end of your panning motion, you might settle on an object—in effect, reframing the shot. In another situation, you might pan to follow someone who is walking or running through a scene, keeping him or her centered in the frame. However they are put to use, panning shots are an essential part of any videographer's visual vocabulary.

Tilts are basically a vertical panning motion along a horizontal axis (see Figure 6.13). By rotating a camera up and down on a fixed axis you can follow the flight of a rocket or show the scale of a tall building. By combining pan

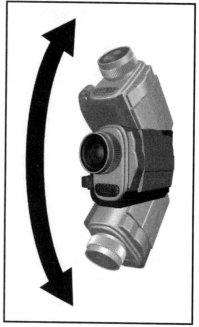

Figure 6.13 *Tilts are the opposite of pans; they move in the vertical direction.*

and tilt motions, you can create complex motions, such as tracking the path of a bird in flight.

HDV CAMERA MOTION

Due to the nature of MPEG-2 compression and the long GOP structure that is utilized by HDV (the properties of MPEG-2 compression are discussed in Chapter 7), fast movements and pans should be avoided whenever possible. The interlaced frames of 60i video may also contribute to unpleasant motion artifacts when quickly moving a camera. Additionally, fast pans can make it harder to achieve a good 60i to 24p conversion, which is essential for transferring video to film. Progressive frame video captures this motion differently than, although not necessary better than, interlaced modes. Panning shots slowly when shooting in a progressive frame mode is particularly important, as it can accentuate the subtle "flicker" experienced by progressive scan video (whether 24p or 30p).

Stabilizing Devices

Stabilizing devices, and more specifically Steadicams (the progenitor of these devices), keep a camera level with the ground while eliminating the shakiness that occurs from holding a camera in hand (see Figure 6.14). Most stabilizing devices require a harness that attaches to the camera operator, although there are many inexpensive versions that consist of only a handheld unit (examples include the Steadicam JR and Merlin). With a Steadicam-type device, you can create smooth motion even if you walk, run, or turn quickly.

Steadicams revolutionized the way movies are made, freeing directors from the constraints of setting up dolly tracks (tracks that are laid down to guide a camera attached to a tripod or other wheeled cart), and allowing them to shoot seamless, smooth video in tight spaces or on location without extra setups. Recently, a Russian director named Alexander Sokurov used a single, unedited Steadicam shot for

Figure 6.14 *Steadicams, including the new Steadicam "Merlin" (which is ideal for HDV), create smooth, natural motion for handheld cameras.*

an entire movie called *Russian Ark*. You might also remember another classic Steadicam shot in Stanley Kubrick's *The Shining* (shot by Garrett Brown—see interview below), in which the camera followed a boy's three-wheeled bike ride through the halls of a haunted hotel. A stabilizing device under $1,000 (and up) may be just what your next production needs, particularly if you are planning to film a tour of a house, business, or other real estate—haunted or otherwise. Steadicams, in particular, can be a great way to add a slick professional quality to any movie.

Interview:
Garrett Brown

Garrett Brown is the inventor of the Steadicam, in addition to several other moving camera devices, and an accomplished camera operator, having worked with the world's best directors. The following is from a phone interview and includes discussion of a new, ultra-compact Steadicam device he developed called "Merlin," which is perfectly suited to the new crop of HDV camcorders (see Figure 6.15). Also, Garrett answers more general questions related to his work in films, as well as speaking about the art and craft of the moving camera.

The Merlin is very compact. What's the limit on weight?

There are handheld stabilizers out there that accept cameras up to 10 pounds; and yes, you can hold something like that briefly, which will then total about 15 pounds in your hand, but in terms of a practical shot of 2 or 3 minutes, the limit for the Merlin that we've designed is 5 pounds. That means you're going to have about 7 pounds in your hand—and 7 pounds is doable. If you're a little tricky with the way you hold it, both hands can contribute to the support, and I have no trouble shooting for 5 or 10 minutes at a time with a 7-pound camera. Obviously somewhere or other, there's a limit.

The Merlin is designed to go from a half-pound camera to 5 pounds, and I suppose if you wanted to add more weight, you could cheat above that, but we wouldn't recommend that. The whole idea is that something like this should be inherently light. It shouldn't weigh a ton. The Merlin weighs under a pound by itself without the weights on it, or the camera, which is less than half what any of the other such devices weigh. So, if we can save you that pound in the total that you're carrying, that gets important about five minutes out when your arms are starting to ache and your wrists are aching and so on.

Part of the question is "What do you want to do with it?" Are you shooting in cuts or are you shooting endless nonstop single shot things? One of the things I like about it is that, if you do put a lightweight mini-DV camera on it, you can get the whole works down under 2 pounds. Then you can shoot skiing, or a sporting application (horseback riding or something), holding it entirely with one hand for long periods of time, anywhere you can reach. In fact, now that this HDV medium exists and has higher resolution (and hopefully is a little more robust) it's just amazing to me, because I'm sure there'll be HDV cameras in this 2–3 pound range.

Last week Sony announced their new A1, a single-chip version of the Z1, which weighs less. There's also talk of another model by late summer or fall[md[a more consumer-oriented, single-chip HDV camcorder (the HC-1).

Well, if you read the articles on the moving camera on my Web site (www.garrettcam.com/movingcamera.shtml), you know that that's a topic that really interests me. No matter what the medium is, it still comes down to the artist who's running it—the quality of the ideas, the quality of the execution of the ideas, the appropriateness of the execution to the idea. So, somebody who's good is never in any jeopardy from the fact that everybody has access to the technology. Somebody who's good does good work, and they'll do good work with whatever technology is out there. So I kind of feel like a—what do you call it—an implementer, I'm hopefully helping people with good ideas to do good work by making sure that the hardware is appropriate.

What is a Steadicam's range of motion, whether it's a JR or a Merlin versus a larger rig?

I'd say much greater with a Merlin-type rig because you can be nearly on the deck and all the way up to as high as you can reach over your head. You have a boom range, depending on your own height, of 6 feet or so, which is twice what even the longest range arm will get you. The only other thing out there that comes close is a new gadget called the AR that will go from low-mode to high-mode, but it's a very particular, complicated object. So, handhelds do give you a tremendous advantage in range of motion, even to the point that you can stick them out windows, or in windows, of cars —or fly them in spaces that are way too constricted for the big rigs. Of course, they're as effective as the big rigs for vehicle shots so you have a great many more vehicles you can fit in with a Merlin-type device than you can fit in with a Steadicam.

(continued on next page)

(continued from previous page)

What is the difference that an arm and vest would make to isolate the camera, as compared with the Steadicam JR or the Merlin, which are strictly handheld?

As the camera's mass gets bigger, it is more inert. One of the things you have to do with the Merlins, and the lighter-weight rigs, is to learn to use a softer touch to pan and tilt. For that reason, we keep shrinking the surface that you're able to get hold of to pan and tilt. The big Steadicams have big handles on them, but of course they weigh a lot and they're floating on the arm and feel very inert. The next rig up from the Merlin is called the Flyer. The Flyer is for cameras from 4 or 5 pounds on up to 15 pounds. The Flyer is amazing because it has a very good arm, and it's very comfortable and you can wear it for hours. So among other things, it holds fatigue at bay for really long setups or if you're working a whole concert or something like that, which improves your performance just by itself, and it allows you to use a camera that's bigger and more inert. So, the Flyer's handle's a little bigger.

But I'd have to say that, if you're good, you can do work that's almost indistinguishable, from the Merlin all the way up to the big stuff, because you're using the appropriate amount of force and grip for the weight and the inertia. The Flyer is handy because it lets you add the camera and the wireless mics and the Obie lights and the spare this-and-that. You can load all the accessories on that you may want—the large, wide-angle adapters and so on.

The Merlin is a more stripped-down phenomenon, but it's also a little less conspicuous. The Merlin is a great documentarian's tool. We're going to do a special LANC control for it, but there are a number of them available even now on the market. If you have control over roll-and-stop while you're using it and control over the zoom, it's a formidable documentary tool because you can go almost anywhere. The eyeline of the people you're interviewing tends to be at you, since you're doing the talking, and the camera has this sense that it's almost invisible to people—because they don't frequently look at it, they look at the guy carrying it, and they're not occupying the same space. It isn't stuck to the front of his face like a camera with a viewfinder. Once you get into the arms and vest and so on, you draw attention to yourself because it's a contraption and it fascinates people. Sometimes, that's a little counter-productive.

In terms of lenses, can you use a wide-angle adapter with the Merlin?

Oh yeah, but I think people have a misconception that a Steadicam needs a wide-angle. The Merlin is designed to be rigid enough for telephoto shooting. Since most of these cameras can be made to auto-focus, which comes into its own in the telephoto world, if you're clever about how you aim and frame, you can use focal lengths that would amaze you—if you're good at it. It's extremely effective that way. I suggest to people that they experiment with the whole range of the zoom, including full tele-photo, and learn what you can and can't do. The Merlin will do wide-angle adaptors, but the weight is the weight. If the total weight creeps up above five, then it's proba-bly more than you would want to do with the Merlin. That would include the Z1 with the wide-angle adaptor or the Z1 with a wireless mic on it—you're pushing it.

On a more general topic, I was reading an article where you talked about this idea you had called the "appearing point." I was wondering if you could talk a little bit about what that means.

Well, we all learn composition related to still frames. It's part of the curriculum—the golden mean, the rule of thirds, etc. It's to do with these masses, these shapes, the ele-ments of a static frame. But I'm kind of interested in something that hasn't been talked to death yet and that is—what are the analogous features of a frame that's in motion and where should they be placed in a frame? One of the things you can say is, if you're headed in a particular direction, looking more or less in the direction you're going, there's only one place in the frame that's not in motion and that's the exact place you're headed toward. You could call that the appearing point, because if you con-tinue infinitely toward that place, everything in the frame appears to grow from that point because you're approaching it, right? So let's call that the appearing point.

Well, now you have another option, which is where do you place that in the screen? It's not written anywhere that it ought to be in the center of the screen. That's what Kubrick liked, for example—he liked these centered compositions, very Palladian kind of balanced frames, and he liked to be heading toward the middle of the frame and to hold people's faces right in there, too. But if you put that point, that so-called appear-ing point, at one of the old rule of third lines—you know, left-third, top-third, bottom-third—I find it very appealing, in some ways, and very intriguing. I like having one side of the frame wiping by you larger than the other side that wipes by you.

The interesting thing is that people watching a moving frame don't take note specifi-cally that, "Oh, we're headed towards the side of the frame." You can have that point way over to the side and people just look at the screen and go, "Yes, we're going that

(continued on next page)

(continued from previous page)

way." They pay no more attention to it, but I've seen some examples that are just striking as hell. The things that you're passing by are appropriately on one side or the other. Likewise, if you're looking back, you could call that the disappearing point, because everything around you eventually approaches that point—if where you're departing from is kept somewhere in your frame. Otherwise, looking ahead or looking behind, if the place you're going to or leaving is not in frame, it is simply wiping going by, and everything is wiping by your frame. If you're looking dead sideways, then it sort of depends on the focal length of the lens how it behaves. If you're looking three quarters to the rear or three quarters ahead, let's say, and where you're headed to isn't in the frame, then there's a kind of "key stoning" of motion that happens as well, because things are expanded and whipping by you more conspicuously on one side vs. the other.

This is a confession of a moving camera junkie. These are the kinds of things that I think about. I try to think about "Why is one moving shot better than another?" Because, no matter what kind of camera you hold in your hand, all the classic dilemmas of filmmaking, movie-making, video-making are presented to you as an artist. You have to find your own way through those dilemmas and come out with a work that people find memorable or interesting. You're swimming in that great stream of movie creativity flowed from Thomas Edison all the way to us.

You had mentioned working with Kubrick. When you're working with a director, do they push you to try new things and reexamine the way that you approach your craft? Can you talk about instances where you may have learned new things about filmmaking in the process?

That relationship, in its ideal form, is collaborative to some extent. Typically, whoever you're working for had the project first. In my profession, as operator, or even if you were a D.P., you are a second hire, you're not in at the beginning. You never quite have a position on the top of that mountain. Somebody has an idea before you have a chance to get in there, so you have the classic choices of, if you have what you think is a better idea, either persuading ahead of time with words—and the words may have to do with practicality—such as "Well if you do that, then we can't do such-and-such; we can't turn around and shoot the other way without a big reset," or something.

In my business, the thing that frequently happens is somebody has a very fixed idea of how they want to do something—some aspect of it is either really tough for you or counterproductive in some way. Sometimes, the best thing to do, since we have this weapon in our hands—the Steadicam—is just to "show & tell." "Look at this," "watch this," and let enthusiasm be your elixir. Let enthusiasm for something that you can demonstrate without having to lay rails and go through all that. So say, "Look at this, look at this, look how this does such-and-such." Even someone like Kubrick sometimes could be persuaded that this would be worth doing. It's so complicated to describe the subtleties of moving an instrument like the Steadicam that, even when somebody exhaustively lays it out, there are indescribable things that you do on instinct. Some of it is extremely subtle, and if you're doing it well (which is to say, you're getting the lens in the place it wants to be in the right moment, at the course and speed that are the most impressive, etc.), sometimes they just sit back with their jaws hanging open and let you go.

My best scene on *The Shining* did not end up in the movie, unfortunately. It was in the very first cut that played in New York and the film wasn't immediately admired by the critics in the first New York screening, which was horrifying to Stanley. He quickly did some editing to shorten it, and this last scene in the movie took place in a small room in a hospital with Shelley in a hospital bed. By that time, I'd been working for Stanley for a year, and it was a sensational relationship. We did stuff in that room with a moving lens that I have never come close to since. I was in great form, it was a great set, it was perfect. Someday I'd love to get a copy of that stuff, on some expanded DVD of *The Shining*, if it isn't out already. That is the culmination of a year's work in which I had the fantastic opportunity to do things 50 and 70 times—not because I didn't do them well, but because Kubrick was looking for something in the performance, or he just didn't feel like moving to another scene for the day and he had the time and the power and he would just do it 50 times.

It's the best thing in the world for the operator; it's like being in a dancing class. By take 14 you're perfect, by take 26 you're beginning to learn new things, like, if my foot's six inches this way, I can do such-and-such. You begin to know the set as if you could do it blind; you know almost the sound of the echoes of it. You begin to have a sixth sense about how the actor's performances are evolving. That's an experience that, unfortunately, most of my contemporaries won't ever have. Nobody has the money or the inclination to be perfect anymore. Boy it's a great experience.

If you admit that something like the Steadicam is more of an instrument than a tool (which I think is true), then you have this fantastic ability to keep improving your playing, as it were. There's only so good you can get with a hammer. But with a violin, we still haven't seen the end of that journey yet. The Steadicam is somewhere in-between.

(continued on next page)

(continued from previous page)

It is an instrument that I think is capable of fantastic music—all sizes of Steadicam, including the big ones, and in some ways the Merlin almost the most interesting, because it's so facile. I've had the most fun in my career with the JR, or the prototype, which preceded the Merlin. It's like jazz—you're improvising. There are no rules, no producers, no hassles. It's just you, the instrument, and something happening in the world.

I was wondering about some of the projects you've worked on recently, such as the new Gilliam film. Also, the opening sequence of Birth was amazing. Was that a difficult shot?

That was extremely difficult. That was supposed to be a SuperFlyCam shot over the trees, and we made a good attempt at that. We scouted it, and we had a park guy with us, and they would not permit one single branch to be broken. To get 1,300 feet of wire—even this lightweight stuff—up, over the trees, meant that you'd have to use cranes in between to get the wire there—because you couldn't just shoot it up over the treetops and then pull it up. What if you broke a branch, right?

I like Jonathan Glazer a lot, I was enjoying the process of interacting with him. I understood completely what he wanted to do with that shot and finally I had to say to him, look, if we do it with SuperFlyCam, which was the whole reason I was there (the SuperFlyCam is this very light gadget that weighs 38 pounds total), it's going to cost X (and it's a very big number). The producer from London was there, whom I knew from the Academy of Film. He was turning slightly pale. I said, suppose we did this much lower, from a Steadicam rig on the back of a truck? One thing that I like is that it'll be close enough so that the wide angle effect really works, and you sense that you're right there (which is why the SkyCam is so good on football; it isn't up over the trees at the equivalent of 40 feet, it's 12 or 15 feet).

I said, let me build up on a vehicle on parallels or something, so that I can get the lens up to just the height that would let me go through these tunnels and look down at this guy at a 40 degree angle, at a wide enough angle that you'll see straight ahead as well. He went for it. Then I found myself standing on this vehicle driving through the slush and the terribly bumpy trails, and I'm using the complete range of the arm to take up these bumps and trying to keep this thing still. "Be careful what you ask for..." I managed it, but that was one of the toughest shots I ever did. But I couldn't explain that to Jonathan. The truck you're on and your body are bouncing 2 1/2 feet, and the lens has to stay the same. And I had to have a guy tap me with a stick, because, if I was too high, the magazine would have hit the top of the tunnel. And they're sitting in the truck watching it on video going, "Wow, this is great."

Was that different than working on an interior set? Was an interior set what you were working on with The Brothers Grimm?

That was all interior forest built on a set. They had 600 pine trees on these giant studios at Barandov in Prague. It was amazing. There the problem is that you're trying to fly cameras and there's no open course for them. I arranged for them to fly a camera on a curved rail flying through the treetops, and they got carried away and made the rail curve every six feet. That was out of control, so we finally ended up doing most stuff on wires there. It's just fun to watch Gilliam in action, he's amazing.

Anything else you've been working on lately?

Mostly, I've been doing new gear. As you saw at NAB, I'm doing the new Steadicam arms, which are kind of revolutionary. And finally, after all these years, the Merlin, which is my dream handheld rig.

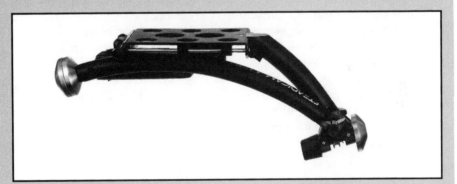

Figure 6.15 *The Steadicam Merlin is extremely compact and folds for travel.*

Image Stabilization

Most video camcorders are equipped with a built-in image stabilization system, which can be turned on and off as required. This type of system helps to alleviate jittery shots caused by sudden movements and shakiness that occurs while shooting without a tripod. For example, if you are shooting in a moving car, your camera is going to move around a lot, possibly making your viewers motion-sick. Although image stabilization does not eliminate the larger camera motions, it does help to soften the minor bumps. Any handheld shots can benefit from this technology; however, it is not a cure-all for shaky video. For moving shots without a tripod or other stationary support systems (like a dolly or jib), a Steadicam-type device is necessary to achieve fluid motion. If using a Steadicam, or similar device, it is often best to turn off the camera's stabilizer feature, so that the two methods do not fight each other and produce unpredictable results (may depend on the type of shot).

USING IMAGE STABILIZATION WITH A TRIPOD

Image stabilization systems built into a camcorder, such as Sony's SteadyShot feature, can be a great way for many users to improve their handheld shots (although it does not remove the larger movements and bumps, it can smooth out jittery motion a little). However, there will be instances in which you would not want to use your camera's stabilization feature. For example, if you are shooting from a tripod, remember to turn off any image stabilization devices. When a camera is locked down on a tripod, image stabilization can cause the video image to "drift" as it's attempting to compensate for tiny vibrations, such as a soft breeze, footsteps on the floor, or a camera operator's finger on the zoom controller. This is also true when using external stabilizing devices, as mentioned earlier.

Shooting People and Places

Different shooting situations often require different solutions for achieving appropriate shot composition. Shooting people can present a number of unique considerations. When framing a shot using the techniques mentioned in the previous sections, you should generally avoid cutting off a person at one of their main joints (neck, waist, knees, and ankles). An example of such a mistake would be placing the bottom of a frame directly on someone's knees when composing a medium shot, thereby creating an awkward and distracting composition that draws attention to the edges of a frame. Try composing the shot so that it eliminates one of these joint lines.

Another important technique for shooting a person is to allow space on the side of a frame for the subject to walk into, move through, or look toward. Generally speaking, the space you create should be on the side of the frame that a person is facing, not the side that is behind him or her. Composing shots with negative space creates anticipation and more visual interest (see Figure 6.16). It also helps to preserve continuity when done correctly. For example, if someone enters a door on the right side of a frame, then the next shot should be of that person entering a door on the left side of a frame. Also, if a person is speaking to someone out of frame to the left, then they should be positioned to the far right of the frame.

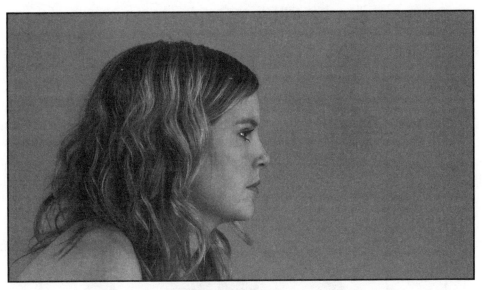

Figure 6.16 *Framing shots with negative space is important to create tension, anticipation, or to preserve continuity (actress Liz MacDonald).*

Regardless of where you are shooting your subject, it is important to properly align your shots. Remember to keep horizontal and vertical lines as straight as possible by lining them up with parallel planes in your frame. For example, use the sides of a frame to line up objects like a light pole, doorway, or a horizon line. This should come naturally to you after a while, and it is important for composing any good shot, whether you are using a tripod or holding a camera. If you need to handhold a camera extensively, consider using a Steadicam or shoulder brace for keeping the camera parallel to the ground. Also, remember that wide-angle lenses can distort the sides of your images, making them an unreliable source with which to judge the alignment of a shot. In this situation, you could line up the frame with an object nearest to the center, or you could compensate for the distortion by balancing the entire frame around the center (you might think of this as a see-saw effect that requires a center point for proper balance).

Reverse Shots

Reverse shots are taken at approximately 180 degrees from the preceding shot. These shots are used frequently in films and television, particularly when conversations are taking place between two people. The best examples of this are the over-the-shoulder shots used in the dialogue scenes of many movies. An over-the-shoulder shot is filmed from behind a person's shoulder, roughly approximating the character's perspective and creating viewer identification with the character. A reverse-angle shot shows the face of the person whose back was previously facing the camera. A scene that incorporates over-the-shoulder and reverse-angle-shots is effective for scenes with a lot of dialogue. It is also a good way to bridge a standard two shot (when two people are placed in a frame and filmed from the side) and a close-up of an actor. _Shooting a reverse_ may also refer to shooting other actions that occur opposite the current shot (see Figure 6.17). For example, if someone is shot throwing a baseball toward the camera, the reverse would be a shot of the ball traveling away from the camera, toward the catcher.

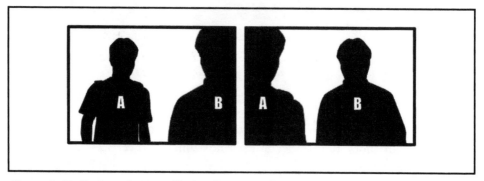

Figure 6.17 _Reverse shots are effective for scenes with dialogue._

While they are not as overt as POVs (discussed next), reverse shots do provide a great way for viewers to understand a character's perspective in a scene. Try looking for these shots in your favorite movies and observe the placement of actors in the frame.

Point-of-View (POV) Shots

Shots that are meant to represent a character's exact vantage point in a film are called *point-of-view* shots, or *POVs*. A POV is a completely subjective viewpoint, and a powerful cinematic device that eliminates the psychological distance of a viewer from the character engaged in the viewing. An example of this technique would be a shot that allows the audience to see exactly what a character on the screen sees—such as the walls moving as he runs down a hall or his hand as he is reaching for an object. POVs are not used very often, as they are most effective when employed sparingly. Directors like Alfred Hitchcock and Brian DePalma have used POV shots to put us in the position of the villain or his victims. Less sinister uses might include a character's POV as he enters a stage, revealing the presence of a large audience facing him.

Recording Time-Lapse Sequences

If you have ever seen a sequence in a movie or on TV where cars, people, or starry skies zoom by at breakneck speed, then you have witnessed a *time-lapse* (or *intervalometer*) effect. By recording individual frames at predetermined intervals that may span seconds, minutes, or even hours, a camera operator can create the effect of time passing very quickly. Some video cameras include a timer option that may be used to simulate these effects (the shortest time span is usually a second or two). Even if you do not have this feature built into your camera, you can record long sequences with your camera and later (while editing) speed up the video to create a similar result. There are also some software applications that can capture images remotely when tethered to your camera through a computer's FireWire or USB 2.0 cable. Currently, most of these applications are for DV-format users only, although you can find many applications that work with digital still cameras. A digital still camera can be an excellent replacement for an HDV or HD camera in this instance, considering that digital still cameras of three megapixels and higher actually surpass the resolution possible with high definition video. After you have shot a sequence of stills, you can import them as an image sequence into your favorite editing or effects software and treat them as a single piece of video. In fact, since the images are often larger than HD resolution, you can even pan across a moving image sequence without losing any resolution, since there is no need to scale up the image.

Try placing your camcorder on a tripod facing out of a window and recording the changes that occur throughout the day. A timer that is set to record once a minute or so can produce exciting results and is an interesting way to illustrate the passage of time.

CALCULATING A TIME-LAPSE SEQUENCE

Although video cameras may have only a few values for time-lapse or interval recording, digital still cameras, together with the appropriate software, enable greater control. To calculate the setting necessary to create the desired speed of the time-lapse sequence (how often your camera should take a picture), you need to know a few values first. For example, if you want to find out the frame rate at which to record your sequence, decide on the period of time that the effect should cover (such as a 12-hour period) and how much screen time you want the finished sequence to fill (such as 10 seconds). Once you have decided on these figures, follow these steps to make your calculations:

1. Convert the number of hours the process should take into minutes by multiplying the number by 60 (12360 =720 minutes).

2. Convert the duration you want the sequence to last into frames (10 seconds 330 frames per second =300 frames).

3. Divide the minute value (for the number of hours the process should take) by the number of frames you want the sequence to fill (720/300=2.4). In this example, the result is 2.4, or 2.4 frames per minute.

4. If your result is greater than one or contains a decimal value, find the common denominator and convert the number into actual seconds (2.4 is actually two minutes and 4/10ths of a minute, or 2:24).

5. Set up your sequence to record with the resulting frame rate (in this example, one frame every two minutes and 24 seconds). Once you are finished recording, your sequence should have condensed the passage for the appropriate amount of screen time (in this case, 12 hours into 10 seconds of screen time).

Shooting Like an Editor

Although it might prove difficult for new filmmakers, it is important to think like an editor when shooting video. Breaking scenes down into a series of shots and getting plenty of coverage (extra footage) helps later in the filmmaking process when you edit the video (Chapter 7 covers the editing process in detail). Having a selection of shots to choose from can help to fill in gaps in a sequence that would otherwise be incomplete or difficult to reshoot. When you are shooting, make sure to get plenty of extra material, such as close-ups of details in a scene. You could also shoot footage of building exteriors and interiors, which may help to establish locations and bridge sequences while editing.

Remember, though, that the more footage you shoot, the more time it will take to sort through. Finding a good balance between the amount of extra footage that you capture and what you ultimately use takes time and is a sign of an experienced shooter. The shooting ratio of a film often varies by genre, with many documentaries producing mountains of footage (over a hundred hours of footage is common, especially since the advent of cheap DV cameras); narrative films, which are generally more focused, generate less.

The following list contains a few suggestions for getting enough shots to assist in the editing process:

◆ Make certain to shoot enough extra material at the beginning and end of a shot to act as *pre-roll* and *post roll* (also known as *heads* and *tails*), which provides flexibility when transitioning between shots. In addition, it is also important to give a deck or camera enough time to sync up the time code, instead of beginning capture on an exact frame of video.

◆ Hold a shot longer than you think is necessary. You can always cut extra material from the beginning and end, but you can never go back and add in more material to extend a shot (slowing down a shot is often noticeable, and is used only as a last resort in editing). You may think you have captured the perfect shot, only to find that it is not long enough to be used effectively in your final edit.

◆ Shoot a scene from as many angles as necessary—within reason. It is often difficult to know which angle on a scene is going to work best until you begin editing. Having extra angles or perspectives to choose from can help you solve problems or smooth shot transitions and make cuts more transparent. However, shooting too much footage can lead to an undisciplined approach. Ideally, you will visualize your shoot ahead of time (the use of storyboards can help), or at least generate a shot list of the items that you need to acquire.

◆ Make certain to shoot a variety of shots in order to include an establishing shot and details in a scene. It is important to have a selection of shots to choose from, as this can help in the construction of a story through the use of alternating shots, such as wide angles and close-ups. Extreme close-ups on objects can be an excellent device for bridging shots.

◆ Shoot a "safety" shot of important takes on a second camera. This is particularly important if shooting narrative drama with actors, since each take of a performance is different, and may be impossible (or expensive) to reproduce. If one camera fails to record, dropouts occur on a tape, dirt appears on the lens, poor audio is recorded, or other problems are found after the shoot ends, you have a backup that you can use.

◆ Pay attention to the eye line when shooting people. When you have actors who are communicating with each other on-screen through the use of connecting shots, it is important to match up where each person is looking. This also applies to the use of the 180-degree rule, which requires that the camera stay on the correct axis of action, based on an imaginary line drawn between the camera and its subjects.

Part III

Editing and Effects for HDV

Chapter 7

Editing HDV

The goal of this chapter is to introduce you to some general editing techniques, as well as specific processes related to HDV. It would be impossible to cover everything you need to know about the subject of editing in these few pages. In fact, entire books are devoted just to this process, and even they do not come close to scratching the surface. For the new filmmaker or editor, this should serve as an introduction, while more experienced readers will find useful information related to HDV and working with high-definition formats. As a supplement to this book's ultimate purpose (filmmaking), interviews with film editors are included, which should provide insight and inspiration for all editors, regardless of expertise. (Make sure to check out the interviews with Paul Hirsch and Steven Gonzales later in the chapter.) I would also recommend picking up a copy of *In the Blink of an Eye* by Walter Murch for more on the creative process of editing.

Also, don't be afraid to play around with your edits, trying out more abstract cutting or simply relying on your intuition. Trying out different ideas is one of the main advantages of editing digitally. You can simply open a new sequence or duplicate an existing sequence, or make changes and try out ideas, while keeping earlier versions intact. The nondestructive nature of an NLE means that your footage is never altered, so fear of making mistakes is removed from the process. Of course, you can always delete the media from your hard drives, but if you have properly logged your footage (as described in this chapter), it should be a simple process to recapture missing media.

While editing HDV can be as simple as editing DV or other standard definition formats, it also possesses some unique qualities that require special attention, particularly if you are working with older software or intend to customize the editing process to suit your specific needs. Before looking more closely at the HDV format and what it means for editing, consider the types of applications that are available for purchase.

HDV Editing Software

Your choice of HDV editing software depends on the type of computer system you own. Options for PC and Mac users vary widely at the moment, although the gap in capabilities has narrowed substantially since the quality and availability of HDV products has matured. Although there are other applications that can work with HDV, such as the KDDI MPEG Edit Studio Pro software included with earlier JVC camcorders, the following applications are the most popular choices for a complete editing system at the time of this writing.

Final Cut Pro 5

Apple's flagship editing product for professionals is Final Cut Pro. In recent years, the popularity of Final Cut Pro has, perhaps, surpassed all other professional software-only NLEs on the market, despite the lack of a version for the PC (see Figure 7.1). Film schools and production companies have chosen Final Cut Pro for its flexibility (it can work smoothly with virtually any format, whether DV, HD, or Film), price, and the solid UNIX based Mac OS X operating system it runs on. The most recent version of Final Cut Pro, version 5, adds support for native HDV formats (in addition to some other nice features, like multicam editing, which works perfectly with the multicamera shooting techniques mentioned in Chapter 4). This means that you can bypass the need for an intermediate codec, like the AIC used by iMovie HD and Final Cut Express HD. If you are still working with Final Cut Pro HD, you will want to upgrade to Mac OS 10.4 Tiger and Final Cut Pro 5, since all earlier versions of Final Cut Pro do not support HDV. Final Cut Pro can be purchased separately or as part of the Final Cut Studio, together with DVD Studio Pro, Motion, SoundTrack Pro, and Compressor.

Figure 7.1 *Final Cut Pro 5 represents a professional NLE that is capable of working with native HDV, as well as many other HD and SD formats. (Courtesy of Apple)*

Lumiere HD

Before Final Cut Pro 5 appeared on the scene, with the ability to edit HDV natively, and even before iMovie HD and Final Cut Express HD added the Apple Intermediate Codec to assist with the capture and editing of HDV material, there was Lumiere HD. This software package permits users to log and capture HDV footage using any number of codecs available on their system, import the data (using XML) into Final Cut Pro, edit it, and then reassemble a high-quality version from the source material.

Since many users of Final Cut Pro may be wondering about the benefits of working with Lumiere HD (especially now that Final Cut Pro 5 can work with HDV natively), the following questions were posed to **Frederic Haubrich**, president of Lumiere Media, LLC.

Can you describe the advantages and workflow for using Lumiere HD with Final Cut Pro? Does this change with the release of Final Cut Pro 5, which supports HDV natively?

There are a few reasons why one would choose to use Lumiere HD rather than just using FCP 5, which works with HDV natively:

1. Modest machine.

Working natively with HDV and FCP 5.0 requires a powerful machine—at least a G5 with much memory and fast drives if you do multilayers of HDV in the Timeline.

Lumiere HD uses the offline/online approach, which has been used by editors editing film and HD for years. It allows for an uncompromised creative flow, while editing in DV and mastering the final output (Auto Conforming) in HDV. Essentially, DV editing workstations can be used to edit HDV content. This is especially relevant for editing solutions that do not have HD resolution monitoring but rather the FCP provided small canvas view. The idea here is, if what you look at is smaller than DV resolution, why go through the pain of editing in HD in the Timeline—as long as the ultimate quality of the original footage isn't compromised throughout the workflow, which it isn't with Lumiere HD.

2. Non-FCP users.

Many users need to capture HDV for other applications than FCP (i.e., After Effects, Shake, etc.). Lumiere HD is an ideal solution for these users and an affordable solution ($179) to work with HDV on a Mac.

3. Not ready to upgrade to FCP 5.0.

Don't break it if it's working is a common practice with professional editing facilities. Many facilities wait a while before upgrading their workstations to HDV. Lumiere HD is a great solution for these facilities until they decide to upgrade to FCP Studio.

4. Uncompressed HD editors.

Lumiere HD captures the HDV footage in its purest form (MPEG2 Transport Stream) and allows you to encode that stream to any codec of your choice, where FCP 5.0 automatically converts the footage to the FCP 5.0 HDV codec. Some may want the flexibility to edit the HDV in uncompressed HD in order to preserve the quality of the footage as much as possible, especially since HDV has been reported to worsen when adding many layers and compositing. This also facilitates multiformat editing in the Timeline (HDCam & HDV).

5. Onlining using uncompressed HD.

Continuing the thought mentioned previously, Lumiere HD recommends an alternate workflow for editors who have FCP 5.0 and do lots of effects and layers. The alternate workflow autoconforms the final edit to uncompressed HD before the final render, in order to alleviate the HDV-generated artifacts. This can be done using the FCP HDV codec or using Lumiere HD as a capturer and encoder to uncompressed HD.

As the first product to market that supports HDV in Final Cut Pro, can you describe some of the challenges involved with designing, testing, and releasing Lumiere HD?

(continued on next page)

(continued from previous page)

The major challenges were working with MPEG2 and making the final stream compatible with different cameras and decks. We designed Lumiere HD, because as filmmakers and editors, we needed it. Other challenges included working with a buggy MPEG2 QT Component, which generated out-of-sync issues because of misinterpretation of 29.97 fps footage. See this write up: http://www.lumierehd.com/audio_drift/

Other challenges involved user training. Editing, especially with new formats, can be an involved discipline. Editors have years of training and experience. Since the cost of professional grade editing solutions has dropped with the introduction of FCP, everyone seems to call him or herself an editor. Too often our customers' questions have little to do with Lumiere HD but with FCP technical issues. So the challenge has been to educate users on the fundamentals of nonlinear editing and the intricacies of FCP. We often recommend using iMovie HD to these users. Some take the advice, some decide to hire a professional editor, and some decide to learn the tool.

Why did you decide to incorporate the MainConcept MPEG-2 Encoder into your product? Can you discuss some of this encoder's features? Does it differ from its PC counterpart?

The MainConcept encoder is very good. It is very similar to the PC counterpart. Features really are unlimited. We have presets for HDV, but the encoder as a stand-alone application allows you to encode about anything you want in the MPEG2 realm.

What are the main advantages, or potential future uses, for the XML Interchange Format, particularly in regards to editing workflow and other video/multimedia applications?

We are planning on incorporating batch encoding and support for the JVC ProHD 24p format. Lumiere HD will become more of an HDV toolkit for Mac users rather than a FCP specific plug-in/app.

iMovie HD and Final Cut Express HD

Several months before the announcement of Final Cut Pro 5, Apple released two consumer-oriented applications that offered support for HDV: iMovie HD (see Figure 7.2), the latest update to the simple, single track video editor that is included in Apple's suite of iLife applications (iMovie, iDVD, iTunes, iPhoto, GarageBand), and Final Cut Express HD, a stripped down version of Final Cut Pro (although it covers most of the features used by the average editor and hobbyist). Both iMovie HD and Final Cut Express HD currently transcode HDV into the Apple Intermediate Codec for easier editing, which is particularly important for slower machines.

Figure 7.2 *iMovie HD was Apple's first application to support HDV. (Courtesy of Apple)*

Avid Xpress Pro

Avid has long represented the standard by which all other editing packages were compared. Only in recent years has Avid seen serious competition in the arena of desktop software applications from competitors like Final Cut Pro. Avid Xpress Pro HD (see Figure 7.3) and previously Avid Xpress DV are an important departure for the company, whose products generally rely heavily upon hardware components that are difficult and expensive to upgrade. With the edition of desktop, or laptop, compatible software, it is now possible for the average user to work with the same system that has been a key factor in the creation of most Hollywood movies and major television productions of the last ten years. If you have been working in the areas of film, news programming, documentaries, or episodic television, then Avid may be your system of choice for professional quality work. However, if you're working on a Mac, Final Cut Pro offers advantages in terms of cost and features. If you intend to edit offline material before passing your project back to an Avid online suite at a post facility, then editing with Avid Xpress Pro is an option you might consider.

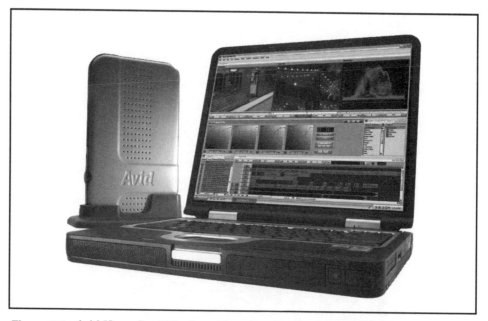

Figure 7.3 *Avid Xpress Pro HD, shown here running on a laptop with Mojo hardware.*

The following questions regarding Avid's HDV offerings were answered by Carter Holland, director of corporate communications for Avid Technology, Inc.

Which Avid products would you recommend for working with HDV?

Avid Xpress Pro HD and Media Composer Adrenaline HD are both scheduled to have full native HDV support in 2005.

What makes Avid's HDV software different or better than other products on the market?

Avid plans to deliver superior native HDV in 2005 that will be worth the wait. One advantage to Avid's native HDV approach includes no time- or storage-consuming transcoding. In addition, Avid systems provide users with the ability to mix HDV with other media formats and resolutions (e.g., DV, SD, HD, etc.) in the same project timeline. Avid systems will also offer real-time effects with HDV, fueling instant creative flow during editing. And while effects output quality can suffer with HDV, Avid solves that issue by allowing native HDV to mix with high-quality effects using Avid DNxHD encoding.

Can you describe a typical HDV workflow using Avid's products?

Typically, users will capture native HDV directly to the Avid system's hard disk via IEEE-1394 (aka FireWire). They can edit native media right in the timeline, including real-time effects, and have the ability to mix other formats and high-quality Avid DNxHD media for effects. There are a variety of HD and SD output choices, depending on whether users want to master to HD or SD tape or to DVD. (Avid expects to support HD DVD creation once standards are finalized.)

How many layers of HDV can you work with simultaneously? Also, what types of effects are applied in "real time"?

There's no limit to the number of HDV layers you can work with simultaneously. Over 100 effects will be real-time.

Does the Avid Mojo hardware improve performance for HDV, in addition to SD material?

Avid Mojo is an SD device, but will be valuable for SD monitoring and output of HDV projects.

Does your software support all current HDV cameras and decks?

Avid is planning support for all popular HDV devices, resolutions, and frame rates, including 24p.

Can you describe Avid DNxHD encoding, including how it can be used, as well as any pertinent technical information?

Most popular compressed HD formats do not natively support the full HD raster. Most of them employ raster downsampling to reduce bandwidth. But downsampling can make HD images look softer, reduce the high frequency detail in the image, and generate unwanted artifacts over multiple generations of post-production processing. Avid DNxHD encoding maintains the full raster of the active video, sampling every available pixel within the image. Avid DNxHD is specifically designed for nonlinear editing and multigeneration compositing, including collaborative postproduction and broadcast news environments. It offers a choice of 8 or 10 bit sampling, three user-selectable bit rates, and the ability to maintain image quality more effectively than other HD codecs.

Some Avid systems can capture Avid DNxHD media to disk in real time from any popular source (Media Composer Adrenaline HD, Avid DS Nitris, and Avid Symphony Nitris). Avid Xpress Pro HD can play and render Avid DNxHD media. In an HDV scenario, Avid DNxHD will be critical for effects and compositing. Native HDV media will not hold up well to heavy postproduction processing, where Avid DNxHD will. Avid systems will let you render effects, titles, graphics, and composites as Avid DNxHD

(continued on next page)

(continued from previous page)

media right in the same timeline mixed with native HDV. Avid DNxHD is 4:2:2 color space, with a range of bit rates from 58 to 220Mbps, depending on frame rate, resolution, and compression ratio.

What type of output options would you currently recommend for an HDV project?

Output depends on client need. Avid systems will support output to HDCAM and DVCPRO HD tape, SD tape, SD DVD, and WMV HD or H.264 for high-definition DVDs that are playable on many computers. Today, HDV is unproven as a mastering format and would not be recommended for best quality and longevity. Avid plans to support HD DVD in the future, as standards become finalized and HD DVD players become available.

Adobe Premiere Pro 1.5

A popular and time-tested video editing package for the PC is Adobe's Premiere Pro software. In the early days of digital video editing, Premiere was one of the first to offer the capability of working with video on the desktop. Today, Premiere has matured into a full-featured, professional application, which also integrates well with Adobe's line of other software, including Photoshop (graphics creation), Encore (DVD authoring), and Audition (audio editing). In recent years, Adobe removed support for Mac users, making Premiere Pro a PC-only application. The addition of an HDV editing component (currently available for download) gives Premiere the ability to work with HDV, which was previously only available by purchasing a separate solution from companies like CineForm. Premiere Pro offers a wide level of support for various video card manufactures, such as Matrox, Canopus, and Pinnacle, to name a few. This software can be purchased as part of a bundle, along with other Adobe products, which makes it a great deal for PC users who want a complete solution for video, audio, graphics, and DVD creation.

Figure 7.4 *Adobe Premiere Pro 1.5.*

The following questions regarding Avid's HDV offerings were answered by Richard Townhill, group product manager, Adobe Digital Video and Audio.

Can you describe the special HDV features of Premiere Pro? Also, what makes Premiere Pro different, or better than, other HDV editing software on the market?

Adobe® Premiere® Pro works with HDV material almost exactly the same as it does with DV material. The editing functionality and features are the same in both cases. Where it varies is that the HDV format is transcoded on capture to a very high-quality digital intermediate format that uses a higher color bit depth to preserve the images when applying filters or transitions. Obviously, one of the biggest areas of difference is when you export your movie. Since there is currently no mass distribution method for high-definition video, the choices are SD (for example, wide screen DVD), Windows Media, back to HDV tape, or up-rezzing the output to another HD format. All of these options are available directly from within Premiere without having to change applications.

Can you describe a typical HDV workflow utilizing Adobe's software line?

Capture and editing are almost exactly the same as DV. The end user should not really notice any difference. However, the output will vary, depending on the production requirements. For example, if the output is intended for DVD, then in the absence of a real high-definition DVD format, you can export the files as a widescreen standard definition DVD. Since the editing was done at a higher resolution, the resulting DVD is very high in picture quality. If you need to distribute in a true HD format, then the most realistic method (other than laying back to tape) is Windows Media 9 Series. Adobe Premiere Pro supports Windows Media directly from the application, allowing you to export directly from within the Premiere interface.

Is it a simple process to move HDV files between Premiere Pro, After Effects, and Encore?

Adobe Premiere Pro can exchange media with Adobe After Effects® easily. Since both applications are capable of working with HD resolution images (for the record, After Effects can go even higher—up to film resolution), moving media between them is simple and painless—the media can even be copied and pasted from a Premiere Pro sequence to an After Effects composition (and vice versa). Since Adobe Encore™ DVD is dedicated to creating DVDs, and DVDs currently do not support high definition video, moving the HDV files to Encore DVD requires that they be first rendered into a suitable format (say, widescreen standard definition MPEG). This can be accomplished directly from either the Premiere or After Effects interface. Additionally, both applications include presets for this, making it a simple process.

(continued on next page)

(continued from previous page)

Does Premiere Pro handle the entire range of HDV formats equally well, including 1080 and 720 line formats (both Sony and JVC cameras)?

Yes, Premiere Pro supports both 1080 and 720 formats. However, it currently does not support the new 24P format from JVC natively. It is supported via the Aspect HD plug-in from Cineform. Adobe demonstrated this during NAB in the JVC booth.

What are the real-time HDV capabilities of Premiere Pro? How does the performance compare with DV or standard definition video?

These are difficult questions to answer with any degree of accuracy, since it depends on so many variables. In general, the HDV performance is slightly less than that of DV. This is because the transcoding process results in a file with a higher data rate than the original HDV format.

Does Premiere Pro use an intermediate codec for HDV editing? Can you describe its GOP structure, color sampling (such as 4:2:0 vs. 4:2:2), and other properties?

Yes, Premiere Pro uses an intermediate codec. The codec is a very high-quality wavelet codec and has a 4:2:2 color sampling. It has a two-frame GOP structure, making it much easier to edit with than the long GOP MPEG format that the original HDV format will use.

Can Premiere Pro work with other HD formats, including DVCPRO HD or uncompressed HD media?

Premiere Pro is able to work with uncompressed HD.

Does Adobe plan to include support for HD-DVD in future releases of Encore?

Adobe does not comment about unannounced products. However, our video products continue to embrace emerging technologies and formats. You certainly don't have to be Nostradamus to predict that at some point high-definition DVD output will be available in Adobe Encore DVD.

Sony Vegas 6

In recent years, Sony entered into the PC software business by purchasing Vegas and several other applications for multimedia production. Vegas is a very powerful and fast video editing application, which includes support for several SD and HD formats, including native HDV—not surprising, considering Sony was the company to break upon the HDV market last year with the introduction of the HDR-FX1. Vegas also has some nice audio editing features, including the ability to mix in 5.1 surround sound, as well as some useful 3D motion effects (see Figure 7.5).

It also supports the use of HD-SDI for hardware like Blackmagic Design's DeckLink card, as well as the inclusion of ITU-R BT.709 color space for HDV (generally standard with true, native HDV support).

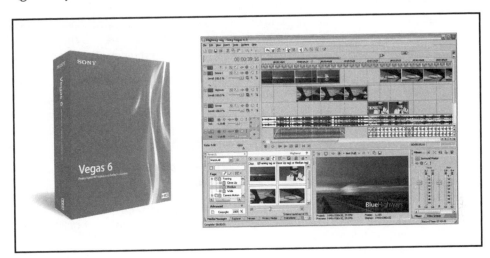

Figure 7.5 *Sony Vegas 6.*

The following questions regarding Sony Vegas were answered by Dave Chaimson of Sony Media Software.

Can you describe a typical HDV workflow utilizing Sony's line of HDV hardware and software?

Plug in the HDV camera or deck and capture from any HDV source to hard drive as native HDV MPEG-2.

Batch transcode selected regions of the captured files to delivery-centric intermediate formats. (For instance, if you are delivering a 60i HDCAM master, you would need to transcode selects to 1920×1080×60i using the Sony YUV codec, or if you were delivering 720p Windows Media HD, you would transcode to 1280×720 24p.) If you need multiple masters in various delivery formats, transcoding to the CineForm codec (our intermediate avi codec) at the source's native HDV resolution and frame rate is advised—up- and downconverting from the native resolution intermediate will be of very high quality.

(continued on next page)

(continued from previous page)

The HDV editing workflow is essentially identical to the DV workflow—just start a new project using the proper HDV project template and edit just like DV. For video monitoring you can use the internal video preview window, the Windows' secondary display option (full-screen timeline output to computer monitor over VGA or DVI), or you can preview the timeline to a broadcast monitor via SDI or a component using a supported Decklink card.

Typical master delivery options include: HD-SDI output (requires a Blackmagic Design DeckLink card and a system that meets the throughput requirements of HD-SDI); Windows Media HD at 1080 30p or 25p, or 720 30, 25, or 24p; Standard definition output to Digibeta or DV; DVD output as 60i, 30p, 25i, 25p, or 24p.

Would you mention some of the features that make Sony Vegas stand out from the competition, particularly in regards to HDV?

Capture, print to tape, batch transcoding to delivery-centric intermediate codecs/resolutions, high-quality 24p conversions, and versatile video monitoring options are all supported, with very lightweight system requirements.

Does Vegas work with JVC's 720p HDV camcorders?

Yes, all HDV cameras and decks shipping as of April 1, 2005 are supported. We plan to support all cameras and decks that conform to the HDV specification.

Does Vegas use an intermediate codec for HDV editing? How do its GOP structure, color sampling (4:2:0), and other important features operate?

Vegas can edit native HDV files; however, using an intermediate codec will greatly improve the timeline playback performance on most systems at a very minimal quality loss. The user has the option to choose which intermediate codec to use, although using a 4:2:2 codec, such as the CineForm CFHD codec (included in Vegas 6) or the Sony YUV codec (if your system is capable of handling HD-SDI files), will typically produce the highest quality output from HDV source material.

What HD distribution options exist for creators of HDV content?

As of April 2005, an HDV master will typically be used for presentations; for instance, the program will be played from an HDV deck to a projector. However, HDV source material can also be up- or downconverted for delivery to HDCAM, Digitbeta, Windows Media HD, DVD, and many other formats.

Ulead MediaStudio Pro 7

Ulead is a PC software company that is known for making their applications easy to use and affordable. This does not imply that their applications are not powerful or lack plenty of features. It is a method that has made them a popular company, particularly with hobbyists, and has given them a sizable user base in the United States, as well as in many Asian countries (the company began in Taiwan). Ulead's MediaStudio Pro is a nice suite of editing, graphics, paint, and DVD authoring applications. Its editing software is on par with Adobe Premiere, and it was also one of the first NLEs to include support for HDV, through the use of an optional HD plug-in (see Figure 7.6).

Figure 7.6 *Ulead MediaStudio Pro 7 and HD Plug-in.*

The following questions were answered by Ulead regarding their current lineup of Ulead MediaStudio Pro software and HD Plug-in.

What are the main features or advantages of using Ulead's MediaStudio Pro over other similar products on the market?

♦ Ulead MediaStudio Pro 7 is a complete, professional digital video post-production suite, including modules for capturing, video editing, audio editing, CG graphics, video painting (rotoscoping), and a DVD authoring tool. It's an all-in-one solution, not just an NLE.

(continued on next page)

(continued from previous page)

◆ Ulead MediaStudio Pro 7 with HD Plug-in 2.0 offers users a complete, native HDV solution—capturing (both JVC & Sony camcorders are supported), editing for native HDV 1080i or 720p MPEG-2 log GOP format, writing back to HDV camcorder, or output high definition MPEG-2 or WMV HD format.

◆ Ulead MediaStudio Pro 7 has an easy-to-use interface and workflow.

◆ Ulead MediaStudio Pro 7 offers flexibility for various capturing tasks. It's capable of capturing video from both digital (IEEE1394) and analog (composite, TV tuner card, and so on) sources. It also offers efficient DV scanning and batch capturing features. The captured video can be saved to various formats on-the-fly, such as DV AVI, MPEG-2, Windows Media, and so on.

Can you describe the features of your HD plug-in for MediaStudio Pro, including how it is implemented into the editing workflow? Does it work with HDV natively or transcode it to an intermediate codec?

Ulead MediaStudio Pro 7 with HD plug-in 2.0 works losslessly with native HDV files, without sacrificing any quality. The step-by-step workflow can be found here at http://www.ulead.com/learning/msp/msp7_11_1.htm.

What are the properties of the HD plug-in's intermediate codec, such as the data rate, color sampling, and GOP structure?

Ulead MediaStudio Pro 7 with HD Plug-in 2.0 utilizes our highly optimized MPEG-1/2 editing engine to work with HDV natively in full quality. It doesn't use any intermediate codec to build large editing files.

What are the real-time performance features of MediaStudio Pro when editing HDV?

Each one has its own definition for so called real-time. From our test, a P4 3.0GHz system with PCI-E VGA card can do HDV720p editing near real time and basic HDV1080i editing. A dual P4 3.6GHz system with PCI-E VGA card can perform HDV1080i editing in about real time. Again, the performance depends on many factors, such as system bus speed, graphics card, hard disk performance, numbers of overlay, and so on.

Are there any plans to incorporate native HDV editing into future software releases without the need for a separate plug-in?

Yes, future versions of MediaStudio Pro will have the HDV editing built in without plug-in required. The next version will also offer our users a unique feature, which we don't want to announce yet, for editing HDV1080i video on midrange equipment or even on notebooks, without sacrificing speed or output quality.

What methods do you offer, or recommend, for outputting HDV projects?

HD DVD or Blu-ray is not available on the market yet, but we can still output HDV project in three formats:

◆ MPEG-2 TS (Transport Stream): The native HDV camcorder file format. Ulead MediaStudio Pro 7 can output the project in MPEG-2 TS file and then write it back to HDV camcorders or decks. We support all HDV camcorders currently available on the market. The full hardware support information can be found on Ulead HD Plug-in 2.0 product page at http://www.ulead.com/msp/plugin.htm.

◆ MPEG-2 PS (Program Steam): Also a native HDV format with full quality, but it's not for camcorder write-back. You can output MPEG-2 PS file to keep the full HD quality for archiving, incorporating into other HD broadcast projects, or play the file on PC.

◆ WMV HD: Microsoft Windows Media Video 9 HD is an ideal solution for delivering high-definition video at the moment. You can capture, edit, and output WMV HD directly from Ulead MediaStudio Pro 7 without opening any other tool. The final result is relatively small in size but keeps almost the full quality. There are also some DVD players that are capable of playing back WMV files.

At the moment, however, most HDV projects end up on standard-definition DVD. With MediaStudio Pro, you can mix and match formats on the timeline, (say, for instance you have DV stock footage you want to include) and eventually output to DV or a normal DVD. One other advantage of shooting on HDV and finishing on DV is that you can pan and zoom on your HDV footage to a large degree without losing resolution in the DV space.

While we cannot announce anything yet, be assured that Ulead will be at the forefront of developing HD-DVD and Blu-ray solutions when the time comes.

Does DVD Workshop 2 handle HDV files directly from MediaStudio Pro? Can you discuss any future plans for HD-DVD or Blu-ray disc support?

DVD Workshop 2 does not support HD format at present. However, the next version will support both HD-DVD and Blu-ray when the spec is finalized and the burners become available.

Canopus Edius

Canopus offers several variations of its Edius software and editing systems that can work with HD and HDV on a PC. The difference between buying a Canopus system instead of an application like Premiere Pro or Final Cut Pro is that the hardware card needed to run the software is included in the package, which also increases the price a bit. However, with a Canopus system, you know that the software and hardware were made to work in tandem from the beginning, which isn't always the case with other third-party vendors. Also, the cards include a variety of options for capturing or converting video from different types of cameras and decks, including some cards with analog to digital conversion built in. Edius NX for HDV allows real-time HDV editing, as well as the mixing of HD and SD content in a timeline. Edius SP for HDV is another option for working with HDV, which also includes hardware acceleration. As with all the other editing systems mentioned in this chapter, make sure to check out their Web site for the most recent product information.

What products do you sell that currently work with HDV and other high-definition formats?

- ◆ EDIUS Pro 3 software only—handles HDV (via system FireWire interface). DVCPRO-HD support is optional with addition of Canopus Codec Option pack.

- ◆ EDIUS NX for HDV—64 bit PCI board + 32 bit PCI board, handles HDV (via its FireWire interface). DVCPRO-HD support optional with addition of Canopus Codec Option pack. Accepts composite and S-Video analog SD input with unbalanced analog audio. Outputs composite, S-Video, and component (Y/Pb/Pr) analog SD, as well as component analog (Y/Pb/Pr) HD with unbalanced analog audio.

- ◆ EDIUS SP for HDV—64 bit PCI board + 32 bit PCI board, handles HDV (via its FireWire interface). DVCPRO-HD support optional with addition of Canopus Codec Option pack. Accepts composite, S-Video, and component (Y/Pb/Pr) analog SD input with balanced or unbalanced analog audio. Outputs composite, S-Video, and component (Y/Pb/Pr) analog SD, as well as component analog (Y/Pb/Pr) HD with balanced or unbalanced analog audio.

- ◆ EDIUS SD—turnkey system, handles HDV (via system FireWire interface), DVCPRO-HD (via system FireWire interface), SD formats via SDI interface. Standard input/output via SDI with optional SDBX-1000 multi-I/O processor unit (3U rackmountable box), also accepts composite, S-Video, and component (Y/Pb/Pr) analog SD input with balanced or unbalanced analog audio or

AES/EBU digital audio. With optional SDBX-1000 multi-I/O processor unit (3U rackmountable box), outputs composite, S-Video, and component (Y/Pb/Pr) analog SD input with balanced or unbalanced analog audio or AES/EBU digital audio.

Can you describe the special HDV features of your software and hardware, including the EDIUS NX, EDIUS SP, and EDIUS HD systems?

EDIUS solutions handle HDV in two manners:

◆ Editing the native HDV MPEG-2 Transport Streams, which provides barely over 1 stream of real-time HD output on a dual Xeon 3.4 GHz machine with 1GB of RAM.

◆ By transcoding to the Canopus HQ codec in real time during capture and editing Canopus HQ codec compressed AVI files, which provides four or more real-time streams of HD output on a dual Xeon 3.4GHz machine with 1GB of RAM. The transcode from HDV to HQ truly happens in real time— there is no additional waiting required after capture before editing can begin.

What makes your products different than other HDV editing software and hardware on the market?

Canopus EDIUS solutions differ from the competition in the fact that they are geared for full-resolution, full-frame rate HD output. There is no "draft" editing—what is processed in real time is what is shown on the video monitor, for true WYSIWYG HD editing.

The Canopus HQ codec provides a quality-preserving, high-bitrate (100–160Mbps variable bitrate) 4:2:2 intra-field encoding for HD video files that are easier for the system to work with, resulting in increased real-time performance compared to native real-time HDV editing. Capturing to the Canopus HQ codec also provides frame-accurate batch capture from HDV sources.

Do your products support the entire range of HDV specifications, including all 720 and 1080 line formats? Will they work with all current HDV cameras and decks?

Currently, our EDIUS hardware solutions only support 1080i hardware output. 720p mode output will be enabled in the future.

In OHCI software-only mode, the EDIUS Pro 3 software can edit and output files in 720/30p mode. Also, 720/30p files can be used in other resolution/frame rate projects. EDIUS will automatically up- or downscale and perform any necessary frame rate conversion in real time during playback. Our EDIUS hardware and software solutions work with all current HDV cameras and decks that we are aware of.

(continued on next page)

(continued from previous page)

How many layers of HDV can you work with simultaneously? Also, what type of effects are applied in "real-time"?

This is completely system-dependent—both CPU speed and disk performance contribute to the number of real-time streams and effects performed. Note that working with native HDV MPEG-2 transport streams is significantly more "difficult" compared to working with Canopus HQ codec compressed streams.

EDIUS Pro 3 does not have any "hard" limits on real-time processing—the more CPU power the system has available, the more it'll be able to do. This is the key aspect of Canopus's Scalable Technology architecture. We do not limit real-time capabilities in our hardware, so the system's capabilities can grow as computer speeds increase.

Does your software (or hardware) use an intermediate codec, or will it work with HDV natively? Do you have the option of transcoding to another HD format for editing and effects, particularly one with an improved 4:2:2 color space?

It can do both. The Canopus HQ codec provides a variable-bitrate 4:2:2 intra-field encoded compression for easier decoding and increased real-time performance. The Canopus HQ codec's 4:2:2 color space is especially useful for capturing from high-quality analog sources as well.

What type of output options would you currently recommend for an HDV project?

As there is no accepted standard for HD content on DVD yet, the major HD distribution formats are output back to HDCAM/DVCPRO HD/HDV tape, Windows Media HD, DivX HD, and D-VHS tape. If space is not of concern, a Canopus HQ codec AVI file would be best for archiving.

Matrox

Although Matrox does not offer its own editing software, its hardware enables the capture, editing, and real-time performance that is similar to other offerings by companies like Canopus, while working together with software from companies such as Adobe. If you are interested in a complete editing package for your PC (and the BlackMagic or AJA cards mentioned earlier in this book do not meet your particular needs), you might consider one of the packages offered by Matrox. These systems include a hardware card and capture device for utilizing video from both analog and digital sources, and sometimes bundle their hardware with Adobe Premiere Pro and other software that ideally matches its capabilities.

Although not currently offering systems that are specifically designed for HDV, Matrox offers systems that are able to work with HD or HDV, while providing other options for editing SD video as well.

What products do you sell that currently work with HDV and other high-definition formats?

Matrox Axio HD provides real-time HD and SD editing with Adobe Premiere Pro. It is designed to give broadcast and post facilities the highest finishing quality, coupled with a comprehensive real-time feature set at an affordable price point. It features no-render HD and SD finishing in compressed and uncompressed formats, superior color correction tools, advanced real-time effects, and a full range of analog and digital audio and video inputs and outputs.

Matrox Axio HD supports the following resolutions and codecs:

HD resolutions and frame rates:

◆ 1080p at 23.98 fps

◆ 1080i at 29.97 fps

◆ 1080p at 25 fps

◆ 1080i at 25 fps

◆ 720p at 59.94 fps

◆ 1080p at 24 fps (planned for a subsequent release)

HD codecs:

◆ Matrox Axio MPEG-2 I-frame HD codec – online quality

◆ Matrox Axio offline HD codec – playback at 1/16 resolution on a laptop or scales up to full size on an Axio system

◆ Uncompressed 8 bit

◆ Uncompressed 10 bit

◆ HDV (planned for a subsequent release)

◆ DVCPRO HD (planned for a subsequent release)

    (In addition to numerous SD resolutions, frame rates, and codecs)

(continued on next page)

(continued from previous page)

Can you describe the special HD and HDV features of your editing and authoring systems, including Matrox Axio HD, as well as the Matrox RT.X100 Xtreme Pro and RT.X10?

Matrox Axio HD provides:

- ◆ Guaranteed full quality, full frame rate, full resolution playback at up to 1080i at 29.97 fps
- ◆ At least two layers of uncompressed 10 bit HD video plus two layers of graphics in real time, with effects
- ◆ At least four layers of uncompressed 10 bit SD video plus six layers of graphics in real time, with effects
- ◆ Real time primary and secondary color correction with shot-to-shot color matching
- ◆ Real time 3D DVEs, chroma/luma keying, speed changes, blur/glow/soft focus, and much more
- ◆ Uncompressed 8 or 10 bit HD and SD editing
- ◆ Compressed HD editing (offline and online finishing quality MPEG-2 I-frame), DV, DVCPRO, DV50, and MPEG-2 I-frame SD editing
- ◆ 24 fps editing in HD and SD with pull-down and reverse pull-down

You can use your Matrox RT.X100 or RT.X10 system for HDV editing with Adobe Premiere Pro 1.5.1 in software-only mode. It's a great way to start working in HDV while taking advantage of all the real-time productivity features of Matrox RT.X100 Xtreme Pro for your day-to-day work in Standard Definition (SD) NTSC or PAL formats. Specifically, Adobe Premiere Pro can use the Matrox 1394 port for HDV acquisition and output. HDV editing is done using the Adobe software plug-ins only. There is no acceleration by the Matrox card. HDV playback is viewable only on the VGA. There is no WYSIWYG output to a video monitor. Matrox real-time inputs, outputs, plug-ins, and effects are only available at SD resolutions.

What software packages do your cards support?

The Matrox Axio software bundle includes Adobe Premiere Pro, Adobe After Effects, Adobe Encore DVD, and Adobe Audition.

What makes your products different than other HD and HDV hardware on the market?

More real-time features (therefore much less rendering) than products such as Final Cut Pro. A more affordable price point than Avid Nitris.

Do your products support the entire range of HD specifications, including all 720 and 1080 line formats? Will they work with all current HDV cameras and decks?

Matrox Axio supports 720 and 1080 line formats at frame rates listed above. Most popular HDV cameras and decks will be supported—validation is underway and will be specified on our Web site.

How many layers of HD and HDV can you work with simultaneously? Also, what type of effects are applied in "real-time"?

At least two layers of uncompressed 10 bit HD video at up to 1080i or 1080p plus two layers of graphics in real time, with effects:

- ◆ Primary color correction
- ◆ Secondary color correction
- ◆ Real-time chroma and luma keying
- ◆ Real-time speed changes
- ◆ Real-time transitions
- ◆ Real-time Adobe Motion effect
- ◆ Real-time advanced 2D/3D DVE
- ◆ Real-time shadow
- ◆ Real-time blur/glow/soft focus
- ◆ Real-time page curl
- ◆ Real-time surface finish
- ◆ Real-time mask
- ◆ Real-time pan & scan

Do your systems use an intermediate codec, or will they work with native HDV formats? Do you have the option of transcoding to another HD format for editing and effects, particularly one with an improved 4:2:2 color space?

Matrox Axio HD will use native HD upscaled to full HD resolution and 4:2:2 at output to HD-SDI—stays native internally.

What type of output options would you currently recommend for an HD or HDV project?

Window Media 9 or back to HD tape.

Pinnacle Liquid Edition 6

Pinnacle is another company that offers HDV editing software for the PC that is both powerful and inexpensive (in its class). With Pinnacle Liquid Edition 6, you can do all of the things you'd expect with native HDV editing software in an easy-to-use package. In addition, Pinnacle is very good at offering real-time speed for its multiple streams of video and graphics (2D and 3D, using "SmartRT"). If you are looking for an alternative to Premiere Pro on the PC, you should check out Pinnacle's offering (now a division of Avid).

MPEG-2 Primer

At this point, we need to consider what makes editing HDV so different than other digital video formats. After all, it is just a high-definition version of DV, right? In fact, HDV has little to do with DV, or even other HD formats for that matter. The difference lies in the method of compression. How do you fit 4.5 times as much information on a standard DV cassette (for 1080i HDV—as compared with NTSC DV—or 2.6 times as much information as 720p HDV) without increasing the file sizes and maintaining the same recording time? The answer is temporal compression, which in this case, is made possible by MPEG-2.

While MPEG-2 is usually associated with DVDs and standard definition video, it is actually a very flexible, and scalable type of compression, which can work at HD resolutions as well. Although MPEG-4 (discussed in Chapter 12, "Delivering HD Content") has become fashionable lately for HD content distribution, MPEG-2 is the format selected for HDV, as well as digital cable and some satellite broadcasts of HD video.

The problem with editing MPEG-2-based video is that it does not contain complete frames. In fact, its GOP structure of 15 frames (for 60i NTSC, 6 frames for 720p, and 12 frames for 1080 50i PAL) means that you only land on an I frame twice every second. Being able to place an edit point on the second or half second is not acceptable for professional editing, which requires frame accurate results.

One method to bypass the limitations of working with MPEG-2, is to transcode your HDV video into an "intermediate" codec, which consists of I frames only and is easier to use for editing. This method is not always ideal, since it often involves a generation loss of quality (at least if you intend to render any effects, transitions, or output back to HDV tape). Of course, some intermediate codes are better than others, and the highest quality codecs may not cause you to lose any information (with uncompressed codecs, for example), although the storage and bandwidth requirements may be steep as a result. Also, the loss of quality that you might see with Apple's AIC intermediate codec may be worse than the loss you would see with a Cineform codec (or vice versa, under the right circumstances). It does however, present an opportunity to improve other qualities of the video in the long run, such as color space. Still, it may require an additional step in the capture process, which can lead to longer capture times and greater storage requirements. iMovie HD, for example, transcodes HDV in nonreal time on slower machines, which means that you have to wait longer for your video to capture and deal with files that more than double the hard drive space of native HDV.

Interframe (Spatial) and Intraframe (Temporal) Compression

MPEG-2 compression (or any other MPEG video format) employs techniques to reduce information within a frame and between frames. Compression that takes place within an individual frame is referred to as *interframe*, or *spatial*, and that which takes place between frames is called *intraframe*, or *temporal*. For MPEG video, a compression algorithm called *DCT* (Discrete Cosine Transform) is used to compress information for a single frame. It is the same technique used to create JPEG images, by processing sections of an image as individual blocks, or "macroblocks," applying a complex algorithm to described sections of an image.

While DCT is a useful technique for reducing information for individual frames, MPEG video requires more. The number of whole frames produced would still require a large amount of storage space for even short clips of video (although DCT compressed formats, such as PhotoJPEG, can make an excellent intermediate codec), although clearly not enough to fit an hour of high-definition video onto a DV cassette tape. For this reason, a more suitable intraframe, or temporal, compression scheme needed to be created if tape capacities and bit-rate limitations were to be maintained. Therefore, it was decided to maximize space by compressing the information that changes significantly over time (as well as using motion vectors to move macroblocks around, making comparisons between their current and original positions, and then encoding any errors with DCT). By looking at information for pictures in a sequence, using motion vectors, writing data for those portions that change from one frame to the next, and filling in the remaining portions from reference frames for that sequence, MPEG-2 was made possible. These sequences are made up of three different frame types, each of which has a special function and assists in the temporal compression scheme.

Group of Pictures (GOP) Structure

Taken together as a whole, groups of frames in MPEG-2 video are known as a *GOP*, or *Group of Pictures*. The three types of frames used by MPEG-2 in a GOP are I, B, and P frames (see Figure 7.7). The number of frames in a GOP, and the order in which frames occur, are referred to as the video's *GOP structure*. The GOP structure for HDV is 15 frames (for NTSC) or 12 frames (for PAL), which is considered a long GOP. HDV also uses a closed GOP, versus an open GOP, which means that no frames are referenced from a previous GOP and the order of frames is not changed for the sake of efficiency.

IBBPBBPBBPBBPBB
(MPEG-2 HDV 1080i60)

IBBPBBPBBPBB
(MPEG-2 HDV 1080i50)

IBBPBB
(MPEG-2 HDV 720p30)

Figure 7.7 *A typical GOP includes a sequence of I, B, and P frames, such as the IBBP structure of MPEG-2 video for HDV.*

I-frames

I-frames, or intra frames, are the only whole frame in an MPEG sequence. They are complete and contain all the information for a picture, without being divided among other frames. They are used as keyframes, which surrounding frames use as a basis for compression, and they employ DCT with a macroblock scheme to reduce their size. While MPEG could technically contain all I-frames (as some MPEG editing software does), this would add significantly to the size of a video file, and as such is avoided in a typical MPEG sequence for capturing and delivering MPEG-2 video, such as that utilized for HDV or a DVD. Conversely, other formats, like DV, lack temporal compression and use all I-frames, which results in larger overall file sizes for video and a higher quality encode.

P-frames

P-frames, or predicted frames, include the data to describe what has changed from an I-frame (using motion vectors). They are the second largest frame in a GOP, after I frames, and are also used as a reference for B-frames.

B-frames

B-frames, or bidirectional frames, compress only the information that changes from surrounding I and P frames. This makes B-frames the smallest of the frame types in a GOP, and the one with the least amount of information.

Editing MPEG-2 and HDV

As discussed, the problem with editing MPEG-2-based video is that it does not contain complete frames (its GOP structure means that you only land on an I-frame twice every second), which is not acceptable for professional editing. In addition, if any of the frames in a GOP are lost, the entire GOP will not play. This means that any dropouts result in the loss of a half-second of video.

There are two alternatives to bypass the editing limitations of MPEG-2 video. The first method (as discussed) is to transcode your HDV video into an "intermediate" codec, which consists of I frames and is easier to use for editing. The next logical alternative to editing with intermediate codecs, and the holy grail of NLE manufactures as of late, is editing HDV natively. This is clearly the simplest method for editors, since it makes editing HDV as simple as working with DV. While you may wonder why this was not always the case, it is because editing native HDV files is extremely taxing on a computer system, which must make all of the calculations regarding I, B, and P frames for each edit decision instantaneously. Although it may seem like you are working with complete frames, all of the calculations are happening under the surface to approximate a seamless experience. This requires a very fast CPU and some intelligent software. Final Cut Pro 5 added this capability with its latest release, and other software, like Sony Vegas, were among the first to offer it.

NATIVE HDV EDITING

Native HDV editing simply means that HDV video is captured and edited in its original format (in this case, MPEG-2), without transcoding to an intermediate format, such as the Apple Intermediate Codec or MainConcept's CineForm. On the surface, editing natively with HDV is as simple and transparent as working with DV, although there are an enormous amount of processor-intensive tasks happening in the background to work with the long GOP structure of the MPEG-2 HDV video. Apart from ease of use, the other benefit to native HDV editing is that less disc space is used, since the low data rate of MPEG-2 is maintained (it requires the same amount of space as DV, or about 12GB per hour of 1080i HDV and 9GB per hour of 720p HDV video). If you plan on outputting back to tape, or utilizing the MPEG video for a DVD, native HDV editing is ideal. In general, native HDV editing is great for cuts-only type of editing, or where only transitions and a few effects are applied.

One of the drawbacks to working with native HDV is that any changes must be rendered and then conformed to the proper GOP structure prior to output (the conforming process can take a long time, and depends on the length of your video and the number or cuts). If you want to bypass the conform process, then you should consider using an intermediate codec, or changing your sequence settings to another format for output. For example, you could edit HDV natively, and then when you are ready to finish and output your video, you could render it as uncompressed and output to HDCAM (as discussed in a tip later in this chapter) or with another QuickTime codec.

The basic process for editing HDV natively is as follows:

1. Connect your HDV camera or deck to your computer with FireWire.

2. Log and capture your HDV (using the appropriate setup for HDV with your editing software—for example, in Final Cut Pro, you can use an "Easy Setup" for HDV).

3. Edit HDV clips in a sequence, as you would any other video (although you may not currently have the same preview options as formats like DV, such as viewing video on an external monitor through FireWire, or as many real-time layers and effects).

4. Output HDV back to tape or export it to a digital format on your computer, such as QuickTime. You can use a "Print to Video" command, although you are not able to "Edit to Tape" with HDV (unless the video is converted to a different format or output to another tape format through a separate hardware card, such as those sold by BlackMagic Design).

Logging Footage

Once you have figured out what software you will use and how to work with MPEG-2 and HDV, it is time to bring some media into your computer for editing. The first step in the editing process involves logging your footage, which is an essential (and often tedious) process that precedes the capture of footage. Logging entails the entering of reel names, clip names, and timecode information for sections of video that you intend to capture from a tape (see Figure 7.8). Entering this information into the Log window of your NLE before capturing clips assists you later on while editing, by reducing the amount of footage you need to capture (instead of capturing an entire tape), breaking up the portions you do need into manageable clips, and identifying individual shots and takes with descriptive names. It is also important when reassembling a project from an old file, or when transferring projects to other editors on a different system.

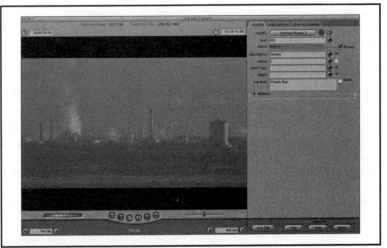

Figure 7.8 *Logging footage requires reel names, clip names, and other important information.*

LOGGING VIDEO WITHOUT A COMPUTER

Timecode information is typically added by using the VCR-style controls in your NLE's log and capture window to mark in and out points for an individual clip. If you would rather begin the logging process before opening your NLE, you can log your footage by notating the timecode on your master tape, or by creating a copy of your tape with timecode burned into it, and then writing down specific times for clips you want to use (a VHS or DVD copy is cheap and does not wear out your master tape through repeated viewings). You may also enter this information into a spreadsheet like Excel, or a database program like Filemaker Pro, using tab-delimited fields for importing into an NLE. (Check with your NLE for the required fields and naming conventions.)

After your footage is logged, the process of capturing, or importing, of video source material from tape or digital media begins. It should be noted that the majority of editors log and capture their footage at the same time, entering information for a tape, and then immediately initiating the capture process. With HDV, this is most often accomplished by using your computer's built-in FireWire connection (also referred to as *i.Link* by Sony). If you are capturing from HDCAM, or another, high-end source, you may need to use HD-SDI, together with a special video-capture card, such as Blackmagic's DeckLink HD, and a special RS-422 device control cable. (Some users may choose to import HDV as well through an HD-SDI converter, in order to "bump up" their video to a higher quality format on capture.)

EDL, AAF, AND XML

An EDL, or Edit Decision List, is a text file that lists all of the edit information and timecode for clips that were added to a sequence. By exporting an EDL for a completed sequence, you can simply import the file into another system and reassemble the project. (Most professional editing software can read an EDL.) An EDL is convenient, since it is a very small file, which can be emailed, transferred, or backed up easily. Although they are most often associated with film or high-end video production (which frequently utilizes the offline process or shares files with clients), you can use an EDL to simply store or back up the basic editing information, such as cuts and transitions, for any type of project. If you lose your original project files, you might still be able to piece together a timeline from an EDL. However, if you decide to use an EDL, try to limit your tracks to one video and two audio, since this is the setup most easily understood by an EDL. If you want to reassemble complex projects, then you will need to consider newer, more advanced data exchange formats, such as AAF (Advanced Authoring Format), or XML (Extensible Markup Language, often used on the Web). Applications like Final Cut Pro make particularly good use of XML, which was actually used in the Lumiere HD software that was originally sold to bring HDV files into Final Cut Pro. Using the XML in Lumiere HD, you can capture clips through the stand-alone software and then easily load and relink clips in Final Cut Pro by importing the XML file.

HDV Timecode

There are a few forms of timecode that you should be familiar with. First, there is SMPTE timecode, which is the professional standard for timecode that measures time in hours, minutes, seconds, and frames, which allows for accurate frame rate information, which is critical for precise editing and broadcast work. If timecode is not already present on a tape, DV or HDV timecode always starts at 00:00:00:00. Most professionals prefer the ability to set their own timecode, which helps to designate the order of tapes (starting a tape on hour 1, 2, or 3, for example, such as 01:00:00:00, 02:00:00:00, or 03:00:00:00). "Professional" camera models, such as the Sony HVR-Z1U, often include the ability to manually set timecode values. Additionally, with HDV (and other formats, like DV), if you accidentally start recording at any point beyond the last recorded frame, you will experience a timecode break, and the timecode automatically resets to zero. You can fix a timecode break on an HDV (or DV) tape by copying it to a new tape. Timecode breaks should be avoided at all costs, since missing or skipping timecode can make logging and capturing footage extremely difficult, due to inconsistent or repeating timecode numbers on a single tape. Some users will "black and code" a tape before recording or shooting, which simply means laying down timecode and a control track on blank media (usually by recording blank, or black, video—done by leaving the lens cap on your camera and pressing the Record button).

Drop Frame and Nondrop Frame Timecode

Drop frame timecode (DF), such as 29.97 NTSC, is the result of the difference between electricity's 60Hz clock time and television's 59.94Hz cycle (doubling 29.97 gives you 59.94, taking into account two "fields" of video, discussed in Chapter 10, "Creating Graphics and Effects for HDV"). This method of timing most closely matches actual time (when looking at a clock on the wall), so that whatever number you see indicated by your counter should be the correct time. Due to the nature of electricity, clock cycles, and our television standards, if you were to count frames normally (as with nondrop frame), from 1 to 30 (for NTSC), over the course of an hour you would have 108 additional frames. This means that you would need to add 3 seconds and 18 frames to an hour-long, nondrop frame program to get an accurate time measurement. Two frame values are dropped each minute to account for this discrepancy (except on every 10th minute), although no actual frames are removed—only the way they are counted changes. This is why you see a drop frame timecode move from 01:04:59:29 to 01:05:02:00, for example.

When someone refers to NTSC timecode as 30fps, it should be noted that is technically 29.97 (although 30 frames is often the shorthand, even for some discussions in this book). Since drop-frame timecode is most closely related to real time, it is the format that is required for delivery to broadcasters. On the other hand, nondrop frame timecode counts every frame equally, from 1 to 30 (for NTSC), without dropping any frame numbers over time. This type of timecode is sometimes used for motion graphics work and animations, where simplicity in counting may be most important, especially when working with video elements intended for compositing, or effects. It should be noted that both drop frame and nondrop frame are equally accurate, since no frames are lost. It is an editor's preference to use one or the other, although broadcast standards, as well as HDV and other formats, most often work strictly with drop frame, 29.97.

Record Run and Free Run Timecode

Record run timecode is generated only while the camera or VTR is recording. This means that if you stop recording and start up again later, the timecode continues where you left off. For example, if you stop recording at 00:05:00:00 and then start up again 20 minutes later, the first new frame you record would be 00:05:00:01. The DV format uses record run timecode, although HDV (with a suitable camera, such as the Sony HVR-Z1U—as mentioned in Chapter 4, "Operating an HDV Camcorder") is able to record free run timecode as well. Free run timecode runs continuously, and it is not affected by starting or stopping recording. Even when a camera is turned off, free run timecode continues to work. You might think of it as a timer, which (once started) continues to advance until it is reset. For example, if a camera with free run timecode is stopped at 00:05:00:00 and then restarted 20 minutes later, the new starting timecode would be 00:25:00:00. This means that you can perform multicamera shoots with ease, particularly when you have synchronized multiple cameras, which can be cut together easily later by lining up the timecode from all cameras. (All timecodes should match perfectly, even if a camera stopped recording and started again later on.) HDV recorded with free run timecode is ideal for editing with the multicam features in Final Cut Pro 5. However, not all users want discontinuous timecode on their tape, which is generally unhelpful for single camera shoots (unless it is also synching with a separate audio recorder or master time code generator). Generally, for most single camera shoots, record run timecode is used, where shooting a slate (especially one with a timecode readout) can help line up video and audio in post.

HDV SCENE BREAKS

The log and capture process for HDV is greatly simplified by utilizing the automatic scene break (scene detection) feature to automatically break up your video into clips, based on the time and date information recorded to your HDV tape. (This information is stored in a special area of the tape, although it is only useful if you remember to set the date and time on your camera.) At each point that you started and stopped recording with your HDV camcorder, a new clip will be made. Most software is set up by default to break your video into clips, based on time and date information, although you may be able to turn off this function if you want to capture your video as larger clips that span the breaks in time. (In Final Cut Pro 5, for example, the default scene break function is set with the "Make New Clip" option for scene and timecode breaks.) This capability is similar to the scene detection feature you may have used already with the DV format.

Capturing Footage

The process of capturing video clips is generally divided into batch captures, clip captures, or capture now. Batch capture is the preferred method, which allows you to import several clips at once using a list of time codes entered into your NLE in the logging phase, or by importing timecode information placed into a spreadsheet or text file. Batch capturing is an enormous time-saver when working with tapes with accurately logged footage. Using device control (included as part of a FireWire connection), your NLE can then import all the video you need at one time. Clip captures trade the batch capture process for more immediacy and occur as you are logging footage. You can instantly capture a single clip from the Log and Capture window after you have set in and out points and entered information for a clip. Capture now (or a similarly named function) is the instantaneous capture or recording of video to your hard drive "on the fly" as you are playing back your tape (sometimes called "crash recording"). This method is rarely used for projects with a lot of footage, but can work if you need to quickly capture a video clip, or if you are not as concerned about accurately logged footage or imprecise clip durations.

ADDING HANDLES

Including additional video at the beginning and end of a clip, called *handles*, can be important in the editing process. Handles can be used to make minor adjustments to a clip once it has been logged and captured. For example, you might decide after capturing a clip that you need additional media at the head (beginning) or tail (end) of the clip to add a dissolve or another transition. By including handles, you can be certain that the extra media is there in case you need it later. Generally, a second or two of handles is enough, although you might choose to include more if you have the space on your hard drive. At least 10 to 20 frames should be standard, even if you have no intention of using handles, since frames are sometimes out of sync when recapturing media and may require some adjustment.

If you are using a separate video capture card on your computer, such as those provided by Blackmagic Design, AJA, Pinnacle, Canopus, or Matrox, make certain that you adjust the project settings in your NLE to match the new hardware. Hopefully, you have checked your hardware card's capabilities carefully before purchasing it to make certain it has all the features you need for the software you are using and the type of HD you want to capture. Most cards include support for a variety of HD and HDV formats. Due to the influx of new HD cameras, decks, and NLE software, it is more than likely that whichever hardware card you choose was made with a wide range of devices, formats, and general compatibility in mind. In fact, the firmware in these cards can usually be updated to add new support for formats like HDV and DVCPRO HD.

When you launch your NLE, make sure to select the right preset for your card. Depending on the card you are using, there may even be specific settings for it in the Presets window (such as the Easy Setup in Final Cut Pro). If this is not the case, or if you want to make manual adjustments to your project, click "custom" and adjust the capture settings in the new Project Settings window that appears. Make certain that the video, audio, and device control settings match your card or the type of video you want to capture.

Troubleshooting Video Capture

Most of the problems that you encounter when capturing video are caused by hardware or software that is improperly configured. This can be the result of many things, whether incorrect capture presets, missing drivers for a particular deck or camera, or even a faulty computer card or loose connection. Before attempting to capture video, make sure your hardware card (if you have one) is properly installed, according to the manufacturer's recommendations. Any drivers or software that you might need to make the card accessible to your computer should be set up and tested. Also, make sure that you are using the latest drivers for any hardware you are using. Most manufacturers keep updated drivers on their Web sites for customers to download. In addition to checking a card, remember to test the deck or camera that you plan to use. Most computers should detect devices that you attach to it and lead you through a series of steps to configure them. This is particularly true for computers with built-in FireWire ports, such as those on a Mac, which automatically detects most FireWire devices attached to it. On either platform, whether Mac or PC, you may need to check for special driver updates to use nonstandard hardware or unsupported devices.

One of the most common problems when capturing a clip is dropped frames. This is often caused by hard drives that cannot write data fast enough to keep up with the incoming video. It can also be caused by not enough memory available for your NLE, due to other open applications using system resources. In this case, you should consider upgrading to a drive with a higher rpm (5400 or 7200 are generally acceptable for HDV over FireWire) and a larger throughput, which is measured in MBps (Megabytes per second). When working with HDV footage, it is important to have a drive that supports a minimum of 4MBps, although a faster drive certainly helps with the overhead of system resources and the fluctuation of actual read and write times. For uncompressed video, you need to have a drive that is capable of at least 140MBps, although more throughput will be important if you are capturing 10 bit uncompressed HD. When it comes to hard drives, the faster, the better. Of course, more storage space does not hurt either.

Online and Offline Editing

In general, there are two ways of working with media that you log and capture. The first, and most understood method, is online editing. Online simply means that the media you are editing is at full quality. When editing online, the media you capture is the same media that will eventually output to tape or the format of your choice. Editing with native HDV files (the way most users are probably accustomed to) is an online process, since the file sizes are small enough to capture and store all of your media on inexpensive drives, which are suitable for low-band width video files (see Figure 7.9). If you had a system that was fast enough, with a fast RAID array, video card, and deck, you could capture and edit with HDCAM or other high-quality formats at online quality. Unfortunately, not all users can afford this way of working. Even for companies that have a fast setup, large projects can eat up space very quickly. In these situations, offline editing may be the answer.

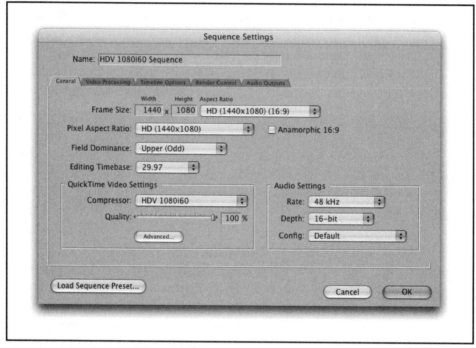

Figure 7.9 *The HDV "Easy Setup" in Final Cut Pro creates settings to work with HDV natively, editing "online" footage that does not need to be recaptured.*

Offline editing means that you are working with a low-quality proxy of your master footage. This is important if you are unable to store all of the video you need on your system (when editing a large project, like a documentary for example, with many hours of footage), particularly if you are working with uncompressed HD. In this case, the speed of your drives may also be another reason for choosing to work offline, since it is difficult or impossible to capture and playback HD video that is not HDV from a FireWire drive, even with a RAID setup. For example, if you need to edit HDCAM footage, you might capture your footage on one computer using a low bit rate format, such as DV, or even DVCPRO HD, put it on a FireWire drive for storage, and edit it at home. In the final process, after you have completed your edit using the lower quality video, the footage is conformed at full quality by recapturing the media from the master tape at full quality. Your NLE makes this possible by utilizing the logged information for your clips, as well as the in and out points set for clips in your timeline. By using the offline process, you could edit a film on your Powerbook, using low quality, standard definition clips of your footage, which can be assembled at high quality when you are finished editing.

Interview:
Paul Hirsch

Paul Hirsch is an Oscar winning film editor whose work includes *Star Wars*, *The Empire Strikes Back*, *Carrie*, *Blow Out*, *Ferris Bueller's Day Off*, *Ray*, and many more.

What role does music and choreography (separately or together) play in your editing?

Editing is similar to choreography at times. Choreography is the organization of movement through a 3D space over a given period of time, usually to music. Editing is the organization of movement in a 2D frame over a period of time, sometimes to music. In a dramatic or comedic scene, the stressed and unstressed syllables in dialogue are analogous to beats and offbeats in music, and provide a rhythm and tempo in the speech of the characters. From this, the editor can derive the rhythm of the cutting. In an action scene, the rhythm can be derived from the length of the events. All actions have a beginning, a middle, and an end; the time between them creates the rhythm. Just as a conductor may get the orchestra to play faster or slower for the appropriate artistic effect, so may the editor change the tempo, while still observing the rhythms of the scene. Actors' pauses can be adjusted to keep the pace of the scene in time to the desired tempo. In an action scene, the time between the events can be compressed, usually, so that the ball never hits the ground, so to speak; the action never gets a chance to rest until the desired moment. These considerations do not, of course, address issues of content, namely character, performance, story, exposition, psychological realism, or stylization, etc.

You mentioned the timing of events in an action scene. What types of editing decisions shaped the cutting of the light saber battles in Star Wars and The Empire Strikes Back?

(continued on next page)

(continued from previous page)

The light saber battle in *Star Wars* between Vader and Obi-Wan was problematical for George. He was unhappy with the way it was cut. All of us took a whack at it, adding pauses, tightening it up, trying different approaches, none of which made him happy. So on *The Empire Strikes Back*, particular attention was paid to the choreography of the fight between Luke and Vader so that we wouldn't have the same problem in the cutting. I'm not sure if that answers your question.

How has the editing of special effects changed for you since working on Star Wars?

When we cut *Star Wars*, the fx shots in the battle scenes consisted of: cockpit interiors, which had actors sitting in sets made of wood, against blue screens seen through cockpit windows, with the camera moving to create some illusion of movement; POV shots through the cockpit windshields, which were simply shots of blue screens framed by the cockpit windscreens; and spaceship exteriors, which didn't exist. To stand in for them, we used stock B/W footage of WWII fighter planes diving, flying, peeling off, etc. Each shot had a "name," such as "435 a" scribed with a sharp instrument (called a "scribe") in one corner of the first frame. This could be referenced (if you stopped the film, pulled it out, and looked at it) against a notebook filled with storyboards that would show the design of the shot, i.e., which ships (intergalactic cruiser, or "X-wing" fighter, etc.), how many, what the action would be (such as flying straight to camera, or L to R, or diving, and so forth), what the BG would be (stars or the surface of the Death Star, for example), and if there were additional elements, such as laser bolts or explosions. But the eventual fx shot might bear no relation to the stock shot standing in for it. So you might have a shot of a Japanese Zero diving to the left representing a shot of Vader's ship coming right at camera. It was very hard to decipher by watching it. You sort of had to analyze it. Pacing it was tricky since you had to imagine how long the desired action might take. Today, animatics are created in computers to stand in for the finished shots. On *Mission to Mars*, ILM provided these, and they were extremely sophisticated animated storyboards, which related closely to the finals.

Do you have any feelings about using HD and video as a replacement for film?

Not in a practical sense, since it is all digital in the cutting. But I worry about the rapid obsolescence of electronic media compared to the technological longevity of film. The chemo-mechanical basis of film lasted long enough for the same methods to be adopted in every corner of the globe. This has meant that films made in China or India could be projected in America or Europe and vice versa. It is hard to imagine a world moving in lock-step from one standard computerized system to the next. Who today can even read what is on a floppy disk? Or a Zip drive? Computers change so quickly that a system two years old is considered ancient. How can we archive material when the platforms to play it on vanish so quickly?

With regard to the movement from traditional film editing practices to modern digital equivalents, have you used an EditDroid, and if so, how does it compare with older flatbed editors and contemporary editing systems like Avid?

I never did. I once visited Ben Burtt, who was cutting on it as a test pilot. He was on the phone with a technician talking about a problem he was having. The technician told him to pick up the control from the table and drop it! I guess they were trying the old "smack the side of the TV set" approach.

In what ways is the overall structure of a film influenced by genre or themes (examples in your work?)? Also, how often do you have to revise the structure of a film from its original script?

The greatest opportunity for restructuring comes from scripts that are sort of episodic, like *Ferris Bueller's Day Off* or *Ray*. In a thriller, suspense film, or mystery, the plotting is usually tighter, and there is less freedom to move scenes around. The information must be revealed in a certain order to keep the audience both aware of what is going on and in the dark about certain things until the right moment. Ferris's day went through heavy reordering that actually strengthened connections between the events. The parade scene had originally been shot for much earlier in the day, before the traffic jam, for example. We moved the parade to the end of the day, in order to create a climax, and intercut a few shots before the scene in the taxi to suggest that the parade was the reason for the traffic jam, as opposed to just another random event. In *Ray*, we moved some of the flashback scenes later in the film, because we felt they were so powerful emotionally, and were over too soon. *Blowout* is the exception to the thriller rule. That was heavily rejiggered so as to introduce the John Lithgow character sooner and create a tension that hadn't existed. If you look carefully, you can tell that a scene between Nancy Allen and Dennis Franz in his hotel room has been cut in half and used in two different places in the film.

(continued on next page)

(continued from previous page)

Do you have any tips, theories, or rules of thumb (particularly in regards to your own decision making processes), which you'd like share with editors?

On the first cut, follow your instinct about how to make the scene better. Don't try to second guess how someone else might cut it. Try to use all the material the director has provided, unless it is impractical. Satisfy your own sensibility as to what is the best way to cut it. Your instinct, ultimately, is what you carry with you through your career. If you can rely on it, you will never be without resources. Keep the film as simple as possible, but not simpler than that. Determining the simplest possible version is the trick. (Hint: It is sometimes very complex.)

What can an editor do to improve his craft?

Cut. Fail. Fix it. Learn from experience. There is only one way to get experience. Cut.

Any anecdotes pertaining to editing/filmmaking that you'd like to share from your past work (something you haven't had the occasion to discuss)?

When I was cutting *The Fury* for DePalma, I wasn't certain how he intended a particular shot to be used. When I asked him, he replied, "You're the editor. You figure it out." So I did. That's been my approach ever since.

Common Editing Techniques

Digital editing has made assembling a home video or even a feature film accessible to the masses. In fact, virtually every major Hollywood production uses a similar nonlinear application to cut scenes together. It's the NLE's ability to work quickly and easily that makes it so appealing, yet creating logic, or poetry out of a series of clips is more important than the technology they rely upon. For this reason, it is important to understand the capabilities of your NLE, while remembering that its purpose is to help you realize your vision for a project. Whether you are simply assembling clips with iMovie, or precisely trimming and editing in Final Cut Pro and Avid, it is important that you familiarize yourself with the digital tools that help you work more efficiently and creatively.

Basic Editing

In order to begin editing, you first need to understand the basics of nonlinear editing using clips and sequences (timelines). The three points listed below are the primary steps in putting together a video using an NLE.

1. Navigating the timeline.

   Begin by opening your source clip in the Viewer window, or source monitor, where you will preview your video before adding it to a sequence (see Figure 7.10). (Opening a clip is usually done by double-clicking it in the browser or file window.) After the clip has opened in the viewer, drag the playhead at the bottom of the window to a new location where you want to start the clip. You may also use the arrow keys on the keyboard to advance one frame at a time or move the sliders to shuttle through the video. Learning to use the playback controls of your NLE is the first step in familiarizing yourself with the world of digital editing. If you have mastered the VCR-style controls that allow you to play, fast forward, rewind, or jump to the beginning and end of a clip or sequence, then you can begin to learn keyboard shortcuts to perform the same tasks. For example, professional editors use a "JKL" keyboard method for stopping, playing, and rewinding their video. The "J" key rewinds, "K" stops, and "L" plays the video forward.

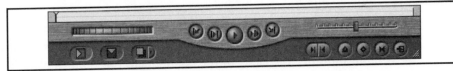

Figure 7.10 *Playback controls and a Viewer window, or source monitor.*

2. Setting in and out points.

   The first step in editing a clip or sequence is the proper placement of in and out points (see Figure 7.11), which determine what portions of your video are added to the Timeline. Marking in and out points is a process that becomes second nature once you have worked with an NLE a few times. In order to perform complex edits, or to even add a simple clip to your sequence, you need to know how this basic task is performed. Keyboard shortcuts, such as pressing the "I" key and the "O" key, are the most common ways for setting in and out points in an NLE.

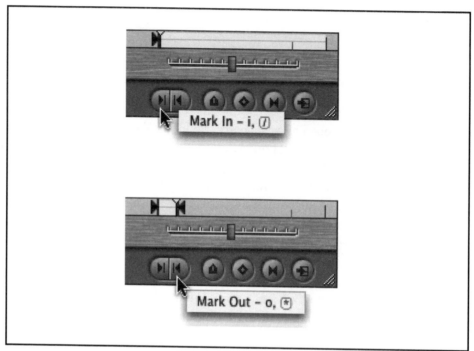

Figure 7.11 *Marking in and out points for a clip.*

3. Adding Clips to the Timeline.

After in and out points have been set for your clip, you are ready to add it to a sequence in the Timeline (see Figure 7.12). Drag the clip from the source window onto the Timeline, to the point where you want to place it. If you have an exact point in the Timeline where you want to add the clip, but it is not at the beginning or end of another clip, it is helpful to place the playhead in the Timeline at the exact point you want the clip to start or end; then drag the clip onto the Timeline. Your clip should automatically "snap" to the line where the playhead is located. You may also use a keyboard shortcut or a special button in your NLE to "insert" or "overwrite" (also called overlay) a clip into your timeline. If you use the insert function, any material located after the clip in the sequence is moved further down the Timeline. This can shift any previously added material and change the synchronization of elements on the Timeline, so make certain to use insert carefully. The overwrite, or overlay, function writes the clip onto the Timeline and does not shift any other clips. Instead, it overwrites any material on the Timeline that occupies the duration of the clip you are adding. Depending on which application you are using, first, you may need to target tracks in order to place clips on a particular track of video or audio. (NLEs have multiple tracks or layers of video and audio, such as V1 and V2, or A1 and A2, which can be stacked on top of each other.)

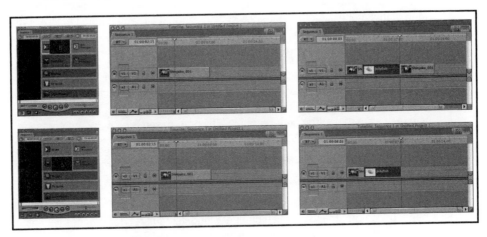

Figure 7.12 *Inserting and overwriting a clip to a Timeline.*

HDV UNCOMPRESSED EDITING WORKFLOW

Even though you might be working with video that originated on HDV, you can convert it to an uncompressed format for output to HDCAM, or to a file type that can be stored or transmitted from a hard drive (such as a QuickTime). If you have a high-end workflow, particularly if you are set up to edit HDCAM or similar material, then you might consider converting your HDV footage to an uncompressed format prior to output. Apart from the ability to mix HDV with other uncompressed material, this method of working also permits the use of "edit to tape" functions you may already be familiar with (ordinarily, HDV only permits "print to video"). Also, moving your HDV footage into an uncompressed sequence improves the quality of your renders—at least it removes the problems of recompressing to HDV, which is an extremely lossy format. The following is one example of a simple workflow (based on Final Cut Pro 5, but generally applicable to other setups) for working with 1080i HDV in an uncompressed HD editing workflow. You may apply a similar approach for converting your project to DVCPRO HD or any other format on which you may want to finish.

(continued on next page)

(continued from previous page)

1. Log and Capture HDV footage using native HDV settings (such as the "HDV-1080 i60" Easy Setup in Final Cut Pro 5).

2. Edit in an HDV sequence, apply effects, but do not render. (You can render if you really want to see a preview, although your effects will need to re-render in the final step of this process.) Your sequence settings should already match the HDV Easy Setup mentioned, including 1440×1080 frame size, HD (1440×1080) pixel aspect ratio, field dominance Upper (Odd), HDV 1080i60 compressor.

3. When you are ready to output or edit to tape, create a NEW uncompressed HD sequence (such as "BlackMagic HDTV 1080i 59.94-8 bit" or similar, depending on your setup). If working in Final Cut Pro 5, even with a BlackMagic or similar card, you may want to use the generic Apple "Uncompressed 8 bit 4:2:2" compressor, located in the QuickTime Video Settings area of your Sequence Settings window.

4. Drag your HDV sequence from the browser into the new uncompressed HD sequence you just created.

5. Render and use like any other uncompressed HD sequence. This will eliminate the need to "conform to HDV," which can be a long, tedious render process with other potential pitfalls, such as mixing of HDV and non-HDV files.

Working with Layers

In order to fully take advantage of the editing and compositing features in your NLE, it is important to understand the value of layers. Layers are an important element of a sequence, especially for complex edits or for projects that use compositing and transparency effects (refer to Chapters 10 and 11). Essentially, the basic concept of layers works the same in any NLE. By placing video and audio elements on separate layers, a variety of different results can be achieved (see Figure 7.13). In the case of video, separate layers (or "tracks") allow the editor to simultaneously view the layout of a complex project and to easily make alterations to a sequence, particularly one with multiple camera angles or footage that is added to separate tracks. By layering video and audio elements, new visual and aural spaces can be created, such as placing text over a moving background or mixing voiceovers with music.

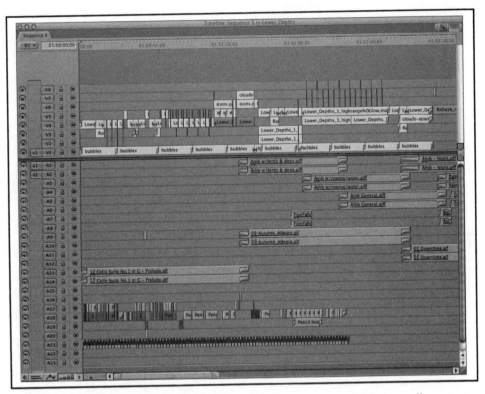

Figure 7.13 *Multiple tracks can be created to hold several layers of video or audio content.*

Professional NLEs allow you to work with several tracks of video and audio. Although you can usually add up to 99 tracks of video and an equal number of audio, it is highly unlikely that you will ever need to use the maximum number of tracks. Just remember that your system's CPU and hard drives are limited in the number of simultaneous tracks they can play back. The addition of a special hardware card can greatly improve your ability to work with several layers of video in real time.

NESTED CLIPS

Nested clips, or collections of clips placed inside another sequence, are useful for many reasons. Although you may never need to use them, they are great for simplifying a complex project or treating large groups of clips as a single unit when applying effects. By using nested clips, it is also possible to create multiple instances of the same sequence in the Timeline, without needing to cut and paste individual clips. You might decide to nest your clips, for example, if you want to apply a broadcast safe filter quickly to an entire sequence, generate output for a timecode printer, or apply other effects to an entire sequence as a group.

Timeline Tools and Trimming Techniques

Professional NLEs include helpful editing tools for use in the Timeline window, some of which are based on trimming techniques (see Figure 7.14). Each of these tools provides a unique way of working with clips added to the Timeline. The Selection tool, which is the default choice when you start up your NLE, is the most common tool. It is primarily used for moving individual clips around the Timeline, and may be used to select multiple clips by holding down the Shift key as you click on them in the Timeline. Since one of the Timeline tools must always be active, the Selection tool is the best one to choose when you do not have a specific need in mind and just want to work with clips in a basic way. Tools like Zoom or the Hand icon are relatively self-explanatory and should be familiar to anyone who has worked in Photoshop or other video and graphics applications. However, in addition to basic timeline tools for selecting ranges, zooming into an edit point, and moving clips with a selection arrow, there are other tools that are less intuitive, which are based on advanced editing techniques that can affect the content and duration of your clips and sequences. Some of these techniques include rolling, rippling, slipping, and sliding.

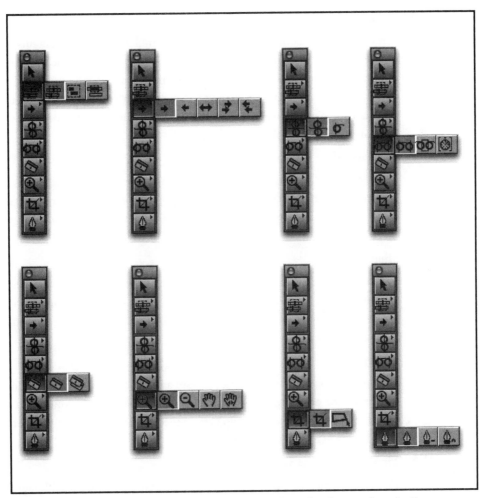

Figure 7.14 *Timeline tools can be useful problem solvers for the experienced editor.*

The following are a few of the tools that you typically find in an NLE for working with clips in the Timeline window. These tools are based on common editing techniques, including single-sided and two-sided trimming, which expand beyond the simple ability to insert or overwrite clips to a sequence. If you are looking for a way to make precise edits or adjustments in the Timeline window, one of these tools, or trimming techniques, might do the trick.

◆ **Rolling Edit**

A roll edit adjusts both sides of an edit point simultaneously. It maintains the duration of your program, as well as the clips you are editing in the timeline, by shortening the previous clip and making the next clip longer by the same amount. A roll edit is frequently used to adjust the in point of a cut, such as when cutting dialogue scenes where you want the video to enter sooner than the audio in order to smooth over the cut.

◆ **Rippling Edit**

This technique "ripples" the edits in your Timeline to fill in the gap that is ordinarily created when adjusting the in or out points of an individual clip. A ripple edit affects the duration of your program, while shortening or lengthening the duration of a clip.

◆ **Slipping**

Slipping only effects the in and out points of a single clip, while not affecting its placement in the Timeline. This means that you can change the content, or portion of your original media, that you want to include in the clip without changing the clip or sequence durations.

◆ **Sliding**

Sliding preserves the duration of a program and the clip being moved, while shortening the preceding clip and lengthening the next one. As you slide a clip, the out point of the preceding clip is shortened as the in point of the next clip is made longer to compensate, and vice versa.

◆ **Time Remap (Rate Stretch)**

The Time Remap tool changes the speed of clip in the Timeline, although it does not affect the source clip. It is a useful tool for matching action to a cut, particularly if you need to expand or shorten the duration between on-screen action and audio events.

◆ **Razor Blade**

The Razor Blade tool slices a clip to produce two clips out of one. It is used for splitting a clip in the Timeline window, which creates separate clips that you may delete (for example, if you want to cut out a portion of a clip from the Timeline), or for adding different effects and speed change to portions of the same clip. There are also "razor blade all" or multiple razor blade tools for splitting clips on all tracks at the same time.

◆ **Pen Tool**

The Pen tool is used for placing and manipulating keyframes in the Timeline or in one of the monitor windows, such as the canvas. This tool is frequently utilized as you work with motion effects, adjust clip opacities, and mix audio levels within your tracks.

Interview:
Steven Gonzales

Steven Gonzales is an editor whose work includes the films of David Gordon Green (*George Washington, All the Real Girls, Undertow*).

What is your working relationship like with David Gordon Green? What is the editing process like?

We've know each other a long time, so I have a good idea of what David likes. I work in tandem with my buddy Zene Baker on David's movies, so we tag team while David decides which scenes he'd like each of us to work on. As the film becomes more finalized, we overlap until we're all in the editing room constantly, tossing around ideas. Then we'll decide to go see a dumb movie at a matinee, goofing off for a while, and then work late into the evening. It is huge hours, but it's broken up by David's occasional impulsive exuberance.

How much has the structure or ideas of the films you've worked on been changed or sculpted in the editing?

The changes during editing have varied over the movies. *Undertow* remained fairly intact throughout the whole process, while *All The Real Girls* had some big changes from the original script. We have been given freedom enough to try out restructuring, mostly because we're also willing to toss out our ideas when they don't work. David takes on the hard task of arguing with producers about what's in or out, so he serves to create an artistic immune system, allowing us editors much room for experimentation. We've done some amazing things that never made it into the final film, mostly because we finally agreed they were too weird for the people putting up the money. But they were awesome ideas.

What principles or techniques do you use to organize clips and sequences while editing?

(continued on next page)

(continued from previous page)

The organization is pretty straightforward; I have bins by scene of picture, bins by scene of sound, bins by scene of sync footage, and miscellaneous second unit stuff organized with informative names. The important thing is to be able to find anything quickly.

How do you decide to time a scene, or an entire movie for that matter? Are there any techniques or approaches you use to determine the correct pacing, or when to let a scene play out?

A lot of the timing depends on the movement of the camera and the performances. You can force timing to some extent in editing, but you can't negate the nature of the footage. The timing comes from an attempt to make the film believable, while still having as much clarity as possible. The tiny choices that seem to make the most difference are reactions: how long do you stay on the person speaking after they've finished, how long before the other character answers, how long does a character think before speaking? A few frames can add a lot of depth to a character. Slight shifts in sound are also very valuable, such as a tiny rush or delay in an off-screen line, which matches it better with the on-screen character. The main principal is to suggest the unspoken intellectual process in the character's mind.

Where does music enter the editing process, and how does it affect the cut?

I personally like to go as long as possible without music. I feel that if the rhythm to the cuts is correct, placing music later will only enhance that. But placing music before the rhythm is correct serves to hide the problems, and to make you think that the scene is working, when actually it is choppy or unnatural. However, other editors I know like to get music in earlier, in order to get a mood. So my method is not for everyone.

Do you have any tips, theories, or rules of thumb (particularly in regards to your own decision making processes), which you'd like share with other editors?

Editing is making choices, so you have to stay focused. Be sure and get some type of physical activity, and you'll be amazed how your stamina will increase. I also like to present ideas to the director as choices: if you choose this take over the other, there is a subtle difference the audience will perceive. This is a much better way to resolve artistic disagreements, because it will force the director to explain his choices. Then further choices are easier for the editor, because he has a greater depth of understanding of the director's point of view. And, of course, sometimes directors are just wrong, but you have to do it their way.

Are there any outside sources, such as music, art, or literature, which influence your style or guide your aesthetic choices?

I'm not the most sociable person in the world, so the arts have always been a strong influence on me. Our gang of filmmakers attended an arts conservatory, so we are all full of ideas gathered from dance, music, staged drama, and design. I could spend all my time in art museums or reading. As a kid I spent most of my time practicing piano (another solitary but immensely interesting activity), so of course music is a very important influence. If you can listen to two different orchestras playing a Mahler symphony, and then explain the emotional difference between the two (and the technical factors which led to that emotional feeling), you would probably make a good editor. I'd also be remiss if I didn't mention the influence of the geniuses I studied with at the North Carolina School of the Arts, all of whom have moved on to other work: Denine Rowan, Jeff Stern, Phil Linson, and Sonya Polonsky.

What is your opinion/experience of using Cinema Tools (formerly Film Logic) to work with film originated material?

Our film *George Washington* was the first movie shot on film (35mm anamorphic) and finished on film using Final Cut Pro and Film Logic back in late 1999. I've watched the whole evolution of Final Cut, and it works great for features, but you have to understand its quirks. I've had a lot of help from great people, including Loran Kary, the creator of Film Logic/Cinema Tools, Daniel Fort, an editor and the wise sage of this technique, and Ramy Katrib and the great folks at Digital Film Tree.

Would you care to share any experiences or anecdotes from the editing of Undertow?

The greatest experience editing *Undertow* was meeting Terrence Malick and Phillip Glass. Also, the fine editor Saar Klein was very generous with his time. Any anecdotes would probably revolve around the building where we edited, the former Frank's Uniforms in Savannah. The rains came down like oceans in Savannah, and this abandoned building had a very leaky roof, so we were working amidst ceiling tiles dipping down under the weight of gallons of water. The building began to look like a hideout in some post apocalypse future. I believe they were going to tear the building down as soon as we finished, and not a moment too soon. Of course, then the rats would have to find somewhere else to live.

(continued on next page)

(continued from previous page)

Did you discuss the film with producer Terrence Malick? What role did he have in the shaping of the film?

Terrence Malick came in during the filming and watched dailies, giving some ideas at that time. Otherwise, the producers all communicated through David's cell phone, filtered by his brain. Us editors really didn't know what ideas came from whom, or how they were filtered before we heard them. This was a fine way to work for me, because I really don't like meetings or talking on the phone.

What is your next project?

I'm working on a film shot on a very low budget in Arkansas, called *Shotgun Stories*. It's directed by another of our gang, Jeff Nichols, and produced by Gary Hawkins, for whom I edited *The Rough South of Larry Brown*. It's an interesting and subtle character study about the feud between two sets of sons from the same man. It's a Cain and Able story placed upon groups of stepbrothers. It shows a strong influence of David Gordon Green, and, of course, they found some amazing locations so it looks great.

Transitions

Transitions can add a great deal to any video program or film. In particular, the use of transitions, such as dissolves and fades, are a staple of just about any project (see Figure 7.15). They can smooth over a rough cut or provide clues about the passage of time. However, some transitions, such as wipes, need to be used judiciously, and only when they suit the project. Using too many transitions, particularly those that resemble a special effect, is distracting and can cheapen a production. In most cases, transitions are added after clips have been placed in the Timeline to help join the video in a smooth manner. When adding transitions, it is important to make certain that there is enough material on either side of an in or out point (an instance where handles are important) to provide a suitable amount of time for the effect to take place. For example, a dissolve requires that enough extra video is present on either side of the edit (the end of the outgoing clip and the beginning of the incoming clip) for the transition to occur. If a one-second dissolve is applied, then each clip needs at least 15 frames to contribute to the transition, when the transition is centered between the two clips. In general, if there is not enough material based on the current edit, a dialog window appears with a warning or asks you if you would like to adjust the edit points for the clips to compensate for the transition. Most transitions require rendering before you can view them, although some faster systems, particularly those with additional hardware, can preview transitions in real time.

Looking to your favorite films for inspiration is a good way to see what transitions work well. The *Star Wars* movies are famous for their use of horizontal wipes (see Akira Kurosawa's *Hidden Fortress* for another example of this effect), although it can appear derivative when used in other movies. You might also try flashes of color to mask an edit, or alpha transitions to add a graphic look to your project (applying images with transparent areas over a cut, which pass through the frame).

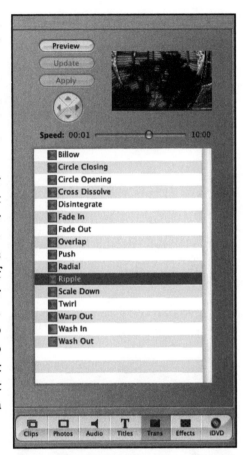

Figure 7.15 *Transitions, such as fades and dissolves, help you get from one clip to the next smoothly, particularly if there is a jump in location or time.*

Chapter 8

Color Correcting Video

olor correction is often the final step for any film or video project, and a necessary (although under appreciated) process. Once the final edit of your movie or commercial project is complete, color correction adds the right amount of polish to blend shots seamlessly together (see Figure 8.1). This process can also be used to create exciting combinations of color that did not exist in the original video or to enhance colors that were already there. In particular, it is an important step to correct flaws in the lighting and color balance of scenes. When properly shot and lit under ideal conditions, some video appears fine to the average viewer. However, professionals, who are accustomed to looking at and evaluating video quality, notice the discrepancies more readily. In both cases, subtle color changes can have a dramatic effect on the feel of a scene or an entire movie, affecting the viewing experience, regardless of the audience's filmmaking knowledge or awareness of the colors that are used.

The importance of color correction cannot be overestimated. Even though your colors may appear acceptable to casual observation, they can almost always benefit from some selective adjustments and special treatment. Also, since your video passes through a number of steps before reaching your audience, it is important to ensure the best possible quality and uniformity of color, whether your project is destined for film, television, DVD, or the Web. (This applies to general image processing considerations as well, such as compression, although color is most apparent.) Beyond maintaining the consistency of your pictures, color correction is also important as an artistic statement that helps to communicate the intentions of a filmmaker. Color grading is used to achieve unique looks that are an important part of today's filmmaking process.

As mentioned, color correction is primarily important for establishing continuity from one shot to the next, which is usually the result of color shifts caused by differing camera settings and lighting setups. Matching the color of shots is critical to maintaining the flow of a movie. Using incongruous shots breaks the flow and pulls a viewer out of the scene. Perhaps the sun was not cooperating on the day of your shoot. Maybe someone gave you b-roll or stock footage from a different camera or another format to cut in with your actors. Color correction can be used to shift the colors from one shot to match another, or to make a shot brighter that was shot under darker conditions, or vice versa.

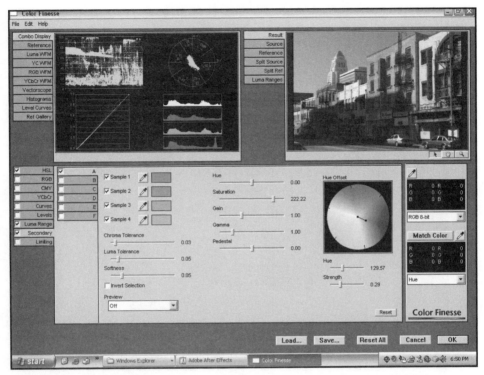

Figure 8.1 *Synthetic Aperture makes a popular color correction plug-in called Color Finesse for Adobe After Effects.*

Utilizing color correction techniques to create a particular feel is another important creative tool that filmmakers have at their disposal in post-production (see Figure 8.2). The look of a video or film, as the result of color, can be essential to establishing a mood or a tone. Using your computer and color correction software, you may decide to modify the results of an on-set lighting decision. This approach of relighting a scene extends the use of the camera, and often involves the input of a cinematographer, broadening their role into the post-production process (a recent evolution of roles, especially with the rise of Digital Intermediates in the film world). A project may be shot with this process in mind, using the lighting setup and set design available on location with the intention of altering it in post. It also allows a director or editor to have the flexibility when assembling a project to try different looks to achieve the tone they are after.

Figure 8.2 *Final Touch HD is a new, relatively inexpensive alternative to the professional color correction systems, like DaVinci (a control surface is optional but highly recommended).*

Color Correction Workflow

Before we get into the specifics of computer software and hardware techniques, it is helpful to review the basic color correction workflow. Although the exact workflow that you use may vary according to your own software or hardware setup, many of these steps (including the order of the process) usually remain the same, with additional steps applied based on experience or the needs of a particular project. For example, most of the steps included here assume that you are not using a chip chart, although they could be modified to include the additional step of using the Eye Dropper tool to match blacks, mids, and whites to the chart you shot on set. (Terms such as blacks, mids, whites, luma, chroma, and others are discussed in greater detail in the following sections of this chapter.)

TAPE TO TAPE COLOR CORRECTION

If you take your video to a high-end facility for color correction, a "colorist" will usually do a tape-to-tape color correction of your video. This process is very fast, since it does not require any re-rendering of clips (everything is recorded in real time back to tape). Although the results are usually very good, the main drawback is price (time spent in the suite can add up), and you are stuck with the changes you have made, unless you decide to bring your tape back to the facility for another round of color correction. (Color correction is also known as "timing.")

For most users, color correcting in an NLE such as Final Cut, Premiere, and Vegas, or using a special plug-in like Color Finesse for Adobe After Effects, is the preferred method, since the color correction can be done on their own machines (although a professional colorist could use an NLE as well). In that case, the effect is only applied to individual clips, which can be changed easily at a later time. (If you're using an After Effects plug-in like Color Finesse, and not editing with Premiere, you might consider a plug-in like Automatic Duck to move clips back and forth to your NLE.) If you do choose a tape-to-tape process, consider up-converting your footage to a sturdier format at the same time, such as HDCAM, HDCAM SR, DVPRO HD, or HD D-5.

A typical color correction workflow for an NLE is as follows:

1. Calibrate your monitor with color bars, if you are using an external video monitor to preview your video, or if you have not adjusted it recently (see Figure 8.3). An external video monitor is a virtual necessity for accurate color correction, particularly if you are preparing video for SD formats like NTSC and PAL. It is also important for HD work as well, although a separate, properly setup LCD screen with adequate resolution can also act as a monitor.

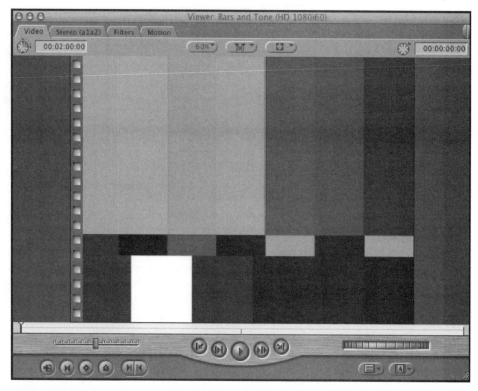

Figure 8.3 *Color bars are used for calibrating a monitor and comparing relative video levels.*

2. Load a clip into your NLE's viewer window.

3. Apply a color correction filter to the clip (see Figure 8.4).

4. Display your video scopes, including the waveform monitor and vectorscope. Video Scopes are part of professional NLEs, such as Final Cut Pro, Vegas (see Figure 8.5), or even specialized color correction software like Color Finesse for Adobe After Effects. You may also have a separate set of video scopes as a hardware display device, which are fed a video signal from your camera, deck, or computer. Use the video scopes to monitor changes to luma (particularly important), as well as changes in chroma.

5. Adjust luma levels for your clip, beginning with whites, then blacks, and possibly mids. Ideally, you are using a three-way color correction filter, which breaks down a signal into blacks, mids, and whites, each with its

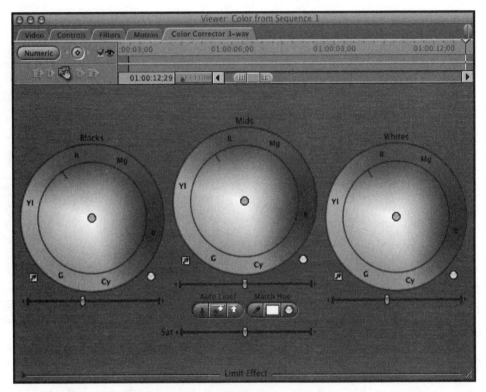

Figure 8.4 *The Color Corrector 3-way filter in Final Cut Pro.*

own luma and corresponding color controls. It is not always necessary to adjust the mids, although if you shot with a chip chart, you could use the gray values in the chart to achieve an accurate match.

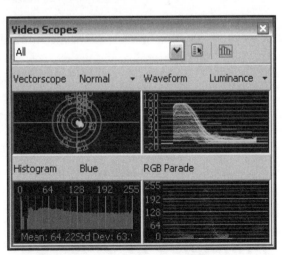

Figure 8.5 *Video scopes in Sony Vegas.*

6. Adjust the white balance of your clip by clicking the Eye Dropper tool (see Figure 8.6) next to the white level controls, and then choose an area of the image that should correspond to pure white, such as a white wall (which may appear yellow, or some other color, if the scene was not shot using the correct temperature of lights). Many times, properly white balancing a shot on-set, or in your color correction software, is all that is necessary for acceptable color correction results. For example, clicking on a wall that should appear white shifts most other colors in a shot back into their proper place. This is the simplest way to achieve correct color balance for a shot.

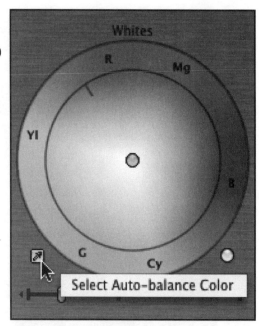

Figure 8.6 *The Eye Dropper tool in Final Cut Pro's Color Corrector 3–way.*

7. Make adjustments to the hue and saturation controls for a particular region of color, or for the entire clip. With individual color wheels for blacks, mids, and whites, you can roughly isolate areas of color based on their luma values. This means that you can shift all of your white values toward blue, for example, or leave your white and black color levels intact while shifting the mids (or the majority of average colors in your scene) to another color. By shifting only your mids toward a color, you can create interesting looks, such as the green cast associated with the Matrix movies. You may also use a hue wheel control (sometimes included as a separate filter) to affect the overall color or tint of your clip.

Principles of Color Correction

Only by understanding the properties of light, from which color is derived, can you properly understand the color correction process as it relates to video. For many readers, the basic concepts of color began in art class with the visual representation of a color wheel, or in science class with the demonstration of a prism. Both of these examples are fundamental to our understanding of color and how we can manipulate it. If you are new to video production, but have worked in print or graphic design, the comparisons should be clear. Colors can be combined, subtracted, made lighter or darker, and shifted up and down the spectrum until you achieve the right look. Although many principles of color are universal, their execution, in terms of digital recording, playback, and monitoring, can differ greatly from the oils and watercolors, or even the Photoshop world you may be accustomed to. For our discussion, the video canvas (and the HDV format in particular) will require some special consideration. However, the most important concepts to understand in this chapter are how brightness, hue, and saturation affect our perception of color, as well as how they can be manipulated to achieve the look you are after.

Luma

Luma (sometimes called luminance, although it is more correct to say luma) is a measure of brightness, or lightness, of an image. This is the value that is most important to the quality of an image, since it is the value that we perceive most readily, even before color. In fact, color would not exist without luma. As such, it is generally the first value that we adjust with color correction. If an image is too dark or too bright, adjusting a particular range of luma values can solve the problem.

Blacks, Mids, and Whites

Generally, the first step in color correction is adjusting the luma values of a clip. In most color correction software, luma values are broken down into their three key ranges of blacks, mids, and whites. Occasionally, these luma values may be the only settings you adjust with color correction software, assuming your video was white balanced properly or fine adjustments are not necessary (particularly if you have a quick turnaround on a project). Many times, it is simply a matter of bringing down the white values to adjust an overexposed image, or bringing the mid values up to return detail while only moderately affecting the surrounding black-and-white levels. Although each range has its own controls, there is an overlap between each of these ranges, which can make it necessary to adjust more than one range, if not all ranges, to isolate the desired amount of luma. This means, that after making an adjustment to one level, you may need to go back and change a different level to compensate. For example, raising the mids too much can cause the black levels to lose their depth or the whites to become overexposed. In this case, it is a balancing act, using your waveform monitor (discussed in a later section of this chapter) to gauge how much you should shift each range.

Black levels affect the darkest areas of an image, such as underexposed objects and portions of the scene that fall into deep shadows (see Figure 8.7).

When black levels are below the acceptable range for video they are often referred to as "crushed." If someone asks you to crush the blacks, they simply mean bring down the black levels and make them darker without affecting the overall brightness of the image.

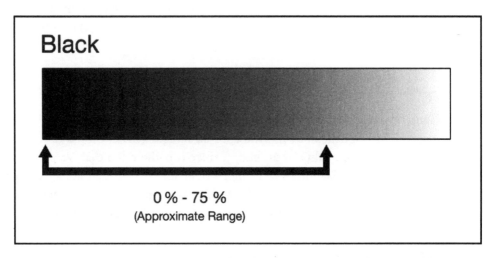

Figure 8.7 *Black levels are at the low end, or left side, of the luma values (image shows approximate values affected by sliders in color corrector).*

Mids affect all of the levels between the blacks and the whites, or the darkest and brightest areas of an image. Most of an image's detail resides in the mid range (see Figure 8.8). By raising the mids, you can often bring out this detail better, such as features on a face.

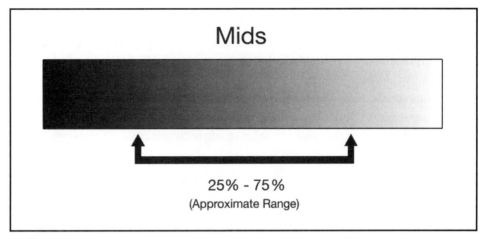

Figure 8.8 *Mids occur in the middle of the luma values and take some information from blacks and whites (image shows approximate values affected by sliders in color corrector).*

White levels affect only the brightest areas of an image, such as windows, reflections, and other bright light sources. See Figure 8.9. When white levels are too low the image appears dim and washed out.

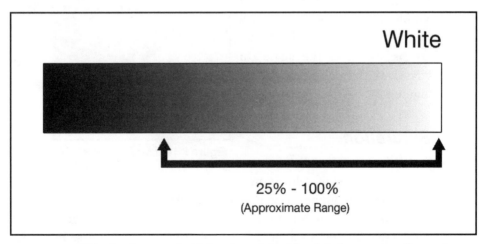

Figure 8.9 *White levels are at the high end, or right side, of the luma values (image shows approximate values affected by sliders in color corrector).*

Chroma

Chroma (sometimes called chrominance, although chroma is more correct and applicable to video) is the color of an image, which is composed of hue and saturation. When an image's chroma is low, it is washed-out and desaturated. Conversely, high chroma images have colors that often bleed into each other. It is important to understand the properties of chroma so that these problems can be avoided, and so that you can achieve the look you need for your project.

Hue

Colors, such as red, green, blue, orange, violet, and yellow, represent hue, which is the most distinctive, perceived property formed from wavelengths of light. The colors of the rainbow represent different hues, as do all of the colors in a box of Crayola crayons. Hue is the gradation of color within the visible spectrum, which (in the digital world of RGB colors) is shown as the angle (or phase) of the color wheel. See Figure 8.10.

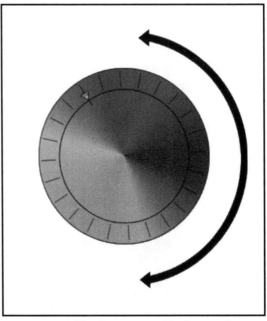

Figure 8.10 *Hue is represented by its angular direction around a color wheel.*

Saturation

Saturation describes the concentration (amount) of color in proportion to its brightness (see Figure 8.11). An image with saturated colors looks more vibrant, although too much saturation can cause an image to lose detail by eliminating differences in gradation. For example, the Chinese movie *Hero* contained many rich, saturated colors (exaggerating certain colors adds dramatic impact), as did the colors (or accents of color) in Technicolor musicals. The less white that is in an image, the more saturated it becomes. When a color is desaturated, it looks light or washed-out. Completely eliminating saturation, by lowering the saturation slider in color correction software, for example, yields a black-and=white image. On a color wheel, saturation is represented by the distance from the center of the wheel (the closer you are to the outer edge of the circle, the more saturated the hue becomes, and vice versa).

Additive and Subtractive Color

Primary colors can be added or subtracted from one another to produce other, more complex colors. In terms of computer displays, red, green, and blue (or RGB col-

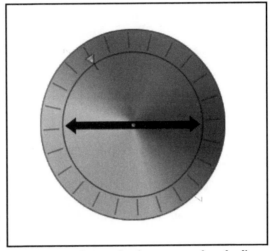

Figure 8.11 *Saturation is represented as the distance from the center of the color wheel.*

ors) are combined in precise quantities to produce virtually any color we can imagine. This system is based closely on the way the human eye sees color with rods and cones. As an additional note, all discussion in this section pertains to the properties of light and the colors it produces.

Adding one color to another produces a completely new "additive" color, while still consisting of the original colors. The principle example of this concept is white light. When red, green, and blue lights are added together, the resulting light appears white. In nature, this phenomenon is exhibited by using a prism to separate white light into its primary colors. I'm sure you remember the acronym for the color spectrum—ROY G. BIV, or red, orange, yellow, green, blue, indigo, violet; a more detailed rendering of color, but analogous to how the human eye and a computer perceive color. In fact, the human eye is more sensitive to green light than red or blue, which means that video and computer displays are biased toward green and mix RGB components in slightly unequal quantities.

By subtracting one of the three primary colors (RGB) from white light, other secondary or "subtractive" colors can be produced as well. For example, when green is subtracted from white light, red and blue are left, producing magenta. The three secondary, or subtractive, colors are magenta, cyan, and yellow.

- Red + Green + Blue = White
- Red + Blue = Magenta
- Blue + Green = Cyan
- Red + Green = Yellow

VIDEO VERSUS PAINT

Colors of light, such as those produced by video and film, differ from paint in the way they interact and are combined. In fact, paint, and similarly applied colors, belong to a different system, which utilizes red, blue, and yellow as its primary colors. When all of these colors are combined, they produce black. Conversely, when all colors of light in video are combined, they produce white.

When a color is subtracted to produce another color, it is called a "complementary" color. For example, magenta's secondary color is green, since magenta is produced by subtracting green from white light. In the same way, cyan's complementary color is red, and yellow's complementary color is blue. You can easily find a specific color complement by looking at a color wheel. Whichever color is directly opposite of another on the wheel (180 degrees around the circle) indicates that it is complementary. If a color is at "3 o'clock" on the wheel, its complementary color is at "9 o'clock." Since the majority of color correction software now includes a visual representation of a color wheel, it is a simple visual process to locate complementary colors. Knowing how to find a complementary color is particularly important in terms of color correction for removing color casts in an image. By shifting a yellowish image toward blue (yellow's complementary color), you can remove the unwanted tinting that typically occurs with indoor lighting when a camera has not been properly white balanced.

Color Space

Color space is the system that describes how color information is represented on a screen. Computers, video cameras, and graphics systems all have a variety of possible color spaces that can be used to display images, depending on the applications that are used and the type of equipment needed to produce the pictures.

ITU-R BT.709 versus ITU-R BT.601

Although video color space is a complex topic, it can be reduced to a few possible systems for our discussion. All video that is HD or HDV conforms to the ITU-R BT.709 standard, which differs from its SD counterpart ITU-R BT.601. Converting between the two color spaces produces unpredictable results, although it is done all the time when down-converting HDV to DV, or when producing DVDs of your finished HD projects. To most viewers, the difference is negligible. However, when color correction is involved, it is much more critical that you stay within the original color space of your video. HDV should remain in the ITU-R BT.709 color space until you have finished editing, color correction, and effects work. Of course, this assumes that your NLE and its intermediate codec (if it uses one) maintains this relationship. Final Cut Pro 5 is one application that intelligently preserves the correct color space when working with HD and SD formats. However, there are some applications that convert ITU-R BT.709 to ITU-R BT.601 when the video is captured. Check with the software manufacturer for the NLE or graphic's application that you use to make certain ITU-R BT.709 is supported.

RGB versus Y'CbCr

Although RGB is the standard additive color model used for computer images, Y'CbCr describes the color space used for digital video images. You may be familiar with the YUV notation used for video as well, although this is just a generic way of describing a system with one luminance and two color differences. Y'CbCr is the more specific and correct notation for digital video formats. Essentially, Y'CbCr consists of luma and chroma information (brightness and color) as three separate components wrapped together, similar to the three separate components of an RGB signal (although encoded differently). In this instance, Y' corresponds to the luma information, or the perceived brightness of individual pixels, while Cb and Cr contain all of the information for hue (chroma). The final image is constructed from a "color difference" process that handles chroma separately from luma and extracts the necessary picture information by relating the different channels to each other. The Y'CbCr system is generally more efficient than RGB for video, where bandwidth can be saved by reducing resolution in the Cb and Cr chroma components while relying more on Y' (luma, or brightness), which human vision is more sensitive to. Overall (by trading luma and chroma information in ways that take advantage of human vision), little if any quality is lost in the final image.

Color Sampling

Color sampling (designated, for example, by 4:2:0 for HDV) is yet another, and very important, way to gauge the quality of color for a particular format. As discussed, the properties of color are composed (primarily) of luma and chroma information. In video devices, chroma information is reduced to make space for more data for a particular format, which is essentially another form of compression. Each video format may sample luma and chroma differently than another, and there can be a significant difference in quality, particularly when comparing highly compressed, low-end formats to less compressed, high-end film and broadcast formats. Since luma information, as perceived by the human eye, is the most important aspect of a color, information for luma is sampled more often than color. In fact, luminance is sampled once for every pixel, while color is usually sampled only in blocks of four or less pixels (the exception is film or formats with 4:4:4 color sampling, such as HDCAM SR, which do not sacrifice any color information). For DV, which uses 4:1:1 color sampling, this means that luminance is sampled for every pixel, while color is sampled for only a single row of four pixels (color resolution is compressed horizontal). Color sampling of 4:2:0, for HDV, indicates that luma is sampled for every pixel, while chroma is sampled for two rows in groups of two pixels each (color resolution is compressed horizontally and vertically). Basically, HDV and DV have about half the color resolution of 4:2:2 formats like DVCPRO HD, while 4:2:2 formats are half of the resolution of full color 4:4:4 formats. The higher the color sampling numbers, the more color resolution exists, which produces better quality images. This is also important for pulling good chroma keys (discussed in Chapter 10 "Creating Graphics and Effects for HDV"), which require greater color resolution to produce smooth edges to extract a subject from a blue or green screen backdrop.

Calibrating an External Monitor

Calibrating a monitor is necessary for maintaining consistent image quality. If you are using a monitor to judge color accuracy, it is important that what you see matches the true levels of your video. It is also important to make certain that it will look the same when displayed on other monitors and televisions. As a measure of accuracy and to assist in the calibration of display devices, color bars were created. Most prosumer and professional video cameras include color bars that can be added to the beginning of a tape. You can then use those color bars when capturing or color correcting your video, to make certain that your display matches the levels for your video.

If you own a professional CRT monitor, apart from an extra computer display, you can follow the steps below to calibrate it properly. For most users, this will probably be a standard definition NTSC or PAL monitor, which can be used to approximate values for HD and to see what a down-converted image will look like before outputting to DVD or another SD format. An SD monitor will never produce the same results as an HD monitor, although it is often close enough for approximating settings (particularly for those who cannot afford a true HD monitor). Before setting up your CRT monitor, and prior to viewing any color critical projects, turn on the monitor and allow it to warm up for at least 15 minutes.

1. Generate SMPTE color bars on your video monitor by using the color bars built into your NLE, video tape, or output by another video application.

   Make certain that the bars are true SMPTE (some of the bars you find on the Internet might not be correct). If you own a camera that can generate true SMPTE color bars, they can be output to a monitor to assist in calibration. Some cameras output full field bars, which are not intended to be used with the "blue only" switch on professional monitors, although they still can be used to help with matching one monitor, camera, or similar videotape to another.

SMPTE

SMPTE, or the Society of Motion Picture and Television Engineers, sets guidelines for the film and video industries with its standards and test materials. You can learn more about SMPTE by visiting their Web site at www.smpte.org.

2. In the bottom right corner of the screen, find the three gray bars of differing shades (these are the PLUGE bars, or Picture Lineup Generating Equipment), which correspond to values for brightness measured in IRE.

   The goal is for the middle bar to be black, the right bar to be a dark gray, and the left bar to be black and blending into the middle bar.

3. Adjust the brightness control (also called *black level*) until the middle gray bar becomes black (the 7.5 PLUGE bar represents absolute black for North America, although even in this country it may vary based on the way digital to analog converters handle their black levels).

4. Turn the contrast all the way up until this gray bar becomes very bright, and then bring it back down until it becomes barely visible (with the correct contrast setting, the bar should be barely visible).

5. Activate the Blue Only button on your monitor.

   Blue Only causes all three CRT guns to show the blue signal, which makes the picture appear black and white (some professional LCD screens, such as Sony's LUMA monitors include a Blue Only button). See Figure 8.12. If you are trying to calibrate a monitor that does not have a Blue Only button, you may look at the monitor through a Wratten 47B deep blue filter, which you can find at a camera store, or by turning off the red and green guns on your monitor (if your monitor is set up with separate red, green, and blue controls). When Blue Only is activated, all of the bars should appear as alternating light and dark lines.

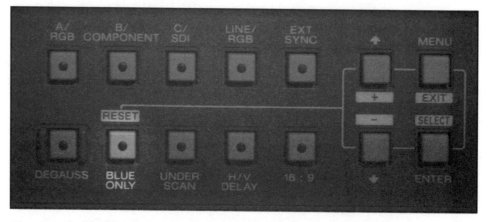

Figure 8.12 *The Blue Only button is used when calibrating a professional monitor.*

6. The monitor is calibrated properly if all of the lines appear evenly gray or black.

   The Chroma control can be adjusted to make the outer gray bars match and the Phase can be adjusted to make the inner bars match.

WHAT IS BROADCAST SAFE?

The term *broadcast safe* is used to describe whether levels are suitable for viewing on a NTSC or PAL television monitor. If you are producing content that will be seen in standard definition formats, such as DV, Digital Betacam, or delivered on a DVD, it is important that your luma and chroma values correspond to correct levels for those formats. Colors that are too bright or outside the limits for that delivery system will either bleed together at the edges (the color red is particularly noticeable) or actually produce an audible buzz in the sound track, caused by the overlap of video information into the audio area (white levels in text are a common culprit).

To insure that your levels are safe for broadcast or viewing on a television, you may choose to apply a broadcast safe filter to your video clip or sequence. These filters clamp down, or restrict, the levels that are too high. HDTV signals are not as restricted as SD formats, such as NTSC or PAL, since HDTV conforms to a digital system with a wider display range (similar to a computer monitor). In Chapter 10 "Creating Graphics and Effects for HDV," specific levels for working with graphics are discussed.

Using Video Scopes

As with any medium that requires a degree of accuracy, it is important to have the right tools for measuring and assisting with adjustments. Carpenters use tape measures and levels; film and video professionals have light meters and video scopes. Without video scopes, we would not have a good way to gauge "correct" color. Scopes are an integral part of the color correction process, and they are necessary for any professional color correction work that you do.

In the past, all video scopes were a piece of hardware that was fed an analog signal from a deck or camera. Although you will still find video scopes sitting next to a camera on a set or mounted next to an editing system, the majority of digital video producers use software to achieve the same results, at a lower cost and with less space. In this section, we'll talk about the most used scopes, the waveform monitor and vectorscope, although other tools, such as the histogram, are available for advanced users.

Waveform Monitor

A waveform monitor is an oscilloscope (a device that represents an electrical signal on a graph), which is specifically designed to show luma levels for a video signal ranging from 0% to 100%. (The scale extends slightly beyond these values in both directions.) See Figure 8.13. As you raise your white values, the waveform monitor shows those values approaching 100%, and as you lower your black levels, they approach 0%. Ideally, all white levels are between 90% and 100%, while black levels are the lowest between 0% and 7.5%, depending on the video standard that is used. Some analog, SD video signals, like NTSC in Japan, use 0% for blacks while the U.S. is restricted to 7.5%. (Video levels are also measured as IRE, which stands for Institute of Radio Engineers—an organization that sets standards for video measurement.) However, these levels are only for analog formats and do not pertain to digital television signals, such as HDTV.

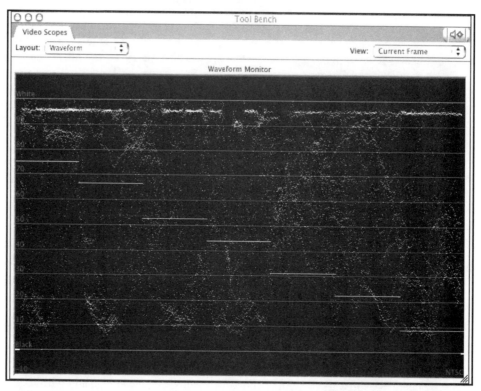

Figure 8.13 *The waveform monitor is useful for checking luma values, or the brightness of your image.*

Based on the way your scopes are set up (see the "Video Scopes and Ranges" note in this section), areas of an image whose white values extend beyond 100% are "blown out" (clipped) or completely white with no detail (such as bright windows, reflections, or other light sources). Since HDTV is a digital system, it can represent a wider range of luma, or brightness, without "clipping." The entire range from 0 to 100 could be used, although it is still smart to keep levels "broadcast safe" for possible NTSC and PAL standard definition delivery. You can tell exactly what levels are assigned to areas of an image by reading the waveform like you would a picture; only instead of color, pixels, and other image details being presented, you simply see the image as a graph of luma levels written left to right, with values on the up and down axis. For example, if there is an overly bright area of your picture in the upper right corner of the frame, the upper right corner of the waveform displays those values with a very high level approaching 100%.

VIDEO SCOPES AND RANGES

Digital video scopes may be set up differently to gauge levels, and may vary from one system or software application to the next. For example, with the video scopes in Final Cut Pro, broadcast safe, 8 bit video values (16 to 235) range from 0% (corresponding to 16) to 100% (equal to 235). Thus, the full scale from 0 to 100 can be used while maintaining "safe" video levels for standard definition formats (simplifying the process of reading scopes). Make certain that you first understand the process that your software (or hardware) uses to gauge your video levels, or make adjustments to match the way you like to work.

Vectorscope

A vectorscope is another type of oscilloscope that represents color, or chroma, instead of luma (see Figure 8.14). Included in this information is the hue and saturation of the colors that are represented on-screen. The main difference in reading a vectorscope is that it is displayed as a color wheel, instead of as a traditional x, y graph (like a waveform monitor). Hue is displayed as the angle, or direction, a line is pointing around the wheel, and saturation is indicated by how far those lines extend from the center of the wheel (less saturated colors are toward the center, and more saturated colors are further from the center).

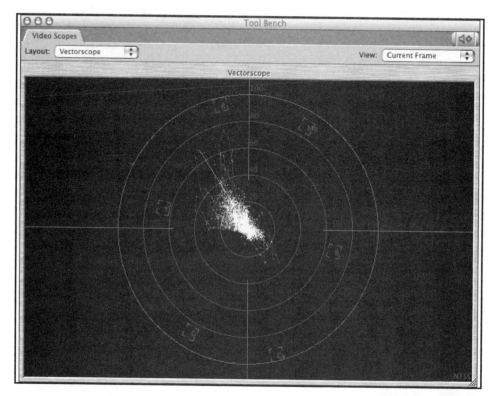

Figure 8.14 *The vectorscope is useful for checking chroma values.*

You can think of a vectorscope like a clock, with colors arranged around the outer edge where the numbers would be located. Red is at 11:30, blue at 3:30, and green at 7:00. The "color vector" is the angle that the hour hand is pointing, while the saturation is represented by the distance from the center of the clock (halfway is 50% saturation, etc.). Black, white, and gray colors are represented as dots in the center of the vectorscope. Color values range from 0 to 360 degrees in a counter-clockwise direction around the wheel. Vectorscopes are particularly useful for telling what areas of an image are oversaturated, and where values need to be lowered to avoid smearing, which occurs most often on SD (NTSC and PAL) monitors.

In addition to judging your levels during color correction, a vectorscope (as well as a waveform monitor) on set is the best way to adjust values while shooting, which can help to correct flaws that are not easy to fix in post. For example, if you are shooting blue screen or green screen shots on a stage, a vectorscope can help you to make sure your screen is evenly lit. By looking for a flat line in the blue range of your vectorscope, you can detect any areas that are not properly lit, resulting in different shades of blue or green, which can make keying difficult.

RANGE CHECKING WITH ZEBRA STRIPES

Range checking luma and chroma information with zebra stripes (see Figure 8.15), the white bars that (when activated) appear over your video image on the screen, can be helpful to avoid overexposing or oversaturating your images. If your white levels are too bright, over 100% for example, zebra stripes will show you where they are on your image, so that you can reduce their values. Ideally, you would look at zebra stripes on your camera while recording your video, in order to avoid overexposing an image, which results in a loss of detail that can never be regained. In post-production, range checking makes certain that your video is properly balanced and safe for viewing on all television sets. (See the previous note on "Broadcast Safe" for further discussion on this topic.)

Figure 8.15 *Zebra stripes are a range checking tool, which helps you avoid overexposing an image.*

Secondary Color Correction

Secondary color correction is the process of changing the color values in one area of an image without affecting other areas. For example, changing the color of someone's shirt from red to blue, without affecting other colors in the scene, is an example of secondary color correction. To achieve this effect, you must first isolate a range of colors that you want to keep (see Figure 8.16). If the shirt you want to change is red, then you can use an Eye Dropper tool or special slider controls to select this range of color. After your color is selected, you can spin the hue wheel or click to select another part of the color spectrum to replace it, in addition to adjusting saturations and luma controls.

While secondary color correction is most often used for subtle color adjustments and enhancement, it can be used to create a dramatic effect. Most famously, the movie *Pleasantville* used secondary color correction to keep certain colors while desaturating the rest of the picture. Recently, *Sin City* used a similar technique (although a bit more advanced) to add impact with colors selectively reintroduced to its black-and-white landscapes (the original video was shot in color and desaturated). This is actually quite easy to do with most NLEs or color correction software. Simply select the color you want to keep, using your secondary color correction tools, and bring down the saturation slider for the rest of your video. (In Final Cut Pro, for example, these tools are found by twirling down the triangle at the bottom of the visual color correction window.)

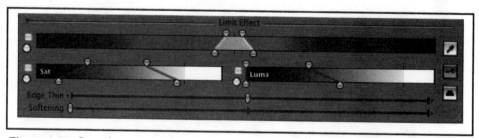

Figure 8.16 *Secondary color correction tools isolate and manipulate specific colors in an image.*

Simulating a Film Look

Film is a medium that produces unique colors, which are difficult to replicate accurately with video. At least, that has been the case in the past. With the latest crop of "film-look" software and plug-ins for your NLE or motion graphics applications, it is possible to create images that appear to have originated on film. Of course, the effect is not always perfect, since the way your scene was lit, as well as the colors you have chosen for your production design, can determine the exact results. Also, the tonal range of video does not match that of film, so the range of luma and chroma information is not as great. Still, these effects are unique and can go a long way toward getting a stylized look for your video.

Magic Bullet Suite and Magic Bullet Editors

Magic Bullet, the most popular film-look software in use today, is an After Effects plug-in created by a visual effects company called "The Orphanage" and sold through Red Giant Software. This software is sold in two versions—one version for After Effects called *Magic Bullet Suite* (see Figure 8.17), and a stripped down version for popular NLEs called *Magic Bullet Editors*. Both sets include a module called *Look Suite* (see Figure 8.18), which provides several practical presets, based on popular movies, for achieving that elusive film look. For example, there are effects called *Neo* (*The Matrix*), *Ohio and Mexicali* (*Traffic*), *Bleach Bypass* (*Saving Private Ryan*), in addition to 50 other looks.

Each of these looks can be customized by opening the effect's controls and adjusting parameters in categories like Subject, Lens Filter, Camera, and Post. There are also simple looks, that are not necessarily based on a particular movie, but can help to create film-like contrast and diffusion, such as Basic Warm, Basic Cool, Basic White Diffusion, Max Contrast, and many others. There are also various tints or sepia looks that can be applied to give your image an overall color cast. The Magic Bullet Editors software, which is actually packaged as a free add-on with some cameras, includes these same looks, although it does not include some of the more advanced effects of the Magic Bullet Suite software for After Effects. However, there is an additional module for Magic Bullet Editors called *MisFire*, which makes it possible to simulate old film that is scratched, dirty, stained, or even jittery. Perhaps most practically, there is a vignette effect, which is seen in many stylized productions, such as music videos.

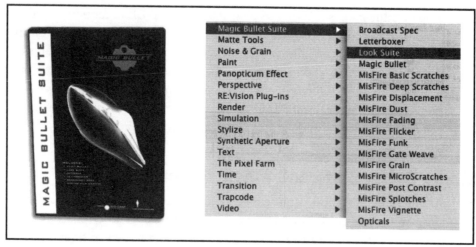

Figure 8.17 *Magic Bullet Suite includes several options for making your video look convincingly like film.*

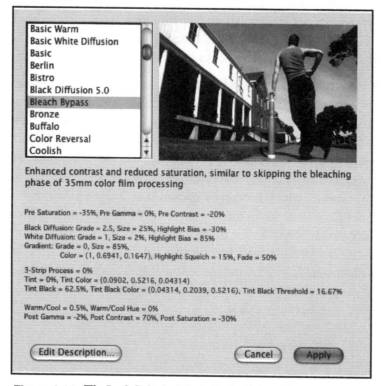

Figure 8.18 *The Look Suite in Magic Bullet Suite software includes presets for achieving specific film looks with little effort.*

In addition to different looks, including film damage, the Magic Bullet Suite set of plug-ins for After Effects includes the ability to remove some digital artifacts and soften sharp edges, which are another clue you are looking at video. It is also able to de-interlace your footage from 60i to 24p or 30p (for example), which can be an important step if you plan on transferring to film, or if you want to replicate film motion, as well as color and contrast. There are also options for applying Broadcast Spec levels to your video, as well as letterboxed looks, and true, film lab style dissolves and fades with opticals.

CineLook 2

DigiEffects CineLook 2 is a faster and more streamlined version of their original CineLook product, which includes various film looks and film motion effects (see Figure 8.19). Like Magic Bullet, the latest version of CineLook supports both SD and HD video. Instead of using unique categories to simulate specific combinations of colors from popular films, CineLook's main purpose is to replicate the look of a particular film stock, such as those from Kodak or Fuji. It comes pretty close to specific stock in many instances by matching the color curves of film, although you might want to dial back the grain a bit. In fact, this plug-in is particularly useful for its control of grain, which can help to simulate 8mm, 16mm, and 35mm stocks, as well as the ability to manually adjust curves, in case you want to create a film stock of your own. In addition to working in After Effects, CineLook 2 will also work within Final Cut Pro and Motion.

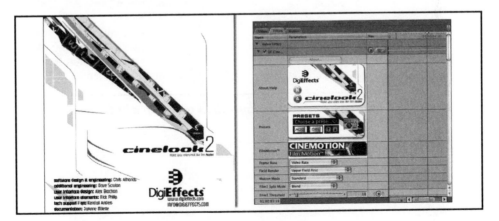

Figure 8.19 *CineLook 2 is good at replicating specific film stocks, which can be selected from a list of presets or created manually.*

Nattress Film Effects

For users of Final Cut Pro, another, inexpensive option is available for reproducing the look of film. The Nattress "Film Effects" plug-ins provide several of the most common treatments (customizable presets), such as Basic Bleach, Basic Sepia, Basic Diffusion, Basic Warm, Basic Cool, Day For Night, and others, as well as conversion of 60i formats to 24p (50i conversion to 25p), for accurate film motion. In addition the G Nicer plug-in, included with Film Effects, can improve your HDV by applying chroma sharpening to your 4:2:0 video. Check out www.nattress.com for more information on these and other plug-ins for Final Cut Pro.

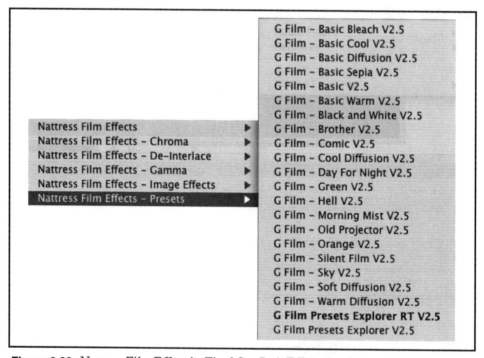

Figure 8.20 *Nattress Film Effects in Final Cut Pro's Effects dropdown menu.*

Chapter 9

Editing and Mixing Audio

An integral part of any successful video program is high quality audio. Like video, this relies not only on what happens in post-production, but also what occurs as it is produced in a studio or real-world environment. Once the material is committed to tape, it's important to understand how to improve the areas where it falls short and enhance the qualities that make it work. In this chapter, we'll discuss some of the areas that should assist you in the creation and editing of good audio. In addition, interviews with audio professionals should enhance your understanding of the creative process and provide you with practical advice and inspiration for improving your own projects.

Each time you begin a new video production, you should consider how to achieve the best possible audio within the budget you are allowed. This sometimes means making due with considerably less equipment and resources than you would like. However, even low budget and no budget productions can achieve good quality audio if you adhere to a few basic principles.

Capturing Audio

After you have acquired audio for your production using built-in or external mics (as discussed in Chapter 4), it is time to capture that material using your computer's microphone input, FireWire, or USB port (if coming from your camera or an external device), or through a separate hardware card. Since the majority of projects use audio from HDV source footage, it is probably safe to assume that most of the audio and video you capture is going to be input from an HDV camera or deck. Since HDV footage amounts to little more than a file transfer, there is less of a need to adjust audio and video as it is being captured. This means that levels do not need to be set or monitored as you are capturing, and the sync between audio and video is locked before it even gets into your system. Just remember that, in some software, you must select whether you want your audio tracks captured as two separate mono tracks or a single stereo pair. For video editing, it is generally easier to deal with audio as a stereo pair. Of course, you can always change your mind later and "unlink" your stereo tracks, in order to work with the left or right channels individually. The majority of work comes later, and includes the editing, mixing, and adding effects to your source material. However, a problem that one might encounter when working with HDV audio involves a difference in the sample rate of the source material and the project settings in your NLE.

Sample Rate Considerations

While it is not so important to monitor levels or make adjustments when capturing HDV audio and video, it is important to consider whether the settings of the camera used to capture audio material match the settings for the editing software you are using. Some HDV cameras may allow you to manually adjust the sample rate at which you record, thereby reducing the quality, but increasing the capacity for additional tracks of simultaneous audio.

For instance, JVC's GY-HD100 provides the capability to record up to four simultaneous tracks of audio onto an HDV tape. It does this by reducing the sample rate for all the tracks to 32kHz, down from the standard 48kHz for HDV. Although this reduces the quality of individual tracks, it does so with little perceptible loss in quality, while providing the ability to use multiple mics for live situations requiring additional coverage. If you have source material that was recorded at a different sample rate than what is typically used, make sure you adjust the audio capture settings in your NLE by selecting either 32kHz, 44.1kHz, or the default 48kHz. In addition, if you are importing audio from a CD (sound effects, music, etc.), you may decide to use a separate application, such as iTunes (see Figure 9.1), to convert your music from 44.1kHz to the correct sample rate for your project, before bringing it into your NLE. Simply make certain to adjust the import settings to the appropriate sample rate, such as 48kHz.

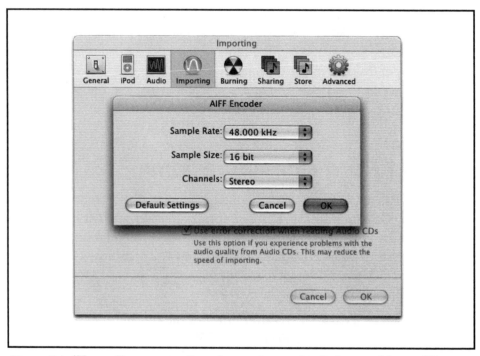

Figure 9.1 *iTunes allows you to adjust the sample rate of audio imported from a CD.*

Editing Multitrack Audio

Editing audio in an NLE is accomplished in much the same way as you would edit video material—the Timeline tools for cutting, inserting, and overlaying remain the same, as do the setting of in and out points. Still, audio is a different beast and requires an editor to not only think about the placement of elements in 2D space but 3D as well. For projects that use several layers of audio tracks, keeping these elements in a sensible order can be an exercise in frustration.

In the sections below, we'll discuss situations and techniques that are practical for your program if you are using an NLE, such as Final Cut Pro, to edit your audio. However, if you are serious about your audio, you may also choose to edit in a specialized application such as ProTools, Logic, SoundTrack Pro, Peak, or Audition. In that case, the tools and setup are a bit different, since video editing is not supported (although, depending on the software, you can view your video track as a guide), and emphasis is placed on tools for accomplishing complex audio editing and mixing tasks. In this section, the basic steps for mixing your audio tracks can be applied generally to most situations.

Although each production has different requirements, these steps should provide an example of what is involved for basic projects.

1. Adding audio to the Timeline.

   The first step of any audio editing project is the importing of materials (as discussed earlier) and the addition of elements to the Timeline. As we mentioned, working with audio clips in an NLE is similar to working with video, especially in instances where the audio and video were shot together. This is the easiest situation for editing audio since, by editing the video, most of the work has already been done for you. However, even in instances such as this, you may decide to add narration or sound effects to enhance the dynamics of your program, or separate out elements from one clip to add with another. This requires the creation of new tracks and methods for properly syncing new elements with material that is already in place.

2. Creating new audio tracks.

   The creation of new audio tracks is important if you want to layer sound elements in your project (see Figure 9.2). For example, if you are creating a documentary with narration, music, and sound effects, then you need at least three separate tracks (probably more, if you are working with stereo pairs) to layer the audio properly. Creating a music video, on the other hand, usually requires a single track for the music (two tracks for stereo), which has already been edited for you. Movies may require many more tracks for separately recorded lines of dialogue (including ADR, additional dialogue recording), music, and potentially many layers of sound effects. An NLE makes creating multiple audio (and video) tracks very easy. Just remember that the number of new tracks you can add is usually limited to approximately 99, or as many as your computer can handle at one time. In the same way that faster storage and CPUs can help with video, audio can benefit from an increase in system performance. If you are running an older machine with a minimum of memory, then you might be frustrated by sluggish performance when you try to preview a complex program with several layers of audio and video material; that is, if it does not crash your computer first.

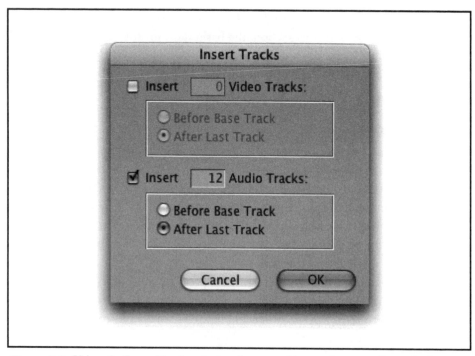

Figure 9.2 *Using the Insert Tracks window lets you add several new audio tracks (and video tracks) at one time.*

3. Syncing audio and video.

Probably the most important step in editing audio with video is the syncing of the two elements. Without proper syncing, the structure of your program falls apart. Therefore, it is important to make sure that all your tracks work in concert with each other.

Aside from the usual techniques of locking tracks as you work with them, which prevents tracks from being shifted or overwritten, and inserting clips into the Timeline, it is important to understand that you can adjust the sync mode, or linking, for clips as well. This means that audio and video can be made to move together as a single clip without the fear or inconvenience of losing their relative positions. In most NLEs, the joining of audio and video elements is handled by a link/unlink function. Using this feature, you can make sure that your original video and audio stay in sync, or you can add new effects and move clips around before linking them together. Linking clips in this way is a great method to insure that associated clips are always moved together. With several audio and video tracks in the Timeline, it is often difficult to keep track of where associated clips are located. For instance, if you had a sound effect on audio track 12 that absolutely needed to remain synced with a clip on video track 4, then you could link them together and move them around the Timeline without affecting their relative position to each other.

In addition to working with individually linked and unlinked clips, you should consider other ways to sync audio that was recorded separately from your video. For instance, if you recorded audio with a Mini-Disc, DAT, or hard disk recorder as you videotaped your actors, you would want to line up the different audio and video clips in the Timeline. This can be easily accomplished by using a "slate" when taping (see Figure 9.3). Slates are famous as the clapboards held in front of the camera before each take on a movie set. The board itself acts as a visual marker of where the scene begins, while the clapping sound, or beep on a digital slate, tells the editor where to line up the audio. To line up audio, you don't need a professional slate, although they can be useful, even for small productions. Instead, you just need to pick an easily distinguishable sound from both audio clips and line them up in the Timeline. If you are good with reading gestures, you might even try lining up audio with visual clues, such as watching the movement of an actor's lips to see where the vowel sounds are placed. After the clips are lined up in the Timeline, use the link/unlink function as described above to link them together, so that there is no danger of having to realign them at a later time.

Figure 9.3 *Slates provide audio and video sync with timecode or an audible sound that matches with the visual cue of snapping shut two boards (represented here by the slate icon for Final Cut Pro).*

4. Adjusting volume and placement.

After all your audio has been added to the Timeline and you are satisfied

with the order of clips, it is
time to make finer adjustments to the volume levels
and aural placement of your
sound (see Figure 9.4). The
first step in the process is to
add any transitions that you
might need between clips,
such as fades and crossfades.
After that comes the difficult
task of mixing all of your
tracks together in a way that
works best for your program.
A documentary, for example,
usually consists of an established structure, such as a
narration track, that plays in
the foreground over a musical
score with environmental
sound effects added as
needed.

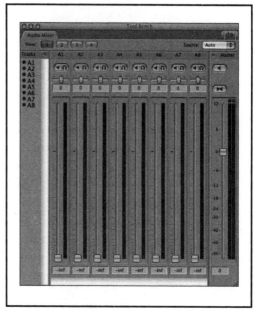

Figure 9.4 *Final Cut Pro provides adequate audio tools for simple editing and mixing tasks.*

5. Using an audio mixer.

When you have edited your audio and video tracks together in the Timeline and are ready to adjust the volume, pan, and balance for your program, it is time to launch an Audio Mixer window, or import your clips into a separate application, such as Logic or ProTools, which can handle the mixing tasks for complex projects better. With an Audio Mixer window opened, make sure that all the tracks you want to monitor are selected. If you want to turn off a track while monitoring, click the Mute button for that track. Use the transport controls to audition the various audio tracks.

As the track plays back, drag the volume fader to adjust levels for the track. Depending on the levels at which your audio was recorded, you might need to raise or lower the slider to compensate for the recording.

Make sure that you keep an eye on the VU meters (audio level meters), so they don't move into the red. In order to avoid distortion caused by "clipping," which is encountered when exceeding ordinary levels, the VU meters need to stay in the yellow (see Figure 9.5). This means that all audio should always remain below 0dB (decibels), while targeting a range of about -12dB for most productions. When you are asked to "master" your audio to a specific level, such as -12dB, you should make sure that your levels always return to this number, although they can go above (for loud sounds in your tracks) or slightly below for quiet moments. Anything above -6 is starting to get hot, although this can be alright as long as there is no clipping. Even if you don't see your audio clip in the meters, you may hear it as a "pop" in the soundtrack.

There is also a special interface in most NLEs and audio applications that is designed to make the process of adjusting the sound in your project easy through the use of automation (see Figure 9.6). This means that while playing back your audio sequence, you can make adjustments on the fly with the audio mixer. Your NLE (or audio application) records the changes and automatically applies them to your clips. The process is intuitive and easy to grasp after a few tries. It is the same method that

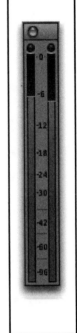

Figure 9.5 *It is important to keep the VU meters in the yellow to avoid clipping.*

is used in professional recording studios with large mixing boards, with faders that can do an eerie dance as the mix plays back. In the case of a documentary, for example, you might have a few tracks, such as narration, music, and sound effects that you want to mix together. In this case, you would need to launch an Audio Mixer window and "ride" the sliders as your sequence plays back. You can then go back and make adjustments while listening to your tracks. You can use the same techniques described to adjust the panning and balance. The Pen tool is also used to place keyframes for points where you want to change audio levels, such as when raising or lowering the volume for a loud noise, or when fading sounds in and out.

Figure 9.6 *Logic Pro's window provides controls for monitoring and adjusting levels for audio tracks. (Courtesy of Apple)*

Choosing an Audio Mixer

Audio mixers are a great help to engineers and even to video editors who are unfamiliar with traditional sound mixing. Using a mixer, you can easily "ride" audio levels as you play back your Timeline in your video or sound editing application, as well as change the panning and other effects that are applied in real time. Having physical sliders and knobs to move, instead of a mouse to move virtual sliders on a computer screen, is quicker, more tactile, and provides better accuracy. Many new devices include touch-sensitive, automated faders (such as the Mackie mentioned below, and other mixers by Tascam), which are motorized audio level sliders that move in tandem with the levels you set in your timeline. This feature insures that your levels on the mixer always match those in your software, while still allowing you to do quick adjustments on the fly.

Additional features include muting (turning tracks off) and soloing tracks (listening to one track, while instantly muting all others) as you preview your mix. Today, you can find many mixing boards that can be connected to your computer through FireWire, which may eliminate the need for a separate audio card or analog I/O (input/output) device. Simply connect the mixer to your computer's FireWire (or i.Link) port and (depending on the number and type of available inputs on the mixer) then connect your audio sources to the inputs on the mixer (including guitars, keyboards, vocal microphones, MIDI devices, and other sources). It may even be possible to send out audio from the mixer to other devices (in case you need to output your audio to CD, DAT, ADAT, or another format).

A good example of a new mixer that works well with most audio applications, as well as video editing software like Final Cut Pro 5 and others, is the Mackie Control Universal. (Although the number of input options is limited, it works well as a mixer, particularly for video applications, or when audio is input through other sources.) Mackie, like Tascam, Edirol, and others, is a respected name in audio circles, particularly with regards to their high-quality, clean-sounding analog and digital mixers (see Figure 9.7). As mentioned, the Mackie MCU device supports Final Cut Pro 5, as well as Apple's SoundTrack Pro application, and includes nice features for video editors, such as a timecode readout (timecode is shown in a separate LED display, while other information is displayed in a backlit LCD screen), transport controls (play, stop, jog, and shuttle), and assignable buttons.

Figure 9.7 *The Mackie Control Universal is an excellent digital mixer, particularly when used with applications like Final Cut Pro 5 and SoundTrack Pro.*

Adding Sound Effects

When working with audio, the last step is usually to enhance the material you have recorded or correct difficult problems with effects. Fortunately, most NLEs (all audio editing/mixing applications) include several useful effects for you to work with. They can be used for a variety of purposes, but are most effective when used to enhance material or to remove unwanted noises in your clips. In the sections below, we mention a few of the most useful effects, such as Reverb and Echo. There are a number of other effects you can apply to your program to improve the quality of your material. These include various EQ controls, delays, chorus, flange, and compressors.

Whichever effects you choose to apply, be certain that you use them in moderation where necessary. You should also be aware that, once several effects are added together, they may cancel each other out, or introduce more noise and distortion than was in your original source material. Keep it simple whenever possible and think about enhancing the material that is already there, rather than adding more effects that may be noticeable to your audience. If you are itching to try something different, work with the edits first, by adding a clip or shifting existing ones; then once you are nearly satisfied with the results, start playing around with some effects to see what works and what doesn't.

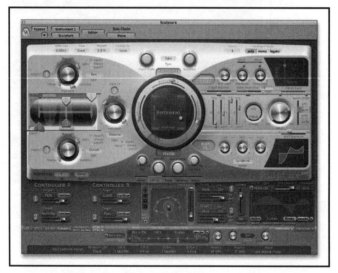

Figure 9.8 *Most NLEs and audio editing software include several audio effects, such as reverb and echo, while some applications include advanced filters that include the ability to finely manipulate sound, such as Sculpture in Logic Pro. (Courtesy of Apple)*

Reverb

Reverb simulates the sound of a particular room size or environment. This can add a feeling of depth or "liveness" to your production, depending on the effect you are trying to achieve. For flat sounding audio, like narration recorded in a vocal booth, or instruments recorded in a small space, reverb can add another dimension that was lacking from the original recording. The Reverb effect in most NLEs is limited in comparison to the range of options you would find in a professional audio editing application like ProTools or Logic. However, for video productions, simple adjustments can be all that are required.

For example, if you want to combine a voice track that you recorded with your computer together with a background of environmental sounds like traffic and city noises, then you should consider using reverb to achieve a more realistic effect. This should help mask the fact that audio was recorded separately and in a dry environment.

The following steps illustrate how you might adjust reverb settings for an audio clip.

1. When in the Reverb setting window, make certain you have chosen the right algorithm for your clip by selecting either Room (Large), Room (Medium), or another type of space. This determines the size of the environment you are attempting to simulate (see Figure 9.9). For natural sounding vocals, a medium room should suffice. Although, if you were working with audio recorded in a gymnasium or large church hall, you should consider using a large room or large hall setting instead.

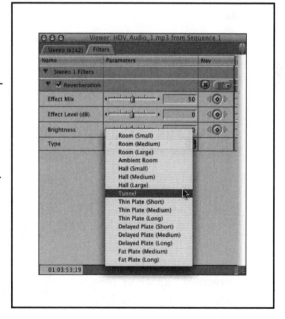

Figure 9.9 *With reverb, you can determine the overall size of the environment you want to simulate.*

2. Adjust the Mix setting to determine the amount of reverb applied to your source (or "dry") material. Audio engineers sometimes refer to an effected clip as "wet," while an unaffected clip is referred to as "dry." For natural sounding vocals, try setting your Mix to between 50 and 75 percent, depending on how pronounced you want the effect to be.

3. Next, set the "decay" to a shorter value and play with the diffusion control to achieve a sound that is a suitable distance from the listener. Decay determines the amount of time it takes a sound to dissipate. This means that a long decay value simulates a larger space. Diffusion determines how much the audio scatters, simulating a new distance between the source audio, such as a narrator, and the microphone. With a high diffusion value, audio that was recorded with a handheld mic can be made to seem like the speaker was standing farther away in the room.

4. Lastly, set the brightness to a slightly muted value. If you want sharper sounding audio, set the brightness to a larger Hz value. Brightness determines the amount of reflectivity, with brighter values simulating rooms with more hard surfaces.

Echo

In addition to reverb, an Echo effect is also available in most applications (see Figure 9.10). Like reverb, this too simulates the properties of a particular space. However, it is capable of creating some subtle ambient effects and other very unnatural results by continuously repeating audio clips. The bouncing effect it creates can be a useful addition if you want to create the illusion of a cavernous space or simply to add a unique rhythm to a sound effect or music clip.

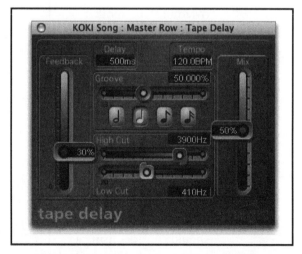

Figure 9.10 *Echo, or delay, allows you to repeat a sound to create rhythm or assist in simulating the properties of a space (especially when used together with reverb—delay is shown here as a "tape delay" effect).*

Other Audio Filters and Effects

The following are a few additional audio filters and effects that you might find in the audio filters portion of your video and audio editing software (listed here alphabetically). Although this list is not all-inclusive, it represents some of the most commonly encountered filters in a mixing environment (in addition to reverb and other effects mentioned elsewhere).

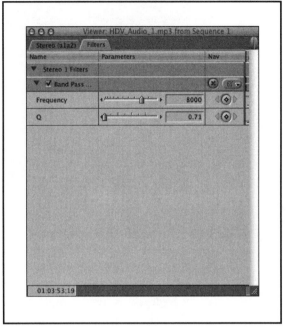

Figure 9.11 *Bandpass settings.*

◆ Bandpass—Modifies a single frequency band by narrowing or widening the range that is audible, thereby allowing only certain frequencies to pass through (hence the name). See Figure 9.11. Lower values provide the greatest audibility over the largest area of the band, while high values are more focused on the center and remove many of the frequencies on either side, above or below the selected band. High Pass, High Shelf, Low Pass, and Low Shelf effects discussed below are based on a Bandpass filter.

◆ Compressor/Limiter—Compresses the volume level over time to smooth out the dynamics of a track, similar to a peak limiter (see Figure 9.12).

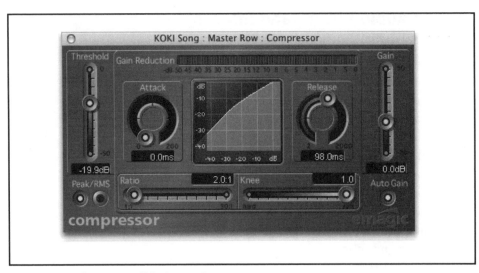

Figure 9.12 *Compressor/Limiter settings.*

◆ Delay—The same as echo (discussed above), which allows you to adjust the amount of repetitions of a sound, including the delay time between repeats and the feedback, or duration of the repeats.

◆ EQ—Divides the audio spectrum into separate frequency bands, which allows you to set a new center frequency for a specific band (ranging, for example, from 20Hz to 20,0000Hz). EQ, or equalization, is one of the most frequently used effects for adjusting the sound and dynamic range of audio, since it provides the greatest amount of control over specific frequencies (see Figure 9.13). A Graphic

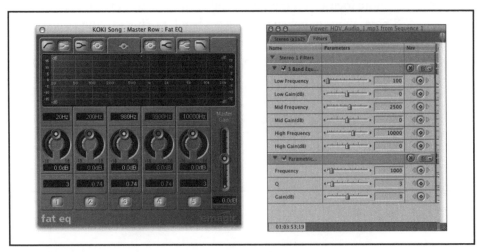

Figure 9.13 *EQ settings.*

EQ divides the spectrum into many frequencies (31 for example), while a 3-Band Equalizer uses three frequency bands—one for treble, mid range, and bass. Parametric EQ is a more specialized version that includes qualities of Bandpass (limiting the range to a single frequency band), as well as Notch and Shelf filters.

◆ High Pass filter—Removes low frequencies, while keeping the high frequencies intact. Useful for reducing low frequency sounds, such as distant traffic. See Figure 9.14.

◆ High Shelf filter—Cuts off the high frequencies, while allowing lower frequencies to pass through unharmed.

◆ Low Pass filter—Reduces high frequencies while allowing low frequencies to pass through without being effected. Although similar to a High Shelf filter, it does not cut the high frequencies as sharply. Useful for removing hiss and other high frequency noise from a clip. See Figure 9.15.

◆ Low Shelf Filter—Cuts off the low frequencies sharply, while allowing the high frequencies through.

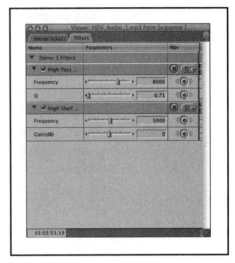

Figure 9.14 *High Pass and High Shelf settings.*

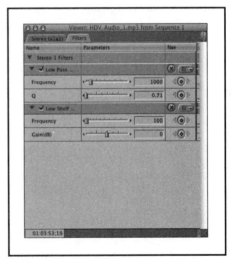

Figure 9.15 *Low Pass and Low Shelf settings.*

◆ Notch—Cuts out specific
frequencies in a narrow range, which
makes it useful for reducing the
loudness of a particular frequency
(such as a single note on an
instrument). See Figure 9.16.

◆ Peak Limiter—Compresses volume
levels over time to limit the loudness
of the audio, using attack and decay
settings to determine the speed of
the response.

◆ Vocal DeEsser—Uses a specialized
EQ to reduce the "s" sound in a
speaker's voice when it is especially
pronounced, particularly when using
a microphone that accentuates high
frequencies. See Figure 9.17.

◆ Vocal DePopper—Reduces the
breath sounds ("p" or puffing
sounds) that can create a popping in
the microphone when it is placed
too closely to a mouth.

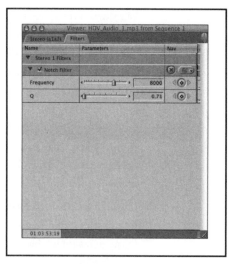

Figure 9.16 *Notch settings.*

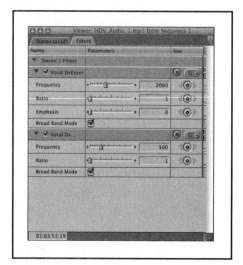

Figure 9.17 *Vocal DeEsser and Vocal DePopper settings.*

Interview:
Brian Emrich

Brian Emrich is a sound designer whose work is featured on director Darren Aronofsky's films (*Pi, Requiem for a Dream, The Fountain*), as well as *One Hour Photo, Wonderland,* and others.

What is your studio setup for working with audio (software and hardware)?

My main hardware tools are a Mac 125MHz DP G4 on OS X along with several FireWire drives, both internal and external, that contain all my sound libraries. I have a Pro Tools 192 HD system with one processing card and one accel card.

My main software is BIAS Peak and Pro Tools TDM. I rely heavily on Peak for most of my sound manipulation. It's also my main audio program for any kind of editing of music to digitizing my LP collection and cleaning up the tracks. I'm also beginning to use more plug-ins in Pro tools for sound design since there are so many nice high-end products available. In Peak and Pro Tools, my main plug-ins would be Pluggo & SFX Machine. I'm not yet a huge fan of soft synths, but I do use SampleTank 2 and Imposcar with decent results. I'm still big on hardware and have been collecting synths for years now—some of my favorites being the Roland Juno-60, Roland JP-8000, Sequential Circuits Pro-One, Moog Voyager, and my Hammond XK-2, which I use as my main controller. I've been composing with MIDI since 1986 and will do so for another 20 years. It's a great tool for creating.

I'm a big fan of vintage drum machines with the Roland TR-808, TR-909, and CR-78 on the top of my list.

With both film and TV commercials, I work to Quick Time movies and output this to a Sony 26" LCD television monitor via a MiroMotion DC30 Plus video card.

For field recording, I have a Sound Devices 722, which is a very high-end 2-Channel Portable Hard Disk Recorder, an HHB MDP500 Portable Minidisc Recorder, and a Sony PCM-M1 DAT Recorder. My main mics are the Neumann KMR-82i shotgun, a Sennheiser ME-66 shotgun, and a Shure VP-88 stereo.

I monitor through an Alesis RA-100 power amp into Alesis Monitor One speakers.

Is sound design for commercials different than long form projects?

(continued on next page)

(continued from previous page)

There are as many differences between the two worlds as there are similarities. The main difference being the time frame you have to work with. A commercial generally takes an average of two weeks for me to complete, while a movie can last around three months, including the final mix. Of course, commercials are only 30 to 60 seconds in length, while features are at least the 90-minute averages. The actual work is pretty much the same from creating my own sounds to recording Foley, but with commercials it's a one-man show and with films, you usually need a sound team to cover all the dialogue, Foley, and effects.

Can you give an example of a unique sound element you created for a commercial?

I just finished up a spot for Gatorade that called for the sound of athlete's bodies "shattering" during a rigorous workout. I temped in some stone crumbling on pavement sounds, but they were just too realistic for what we needed. The director really wanted to go all out with the design and make things more subjective, so I was able to let loose. This is a rarity in commercials and to top it off there was no music, just sound effects. I wanted to try out something new in the plug-in department, so I called up a plug-in Pro Tools called *Sci-Fi*, created by Digidesign. Sci-Fi adds analog synth-type ring modulation, frequency modulation, and variable frequency resonators to your audio. I applied it to the crumbling stone effect and within minutes I had what I needed—a great sizzling cracking sound with an amazing whiplike attack that brings you into it. Everyone in the mix was asking, "Where did you get that sound from?" I guess it was my secret until now!

What are some examples of unique sound elements you created for "Requiem for a Dream"? How were they created and mixed together?

When I work with sound I tend to use (or at least start) with organic sounds as much as possible. Overall, I don't like things sounding too processed and synthetic. So with the drug sequences in *Requiem*, I chose to use straightforward "real-life" sounds along with a few more designed sounds. I wanted the real sounds to match the actual picture and to ground the sequence in the beginning of the film—then to have it gradually morph into more designed and intense sounds as the movie progressed. It was my idea to complement the film with sound to help carry the listener/viewer on a journey deep into the dark side of chaos.

A lot of the root sounds in each of the drug sequences are the same, but I would use certain plug-ins to distort their character a bit more in each new sequence. I also reversed several sounds and spent hours upon hours trying different effects until I got a satisfying result. I'm very picky so sometimes it takes a while to nail what I want. I even used a kick drum from my Roland TR-909 drum machine to beef up the pills hitting Sara's hand. The LP-scratching type sounds and the kick drum ideas were chosen because Darren wanted to have a hip-hop feel with the editing, so I thought taking sound into this direction would help relay that feel much better, giving it an almost percussive element.

My most ambitious creation for *Requiem* was on a lake in a boat with an underwater mic hanging fifteen feet off the side. I then took a solid fuel rocket engine (the type used for model rocket enthusiasts), attached it to a wooden dowel for stability, and launched it into the water. I captured the engine fuel burning underwater and used this sound for the hypo-needle injection bubbling images.

One Hour Photo has a distinctive sound quality as well. What was it like creating sounds for that film?

One Hour Photo was a bit different to deal with because of director Mark Romanek and his way of working. He's a very talented music video director who made his film debut with OHP.

He tended to be more hands-on in every aspect of the film, so as to have more control over what was being created. When I first started on the film, I was able to create all kinds of really interesting soundscapes that he approved of highly. But when we got into the mix, he started pulling back quite a bit with what I had done and had the film take on a more subtle approach than he probably originally planned. I think he really wanted to have all the bases covered when we got to the mix and then sorted it out on the stage.

Overall, I took the same approach as in *Requiem* and worked with organic sounds for OHP. But what's different from *Requiem* was that I used a lot of synth drones that I manipulated to create certain moods, which complimented the music so much that it ended up sounding like part of the score.

(continued on next page)

(continued from previous page)

What is your approach to recording new sounds and creating Foley on a film?

With film I actually don't get too involved with the Foley aspect. That's a whole different world. Of course, there are times that I need to record specifics that I have to incorporate into my work and then possibly manipulate to get the results I need. I'll brainstorm until I get some ideas of what and where I have to record and then head out with my gear and capture what I need. I'll be heading down to Guatemala soon to record jungle ambience and Howler monkeys for Darren's film.

With commercials I tend to do a lot more Foley. With such a quick turnover time I need to get a list going of all the actions occurring in the spot and then decide where I'm going to record what I need. It can be anything from racing bikes to tennis playing to walking in the snow. I usually try to find the same type of environment as the commercial spot has just to keep things as realistic as possible.

Do you have a process, or systematic method, when creating sound design for a film?

I usually like to get involved with a film as early into the game as possible. This is not always the case, though. I might get hired close to the point of final picture lock and have to jump right in. What I do first is watch a tape of the most recent version of the film a couple times and take down notes and ideas. I then have some kind of spotting session with the director and get their input while giving my ideas up to this point. Then it's off to my home studio and sound library to assemble a palette of sounds I might need. This is a very important step to my work method, and it can take a solid couple of days' work to put together. I go through my fairly extensive library of prerecorded sounds, which range from the everyday stuff to the more off-the-wall stuff like drones and ambiences. I also have my libraries created from past projects, which do contain many unused sounds that I can put to good use. And if I need to go out and record some other live sounds, I will do so. Now that I have this large database of sounds together, I can dig in and begin my manipulation. It is at this stage that I really begin to put my imagination to work.

Do you discuss the sound elements in detail with the director or editor before work begins on a project?

With *Requiem* I was given the freedom to tackle all the obvious and not-so-obvious scenes and do my thing. Darren had complete trust in me and let me be as creative as I wanted. We had several spotting sessions, and my friend Craig Henighan at Sound

Dogs tackled all the other elements, excluding dialog and Foley. He also took on a few scenes that allowed him to be creative as well. We just kept in close contact— with me sending my sessions to Toronto to have everything merged together and checked out to make sure every aspect was covered. I have also been in the situation of never talking to the other sound designer/editors and having to create completely in my own environment. I then bring my files to the final mix and everything sorts itself out there. A bit scary, but it does happen.

I also like to be in contact with the composer as much as possible so I know what areas they are covering so I know to be prepared to have my stuff complement the score and not conflict with it. Chances are that if there is a conflict, the sound design is the first to go.

Do you have any special techniques or principals for editing audio?

I really like to work with sounds by putting together several separate bits of audio and sculpting one specific piece via Peak. Maybe this cuts out my options in a final mix, but I really feel more satisfied having created these "sound sculptures" that fit into place.

And if something doesn't sound quite right in a scene, I need to redo it. Everything has to feel right to me in order to make the grade.

Can you describe a particularly problematic audio editing/mixing situation that you have encountered?

My worst experience was when I started work on *Requiem for a Dream*. I was using Pro Tools Free slaved to a consumer VCR. Talk about a nightmare! Trying to cue up all those quick cuts in the drug sequences was almost impossible. At least a dozen or so edits back-to-back of ten frames each that needed specific sound cues. Boy, did I panic. Luckily, the guys up at Sound Dogs in Toronto, who were covering the rest of the sound, came to my rescue with an install for Pro Tools Power Mix, which allowed me to use QuickTime movies instead of tape. This saved me. I was still limited to only eight voices playing at one time, making it very tricky in trying to monitor a proper mix. On top of this, it was the first time I'd ever used Pro Tools, so I had the learning curve to deal with, not to mention the most important aspect of being creative. Up until now, I have done all my films with this setup, and I've somehow managed to pull it off.

(continued on next page)

(continued from previous page)

How do you manage large projects with many elements and tracks?

So far all the projects I've been on allow me to dictate the intensity of the elements. I tend to keep things more or less manageable when it comes to track count. I don't like a lot of clutter. And I don't like to make too many options either. When I spend time developing a sound for a certain event, then that's what I want for that event. Sure there might be several other elements that work together, but I don't go crazy with options. I make the decision from the start with what I want to hear. If the director wants me to change it at some point, then I'll have to make the changes needed. And some directors cringe if there is too much to wade through in the F/X department during a final mix.

Where do you find inspiration for your work?

That's a hard one to nail down for me. First and foremost, I'm a musician, and I think I pull a lot of ideas and applications from a musical standpoint. Maybe I'm a sound designer crying out for the attention that a composer gets so I push the boundaries a bit farther than normal. I also have a dark side to myself, and I tend to veer towards moodier and even scarier sounding elements. This is the sort of stuff that comes very easy to me.

What projects have you been working on lately?

Lately, I've been quite busy with TV commercials. I've been doing a lot of high-end jobs like Nike, Gatorade, Coke, and Propel Sports Water. All of these called for a fair amount of work. Especially the Nike and Gatorade. Lots of sports-related effects and crowd reactions. I'm also in the beginning stages of work on Darren Aronofsky's next feature called *The Fountain*. It's his biggest and most ambitious movie to date. It's been in the works for several years now and at this point they are just beginning to edit picture. I'll be involved now for the next six months as sound designer and co-supervising sound editor. A very intense project that will definitely turn some heads.

Do you have any anecdotes or other interesting experiences relating to sound design that you would like to share (something you haven't had the occasion to discuss)?

Last year I worked on a very interesting and challenging project for the National Underground Railroad Freedom Center in Cincinnati Ohio that recently opened its doors last summer. I was hired to do the sound design for three pieces of animation that are now being shown in the main theater of the museum. They were each created by artists from different parts of the world and had to do with the subject of slavery and the Underground Railroad in America. The total time of all three pieces combined is about 12 minutes long. This didn't seem like a lot to me, but when I started to get into it, I realized how time consuming doing sound for animation could be. I traveled to several locations within a 200 mile radius of my studio and even went to Florida to record sound for this. Since there is no production sound existing in animation like in film and sometimes commercials, I naturally had to cover every aspect of these animation pieces. And two of them were basically real life episodes of slaves and their escape to the north during the 1800s. It was probably the most time-consuming job to date for me, but also one of the most rewarding. I had to go swimming in an outdoor pool in March to record myself kicking around in the water and almost froze to death! I had to climb trees, make fires, find an old cabin in the woods to record in, run through weeds, rattle chains, walk through foot deep mud and swampland, rattle dishes, peel potatoes, you name it I did it. At one point, I was out in the boonies on a nature trail recording myself running in place with bare feet, and the mic was picking up my pants rubbing together. I had to take my pants off and re-record, so there I was standing in the middle of nowhere in my underwear running in place thinking to myself, that if anyone were to walk down that trail and see me, I'd probably be spending the rest of the day in jail explaining what I was doing.

Composing a Score

The composition, or creation, of a musical score may be achieved in a number of ways. For professional musicians and others familiar with music theory and composition, the creation of a soundtrack may begin with pen and paper, timing bars of music to action on-screen. Additionally, musicians may play along with the movie, overlaying tracks of synthesizers, guitars, or orchestral instruments in multiple passes, until they arrive at the best emotional and dramatic results. Usually, looking at timecode readouts and syncing audio with a master video clip is a good method for today's digital musician (for example, Logic and SoundTrack Pro are two applications that include the ability to sync a video clip with your audio tracks).

For those who do not have the musical background or time to create a score from scratch, licensing music from a sound library is an option. (Make certain to carefully check the terms and usage rights for any audio, even if it is listed as royalty-free.) There are a number of "stock" audio companies that specialize in music for films and short programs. Of course, the main drawback to using purchased music is the fact that it is not original, and has probably been used in several other productions already. You may also consider enlisting an unsigned band or musical group eager for exposure to come up with some music for your production, although you should always make sure to obtain signed agreements (to avoid legal disputes over future royalties—for example, if your film gets picked up by a studio—and battles with record labels that may sign a band or artist).

There is also another option to creating a musical score (even for the "un-musically" inclined), and that is the use of audio loops, assembled in software such as Acid, SoundTrack Pro, and GarageBand. With loops, you can easily lay down a drum track, strings, and other instruments, which play continually in sync with your music. You may change the pitch, duration, and tempo of a track with loops, and easily line up audio with your video. Loops may also be used to throw together a temporary score quickly as a reference for an editor or composer, which is later replaced by a more professional soundtrack. Once again, using loops can sound "canned," particularly if you are using loops included with the software. If you are using loop-based audio to create the final score for a film, consider building up your tracks with original loops that you, or another composer, has created specifically for the project, or stick with beats and less recognizable sounds, while adding original melodies with other instruments on top.

Figure 9.18 *GarageBand (included as part of Apple's iLife suite of software) is an inexpensive application for creating soundtracks with loops, although you may also add guitars, MIDI devices, and other instruments to the mix. (Courtesy of Apple)*

Interview:
Robert Hill

Robert Hill is an audio producer and engineer who has worked with several recording artists, including Peter Gabriel, Seal, Madonna, William Orbit, Korn, Bush, Beth Orton, and Marz, in addition to work on films and British TV ads.

Do you have any tips for creating custom audio loops from sampled instruments, percussion, or bits of dialogue?

To start with, make sure you legally own the sample, or you can disguise it enough that it won't be recognized. Then, realize that in the digital domain the more you treat audio, the more affected it will sound, so keep that in mind when selecting samples you are going to loop. Whether you're changing tempo and pitch, or just tempo—the further you go from the tempo of the sample, the more the sound will change. However, speeding a sample up is easier for a computer to do and will sound more authentic than slowing one down.

If you are looping a sound that runs into itself, like a drum loop or something similar, it is imperative that you make sure the transition is smooth and feels natural. If your sample is edited to the correct length (and if it is always played at this length), that will govern whether you play the sample to the end, or if you a note on a MIDI keyboard trigger the length to be played. If the latter is the case, adjusting the MIDI note length and the sample release should give you the feel you want. Chopping up your sample, either by hand or with an application like Re-cycle, can give you a different feel and more playback flexibility.

How do you usually remove noise or unwanted sounds from a prerecorded track?

This depends on how much noise you have, in addition to the amount and type of audio. First, go down the processor avenue. For vocals, and a more delicate noise reduction, try an expander. For a more severe effect, use a gate—giving the gate an external trigger may be worth playing with. You can trigger the gate by using other audio or MIDI, which is useful for drums or situations where the attack is causing problems (you can shift the trigger forward by a few milliseconds).

The software you have may give you some other options. For instance, in Logic you can "Strip Silence" by adjusting threshold, pre and post times and cut one piece of

(continued on next page)

(continued from previous page)

audio into many, ideally not including the noise. These methods generally work for instrumentation; however, vocals usually need a more personal touch. So, roll up your sleeves and be prepared to spend a few hours editing a vocal that may have only taken 10 minutes to record. Also, remember that noise, and the frequencies it takes up, is relative to what else you have going on in the mix. Some subtle EQ or a high or low pass filter may work. Even recording a track of just the noise and placing it out of phase can help cancel out the original noise.

Your work with audio shouldn't be handicapped by poor quality recordings. A little planning and foresight can help reduce this type of work and enable you to spend your time enhancing your audio, not fixing it. With digital, the greater your signal, the better the sound (while obviously avoiding clipping). This is to do with the way the converters work. However, be aware of your source and your signal path. Keep it simple. If recording, use the right type of mic and go through as little gear as possible before your computer. Obviously, this only applies if you're using low-end equipment. For example, you can use a mic, pre-amp, and compressor before going into your computer. Depending on what you're recording, the quality of the compressor, and your options on mixdown, you may be able to leave the compressor out of the chain.

I try not to EQ what is being recorded; on most occasions, I won't go through a mixing desk, just an independent pre-amp. There are many schools of thought on this. Some engineers compress and EQ real hard on the way in, but if that is the case, they will have a clean signal to start with. If in doubt, less is more.

What are some of the challenges you face when mixing music with dialogue or other sound effects?

There is only a certain amount of space in the frequency spectrum that the ear will hear. So the more audio you have, the harder it is to place everything so it can be heard. Simply increasing the volume of one sound can make another disappear, while EQ'ing some frequencies out of the disappearing sound will have the effect of enhancing the other. I'm saying this to illustrate the relationship between all of your tracks, regardless of what they are. The advantage of working with a song is that everything is recorded from the start to fit together; with film you may have music, dialogue, and sound effects not necessarily recorded to fit with each other.

What I love about working with computers is the ability to loop sections of audio. Take advantage of this ability and spend your time balancing your audio—take it slowly and let it all settle into its place. Create space in the mix, especially for your dialogue. When mixing for live shows, I will sometimes sound check the vocals first and fit everything around them. With dialogue in movies (surrounded by music and sound effects), it may be worth trying this approach. It's hard to be technical without knowing the specifics of the project; however, remember once again "less is more."

Do you have a method for organizing media for large projects?

Make sure you always back up your audio. You can use a program like Retrospect to keep that side of the project under control. Then be brutal and delete the crap you aren't using—if you have a lot of audio in a project, the last thing you want is audio floating around that isn't being used.

I've always been bad at naming audio. If recording or working at a good pace, I am loath to stop and name or rename. Instead, I will group "like" instruments and dump them into their own folders. This is quicker for how I work, especially as there is a high chance that it will be a while until I get round to actually organizing everything. Whatever system you create for yourself, make sure to utilize your software and operating system, since most software has certain built-in functions that will help you out.

Is there a limit to the amount of instrumentation or parts in a soundtrack before it becomes too busy or overwhelms the listener? Also, is there a minimum number of channels that a mixer should have for this type of work?

One badly recorded track can overwhelm the listener. However, if recorded and mixed well, your possibilities are nearly endless. I've worked on songs with over 100 tracks and, although they sound big, they don't overwhelm. Take a major movie soundtrack. You may have a couple of engineers mixing the music, which could be a 60-piece orchestra and a band, another engineer handling a couple of dozen sound effect tracks, and then another dealing with the dialogue—all of this mixing down for surround sound. Logic audio software's mixing capabilities will enable you to mixdown well over 100 tracks for surround sound; you can automate everything from volume to your effects—only your computer and your imagination will limit you. All of this is being done internally on your computer, preventing you from buying a $200,000 mixing console. There is an abundant amount of software with various mixing capabilities available on the market.

(continued on next page)

(continued from previous page)

However, if you want to take things further, you need to decide on a budget (obviously) and whether you want to remain in the digital domain or mix in analog. It would take a whole book to discuss the pros and cons of both. How much flexibility do you need? Are your projects of a similar type and size? Does what you do need to be broadcast quality? Generally speaking, the better your equipment, the more sophisticated you can make your audio. If you're on a budget and most of your projects end up on DVD, it makes sense to stay in the digital domain. Use your mic and pre-amp to record and monitor via a small analog console. It's a jump from there, as the next level up would be a digital or analog desk to mix through. This would enable a little more flexibility and would make the mixing easier (i.e., using faders for riding levels, as well as proper controls for EQ and effects). However, you will need an audio interface with enough outputs to make this worthwhile for you.

The system that is best for me is to have fewer inputs and outputs on the computer, but a high quality converter. I will then do good rough mixes on the computer, and when I need something better, go into a professional studio to lay down the masters. This has enabled me not to have to compromise on quality over equipment. Once again, less is more.

How do you make tracks sound fuller and more organic? For example, how can you add dimension to vocal performances or enhance instruments, such as guitars and strings?

While recording, try stacking up some of your takes. If it's vocals or instrumentation, get the performer to keep repeating the takes and record onto new tracks, and then pan your takes to create a stereo image. The type of sound you want will determine how many times you track something up and how tight you want the takes. Experiment and keep checking what you are doing in conjunction with the rest of your audio.

Once again, bear in mind the relationship between your audio. Stacking things up can make it sound fuller, but also make other things sound smaller—it can even cancel itself out or just sound sloppy. Due to the nature of analog recording and processing, the physical properties of sound are changed just by passing through the analog domain. This can be used to your advantage, especially with the truthfulness of digital recording, which can be interpreted as clinical sounding. Tube processors or the tape compression in analog recording can all color your sound and give it warmth. Putting a keyboard or samples sound through an amp and re-recording is worth experimenting with. It all really depends where your source audio came from. If you don't use good equipment, taking a sound out of the digital domain (if that's where it started) to try and give it something you think it's lacking, is probably going to be self-defeating. This is especially true if you're trying to add to your sound without taking it too far away from the original.

In certain circumstances, if you are after a severe effect, taking your sound and putting through analog effects (maybe some pedals) can give you an original and dramatic result. If your sound was from an external sound source, this once again endorses the argument to get it right on the way in. Without good equipment, going through cheap processing and converters will not give you a fuller or more organic sound. Organic by definition means close to the origin—just don't get this confused with not being able to play with a sound before recording.

In general, are there rules for where to place vocals, drums, and other instruments in the mix? Is it different for surround sound than with stereo (if you've worked with it)?

No, there are no rules. However, there are certain things you should keep in mind if you're looking for commercial success. The ear of the listener has been trained over time to expect to hear things in a certain way, so basically, you should model mixes you respect. If you're trying to do something that is strictly artistic, then you can play around a lot more. If you listen to a lot of old music, you will have heard early stereo tracks with the drums panned to one side and instruments and vocals panned to the other—or variations of that. It didn't catch on, as it doesn't sound balanced and that is what you're after. So the more severe the placement of your audio, and the more it grabs your attention, the more it will take away from the song itself. That is the effect you are after when mixing sound effects, so bear it in mind.

To be more detailed, you can create the feeling of depth and movement. If dealing with just stereo, you can still make a sound feel like it is moving from back to front, or more distant, or up or down. This can be achieved with reverbs, delays, EQ, and a host of other outboard gear. It can take years to learn how to mix with depth and good placement, so learn from people whose work you respect. Also, model their good

(continued on next page)

(continued from previous page)

mixes, and it will help your learning curve. All that being said, (once again) less is definitely more in mixing. Having watched some great engineers over the years, they get great results with very simple approaches—subtle balancing, EQ'ing, and compression, with limited use of effects.

Are there any special tricks or rules of thumb for the creation and placement of beats and electronic percussion?

When watching shows, the drummer is in the middle for a reason—it sounds better. Spread your drums out like a real drum kit—bass drum, snare centered, toms panning, hi-hat to one side, and cymbals with a stereo spread. For percussion, try to get a stereo spread—for stuff like congas and bongos, with a little pull to one side. Balance out the hi-hat by placing some hi percussion on the other side. Once again, use other songs as your model.

Removing Unwanted Noise

The removal of unwanted noise is a constant struggle for producers of location audio. First, there are the atmospheric sounds that are difficult to avoid, such as traffic, crowd noises, and airplanes flying by. On top of that, there are more subtle sounds, such as an air conditioner, the buzz of an overhead lamp, or poorly grounded electrical lines. Old, analog recordings that are transferred to digital also exhibit static, scratches, and other sounds associated with degraded audio. There are special tools built into audio editing software, such as Logic and Soundtrack Pro, which assist in the removal of these noises. Stand-alone software, such as Bias' Sound Soap, are also created for this purpose.

Eliminating Hums

When recording audio, a humming noise may be introduced into the signal by power lines, improperly shielded cables, or other forms of electronic interference, like a buzzing speaker, a mic, or the camera itself. To remove these unwanted noises, you can employ a notch filter, sometimes referred to as a hum eliminator, which removes sound at specific frequencies (see

Figure 9.19). For example, power lines and electrical systems in the United States tend to hum at approximately 60Hz. If you were taping an interview in a quiet office, you might experience hum from other electrical devices in the room, such as computers or lights.

Most software that includes audio effects provides a notch/hum filter, which might also be located in a Bandpass filter category. To use a notch/hum filter, enter a frequency that you want to remove, such as 60Hz for line noise in the United States, or move a slider until the noise disappears. You can usually use a preview function to hear a playback of the changes as you make them to a clip.

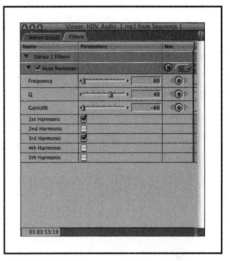

Figure 9.19 *The notch or hum filter (hum remover) helps to eliminate unwanted noises from power lines in a room.*

REMOVING NOISE WITH SOUNDTRACK PRO

The latest edition of Apple's SoundTrack Pro application includes several useful tools for cleaning up unwanted sounds (see Figure 9.20). It also allows you to add noise back into a recording, which can be useful for keeping a consistent room tone or other ambience, which is critical to maintaining the consistency of your audio edits (prevents background noise from cutting in and out). To remove unwanted noise (such as a hiss, buzz, or other persistent sound), first identify a "noise print," which represents a good example of the sound by itself, such as when a speaker pauses for a moment, or any other time you can isolate the noise without additional sounds on top. Once the noise print has been set, it can be applied to a clip and used to eliminate that same range of sound in your existing audio. Similarly, a portion of a clip may be identified and used to add an ambient tone to the rest of your clip (such as room tone).

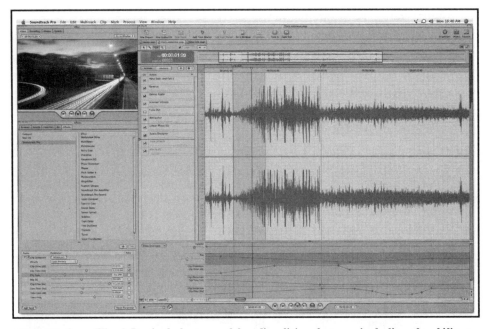

Fig 9.20 *SoundTrack Pro includes powerful audio editing features, including the ability to easily add or remove noise. (Courtesy of Apple)*

Audio Editing Tips

The following are a few additional tips to consider for editing audio, particularly if you are working with your audio in an NLE along with your video. Most of these tips are oriented toward dialogue, but may also be applied to editing tracks of music and sound effects.

◆ Smooth out audio transitions from one clip to another with a crossfade, instead of a straight cut. This is particularly helpful with dialogue tracks, and may also work well for music. If you are experiencing pops at the beginning or end of a clip, try adding a two-frame fade to smooth it out.

◆ Split your audio into multiple tracks. It is often best to place clips on separate tracks to make them easier to adjust (crossfading using keyframes, instead of an effect, presents more options, and shifting a clip a few frames in one direction or the other is easier). Having clips on multiple tracks also allows you to visualize better where one sound starts and the next one begins, in case you need to make an edit, apply an effect, or swap out a single instance of a clip.

◆ Keep your tracks organized. This is particularly important for larger projects with a lot of tracks, although any project can benefit from careful organization. At some point, you will need to make adjustments to audio levels, effects, and placement, or swap out one clip for another. If you keep your tracks grouped according to type, they are easier to locate. Usually, dialogue, voiceover, music, and sound effects are separated from each other. This makes it easier to apply the necessary EQ settings and other effects (which differ between voice and music, for example), while also making adjustments easier if changes need to be made to the final mix. If you are mixing audio for a movie, then you would want to separate these elements in the final mixdown, since you may need to swap out dialogue (for example) for foreign distribution.

◆ Cut the sound from one take and paste it into another to salvage a bad take. You can often get away with this, as long as you pay attention to the beginnings and ending of words, which can run into each other (particularly if a speaker is talking quickly). In general, feel free to swap the audio from one take with the video from another. Just because your audio came in attached to a particular clip of video does not mean it has to stay there. If you can get away with it, feel free to use the audio from one take with any other video where it is most appropriate. Just make certain that you match the room tone with each take.

◆ Break up your audio to create more space in your dialogue. You can slow down or create gaps in speech by spacing out dialogue through the use of cuts. This works as long as the speaker is off-screen, and is a very common way to cut a documentary, especially when you want to cut away to something or need more time to provide video that supports what the speaker is saying.

Chapter 10

Creating Graphics and Effects for HDV

Completing most film or video projects requires the addition of titles and, in many cases, some sort of effect, whether simply changing the speed of a clip or compositing an actor onto a new background. In this chapter, topics related to the application of special effects and, more generally, the improvement of an HDV project are discussed. Using special software and other digital tools provides a wide range of options for improving or enhancing a project in post-production. In addition to providing video editing capabilities, most of today's NLEs (such as Final Cut Pro and Premiere) are also powerful applications for adding effects and manipulating images, including projects in need of animation and compositing tasks.

Although the usual process is to complete an effects shot after the film or video has been shot or edited, it is often important and helpful to plan for effects while shooting, which can improve results and eliminate potential headaches later on. This is especially the case with blue or green screen shoots, discussed in this chapter, although it can be equally important when shooting credit sequences and shots that require graphics placed over video (perhaps more so for 3D animations, discussed in the next chapter, although 2D particle effects and other composited elements as well).

In order to be prepared better and eliminate difficulties when finishing a film, it is important for directors, producers, cinematographers, and just about anyone else working on a film to have a basic understanding of what is involved with graphics and effects production for their project. As with editing, an understanding of the video format you have chosen is the first step to deciding how you will approach working with the medium. This process should begin with an understanding of some basic properties, such as frame rates (discussion of HDV frame rates is included in Chapter 1, "Understanding High-Definition Video Format"), as well as scan rates, pixel dimensions, and other features of video technology.

Interlaced and Progressive Scan Video

The majority of video formats are based on fields instead of complete frames. Video that consists of separate fields rather than full frames is considered "interlaced." HDV, in its 1080i format, is interlaced, as are some other HDTV standards.

Each frame of interlaced video consists of two interleaved fields, one even and the other odd, played back in quick succession, which creates the illusion of smooth motion and complete frames (see Figure 10.1). Although NTSC HDV at 1080i has a frame rate of 30 frames per second (technically 29.97), each of those frames is split into two fields, yielding a 60 fields per second video image, which is also referred to as 60i. In general, it is more accurate to refer to NTSC video as 59.94 fields per second (29.97 odd fields and 29.97 even fields per second) and PAL as 50 fields per second (25 odd fields and 25 even fields per second). You may also surmise that each field contains half the vertical resolution of a full frame, since only 540 scan lines (one complete field) is shown at a time.

Depending on the format that is used, these fields may start with even or odd numbered lines. It is important for digital video producers and artists to be aware of the field order of their video, since it can have an impact on the creation of graphics, the application of effects, and other post-production processes. Interlaced HDV (and HD in general) is odd, or upper field first, while DV is always even, or lower field first (other standard definition PAL and NTSC formats are usually lower field first). This refers to the order that fields are played back, beginning at the top and working its way down to the bottom of the screen. Imagine a screen with each horizontal scan line numbered sequentially from 1 to 1080. For interlaced HDV, the first set of 540 scan lines would include lines 1, 3, 5, 7, and so on, followed by the last set starting with 2, 4, 6, 8, etc. When making settings in your editing or effects software, the order of fields has a significant result. Although capturing HDV using the traditional FireWire method keeps the field order consistent, the order of your fields may be changed inadvertently if you are using a special capture card that converts your video to another digital or analog signal during capture. Improper sequence or project settings in your editing or effects software may be problematic also. Make certain that you check the default settings for the capture cards and software applications you have chosen.

FIXING FIELD ORDER

If your video exhibits "jitter" upon playback, you may have set the field order incorrectly. When watching your video frame by frame, if you notice a "two steps forward and one step back" pattern, this means that your field order was not set properly. Either recapture your video with upper/odd field first (for all HD formats) or change the settings in your Timeline to match the source video.

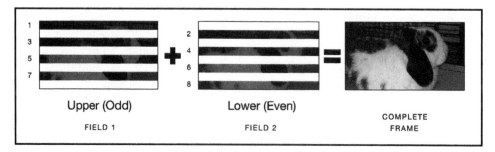

Figure 10.1 *An interlaced frame of video is composed of two fields, one odd and the other even, which are combined to produce a complete picture.*

Although interlaced video's temporal, or motion, information contributes to its realism, there are reasons why you might not prefer to view interlaced images. Still images (freeze frames) taken from interlaced video with a lot of motion often exhibit a "comb" or stepped pattern, which results from the overlap of even and odd fields (see Figure 10.2). Upon closer inspection, this pattern may also be seen in the moving video. The use of interlacing can be particularly noticeable in high motion shots, which is why viewers often find progressive scan imagery most pleasing to look at. However, the greater amount of motion information in interlaced video makes it a good choice for documentary, sports, and other situations that require natural motion without the flicker sometimes associated with progressive scan images.

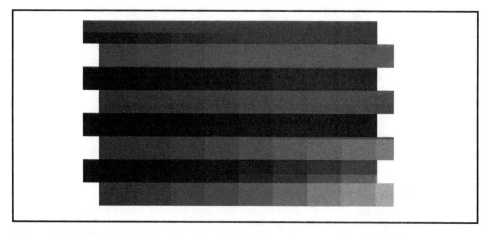

Figure 10.2 *"Combing" in an interlaced video image is most noticeable in high motion shots.*

Progressive images, on the other hand, are captured as complete frames, without interlacing. The most cited example of progressive imagery is film, which consists of a single image playing 24 times a second (and captured at 18, 24, 48, or 125, etc. frames per second, depending on the needs of a production). The image is captured photographically using the interaction of light with chemicals and emulsion, although the same can be accomplished electronically using a CCD or CMOS image sensor that captures an entire image at once. JVC's GY-HD100 is an HDV camcorder that offers true progressive scan recording capabilities, producing 24p or 30p images, depending on the needs of the shooter. Panasonic's Varicam series of DVCPRO HD cameras, as well as their new HVX-200 camcorder, are also capable of capturing 720 60p images, which means that 60 full frames of video may be captured each second. This feature allows for dramatic speed changes, slowing shots down by 50 percent or more with no sacrifice of quality. In fact, the HVX-200 DVCPRO HD camcorder that records to P2 cards is able to acquire 1080 30p and even 1080 24p as well—a capability that, until recently, was only found on high-end cameras costing upwards of $100,000. As discussed in Chapter 12, "Delivering HDV Content," 24p video is ideal if you intend to transfer your movie to film, although interlaced footage can be transferred as well with some additional processing.

Traditionally, camcorders and other video devices are interlaced, although in recent years there has been a trend toward progressive scan devices, including DVD players, digital televisions, and camcorders. As more people witness the potential that is locked within their DVD collections, the proliferation of digital televisions and HDTVs are sure to rise. (A trip to your local AV dealer helps to sort out the advantage in quality.) Although a video device might record progressive scan images or even claim to offer progressive output, the use of an interlaced display device (such as the majority of televisions in use today) requires them to output interlaced as well. For a complete film-like, progressive scan environment, make certain your camcorder, DVD player, television, and other devices are capable of inputting and outputting progressive images.

De-interlacing Footage

Unless you are shooting with a true progressive scan video camera, such as the JVC GY-HD100 (HDV) or the Panasonic HVX-200 (DVCPRO HD), you will be dealing with footage that is interlaced. Interlacing, as discussed in the previous section, is when a single frame is captured as two separate fields, either odd (upper) fields first or even (lower) fields first. In order to achieve a look closer to film motion, these interlaced frames must be recombined to form a single, progressive frame. This is an optional step, and one that is not necessarily advised, particularly if you are delivering your video for broadcast or viewing on a 1080i monitor or television. However, if you are creating video for the Web, transferring to film, or simply want to add a more film-like motion to your images, then progressive is the way to go. Also, de-interlacing footage can help considerably when using motion tracking tools to analyze your video (mentioned in Chapter 11, "Working with 3D Animation and Effects"). De-interlacing can create smoother edges, with features that are easier to follow for both matchmoving purposes, as well as more accurate speed changes applied to a clip. Fortunately, there

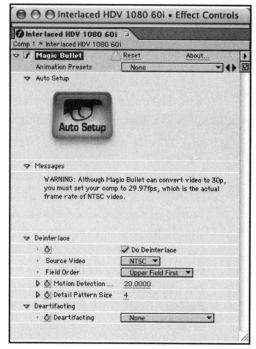

Figure 10.3 *The de-interlacing options in Magic Bullet Suite convert interlaced video to progressive scan video (www.redgiantsoftware.com), in addition to removing many of the "artifacts" that are the hallmark of interlaced and highly compressed video.*

are now a variety of tools available to do this. Knowing which tools will work with your favorite software and are able to produce acceptable results is the only test.

Most de-interlacing software simply blends the two fields together. This is the nonintelligent method, which yields acceptable results for simple footage, but cannot handle the complexity of footage with a lot of motion. The use of a more intelligent application is important for the best results and is most evident when trying to slow down or speed up footage. Most NLEs include a de-interlace filter that does a decent job for general use, although there are also professional applications for this purpose.

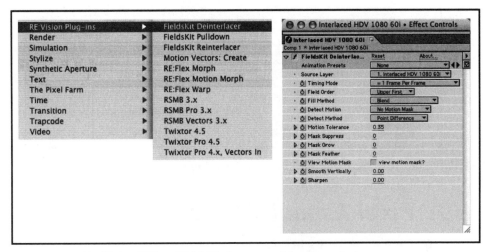

Figure 10.4 *Re:Vision Effects FieldsKit (www.revisionfx.com).*

There are a variety of applications that specialize in the de-interlacing of footage. Two of the most popular options for After Effects (plug-ins) and other similarly supported animation/effects software are Magic Bullet Suite (www.redgiantsoftware.com, see Figure 10.3) and Re:Vision FieldsKit (www.revisionfx.com, see Figure 10.4). Both of these plug-ins are able to convert interlaced video to progressive scan output at a variety of frame rates, even converting your 29.97 frames per second, NTSC video (or 59.94 field per second) into a 24p, film-ready format. Additionally, Magic Bullet is able to do this while also applying other "optical" effects, film transitions, and special "looks" to better approximate the nature of film, in addition to helping remove "artifacts" associated with HDV footage (softening pixilated edges, while maintaining sharpness). If you are working in Final Cut Pro, you should also consider Nattress Film Effects (see Figure 10.5), which includes high-quality and fast de-interlacing capabilities, as well as standards conversion (converting NTSC to PAL, for example) and film-looks that render very quickly, especially when compared with other plug-ins. *DV*Film (www.dvfilm.com) is yet another option for converting your HDV and NTSC or PAL video sources to true 24p film motion. Additionally, the CineLook 2 set of plug-ins offers film motion effects for simulating the look of 24 frame material for an interlaced project. You can check out the DigiEffects Web site (www.digieffects.com) for more information on CineLook 2.

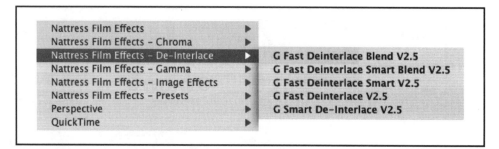

Figure 10.5 *Nattress Film Effects for Final Cut Pro.*

HDV Pixel Aspect Ratios

As mentioned in earlier chapters, the 1080i HDV format consists of a 1440×1080 frame size with nonsquare pixel dimensions. 1080i HDV is anamorphic, like DV, and thus it is exists as a 4:3 aspect ratio image (or 1:1.333 pixel aspect ratio) until it is stretched back out to fill a square pixel, 16:9 aspect ratio display (see Figure 10.6). Basically, a nonsquare pixel is taller than it is wide, resulting in a stretched image that only appears correct when it is expanded horizontally to fill a widescreen frame. If you have worked with the DV format or other standard definition video formats, this type of pixel dimension should already be familiar to you. When working with HDV in your NLE or effects software, make certain the pixel aspect ratios you are using match those of the HDV format. The only exception is for 720p HDV formats, which have a 1:1, square pixel ratio.

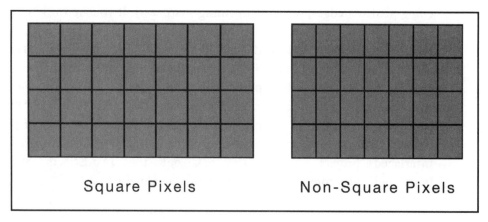

Figure 10.6 *HDV uses nonsquare pixel dimensions to record and store video images, although they can be stretched out to fill a standard, 1920×1080 HD frame.*

WORKING WITH HDV IN AFTER EFFECTS

Although you may choose to work with graphics and animations at native HDV resolutions and pixel dimensions in After Effects (or any other application for that matter), there is an alternative, which can make your job easier and produce better results when compositing, animating, and applying effects. When working with 1080i HDV in an application like After Effects, it is often best to use square pixel dimensions and full HDTV frame sizes (1920×1080 square pixels). For example, if you are using HDV footage in an animation or as part of a composite, try working with it in a standard 1920×1080 composition with a square pixel aspect ratio and a frame rate of 29.97 (or whatever frame rate matches your source video). If your footage is "interpreted" correctly and then used to create a matching composition, your project should be easier to deal with, as it is now a square pixel format, which works perfectly with graphics and other animations created on a computer. Working in square pixel dimensions eliminates any confusion about how to combine video- and computer-based imagery, a clear advantage to using other HD formats, particularly the uncompressed variety. (DVCPRO HD has its own unique properties, similar to HDV.)

The following is a basic workflow for importing HDV footage into After Effects, interpreting the footage, and setting up a composition to work most easily with your video.

1. Start up After Effects and proceed to its main application screen, bypassing any pop-up windows with presets that might appear. The current version of After Effects (6.5) does not offer an HDV preset, and even if it did, we may want to create our own settings for a square composition at the appropriate frame rate and duration.

2. Drag and drop an HDV clip into the Project window, or choose File > Import > File to select a video clip on your computer's hard drive.

3. Control-click (Mac) or right-click (PC) onto the HDV clip in the Project window and choose Interpret Footage > Main from the context-sensitive menu that appears, or choose File > Interpret Footage > Main.

4. In the Other Options area of the Interpret Footage dialog box, choose Square Pixels from the Pixel Aspect Ratio drop-down menu.

5. Click OK to accept your new settings and close the Interpret Footage window.

6. Drag your HDV clip onto the Create New Composition button at the bottom of the Project window. A new composition is created for you automatically with settings that match your clip exactly, including the new pixel aspect ratio as defined in the Interpret Footage menu. At this point, you can treat your project like any other square pixel, HD composition, creating all of your full frame graphics as 1920×1080 pixels and rendering out to your HD format of choice, whether uncompressed (Animation, Uncompressed 8 bit 4:2:2, etc.) or even to HDV and DVCPRO HD.

Working with Text and Graphics

Adding text and graphics to video for use as titles or in other broadcast designs requires some special consideration, as compared with simply designing for print or the Web. Fortunately, HD formats remove some of the constraints placed on comparatively low-resolution SD formats, such as DV. For instance, HDV's increased resolution permits more detailed images with greater complexity, approaching that of film (at least in comparison to standard definition formats). Still, there are issues to be aware of and pitfalls to avoid. For many multimedia creators, the first step of any project begins in Photoshop. This may include everything from the initial storyboard stages to the final creation of graphic images for a composite. When piecing together the elements of a composite, Photoshop is an invaluable tool, with which you should acquaint yourself. Even if you haven't worked with Photoshop before, you should be familiar with a few principles for creating images to composite in After Effects or a similar application, including Final Cut Pro, Vegas, or Premiere.

Although HDV has greater resolution than SD formats like DV, it is still interlaced video, at least in its 1080i iteration. For this reason, it is important to watch the thickness of the lines in your graphics, since horizontal lines that are two pixels and under in thickness can flicker as a result of the interlacing. However, since the amount of space you have to fill is larger with HD, you are less likely to create these types of images inadvertently, since even the thinnest lines must be slightly thicker to make them visible on such a large screen. The same principle applies to text. Although for standard definition formats, you should generally avoid serif fonts (fonts with curls and other embellishments, such as Times New Roman) in smaller type sizes, HDV and other HD formats can easily handle most serif fonts, since the size of text is necessarily larger at HD resolutions.

When working with photos, it is usually best to scale them to the proper frame sizes or aspect ratio before importing them into an NLE. Using images that have greater resolution than your video project are only a good idea when you want to scale or realign an image in the frame. Larger images are great for doing pans and other moves across an image. Otherwise, sizing your photos to the correct resolution and 16:9 aspect ratio prior to import is best to avoid flicker in finely detailed or patterned images. If you have a lot of photos to import and use in an edit, you might consider using a Photoshop "action," or automated process that you can create, to crop and resize your pictures. Of course, many NLEs will also accept images of various resolutions and instantly resize them to fit within the frame, which can be a great timesaver. When importing images in this way, it is often important to make sure that they all conform to the 16:9 aspect ratio for HD and are the same size or larger than your project, to avoid empty spaces on the top, bottom, or sides of the frame, and (in the case of smaller than normal images) to prevent scaling images up and losing detail.

Although most NLEs are capable of importing Photoshop files, some may only be able to import one layer at a time from a multilayer image. However, they are capable of importing and preserving alpha channels, which store the transparency information for a picture. For complex projects requiring the manipulation of multiple Photoshop layers, you should consider creating your project in After Effects and then importing the completed animation into the NLE of your choice for editing. If you are working with a suite of applications, such as a set of Adobe software (Premiere Pro, After Effects, and Photoshop, etc.) or Apple's Final Cut Studio (Final Cut Pro, Motion, etc.), you can easily send projects that require complex graphics and animations back and forth without needing to render them first. Final Cut Pro 5, for example, is able to move clips and sequences back and forth between its Timeline and the Timeline in Motion 2, which is able to create sophisticated 2D animations and titles for your production. A seamless workflow between editing, effects, and animation software (as well as sound editing applications like Soundtrack 2 and DVD authoring software like DVD Studio Pro 4) is the ideal, although certainly not necessary or appropriate in every situation. For users of After Effects, an application called *Automatic Duck* will also move projects back and forth to your NLE, while retaining clip and layer information.

When you attempt to import a Photoshop file with more than one layer, your NLE or animation/effects software may ask you to choose a single layer to work with. If you require more than one layer from a file, you may need to import each additional layer individually and then composite them using separate video tracks. Some software will import a layered Photoshop file as a new sequence, with layers stacked sequentially. If you do not require separate images for each layer, choose merged layers (if the option is provided), which flatten the image upon import. Any images, aside from the background layer (unless the original background was deleted), that you create as part of a multilayered Photoshop file retain their alpha channel values when imported into other software.

It is important to note that layer effects and type (in most cases) should be rasterized before importing them into your NLE or effects software. Also, remember to consider the difference between the square pixel images you create in Photoshop and the nonsquare pixel images used for video purposes. You should make certain that your project settings match the formats you are working with. Current versions of Photoshop allow you to work with nonsquare pixel format while previewing them in square pixel dimensions. This may eliminate some of the confusion when mixing square and nonsquare formats, although you might choose to convert all your media to square pixels for editing and animation, prior to editing in an NLE or outputting back to HDV or another video format.

In terms of color, the graphics that you create are a bit more flexible with HD, as opposed to standard definition formats like DV. Although any video destined for standard definition formats, such as NTSC DVD, should conform to the video and broadcast safe range of colors, digital TV formats, which include any HD or HDV televisions and monitors, are able to represent more accurate color values without smearing or creating other problems. (Broadcast safe values are from 16 to 235 on an 8 bit scale, rather than 0 to 255, although applications like Final Cut Pro make the adjustment transparent, keeping the 0 to 255 within broadcast safe limits.) Still, HDV and the majority of other HD formats have an 8 bit color depth, and as such you should be cautious when using gradients (or other fine gradations of color) to avoid "banding." Banding can be a real problem, particularly for graphics created on a computer. Whenever possible, use solid areas of simple color rather than subtle gradients to prevent banding from occurring in 8 bit graphics. Previewing your graphics on a separate video monitor (such as a CRT, NTSC or PAL broadcast monitor) is the best way to check for this. To avoid banding altogether, you need to work with 10 bit graphics or linear float space (32 bit) images and then master to a suitable format like D5-HD, HDCAM SR, or film. Any time you return to the 8 bit world, banding may occur. In general, since you never know how your video will be displayed in the future, it is best not to get too wild with colors and stick within safe limits, often by applying a broadcast safe filter when appropriate.

TITLE SAFE AND ACTION SAFE AREAS

In broadcast designs, the title safe and action safe areas are those portions of a frame that always fall within visible areas of the screen (approximately 80 percent of the screen, reaching from the center outward) and are not affected by overscan on a CRT television or monitor (see Figure 10.7). Overscan is the edge of a CRT video screen not seen by a viewer. Pressing the "underscan" button on a professional video monitor will show you exactly how much of the full raster image you are missing on a CRT. LCDs do not scan and thus do not have a true overscan area outside the frame. The title safe and action safe areas for HDV may be relaxed a bit, as compared with standard definition video formats. Digital televisions have little or no overscan area (depending on the quality of the monitor and whether it is a CRT), although you should still use title and action safe as a guideline for placing text.

It almost always looks better when text and other critical designs are farther from the edge of the screen, while also ensuring safety on lesser monitors. This is especially important when you consider that the majority of video productions, whether they were shot on HDV or DV, are still viewed on older, standard definition televisions. In this case, you may also want to "protect" for a 4:3 image, in case you want to crop your video for display in some broadcast situations or for DVD purposes (notice the widescreen versus full screen options for major DVD releases), although it is certainly not necessary. In fact, having a widescreen, 16:9 aspect ratio to work with is another advantage to HD formats, and it should be utilized to the fullest. When viewed on a computer or a good digital television, one can appreciate the image range you have to work with.

Most NLEs and animation/effects software have built-in title safe and action safe area guides that can be turned on or off. As long as you keep your text and most important elements within these lines, you will be fine. Of course, viewing on a computer is the exception, since the overscan properties of televisions do not apply. In fact, as more LCD TVs hit the market (which are essentially computer monitors with video inputs and, in some cases, an HDTV tuner), these safe areas become less important, although still useful for creating attractive designs.

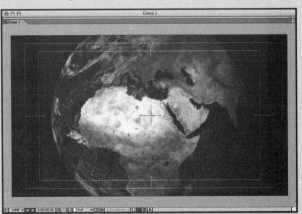

Figure 10.7 *Title Safe (inner set of lines) and action safe (outer set of lines) are most important when viewing material on CRT monitors.*

Compositing

Compositing is the art of combining layers of video and graphic elements to form a single image (see Figure 10.8). This involves a variety of techniques, but primarily relies on using foreground images with a transparent "alpha channel" applied, which are placed onto a static or moving background. The effect can range from the ordinary (the classic example is a television meteorologist standing in front of a weather map) to extremely complex, such as the many layers of action in a science fiction film like *Star Wars*.

In the early days of film, the best way to place actors or objects onto a new background was through the use of rear projection, which simply involved the projection of a film element onto a screen behind the actors. Directors used this technique frequently for driving sequences to show trees and roads moving past the outside of a prop car and actors on a stage. Today, the majority of background replacements are done with blue or green screens, which allows artists to change and manipulate a shot as much as they want after a production has wrapped shooting. Working in this way also allows objects to be moved around, animated, and used in more complex ways than were originally possible. Additionally, compositing encompasses the use of graphics, text, 3D animations, and any other number of elements that are layered in a shot, not just live action elements. In this section, I discuss a few of the simplest concepts related to compositing, although there are an extraordinary number of options and techniques utilized by professionals working on feature films and other high-end projects that mix 2D and 3D elements, motion control, and other special effects.

ALPHA CHANNELS

Computer images contain at least three basic channels of color information—red, green, and blue—which are combined to create a complete, natural looking image. For compositing purposes, a fourth channel, called the *alpha channel* can be utilized. Instead of color, an alpha channel contains transparency information that describes which parts of an image should appear transparent or opaque. When selecting a color depth for your image, make sure to select "Millions +" if you want to retain the alpha channel in your image. Not all video and still image formats support the use of an alpha channel. If you are rendering from After Effects, the default animation setting is one format that will retain your alpha information. (Just make certain that the "Millions +" colors option is selected when setting up your render queue.) If working with still images, PSD (Photoshop), TIFF, and PNG are some of the most common formats that can carry a separate alpha channel.

Empty portions of an image in Photoshop, created by cutting or deleting areas of a layer, may be considered alpha information and utilized for compositing. Black, white, and grayscale images may also be used to define alpha values in compositing applications. For example, you can create a black or white mask in Photoshop over portions of a reference image from your video, which can be imported into an NLE and used to define the visible portions of your video (an alpha mask or matte that determines portions to keep and areas to remove for assisting in compositing). In fact, in terms of alpha, black areas would define opaque portions of an image and white areas would indicate areas that are fully transparent (gray indicates varying degrees of opacity).

An image doesn't need to be black or white to preserve alpha channel information, but it does makes sense in many instances to create an image in this way if it is intended solely as a matte for another layer or video clip. This makes it easier to determine the transparency values for a layer. When working with chroma key effects, for example, you can often view the portions of an image that are being keyed out by switching to a black-and-white matte view.

Figure 10.8 *Compositing creates layers of images.*

There are many practical uses for composited images, including special effects work for movies or adding an interesting background behind interview subjects. In fact, the majority of video and film programs or media you watch include some form of compositing, whether it's a simple title sequence or brand logo, a DVD motion menu, or a brightly colored super hero swinging through the streets of New York city. Apart from using text, graphics, or animations produced using a computer, blue screens and green screens are most frequently used to place a subject into a composite shot.

ROTOSCOPING

When a subject must be removed from its background, without the use of a special blue or green screen effect, one must often utilize a sometimes arduous process called *rotoscoping*. Rotoscoping is simply the manual extraction of a subject from a piece of film or video by tracing its outline over time, creating a special matte that moves along with your subject like an animated movie. With a carefully performed rotoscoping job, any actor or prop can be removed from one background and placed into another, or wires and other distracting set elements can be eliminated from a shot. (You may have to "clone" areas of the background to fill in gaps where you have removed a subject.) While this technique can be ideal for shorter shots (around a couple of seconds in length), it is often impractical for longer takes. However, the ability to work with a subject in a natural setting, with real world lighting, can make it an excellent choice for a professional production with the time and talent to make it work.

In After Effects, as one example, you can paint over a subject and use "onion-skinning" (a technique borrowed from traditional cel animation to plot the course of an animation over time), which allows you to check the progress of your custom matte. You could also open an image sequence in Photoshop and use its tools to extract an object one frame at a time. Special software or plug-ins, such as Silhouette Roto for Final Cut Pro, are another option. Rotoscoping is generally reserved for those difficult shots that require special attention or where a screen could not be used. In general, if you need to extract an actor or other subject from a shot and place them into a new background, use keying techniques, as discussed in the blue screen and green screen section that follows, rather than investing the time needed to rotoscope. In case you find rotoscoping necessary for your project, you may also consider using software like Combustion or Shake, which are just two applications known for their excellent rotoscoping toolsets.

Keying with Blue and Green Screens

Since the days of Meliés, filmmakers have sought new techniques and special effects for expanding the visual vocabulary of their medium. One of the most common effects for both film and video involves shooting a foreground element shot against a colored background, which is then placed (composited) onto a separately created backdrop or scene. This is the same effect we first noticed in movies like *Superman* and *Star Wars*, although it is used much more extensively today, due to digital tools that produce better results in less time and with less expense. In fact, it is used to some extent in most Hollywood movies made today, even on small productions. Most surprising of all is that the average consumer is able to reproduce the effect using a consumer camcorder and inexpensive editing software.

One example where this technique may be used effectively by the average film-maker is for "talking head" shots. By shooting an interviewee or actor against a blue or green screen, you can decide later what type of background you want to place behind them, whether purely graphic (moving shapes and patterns) or natu-ralistic (forest, sky, or a shot from their latest movie). The technique that is employed here is called a *color* or *chroma* "*key*," which refers to the color that is cho-sen to drop out of the picture. For example, a green background is "keyed" out in order to replace it with a new backdrop. With a little experimentation and atten-tion to its use in other productions, you can find a number of ways to utilize this technique. However, to achieve acceptable results for a professional production, you should pay close attention to some basic principles, some of which are described below. Additionally, the more color and image information that your camera is able to produce can help immensely. A DV camcorder, for instance, is notoriously inept at producing high-quality keys, due to its lack of sufficient color information (4:1:1 color sampling) and the format's artifacting (due to compres-sion) that tends to create jagged edges.

Some of these limitations could be lessened through the use of special software, like Magic Bullet, Nattress Film Effects, and others, applying a softer edge or blur, and even closer attention to lighting. For most general keying purposes, it is fine. HDV uses 4:2:0 color sampling, which is also less than ideal for keying pur-poses, although it can be made to work with some extra attention, just like DV, most of which involves careful attention to lighting and tweaking the image and keying effect in post. The highly compressed MPEG-2 format utilized by HDV also adds to the number of potential keying problems that result from rough edges. In general, HDV can work for producing good keys, just like DV can with a little extra attention. If you have the budget, consider shooting all of your blue or green screen footage with a higher quality format, and then adding that to your HDV project. Ideally, you would work with a 4:4:4 format, if available, but that is currently expensive and an unlikely choice for lower budget productions.

USING ALTERNATE KEY COLORS

Although blue and green screens are the most common type of backdrop for keying purposes, black is often the ideal color for shooting smoke and water. Early BBC chroma keyers experimented by using yellow as a key color together with a Color Separation Overlay (CSO) system. In fact, depending on what you are shooting, it is sometimes best to select a background color based on the furthest color from your foreground subject and suited to the type of camera you are using. If an object in the foreground contains both green and blue colors, it may be best to select another color instead, unless you can easily matte out the objects (if they are static), in which case you may not need to use keying at all. This may also depend on the keying software you are using, since specialized software is often ideally tuned to particular frequencies of green and blue and is good at keying them out quickly and painlessly. In general, stick with blue or green screens for the majority of your shoots, although keep your mind open to alternate key colors as well.

In most instances, either a blue or a green backdrop is used to shoot against, although other colors may be used as well, such as black or (in rare occasions) red. This often takes place on a stage with special lighting that evenly illuminates a cloth material or painted surface. When it comes time to separate the subject from the background, keying software can be used simply to eliminate a particular shade of blue or green (or any other color for that matter) from the picture. Using the right color of paint or type of fabric is crucial to "pulling" a good key (in this context, the term "pull" refers to the process of extracting a subject from the background). See Figure 10.9. If the screen is not properly lit, shadows and other areas of nonuniform color can also make it exceedingly difficult to key out a single color. Most keying software is calibrated for special colors that are best matched with professional paints and screens. Additionally, your screen should have been illuminated evenly, to eliminate shadows, creases, and other dark areas or abnormalities that can turn a seemingly simple keying project into a nightmare job. Green or blue "spill," or color that reflects off the background and onto your subject, can add considerable difficulty to the keying process. It is common to receive a shot that is too dark with the subject too close to the screen (causing spill) and with varying shades of green or blue created by shadows or by mixing different types of cloth and paint. In short, the best keys are achieved by proper lighting and good shooting first and foremost. Some keys are next to impossible to pull without considerable time spent matting out areas of an image and making all sorts of adjustments. Even the best effects artists may not be able to pull a perfect key on a badly lit or planned shot.

Fig 10.9 *Blue screens and green screens are used for shooting a subject that is later composited onto another background using chroma keying software, such as Keylight in After Effects. (actress Liz MacDonald)*

The selection of a blue screen or a green screen is often based on the color palette of foreground objects and vice versa. For instance, if a subject you are going to shoot is wearing clothing that contains blue elements, you may want to try shooting in front of a green screen instead. If you do not, the blue in their wardrobe may be eliminated along with the blue screen when it comes time to key them out. Alternately, you could plan your wardrobe and props around the color of your screen. Although blue screens have been popular since the early days of science fiction movies, green screens have gained popularity since they are sometimes better suited to skin tones and other naturally occurring elements. In addition, green is most often used with DV and HDV since it has the potential for slightly higher luma content and requires less light to illuminate, which is especially good for keying with 4:1:1 (DV) or 4:2:0 (HDV) color sampled video. Also, it is thought that green may be best for brunettes and blue for blondes, but either can work as long as they are lit properly. Originally, film projects used blue screens since the color was absent from skin tones and (more technically) the blue layer of film stock was the sharpest. For digital formats, it is the opposite, since the blue channel tends to be the noisiest, thus another reason for choosing green for formats like DV and HDV. In the end, it all depends on the needs of your shoot, the format that you require, and the colors used on a set.

The following are some suggestions for setting up a successful blue screen or green screen shoot.

◆ Choose the format with the best possible quality to shoot in, even if you will eventually incorporate it into an HDV project. For example, HDCAM and DVCPRO HD are better than HDV for this purpose, although you can still do a good job with HDV when shot and keyed properly. 4:4:4 (HDCAM SR) color sampling is better than 4:2:2 (DVCPRO HD), and 4:2:2 is better than 4:2:0 (HDV) or 4:1:1 (DV). HDCAM falls somewhere between 4:1:1: and 4:2:2 for keying purposes, since it uses 3:1:1 color sampling.

◆ Select a wardrobe for your actors that is as far as possible from the key colors you are using for your background. Tell your actors to avoid any blue or green in their clothes, as well as in any set decoration (although immobile objects are easier to matte out when a key cannot be pulled properly for them).

◆ Keep your subject as far away from the screen as possible to avoid blue or green spill reflecting off the screen and onto your subject (often six feet or more).

◆ Use a single shade of colored fabric or paint for each area of your image that needs to be keyed. You can carefully mix different shades of green and blue (for instance) when the shot calls for it, but "patches" of color from overlapping cloth or paint should be avoided.

◆ The screen should be as smooth as possible. Remove all wrinkles, folds, and creases from your screen, which will cause shadows and other varying shades of color.

◆ Lighting is critical. Make certain to light your screen as evenly and brightly as possible without creating spill. (Avoid spill on actors, as mentioned, by placing them at a safe distance and beware of "hot spots" in your image brightness.)

◆ When lighting your subject, try to match the shadow direction of the scene into which you intend to composite them. Pay careful attention to the lighting of your subject, since the believability of their lighting is crucial to selling the final composited shot.

◆ Do not use diffusion on your camera, since it can smear edges, making the edge between foreground and background softer and difficult to separate when keying.

◆ Avoid reflective surfaces that may pick up the background color. Glass (such as windows) and reflective metal can be problematic. If you need windows for your final shot, consider creating them separately in After Effect or another 3D or 2D application.

◆ If you can, have a laptop or other computer on set to test pulling a key from material as you shoot. It is better to find problems on set rather than have to come back later and reshoot. Compositing test shots may also help you to line up your actors better or to match them more accurately with artificial environments.

PULLING DIFFICULT KEYS

Sometimes, no matter how hard you try, you cannot pull a good key from the blue or green screen footage you have shot. If you can't achieve a good key using a one-click method, where a single key effect is added to a clip, you should try using multiple key effects. Stacking up the chroma keyers allows you to make multiple color selections with an Eye Drop tool, isolating individual ranges of color, rather than a single large range. By carefully adjusting the Tolerance, Edge thin, and Feather sliders on each effect, you can usually get the rest of the way to a good key (often after a few attempts). Whether multiple keyers are doing the trick or not, you should also consider using garbage mattes to isolate or exclude areas of a frame, which means keeping only the areas immediately surrounding the subject you are trying to key out. Not only do mattes like this make color selection more precise, but they can also eliminate light stands or other objects and areas outside the screen that were set up while shooting and included in the frame.

Applications such as After Effects, Combustion, and Shake come standard with several useful features for working with blue and green screen material. Even though an application like After Effects is great for this sort of thing (especially on complex projects), an NLE like Final Cut Pro is often capable of handling simple keying tasks as well. In fact, it is sometimes easier to do this work in an NLE so that you can bypass the exporting of material to another application and then reimport it into your editing software. For the majority of simple jobs that require the removal of a properly lit background, the keying settings in Final Cut Pro, Premiere Pro, Avid, and Vegas may do the trick. For projects with a higher degree of complexity or professionalism, dedicated keying and compositing software is preferable. Keylight for After Effects is a good choice and software such as Ultimatte and Primatte Keyer are industry standards.

Composite Modes

Composite modes, also called *transfer modes* or *blend modes*, are a simple, useful method for affecting the interaction of layered video and graphic elements. While the simplest method for creating an interaction between two superimposed clips is to adjust the clip opacity for the layer on top (by varying the amount of transparency), there are often more interesting ways to work with layers of video. Often, much more useful and complex interactions between clips can be achieved by selecting one of a variety of special composite or transfer modes, such as those discussed in this section. Basically, composite modes work by comparing pixels from one image to pixels from another. When two layers are stacked on top of each other in the Timeline, each clip will have a corresponding pixel in the clip directly beneath it. By adding, subtracting, dividing, and multiplying the values of pixels (or using other mathematical formulas), new color values, and thus new effects are achieved.

You can create unique looks for your video in this way, or quickly composite two elements without needing to key out a blue screen or green screen backdrop. In fact, composite modes can be used with any type of video, no matter how it was shot. However, in most cases, only one or two different composite modes will come close to suiting the look you are after. At other times, composite modes may not be appropriate at all, or may require adjustments to the colors, transparency, or other properties of your source footage before the desired effect is achieved. (Composite modes are simple operations and do not have any parameters of their own that can be adjusted.) At the very least, composite modes provide one more tool to help you find the right look for your video. Whether you are creating "abstract" animations, intricate title sequences, or simply altering the colors of your clips, you might try out different composite modes to find the perfect look. Play with the composite modes that are available to you, even if you are not sure what effect you are after. The best way to find the right effect is to simply try out all of them.

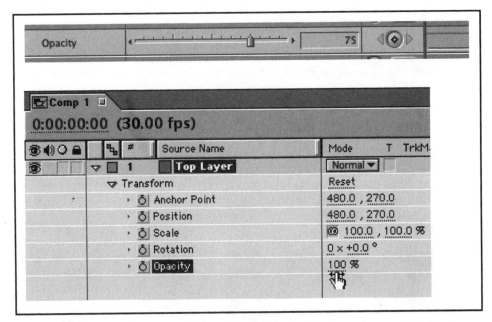

Figure 10.10 *The simplest type of layer (or clip) interaction is opacity, or transparency, which adjusts the visibility of the top layer in relation to the layer underneath. The amount of each layer that is visible depends on the percentage of opacity of transparency that is selected.*

You can usually find a list of composite modes in the Timeline, layer, or modify menus of your favorite NLE or animation software, although they are sometimes accessible through "context sensitive" menus by right-clicking (PC) or Control-clicking (Mac). In Final Cut Pro, for example, composite modes can be accessed by Control-clicking on a clip in the Timeline and selecting Composite Mode, or by selecting a clip and choosing Modify > Composite Mode. In After Effects, they are called *Transfer Modes*, and can be accessed by clicking on the Switches/Modes button at the bottom of the Timeline window and then selecting the appropriate mode for a particular layer.

To begin using a composite mode, set up two tracks of video in your NLE (as discussed earlier). Place one clip of video on Track 1 and another on video Track 2.

The clips that you choose do not need an alpha channel (although there are composite modes that can use an alpha channel), since the composite mode will determine the amount of transparency, if any. With your two clips in the Timeline, select the top layer (Layer 2) and apply one of the following composite or transfer modes as your particular software allows. After composite modes are applied, you can use separate brightness or contrast controls (for example) to adjust the results, which may work best by first nesting the clips.

The following are some of the most common composite modes found in NLE software like Final Cut Pro. Special effects software, such as After Effects, include more options than those seen here, although these represent the type of layer interactions that you are more likely to use for a video project.

◆ **Normal or None**—This is the default setting for all clips and layers of video. No effect is applied. See Figure 10.11 for an example.

Figure 10.11 *A "Normal" composite mode is the default settings and produces no interaction between clips.*

◆ **Add**—Combines the color values of both clips together, creating a brighter composite image (see Figure 10.12). Light, or white, areas of the original image are turned completely white and sometimes "blown out" (at a maximum value of 255, color values may exceed broadcast safe), which makes this mode best for darker source images. This mode may be useful for adding glows, highlights, and otherwise brightening dark composites.

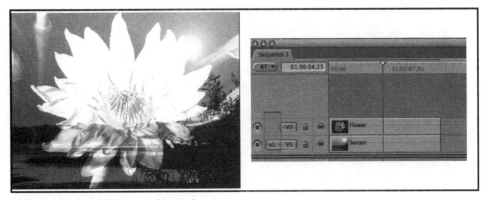

Figure 10.12 *"Add" composite mode.*

◆ **Subtract**—Color values from each clip are subtracted from each other, producing a darker final image (color values can approach 0, which may be outside of broadcast safe). Darker areas of the original clips turn black, which makes this mode best for brighter images, as in Figure 10.13.

Figure 10.13 *"Subtract" composite mode.*

◆ **Difference**—Color values from video Track 1 (the clip on bottom) are subtracted from the color values of video Track 2 (the clip on top), with color information that is inverted if the value is less than zero. See Figure 10.14.

Figure 10.14 *"Difference" composite mode.*

◆ **Multiply**—Multiplies the color values from one clip with the color values from another, producing a composite with dark areas that remain dark and white areas that become darker. This mode can be good for layering an image over a background texture or for enhancing colors in the original image (see Figure 10.15).

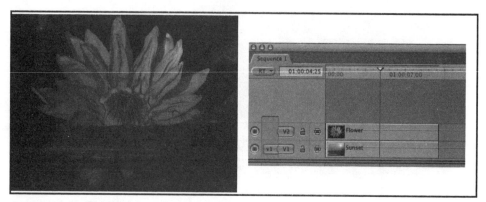

Figure 10.15 *"Multiply" composite mode.*

◆ **Screen**—Multiplies the inverse color value of pixels (inverts values, multiplies them together, and then inverts again), leaving light areas intact while making dark areas lighter. Screen is similar in some ways to Add mode, but less extreme. This mode is particularly useful for placing images with a black background over a video clip. (The darker areas will become transparent, leaving the brighter areas on top.) See Figure 10.16.

Figure 10.16 *"Screen" composite mode.*

◆ **Overlay**—Combines properties of the Screen and Multiply modes. The Screen mode is applied when a pixel's color value exceeds 50% gray (the middle gray value is 128, for an 8 bit image) and the Multiply mode is applied when the color value is lower than 50% gray (see Figure 10.17).

Figure 10.17 *"Overlay" composite mode.*

◆ **Hard Light**—Lighter areas of an image become lighter and darker areas become darker, emphasizing the division between light and dark areas of an image (higher contrast). See Figure 10.18.

Figure 10.18 *"Hard Light" composite mode.*

◆ **Soft Light**—Similar to Hard Light mode, although the division between light and dark is softer and less pronounced (softer shadows, diffused light). See Figure 10.19.

Figure 10.19 *"Soft Light" composite mode.*

◆ **Darken**—Compares the color values of both images and keeps the pixels with the darker value, as long as it is above 50% gray. See Figure 10.20.

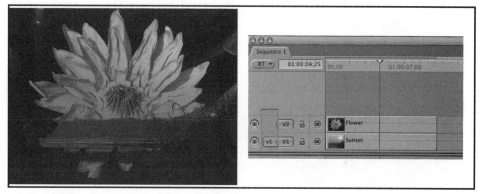

Figure 10.20 *"Darken" composite mode.*

◆ **Lighten**—Compares the color values of both images and keeps the pixels with the lighter value, affecting values less than 50% gray. See Figure 10.21.

Figure 10.21 *"Lighten" composite mode.*

◆ **Alpha**—Also referred to as a Travel Matte Alpha, this mode is different from the previous modes discussed, as it derives its information from the alpha channel of the lower clip (video Track 1) to decide what part of the top clip (video Track 2) is visible. See Figure 10.22. As determined by the alpha channel, black areas are transparent, white areas opaque, and gray values have varying degrees of transparency. A travel matte that uses an alpha channel is particularly useful for placing video inside text or for creating custom transitions. (Apple's DVD Studio Pro uses a similar method to achieve its alpha transitions between elements on a DVD.)

Figure 10.22 *The "Alpha" composite mode is a travel matte that takes its opacity information from the lower clip to determine what portions of the top clip should be visible.*

◆ **Luma**—Also referred to as a Travel Matte Luma, this mode is also different from the previous modes discussed (but similar to an Alpha mode). The luminance (brightness) information from the lower clip (video Track 1) determines what portions of the top clip are visible. Black areas will be transparent, white areas opaque, and gray values will have varying degrees of transparency.

Working with 2D Animations and Effects

After you have created a composite of layers for your project, you may decide to animate them to move across the screen or interact with each other. For example, you might choose to composite a spaceship shot with a blue screen onto a background of stars and then animate the clip for your spaceship to fly across the screen. You can achieve this affect by using keyframes and other motion control tools. The following section introduces the concept of keyframes, although you should refer to the specific software you use for details on creating and working with keyframes and effects. There are a number of resources out there for learning animation and effects for motion graphics, video, and film work. Visit www.hdv-filmmaking.com for tutorials, news, and links to other sources of detailed information.

Keyframes and Motion Control

Adobe After Effects and similar applications include the ability to control the animation of video clips and graphics by using a timeline-based interface to control their motion. The most basic use of this feature is the ability to set a motion path for a video clip, moving it from one part of the screen to another. This is great for making a clip move across the screen or revealing parts of another layer using a mask. It even works on clips that have transparencies applied, as described in the last section. For instance, you could key out an image from a blue screen and move the clip across a new background.

The foundation of any animation, motion control, or complex effect is the keyframe (see Figure 10.23). Keyframes are specific values that change an animation, effect, or other value over time. By moving a keyframe you are changing its value, which can affect the position and duration of an animation. There is usually a small dot or triangle to indicate the existence of a keyframe for a property at a particular moment in time. To add a keyframe you need to have a clip selected in your Timeline first. Choose the clip that you want to move, whether it is on your first video track or on a superimposed track. In the Timeline, or your application's Motion Settings window, you can place keyframes at each moment in time that a particular parameter should change, such as the position property. You need at least two keyframes to create motion or to change a parameter over time. One is the beginning keyframe, where the value starts, and the other keyframe indicates where it should end. A Pen tool can be used to place keyframes on a Timeline, or a button can be pushed to add or delete a keyframe.

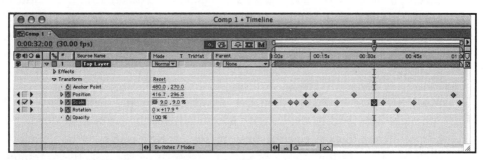

Figure 10.23 *Keyframes in the After Effect's Timeline.*

The motion paths for your clip can extend beyond the boundaries of the visible video area (an area that is defined by a television screen or monitor), so that you can make a subject enter and leave a scene. The classic example is a car driving into a frame on the right and then out of the frame on the left. In two-dimensional (2D) space, a clip can move across the screen from left to right and up and down (x and y coordinates), although it can also scale to create the illusion of moving closer or farther away from the viewer. True, three-dimensional (3D) motion (as described in Chapter 11, "Working with 3D Animation and Effects") is often necessary for realistic movement in a complex environment. After Effects includes the ability to work with 3D space in addition to 2D by turning on the 3D properties for a layer. You can create several keyframes to construct complex motion patterns or effects for your clip. Also, complex animations can be achieved by combining various attributes of a clip, such as position, rotation, scale, and others. Each of these values is associated with specific keyframes placed on a Timeline. Other properties, such as distortion (which affects the shape of a clip), can be keyframed as well. In fact, just about any property that you are able to set, whether a built-in effect or one added by a special plug-in can be keyframed. The number of options that you have for animation and effects is almost limitless.

Speeding Up and Slowing Down Video

Speed changes are often done to slow a clip down so that it fits into the allotted time or to achieve a dramatic or stylistic effect that simulates the variable speed effects possible in a film camera (or a 720 60p HD camera). Minor adjustments in speed, especially when only by a few percentage points, may be entirely invisible to a viewer, and even larger changes in speed may go unnoticed, depending on the type of footage (if there is not a lot of motion in a frame or a lot of grain and noise in the image).

Most NLEs use frame blending as a means to make smoother changes in speed, although there is software designed specifically for the purpose of slowing down or speeding up footage. Special software, such as Re:Visions Twixtor, functions by analyzing the position of each pixel and interpolating the in-between frames (see Figure 10.24). Although this degree of control is not always necessary for minor adjustments, extreme changes in speed require this sort of analysis. Most NLEs simply duplicate frames and blend fields together in different proportions to arrive at their speed changes, which can produce jerky or less than satisfying results. Using a plug-in like Twixtor in After Effects or a similar application can stretch your video a long way with excellent results. In general, once you drop below 50 percent or more (sometimes 33 to 25 percent can look acceptable) in most NLEs, the speed of a clip starts to appear jerky. The speed of a clip is usually linear (does not change speed over time), although it can be variable as well, which means it can accelerate or decelerate from one keyframe to the next. The default is linear, although applications like Twixtor, or even the capabilities built into software like Final Cut Pro, allow you to ramp speeds up or down across the duration of a clip. Of course, speeding up and slowing down video in a sequence will affect the surrounding clips and may push other material out of sync, so be careful when applying speed changes to video already in a Timeline with other material.

Using Plug-ins

The majority of video editing and effects applications are compatible with a wide selection of third-party plug-ins, or special software add-ons that can be used to augment the capabilities of your existing software. In fact, many of the best and most sophisticated effects are produced with plug-ins. Plug-ins are often created to solve very specific problems or situations that a host application is less adept or incapable of achieving. In this section, a few popular plug-in packages are discussed to give you an idea of the many possibilities that are available. For more information on the various plug-ins and software applications that are available for filmmakers (including tutorials), check out this book's Web site at www.hdvfilmmaking.com.

Trapcode makes some of the most useful and interesting plug-ins for Adobe After Effects and Combustion. You can see them being used in all kinds of commercials and motion graphics projects, including MTV-style spots. Their current lineup includes Particular (a surprising 3D particle generator), Shine, Starglow, 3D Stroke, Sound Keys, and Lux. Each of these plug-ins produces a truly unique effect. For example, 3D Stroke turns any path on a layer (created by a Pen tool in

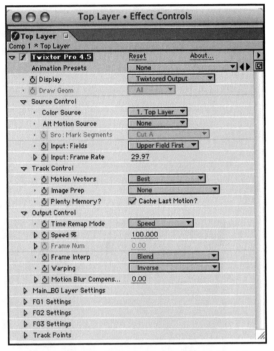

Figure 10.24 *Re:Visions Twixtor specializes in applying speed changes to video by analyzing individual pixels over time and creating new in-between frames.*

After Effects or Illustrator) into an animatable, three-dimensional line that can be tapered, twisted, and replicated in all sorts of ways. You can use the effect on vector artwork as well, which allows you to fly around the graphic and animate the path to write on or off the screen. Applying the Shine effect to the stroke adds a light effect that appears to have volumetric properties. Starglow makes highlights (light areas) in darker source footage glow and sparkle (similar to using a star filter on your camera). Lux simulates visible light, particularly in a foggy environment, and Sound Keys links any After Effects parameter (such as Scale) to specific audio frequencies. Make sure to check out the plug-ins at www.trapcode.com and download the demos (see Figure 10.25).

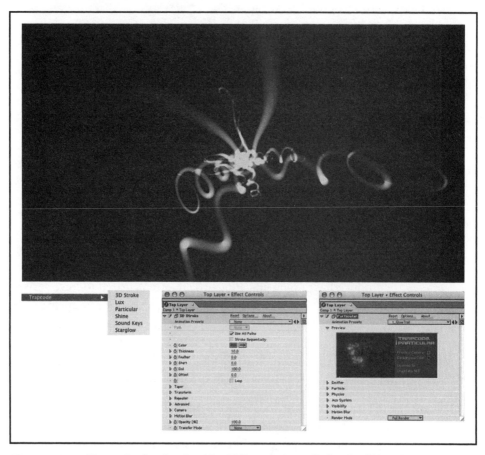

Figure 10.25 *Trapcode plug-ins for After Effects, such as 3D Stroke, Shine, Lux, Starglow, and Sound Keys, can add style and unique capabilities not found anywhere else, especially in 2D applications.*

Cycore FX also makes some excellent plug-ins for After Effects (see Figure 10.26). Their Cycore FX HD set of plug-ins (the "HD" refers to the image quality, not a particular resolution) includes 16 bit versions of their standard effects (the standard version is included with After Effects 6.5 Professional). The package contains 62 professional effects for creating particles, altering colors, adding blurs, distorting image layers (including the creation of spheres, tunnels, and cubes), as well as breaking up an image in various ways. It is a complete set of effects that can add a lot to After Effects, and the HD set offers improved versions of Particle World and Particle Systems II effects, as well as a few new effects, such as the ability to animate a spherical panorama (a navigable panorama contained in a QuickTime movie). Visit www.cycorefx.com to check out their products and download a demo.

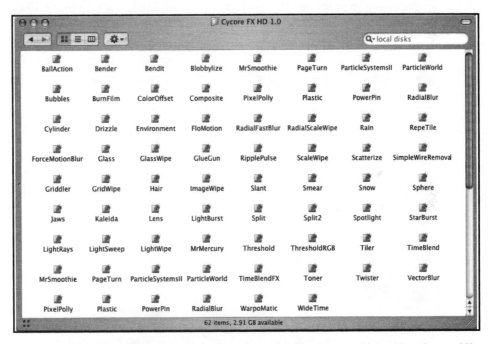

Figure 10.26 *Cycore FX HD offers a complete set of effect filters, which add to the capabilities of After Effects.*

USING LOW-RESOLUTION FOOTAGE IN HIGH-DEFINITION PROJECTS

One of the greatest frustrations when moving from standard definition to high-definition formats like HDV, is that all of your older material (whether shot on DV, Betacam SP, Digital Betacam, or any other SD format) is not easily utilized in an HD project. In general, scaling produces terrible results, although if transferring to film or remastering back to SD (for DVD, etc.), the lack of quality should be less noticeable. Professional scalers (particularly the hardware variety) will help, but the lack of resolution remains the main issue, even when line doublers are used.

As a stylistic choice, you may choose to vectorize video and scale it up, producing images that remain clear and sharp, even though they began much smaller in size. Even video that originated on the Web can be scaled up when vectorized. However, the video will almost always be cartoon-like in appearance (unless a high degree of vectorizes and long render times are used), similar to Flash animations you may see on the Web.

Synthetik Software's Studio Artist for the Mac is one application that can be used to create vectorized video that can be scaled up to HD resolutions, or even film, for that matter (see Figure 10.27). The render times can be long and impractical for general use, especially when using the paint effects, although it is a truly unique application that is also good for producing original image paintings and animations that move. The number of different looks that you can achieve is impressive. Scaling source video up to HD from SD and then applying a series of paint effects in Studio Artist is another alternative, although, as with vectorizing, it is also only suitable for graphic and artistic effects, not general uprezing purposes. If you would like to check out some of the interesting and fun effects you can produce with Studio Artist (including the ability to create custom brushes and layered effects), check out www.synthetik.com.

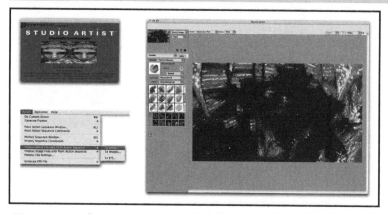

Figure 10.27 *Synthetik Software's "Studio Artist" for the Mac is graphic software for producing painterly effects, which can also be applied to low-resolution footage that is scaled up to HD frame sizes.*

Chapter 11

Working with 3D Animation and Effects

It is important for today's filmmakers (particularly those working with digital formats) to be aware of the possibilities for including 3D in their work. Even if you have never used a 3D application before, or you do not intend to do so in the near future, a general knowledge of this increasingly, ever-present form is important. Every time you turn on the TV, open a magazine, or power-up your mobile phone, you are likely to see 3D images in use. Filmmakers are constantly finding new ways to use 3D tools to solve problems or make their movies more exciting. Most editors and illustrators are used to working in a two-dimensional space, which is defined by the "x" and "y" coordinates of a photo, video, or film frame. Adding a third dimension, represented by the z-axis (depth), introduces incredible possibilities for more accurately representing the real world. This chapter is a brief primer for filmmakers who are considering a move into the world of 3D animations and effects.

Introduction to 3D

In this chapter, our discussion focuses on ways to utilize 3D graphics and related approaches to enhance your own high-definition projects. This should serve as an introduction and a jumping-off point for the subject. Topics range from general 3D concepts, such as modeling, texturing, and lighting, to the more esoteric, like image based modeling and the creation of HDRI images. In general, a single 3D application, Maxon's Cinema 4D (www.maxon.net), is used to illustrate the topics in this chapter, although the same techniques can be applied to any number of other 3D software, such as Maya, 3D Studio Max, or Lightwave (see Figure 11.1). I have chosen Cinema 4D for its comparative ease of use and fast render times, as well as its special integration with Adobe After Effects. It is particularly suited to video work, although it is equally capable for use in feature films. In general, beginning 3D artists should choose a package that will be useful for them in the long term and stick with it. Even though the essential concepts of 3D remain the same regardless of platform, each set of software has its own learning curve which requires time to master. Maya for example, is a very robust 3D package, yet may require advance knowledge of a special scripting language (MEL) to accomplish certain tasks. Professionals tend to prefer it for feature film projects, since it offers a greater amount of control and customization than is often required to solve problems in that field. However, graphic artists and designers, who are (perhaps) less technically inclined, may have different requirements. Cinema 4D offers a good balance of both intuitive procedures and advanced features when you need them, and its feature set continues to grow (see Figure 11.2).

Figure 11.1 *Maxon's Cinema 4D (for both PC and Mac users) is one of the more intuitive 3D applications on the market for creating professional 3D animations. (Courtesy of Maxon)*

Figure 11.2 *The Cinema 4D interface provides a variety of tools to help you create any type of 3D models or environments you can imagine. (Courtesy of Maxon)*

Modeling

The practice of creating 3D models can be as complex as you make it. For those with a high degree of technical proficiency and artist talent, anything is possible. A great amount can also be done by even the least experienced 3D user. Beginners tend to work strictly with text (3D titles can add a lot to a production) and "primitive" 3D shapes (primitives are basic, ready-made objects such as cubes, spheres, cones, planes, etc., which can be manipulated and assembled to create more complex models - see Figure 11.3). As your knowledge of 3D progresses, you can begin to use more complex methods for creating shapes. The first concept to understand is that you are working with a three coordinate system (x, y, and z) that represents three-dimensional space. Navigating within this world is the first hurdle to overcome, but you should quickly get the hang of it. Once you are familiar with the different viewing and navigating options, you can begin to assemble your models from a wide variety of 3D modeling tools. Make sure you work through the tutorials provided by your software's manufacturer or, optionally, take a class on the fundamentals to get off to a good start.

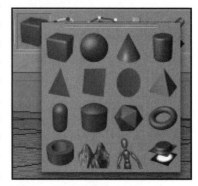

Figure 11.3 *Shown here is a selection of primitive shapes in Cinema 4D, which are the starting point for many modeling tasks.*

The following terms represent just a few types of geometries and tools to assist with modeling, although many more types exist for 3D applications.

◆ **Polygons**—Polygon modeling consists of geometry created by connecting points to form surfaces. When several polygons are put together, complex shapes and surfaces can emerge. Usually, polygonal modeling begins by working with primitives, which are simple shapes, such as cubes, spheres, cones, planes, and other rudimentary forms that can be assembled into more complex objects. For example, a building might be constructed from several cubes stacked together. Several triangles or cubes, created with points and lines, can also be combined to form a face or other geometry, which (when utilizing fewer polygons) can look something like a patchwork quilt upon closer inspection.

◆ **Curves and NURBS**—In order to form smooth geometry, a lot of polygons are necessary, which is why a different approach to modeling geometry was created utilizing curves. Curves are not restricted by the flat surfaces of polygons, which are only smooth in extremely large numbers. This approach makes all types of shapes possible, adding to the realism of objects, particularly organic shapes. By connecting points together, curves are drawn and form elegant shapes using special subdivision surfaces to smooth out the underlying geometry. (The application still starts with polygons and subdivides for you until they are smooth.) You can also work with special 3D tools like Extrude, Lathe, Sweep, Loft, and others to modify the geometry or form new shapes that are not possible by only using primitives. NURBS are a modeling form to use curves. Using a Hyper NURBS object (see Figure 11.4), you can even smooth out the edges of existing polygons or primitive shapes that you create, which is a simple way for beginners to see what NURBS and curves are about. Simply take a cube, extrude it a bit, and drop it into a Hyper NURBS object. You should notice that its edges have become smoother.

Figure 11.4 *A Hyper NURBS object uses curves to create smooth edges and organic shapes.*

◆ **Deformers**— Once you have some geometry to work with, you can modify it in a number of ways, using deform tools, such as Bend, Twist, Bulge, Shear, Wind, and Stretch, to name a few.

◆ **Booleans**—Using Boolean, you can affect the interaction of different objects by using operations such as Add or Subtract. They can be used, for example, to cut out a shape from one object by using another, intersecting object.

◆ **Metaballs**—Metaballs are another type of geometry formed by molding objects together like clay. For example, you can place several spheres into a metaball object, and it will blend them together in organic ways.

Creating Textures and Materials

After you have created a 3D model, you will need something to cover it, whether fabric for a character, metal, brick, or glass for a building, or carpet, pavement, and grass for a floor. You can create textures from photographs and edit them in Photoshop, which adds to the realism of a 3D object, or you can manufacture materials using the many parameters built into your 3D application. By using color, luminance, transparency, reflections, bump maps, specular features, and many other properties, you can create an infinite number of materials to simulate things like water, clouds, skin, rocks, glass, and numerous other surfaces. You may also use applications such as Maxon's Body Paint 3D to paint complex textures onto models in real time (see Figure 11.5).

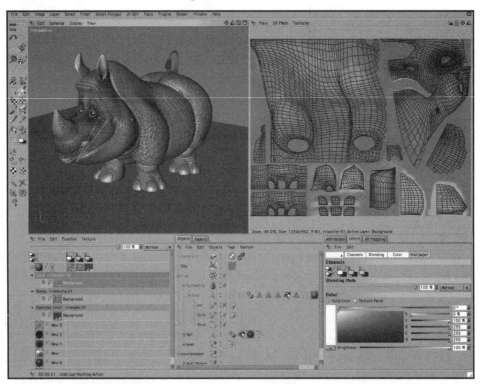

Figure 11.5 *Body Paint 3D is an interactive texturing application that paints complex surface textures directly onto 3D models. (Courtesy of Maxon)*

If creating your own textures is too time intensive or difficult (see Figure 11.6), you can often find the materials that you need online, either by purchasing them in CD/DVD sets or by downloading them from user forums and Web sites like www.turbosquid.com, to name just one example. (You can find a wide variety of ready-made models on these sites as well.) There are several books out there on the subject, including *Inspired 3D Modeling and Texture Mapping* by Tom Capizzi. For links to other resources, check out www.hdv-filmmaking.com.

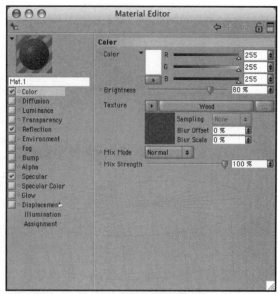

Figure 11.6 *In Cinema 4D's Material Editor window, you can create and modify textures that may be applied to 3D models.*

Lighting

As with shooting film and video in the "real" world, lighting for a 3D project is just as important, if not more difficult in some ways. In fact, lighting can be a tricky concept to grasp for new users, although with some experimentation, you should be able to appreciate the flexibility you have in creating realistic or mood-driven lighting (see Figure 11.7). Begin by studying traditional lighting techniques, used by other filmmakers and apply it to your 3D environments. Perhaps you could start out by creating a simple three-point lighting setup (as described in Chapter 5, "Lighting for HDV") and then modifying it from there. Difficulties are often the result of too many options, settings, and variables that you must design for and set up for a project. For example, you must take the surfaces and textures of your objects into account, such as their reflectivity (which also relates to rendering, discussed later), as well as the distance of a light from an object or camera (all considerations for the real world as well), the type of light used (omni, spot, distant, parallel, etc.), whether it casts shadows, and other variables. Developing reusable lighting rigs is one possibility if you do a lot of modeling, and you can also find suggestions for specific setups online.

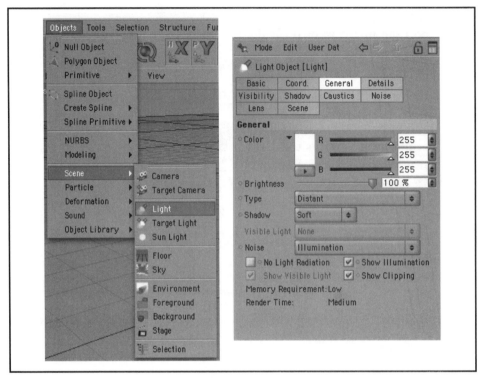

Figure 11.7 *Shown here are a few of the parameters for lights in Cinema 4D.*

HDRI AND IMAGE-BASED LIGHTING

HDRI, or High Dynamic Range Images, have become a real asset for 3D and special effects artists in recent years, and are particularly useful as a means of image-based lighting for quickly and realistically lighting a scene to match real-world environments. These images use floating-point math to include more information in an image than is possible with the 8 and 16 bit images with which we are familiar. With an expanded amount of visual information at their disposal, HDR images can also be used to make extreme exposure adjustments without losing detail. Using a spherical image of an environment, while bracketing exposures on a number of images, you can bring the photos into special software that compiles the multiple, low dynamic range exposures into a single, high dynamic range image.

For more information on applications and techniques for creating and working with HDRI, floating-point images, and formats like Open EXR, visit this book's Web site at www.hdvfilmmaking.com, or check out Paul Debevec's Web site (the HDR master) at www.debevec.org, or download his HDR Shop application for the PC at www. hdrshop.com.

Animation

After you have created a 3D model, textured, and lighted it, it is time to animate. You can choose to animate an object, such as a character walking or interacting with other objects, or you can simply animate the camera through a scene. Good character animation takes considerable knowledge and talent to pull off, although anyone can learn the basics. Begin by studying the "classics," taking lessons from traditional 2D cel animation, such as early Walt Disney (check out the wonderfully illustrated *The Illusion of Life: Disney Animation*) and watching a lot of animated films from a variety of sources. Books by Don Bluth, such as *The Art of Storyboard*, as mentioned in Chapter 6, "Designing Effective Compositions" (see interview), and *The Art of Animation Drawing*, are another source with a focus on film concepts. Study real-world actions and incorporate those into your animation as well, which can be documented with a video camera and used as a reference. Animating with a camera, on the other hand, is quite simple to learn by comparison. If you are already familiar with ways to move a real-world camera, you are halfway there. However, 3D allows an infinite range of motion, not limited by gravity or mechanics, although it is usually best to start with a grounded approach that approximates the look of film motion and real world physics and start from there.

Using a Timeline interface and keyframes, you can create an unlimited amount of motions. Although keyframe animation is the most common, larger productions may also consider using motion capture data to drive an animation. Motion capture (or "mocap") is made possible by special sensors that read the motion of markers placed on a subject whose movements you want to capture and apply to a model. This can be an excellent way to capture and create movement quickly that corresponds to real-world actions. Video game companies use this a lot to build libraries of human motion. The performance of the character Gollum in the *Lord of the Rings* (and more recently *King Kong*) was partially created by capturing the motions of a live actor and applying them to a 3D model. However, for the majority of productions, keyframing the motion of a character manually is the best solution even if it isn't necessarily realistic.

Rendering

Rendering is more than simply clicking a button to output your finished animation. When a 3D project has been constructed, lit, and animated, you still have several decisions to make before finishing it and flattening it into a 2D movie (see Figure 11.8). All of the final calculations for details, such as shadows, reflections, refractions, and volumetric effects (to name just a few), are processed at maximum quality when they are rendered for output. At this stage, you may choose to apply radiosity, subsurface scattering, lens effects, and a whole host of other special effects to add realism to your movie. Unfortunately, the more detail that you include in your render, the longer it will take to process. In fact, 3D animations (even a seemingly simple one) can take hours, days, weeks, or even months to render, particularly when only a single processor is used—no matter how fast it may be. Movie studios and production companies use several machines linked together into a "render farm" to distribute the processing tasks among several computers. While you may not be able to afford a large render farm of your own (some companies use over a thousand CPUs to render animations and effects), you may be able to hook up a few of your own computers into a small render farm using special modules provided by your 3D software's company, such as NET render for Cinema 4D, and a fast Ethernet connection between machines. Additionally, for the greatest amount of control, professionals prefer special rendering engines, such as RenderMan (developed by Pixar), Mental Ray, Brazil, or Cinema 4D's Advanced Render Module, to achieve the best results.

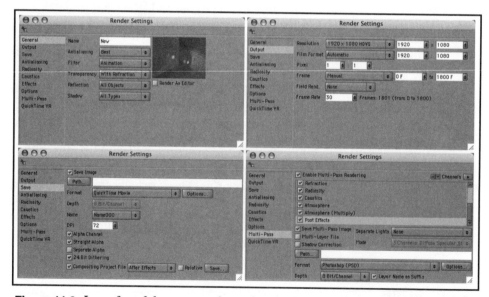

Figure 11.8 *Just a few of the many render settings in Cinema 4D's XL Bundle.*

Advanced 3D Compositing Tips and Techniques

In addition to the basic capabilities of 3D applications, there are other techniques that can be used to add to the believability or complexity of a 3D project. This is especially the case when combining 3D with live action footage, an effect seen all over television and feature films. Compositing 3D graphics into real-world environments adds yet another technique to the filmmaker's tool box and can be an excellent problem solver in addition to looking really cool. Using off-the-shelf software, you can accomplish a great degree of realism rivaling the big Hollywood studios. Some of these techniques require forethought or planning prior to shooting, although the extra effort is definitely worth the end result.

Combining Video with 3D Animations and Environments

The majority of films that include 3D animations or effects do so by incorporating them into existing footage, rather than creating entire scenes from scratch in a 3D application. When designing your shots, it is usually best to have an idea of what you need prior to shooting. This will give you an idea of where lights should be placed, whether you will need tracking markers (for matchmoving), blue or green screen elements, prop and set measurements, as well as any other information that may make the construction and integration of 3D elements easier. In general, locked off shots (tripod shots) are simpler to deal with than moving shots, since it is easier to create mattes and add or remove objects with less difficulty (although matchmoving, discussed next, allows for more flexibility). When possible, write down the settings you used on your camera (focal length, shutter speed, etc.), as well as any notes about the environments you are in, such as the direction of the sun and other details that may assist with lighting and setting up a virtual camera in a 3D application. Once you have your live action "plate" (live action backdrop), you can assemble your 3D animations and other graphic elements and effects on top, using software such as After Effects, Combustion, or Shake. The better your environments and animations match up before putting them together, the easier compositing them into a seamless movie will be.

Matchmoving and Motion Tracking

Video or film that contains movement may be analyzed to determine the position and orientation of objects in the frame. Objects may be "tracked," or followed, in order to match the movement of new graphics and animations to them or to add artificial 2D or 3D elements into the environment. For example, you might want to track the motion of a truck in a shot in order to pin a new billboard or logo onto the side of it. You may also decide that you want to cover up a light pole with a tree created in a 3D application, or apply a new background outside of a window that changes perspective to match the camera's movement. You can track objects with 2D motion tracking tools, such as the tracking features in After Effects, although the inclusion of complex three-dimensional objects in a shot requires 3D motion tracking capabilities. Software like 2d3's Boujou, Pixel Farm's PFTrack, Realviz MatchMover Pro, Realviz MMTrack, and others can be used for this purpose, and are utilized by major feature films. A powerful, yet inexpensive application (under $400) that is available for both Mac and PC users is called SynthEyes (www.ssontech.com), which has been utilized on several large movies (see Figure 11.9). Although the interface design may not be as attractive as other applications costing several times as much, it is able to produce results that rival or surpass its competitors.

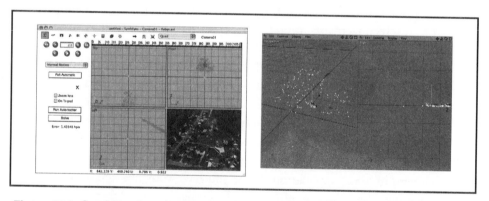

Figure 11.9 *SynthEyes is an inexpensive application for professional, 3D matchmoving of unlimited resolution footage, which can be incorporated into almost any 3D application, such as Cinema 4D. In the image above, a scene that was analyzed by SynthEyes (one panel of the SynthEyes interface is shown on the left) has been imported into Cinema 4D on the right, where a model is added to the scene.*

After a scene has been analyzed and 3D data extracted from it, which determines the real world camera's position and applies it to a virtual camera, you can then integrate that information with a model in your 3D application of choice. Using special tracking markers on the set can greatly improve the results of a track. Making sure that the camera moves enough to extrapolate shifts in perspective is also important. In general, for a good 3D track, keep the object of interest focused in the frame when you are moving toward or away from it. Also, smooth out the camera's motion as much as possible by utilizing dolly tracks or Steadicam shots. The more fluid the motion, the easier it will be to track. Do not shoot in a room with solid colored walls (or blue and green screen), unless special tracking markers have been added, or there are other features you are able to track. Additionally, do make sure that trackable features are spread throughout the frame and are not just concentrated in one area, where shifts in perspective and larger motions will be difficult to accurately determine.

After a shot has been imported into an application like SynthEyes, it is analyzed (automatically or manually, by choosing your own tracking points) and a project file containing camera data and tracking points for your 3D application is produced and imported into your 3D software. Then your model can be placed into the project (the new 3D camera determines where to look, so your object stays exactly where you want it while the camera does the moving). Then the animation can be rendered and exported into a compositing application, such as After Effects or Shake, to be combined with the live action background. Once you have tried the process for yourself (download demo versions of the software before purchasing), you will see that it is actually quite simple, although a poor track will be instantly noticeable, since objects will appear to float freely around the screen. Even subtle misalignments give away the effect, which is why much care may be required to create a convincing shot.

For more information and tutorials on matchmoving visit this book's Web site at www.hdvfilmmaking.com. Also check out *Matchmoving: The Invisible Art of Camera Tracking* by Tim Dobbert.

Image-Based Modeling

Image-based modeling, or photogrammetry, is the construction of 3D models based on photographs taken from real objects. Using this method, you can quickly create realistic objects, such as interior and exterior architecture or even facial captures. You may take the models and apply them back into another real-world environment, where the results can be quite striking. The limits of image-based modeling have yet to be tested, and you can purchase applications to help you create models from photographs with the least amount of difficulty. Realviz ImageModeler (see Figure 11.10) is an excellent application for this purpose, which allows you to extract 3D information from stills by importing, calibrating, aligning, and creating textures mapped to geometry that you specify from corresponding photos with different camera angles. Models created from photos can then be exported to your 3D software, animated, and added to a scene. You may even use the application to measure scene details for use in forensics or other scene recreation purposes. Of course, simple architectural rendering can be created quickly, although detailed structures may take a bit longer, but would be much more difficult to create in a standard 3D application. Try combining image-based modeling with matchmoving for impressive results.

Figure 11.10 *Realviz ImageModeler is one application for creating detailed 3D models from photographs, such as architectural (see above) and archaeological reconstructions (the example shown here illustrates parts of the PC interface as well). (Courtesy of Realviz)*

Using 2D and 3D Particles

Particles are objects that are sent out of an emitter. The speed, rotation, and amount of particles that are emitted can be controlled to produce all kinds of results, such as realistic rain, snow, fog, sparks, fireworks, and numerous interesting effects. Other applications and plug-ins offer particle effects, such as Apple's Motion (see Figure 11.11), Adobe After Effects, and third-party software like Particle Illusion (www.wondertouch.com), although Trapcode's Particular (www.trapcode.com) is one of the only 3D particle generators for use in a 2D application such as After Effects (mentioned in the last chapter). Most professional 3D applications, like Cinema 4D, also offer more complex 3D particles that can interact with models and their environments. Thinking Particles, for example, is Cinema 4D's advanced particle system for creating all types of complex interactions between particle effects and a 3D environment. If you are creating streams of particles to composite on top of a live action background (for example, to add rain to a scene), then make sure to use appropriate dimensions, camera angles, speed, wind motion, and gravity (if available) to sell the effect. You might even try combining particle effects in a 3D application with matchmoving techniques to match the camera movement (walking through the snow, for example) or in a 2D application such as After Effects to anchor plumes of smoke to a passing locomotive.

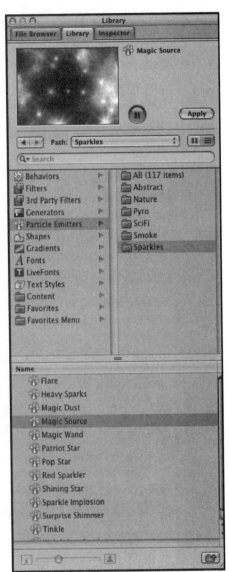

Figure 11.11 *Apple's Motion application has many built-in 2D particle effects.*

SIMULATING 3D IN A 2D ENVIRONMENT

Although 2D applications like After Effects are generally thought of as being used for compositing and animating two-dimensional movies, they can be used to simulate 3D space as well, even working with cameras imported from software like Cinema 4D. By activating its 3D option, a layer can be positioned along the x, y, and z axes, just like in true 3D software. This allows entire environments to be created and flown through with an After Effects camera. Distance effects can be achieved, as well as the creation of simple models from 2D planes, such as the sides of a box (to create a television model, for example). You might think of these models as paper cutouts, rather than objects containing volume like they do in 3D modeling software. You can use special plug-ins, such as Digital Anarchy's "3D Layer," to add dimension to your 2D layers, which creates thickness for a flat plane in After Effects (even 3D layers in After Effects are still two-dimensional, which is where this type of plug-in can help).

In addition, expressions in After Effects are extremely useful for a variety of purposes, one of which is the automation of difficult tasks. Digital Anarchy's "3D Assistants" is a plug-in for After Effects that allows you to take advantage of expressions by quickly creating boxes or other simple shapes and distributing them in 3D space (2.5D, as After Effects calls it). You can do this manually yourself, although automating the process can save considerable time.

If you are looking for a way to greatly improve your After Effects knowledge and experience, you should check out what expressions (custom scripts that are written to create advanced interactivity) have to offer. For more information on how you can use expressions, as well as other links to After Effects tutorials and news, visit www.hdv-filmmaking.com, or check out the wide variety of After Effects (and other) information on the Creative Cow Web site, www.creativecow.net.

Creating Backdrops and Digital Matte Paintings

Artificial backgrounds and set extensions have been used in movies since the early days of film. With digital tools, the artist's job has become easier in some respects, since we no longer need to paint backgrounds by hand on glass or other physical surfaces. Instead, a subject can be keyed out using a blue or green screen, or rotoscoped and dropped into a new setting courtesy of Photoshop or any number of image creation software. Painted backdrops for a film are called *matte paintings*, and today's digital matte "paintings" may consist of either 2D or 3D elements. A new backdrop may simply consist of a sky or some artificial water, or it may be entire cityscapes and environments created in 3D software and placed outside the windows of a house, car, or any other setting. Software like Aurora Sky and Water may be used inside After Effects or Final Cut Pro, for example, to create artificial sky and water backgrounds that can be customized to suit a project. Actual backgrounds created in 3D or even 2D software may also be motion tracked to remain locked to a particular set location or to follow the path of a camera.

Actual photographs may also be used as a backdrop and are often placed behind keyed footage. Using Realviz Stitcher (see Figure 11.12) and a series of panoramic photos, you could create a 360-degree environment based on real places. Stitcher is a great tool for this purpose. You could even create HDRI images, align them in Stitcher, and then compile them in HDR Shop, apply them to a 3D environment in an application like Cinema 4D, which is then combined with matchmoving data to incorporate the real-world camera movements into the rotation and perspective of a virtual camera. This is one complex way a stitched background could be used. Of course, you could simply construct a static or moving 2D backdrop in Photoshop or After Effects and place it behind some keyed footage. To add a little extra interest, you might even apply a particle effect, like rain or snow. Additionally, photographs could be cut into separate layers that can be positioned in 3D space to create the illusion of depth.

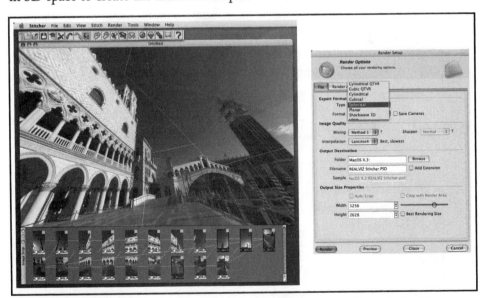

Figure 11.12 *Realviz Stitcher can be used to assemble panoramas for use in backdrops. (Courtesy of Realviz)*

Interview:
John Dames

The following is an interview with John Dames at coreaudiovisual (www.coreaudiovisual.com), where they create commercials and other projects for clients like Nike, Pontiac, and others. In addition, they are the creators of several useful plug-ins for Maxon's Cinema 4D application.

What types of problems have you encountered when integrating 3D with live action elements?

Matching live action and 3D elements is always a tricky task, but it is made especially difficult when you are not in control of the live action shoot. Typically, you get some shots, with no technical reference as far as camera, lenses, and lighting, and are asked to "integrate stuff."

When we worked on the Nike/Champs "Style Wars" spot, we were asked to integrate existing NBA footage of Charles Barkley and Dirk Nowescki with a stylized 3D environment and characters we had created. The footage was delivered two weeks late, didn't contain the shots we requested, and was on Beta SP (not D1). It was a problem.

We attempted a number of tricks, but even matchmoving in some of the more popular apps was made difficult by the awful quality of the footage. Our TD, Darf, quickly whipped up a solution and started development of "Skrub." Skrub allowed us to take our rotoscoped d1 footage and play it real-time, with full alpha, in a C4D viewport. All of the camera and matchmoves were then hand-keyframed to fit the shot.

We now refer to this technique as "perceptual matchmoving," in that it may not be technically perfect but it works great. In the end, it helped us create an even more surreal universe for the spot.

http://www.coreaudiovisual.com/spotpages/nk_stylewars.html

Do you have any tips for users who want to work with 3D animation and effects, particularly with HD video or other high-resolution projects (reducing render times, etc.)?

Problems in your 3D workflow are magnified tenfold when you move to HD. It really forced us to pay attention to the smallest efficiencies and optimizations, and in the end really helped refine our process.

Here are some general tips.

1. Learn to work with proxies: Most compositing and editing apps out there make it fairly easy to build at one resolution and change it for the final output. Just remember when building your proxy project to account for your final output aspect ratio and frame rates.

2. Design for post: 3D rendering, in any app, is the most time-consuming part of any project. HD render times are literally exponentially longer when it comes to volumetric effects, photon/caustics generation, etc. By breaking your renders into multiple passes, such as ambient, shadow, specular, effects, etc., you have much more control and flexibility in achieving your desired look in post without having to re-render for tweaks.

3. Design for your vision, not the format. Yes, you now have 1920×1080 pixels to play with, but you don't have to use every one of them. Too many artists believe they must increase the complexity of their work to "fill" the new formats, but in reality people perceive and process HD images just like standard D1 images. At the end of the day, this is still filmmaking and all the old rules apply.

In what ways have you found 3D particles useful?

At coreaudiovisual, we are technology driven. That drive is expressed in our software division, corearsenal. It's a totally symbiotic relationship, and each drives the other. So when we got into particles, we started exploiting the technology and writing software to allow new possibilities. We use 3D particles for everything from standard explosions to type FX to recreating paintings to generating complex geometry. One of our customers even uses our COREPARTICLETOOLS plug-in for C4D to create hair for a character.

Particles are really useful for all of these things because you can give them behaviors and let them drive the animation. All you do is set up the conditions for them to work with and animate the changes to their environment or how they react to it.

One use we have for particles is to "hold" a camera while flying around a scene. The particle gets attracted to some things, repulsed by others, and maintains a tenuous control over the camera like it's on a bungie cord. Now if I were to try and keyframe that camera, it would never feel the same. It wouldn't have the "intelligence" that the particle brings to it.

(continued on next page)

(continued from previous page)

http://www.coreaudiovisual.com/pcam.html

This same standard applies to more traditional uses of particles—they easily convey natural processes in an unnatural (3D software) environment.

Chapter 12

Delivering HDV Content

Considering the complexity and general confusion surrounding the latest high-definition formats, deciding how to output your finished masterpiece can be a challenge. Currently, a debate is taking place among the big video and computer companies, such as Toshiba and Sony, regarding the adoption of HD-DVD or Blu-ray disc formats. The imminent release of high-definition DVDs promises a better home video experience that includes sharper images and greater interactivity. Meanwhile, consumers and production professionals are left wondering what they should do with their HD video today. If you are reading this in 2006 and beyond, most of the confusion should have been sorted out. Fortunately, there are other ways to deliver HDV content, including a variety of HD resolution options, standard definition formats (such as DVD), and as Web-ready files.

Outputting HDV

As of this writing, there are only a few options for outputting HD or HDV to a disc-based format for playback on a computer or set-top player. In fact, no set-top HD-DVD or Blu-ray players (the top HD disc delivery formats) are currently sold (at least in the U.S.), although this should have changed by the fall or winter of 2005. Applications like DVD Studio Pro 4 and Sonic Scenarist HD offer the ability to author HD DVD-ROMS, although burning a disc that will play in a set-top player is currently not possible (at least without one of the expensive recorders/players available in Japan). You can, however, author an HD-DVD that plays on a suitably equipped computer, a stopgap that may be worthwhile for archiving and transmitting video to clients, or for high-definition presentations. This does not mean that other options for outputting HD do not exist. JVC recently introduced a device for playing HDV on a disc; JVC has its D-VHS tape format; and the full range of ROM, Web, and other standard definition output options are still available. This means that there are a variety of encoding options to select for an HD or HDV project, although none that is as ideally suited to home viewing as the current standard definition video discs.

As more people adopt high-definition formats like HDV, the number of available options and their ease of use will increase considerably. If you think back a few years, it was hard to imagine a time when millions of ordinary homes would have the ability to burn their own DVDs, much less design and author beautiful discs on their home computer. Copying television programs or home movies onto a recordable disc is now as simple as using a VCR. In time, HD-DVDs (or Blu-ray discs) will become the preferred recording medium for storing and sharing your video. It is important for professionals to acknowledge the use of HD technology by consumers, since it is what drives the market for HD content, as well as the creation and support of HD devices by the world's hardware and software manufacturers.

First, it is important to understand the process before outputting a video project for any of the formats mentioned, even though many of the steps may remain similar to delivering standard-definition projects. For example, the first step in preparing video for delivery on disc-based media or over the Web is encoding. The encoding process entails taking your source video (usually in some uncompressed, or relatively low-compressed form) and converting it to some other format through the use of advanced compression schemes. There are applications, such as Apple's Compressor 2, that can create these files using simple presets, which can be used "as is" or modified to meet your project's needs. The accessibility and efficiency of delivery depends greatly on which encoding options you choose.

Standards for Output

There are currently three main encoding options for outputting HD video for playback on a computer or a disc. Each of these standards may relate differently to the media that it is eventually distributed on (HD-DVD, Blu-ray, etc.), although if your computer can produce these files, you will likely be able to play them back without too much difficulty. (However, machines may experience intermittent playback problems, particularly with 1080i 60 formats, even when running on a fast computer.)

H.264

Also known as MPEG-4 Part 10 or AVC (Advanced Video Coding), H.264 is the basis for the majority of HD-DVD and Blu-Ray disc content. In fact, H.264 is a mandatory standard for HD players for delivering high-definition movies on disc (players must support it, although they can support other standards as well).

Due to its unique scalability, H.264 is an ideal format for all sorts of applications, ranging from HD-DVD to video for mobile phones. It is extremely efficient, providing at least twice the space savings (half the bit rate or better) of a comparable MPEG-2. In addition, H.264 has seen adoption by computer software and hardware makers, including use as part of Apple's new operating system, OS 10.4 Tiger. Even Sony's new Playstation Portable has hardware decoding that allows it to play video files in the H.264 format (albeit at smaller resolutions). For content producers, H.264/AVC is the format to watch. For a look at some H.264 content online, check out Apple's Web site at www.apple.com/quicktime/hdgallery/.

One element of the H.264 codec that assists in the creation of extremely small and efficient files is the method it uses for its B-frames (a discussion of I, B, and P frames for MPEG-2 is discussed in Chapter 7). In an MPEG-2 file, such as those used by a standard definition DVD, B-frames are created by looking at the previous or next frames (referring to frames that are immediately to the left or right). An H.264 file, on the other hand, creates its B-frames by referring to groups of frames that can be located earlier or later in time, as well as being used as reference frames themselves for other B-frames. The result is a more efficient encode that is also more accurate, since it is drawing information from multiple locations to arrive at the best frame using the least amount of space. This means lower data rates and potentially better looking video than MPEG-2 (at least at the same data rates). In addition, H.264 utilizes the AAC audio file format, which is comparable to an MP3, although higher quality (ideal for the Web and other services that lack bandwidth) and capable of sample rates up to 96kHz (CDs use a 44.1kHz sample rate, while standard definition DVDs utilize 48kHz—although DVD-audio discs are capable of more than 96kHz).

MPEG-2

When Blu-ray was first introduced, MPEG-2 was the only HD video format it supported for playback from set-top players. It didn't take long for Sony to adopt the other HD formats (H.264 and VC-1). MPEG-2, the format used by today's standard definition DVDs, is scalable, much like H.264, and can be used for HD resolution video. (Remember, it is the format used to record and transmit HDV.) Since HDV is MPEG-2, it can be included in an HD-DVD project that you create without the need for additional compression, although it will not be as efficient as H.264. Currently, JVC offers a special player to read conventional red laser discs with MPEG-2 HDV content recorded on them (JVC SRDVD-100U ProHD, see Figure 12.1), although it may be supported in future players by other manufacturers as well.

Figure 12.1 *The JVC SRDVD-100U provides inexpensive playback of HDV media (MPEG-2) from current, recordable DVD discs.*

VC-1

The VC-1 encoding option is based on Microsoft's Windows Media Video 9 codec (WM9), and several companies produce software and offer export options that support it. It is similar to H.264 in many ways, and is even included as part of the requirements for HD-DVD players. Although it may be based on Windows technology, you can encode VC-1 (or Windows Media Video 9) content on Macs as well as PCs. As with H.264, Windows Media Video 9 is used for a variety of applications, including (but not limited to) delivery of HD content on DVD-ROMs, theatrical projection of HD video (digital cinema), and creation of HD dailies for film productions (real-time encoding of HD content using special hardware makes this possible).

DVD-ROM Presentations

Before the advent of recordable HD-DVDs and Blu-Ray discs, the only option for someone to put HD and HDV video on a disc was as a data file compressed with any number of HD formats that a computer could read (MPEG-4, MPEG-2, VC-1). If you have a fast computer and a monitor that is big enough, you can experience an early version of high-definition DVDs on DVD-ROM discs, such as those sold through Microsoft, or even a few Hollywood titles. A past DVD edition of *Terminator 2* came with a second, bonus disc that included the film in

WM9 format for playback on a suitably equipped computer. To find out more about which HD DVD-ROMS are available for your computer, check out Microsoft's Web site (http://www.microsoft.com/windows/windowsmedia/content_provider/film/HDVideo.aspx). For the near future, HD on DVD-ROMs may be an option to consider, and even when HD-DVD and Blu-ray reach consumers, an adequate way to deliver video for HD resolution training materials, presentations, or multimedia kiosks.

Figure 12.2 *Until HD-DVD and Blu-ray recorders become available, Apple's DVD Studio Pro 4 allows you to create HD-DVD projects that play back on current red-laser media, using a computer with a software DVD player that supports the format. Apple's DVD Player 4.6 is required on the Mac. (Courtesy Apple)*

Apple's DVD Studio Pro 4 is one of the early supporters of HD-DVD, allowing you to author a disc using HD video (HDV or otherwise), which can be compressed and placed onto current recordable DVDs (see Figure 12.2). Of course, DVD-ROMS do not have the capacity of the newer HD-DVD and Blu-ray formats, discussed in this chapter. When those formats do become available, it should be a seamless process to make a new copy of your project that takes advantage of the HD-DVD set top players.

Windows Media Video 9

Windows Media Video 9, on which the VC-1 codec is based, is another option for the delivery of HD video content, particularly for computer-based purposes or distribution on DVD-ROMs. Since WMV9 HD discs are not limited by the traditional DVD specifications, it is possible to include data rates on the discs as high as 22Mbps, as compared with the 9.8Mbps of traditional DVDs. As mentioned earlier, it is even used for select digital cinema applications. Some Landmark Century Theatres have used Windows Media Video 9 playing off of a hard drive to project independent films transferred to this digital format (initially playing from 2.8GHz Pentium 4's using 8Mbps data streams), reducing the cost and impracticality of distributing film prints for short-run and independently-funded projects.

Several companies provide tools for the creation of WMV9 content, many of which can be found by visiting Microsoft's Web site or checking with the companies that produce the software you use every day (Adobe, Avid, Apple, etc.). The following example demonstrates some of the options for the Windows Media Export settings included in the Flip4Mac Windows Media Video 9 Pro edition (see Figure 12.3). These options are reached through the standard QuickTime Export window (choose File→Export→Export: Movie to Windows Media, and then click the Options button), which is available in just about any application that supports QuickTime, including the stand-alone QuickTime Pro player.

Figure 12.3 *Flip4Mac's Windows Media Video 9 export option in QuickTime Pro.*

Most of these settings should translate to whichever software you use to export Windows Media Video 9. Some of these topics (including bit rate and CBR/VBR) are discussed in Chapter 7. In addition, Windows Media Video 9 is also able to export video for the Web and a variety of other applications, which are mentioned here together with HD (even HD can be placed on the Web, either for client approvals or for showcasing your work). The following settings represent a selection of parameters from the Flip4Mac software, although they do not necessarily include every option you will encounter.

Video Tab

If you are using an application like Flip4Mac to assist with the encoding of Windows Media Video 9, you may have an option of choosing a particular export module for your video. Make sure you check the option to include video, whether using standard or professional output. (Professional options usually denote support for greater HD resolution support, rather than standard definition and Web-only features, - see Figure 12.4.) In this case, options include WMV 9 Standard and WMW 9 Advanced (for more HD specific features). If you are on the Mac, the Windows Media Advanced features will not play back in the Mac version of the Windows Media 9 Player, although you can still use this option to create content for Windows PCs.

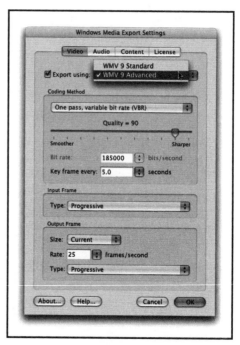

Figure 12.4 *Windows Media 9 Standard and Windows Media 9 Advanced in the Flip4Mac Export window.*

Coding Method

The coding method refers to the compression settings that affect the data rate and processing methods for your video. The two main options are CBR (constant bit rate) and VBR (variable bit rate), which control how data is assigned at any given moment in your video, based (generally) on the complexity of the image. VBR is more efficient and works well for the majority of HD video encoding needs, particularly in two-pass mode (as described in Figure 12.5). Although Windows Media Video 9 is great for HD, it can also be used to deliver a copy of your project for viewing on the Web. In general, CBR works well for Web video that is used on a streaming server (probably something you do not encounter often) since it restricts the bandwidth better than VBR. Alternately, VBR works best for progressive downloads, where data can vary according to the complexity of your video. VBR is most important when trying to maximize space while not sacrificing quality. A two-pass encoder uses a first pass to analyze the video to make better decisions about what information needs to be thrown out in order to maintain the constant or variable bit rate, and the second pass does the actual encoding. It takes longer to encode with two-pass encoding, but should look better than one-pass CBR or VBR.

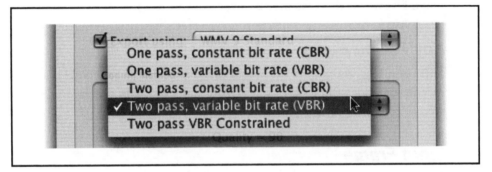

Figure 12.5 *Coding methods include the type of bit rate processing and quality settings that are used.*

Quality

Quality settings determine the visual excellence of the output, based on where the emphasis is placed on the analysis and processing of video to achieve the best results. The main factors that determine quality (in this instance) are image sharpness and smoothness of motion. To increase the value of one, decreases the results of the other—to what degree is determined by the quality setting (controlled here as a slider). For example, if you were more concerned with the fluidity and smoothness of your video then the quality setting should be moved to the left toward the "Smoother" setting, which lessens the integrity of individual pictures, leaving more bits for higher frame rates and reliable motion. If sharpness is more important in your video, then move the slider toward the "Sharper" setting (one instance would be text or detailed graphic images and designs). In general, it is better to keep the quality setting set toward Sharpness (the default might be between 75 and 90). For high bit rate HD video, the differences are probably negligible, although video for the Web suffers much more, and the differences are more apparent. In addition, the better the quality, the more bits that are used, and the more time it takes to create a file.

Bit rate

The amount of data, in bits, that is transmitted every second determines the quality (and size) of the video you output to a great degree. In fact, it is one of the main limiting factors for achieving the best possible quality, and a large part of the difference between physical formats like HDV and HDCAM, or video on a DVD, as opposed to video on a mobile phone. Generally, high bit rates mean good quality, while low bit rates mean less quality. However, bit rates are relative to the type of project you are creating (HD versus Web files for example), so that a high bit rate for the Web may be a very low bit rate for HD.

Key Frame Every

This option determines the amount of time between each keyframe that is used to encode your video (more keyframes create larger file sizes and may take longer to process).

Input Frame

The input frame type is where you can tell the software what kind of images (in terms of field order) it can expect to work with, so that it can create the optimal settings better to match it. The input frame is important so that the encoder knows exactly what type of video it is being fed. Choices include progressive (for 24p and 30p material, such as those produced by the JVC HDV cameras or produced with Magic Bullet Suite or a Nattress plug-in) and interlace (either upper or lower field, although upper field is the correct choice for HDV, see Figure 12.6).

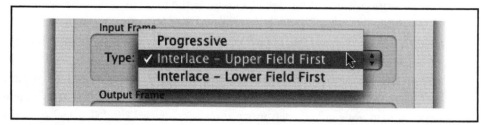

Figure 12.6 *The Input Frame tells the encoder what field order your source video uses.*

Output Frame

The output frame determines the frame size, frame rate, and field order of the video you want to output, and is more specific than input frame, since you have a variety of options to choose from (see Figure 12.7). Using these controls, you can scale the video you have input to a larger or smaller frame size (including up-rezing video to HD, or lowering its size for use on the Web), while adjusting frame rates to hit your target bit rate with better results.

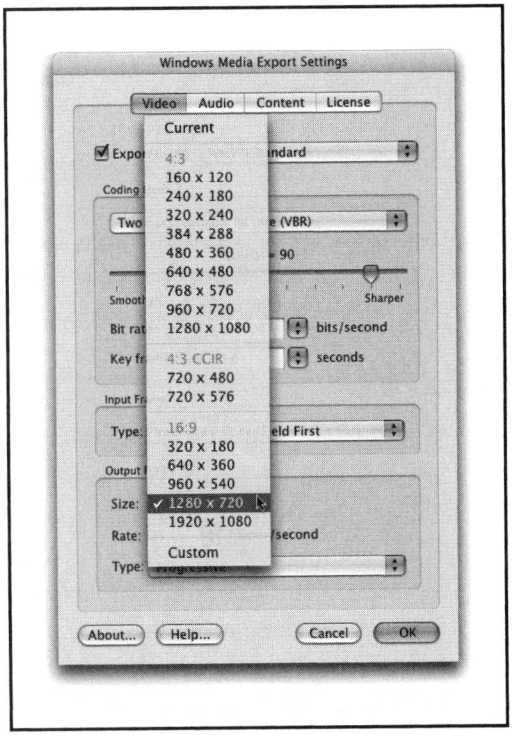

Size

The frame size of the video you output might range from 160×120 (smallest video size for the Web) up to 1920×1080 HD frame sizes. For 16:9 HDV images scaled down for the Web, you should consider using a widescreen frame size, such as 320×180.

Figure 12.7 *Output Frame determines the size, frame rate, and field order of the video you output.*

Rate

The frame rate of the video you output has a great effect on the size of the file you output. This is particularly important for Web video, which generally requires fewer frames per second to play smoothly. In general, 15fps usually works for 30fps NTSC media (although for 25fps PAL media, and 24p material, 12fps is the correct choice), although broadband connections might handle more, especially as a progressive download. Choices range from 5 frames to 60 frames per second.

Type

Once again, you should specify the frame order for your video output, whether progressive or interlaced. Video that is destined for the Web works best as progressive, since it compresses better and provides smoother playback on video monitors, while interlace is fine if you are going back out to video (such as when producing a WMV9 DVD-ROM for HDV content you have shot with a Sony HDV camera).

> ### DIVX
>
> As an alternative to H.263, VC-1 (WMV-9), and MPEG-2, DivX allows you to compress a movie small enough to fit on a standard, red laser DVD disc at file sizes that are often smaller than all other HD compression formats. DivX-capable HD-DVD players for the home have been available before any Blu-ray or HD-DVD format players. Visit www.divx.com to find out more about the format, including information on software and hardware that will create and play HD video. The newest versions of applications like Toast should also be able to burn DivX HD discs.

HD-DVD

HD-DVD (High-Density Digital Versatile Disc) is an optical media, championed by Toshiba, NEC, Sanyo, and several major film studios (see Figure 12.8). It is one of the main standards for the delivery of high-definition video content (the DVD Forum voted to make it the official successor of DVD), although it can also be used to store data, similar to a DVD-ROM (basically, any disc that can deliver video stores data in one form or another, so it can be used for general storage needs as well). HD-DVDs, like Blu-ray, are able to use H.264, VC-1, and MPEG-2-based video, although H.264 is the standard, being used to deliver most movies in high-definition. All current HD disc formats, including HD-DVD, use a blue laser (blue-violet, actually) that operates at a wavelength of 405nm, as opposed to the red laser technology that operates with a 650nm wavelength, which is used by standard definition DVDs. The benefit of the blue laser is that it is a shorter wavelength (405nm compared with 650nm), which means it can read smaller pit sizes on a denser disc with more data.

The HD-DVD format currently supports a maximum of 45GB on triple-layer, read-only discs (or HD DVD-ROM), or 50% more than the 30GB dual-layer discs (see

Figure 12.8 *HD-DVD recorder prototype from Toshiba.*

Figure 12.9), a capacity that comes closer to meeting Blu-ray's current 50GB threshold. This added capacity makes the format even more enticing to movie studios and others who are attracted to Blu-ray's larger storage capacities, but prefer the production methods for HD-DVD, which are similar to current DVD processes. Much of the compatibility in replication is due to the physi-

Figure 12.9 *Toshiba HD-DVD player and 30GB dual-layer disc.*

cal structure of the HD-DVD discs, which consist of two 0.6mm thick discs (layer depth) that are bonded together back to back, the same as all current DVD formats. (Blu-ray, as mentioned in the next section, is handled differently.)

In addition to its HD-DVD ROMs, Toshiba has been busy working on its recordable technology, largely to outdo the competing Blu-ray format. They will sell a recordable high-definition HD-DVD, which (as of this writing) is expected

to ship in spring of 2006, along with an HD-DVD recorder. These discs are write-once, and have a 15GB storage capacity, as compared to the current maximum of 45GB for a three-layer HD-DVD disc. See Figure 12.10.

Figure 12.10 *15GB write-once, recordable HD-DVD media (HD DVD-ROM).*

Although HD-DVD is similar in many ways to the Blu-ray disc format introduced by Sony, there are differences between the formats, including the methods used to produce the discs. In HD-DVD's favor, its discs can be replicated using existing DVD technology, which means that disc manufacturing plants do not need to drastically overhaul their current processes. This relatively seamless transition reduces the cost and risks associated with migrating to a new format. It also means that producing HD-DVD discs may be less expensive than an equivalent Blu-ray disc (new processes for creating Blu-ray discs may eliminate the price gap). Fortunately for today's consumers, both HD-DVD and Blu-ray players are backward compatible with earlier formats and are expected to play standard definition DVDs. It has even been suggested that dual-format DVDs could be sold that include HD-DVD discs on one side and standard definition DVDs on the other, so that consumers are only presented with one choice, which gains usefulness as they upgrade to newer televisions and DVD players. Optimistic, perhaps, yet it reminds content producers of the importance of catering to both HD and SD audiences. In fact, Toshiba has also announced a double-sided, dual-layer hybrid disc that holds 30GB of HD-DVD content on one side and 8.5GB of DVD material on the other. Hopefully, these efforts will make the transition to HD-DVD smoother.

Figure 12.11 *An early model HD-DVD drive from NEC.*

It remains to be seen whether a compromise will be reached between the creators of HD-DVD (Toshiba and NEC, see Figure 12.11) and Blu-ray (Sony) regarding the union of these two formats (a difficult task, considering the differing layer depths and manufacturing processes). Many talks have taken place, attempting to arrive at a single standard for high-definition DVDs, in order to avoid the confusion that took place with VHS and Betamax, and more recently DVD-Audio and SACD. It is in the best interest of consumers to have a single standard, although the possibility of a dual-format player is another option for improving compatibility. A few of the film studios that currently support HD-DVD include Warner Brothers, Universal Studios, Paramount Pictures, and New Line Cinema, although many of these also will back Blu-ray releases.

The following is a breakdown of currently announced, HD DVD-ROM discs (as provided by Toshiba).

◆ **Single-sided, single-layer**—15GB 0.6mm discs are the smallest HD DVD-ROMS, yet provide enough space to hold an entire HD movie and bonus material. Depending on the bit rate used to encode your video (with MPEG-4 or VC-1), you can fit about four hours of HD video onto one of these discs. See Figure 12.12.

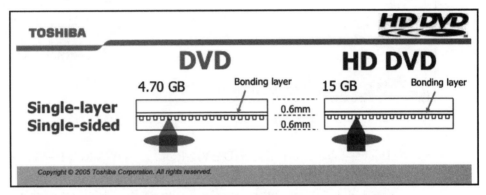

Figure 12.12 *Single-sided, single-layer HD–DVD . (Courtesy of Toshiba)*

◆ **Single-sided, dual-layer**—30GB 0.6mm discs (15GB per layer) provide more than enough space for a few HD-DVD movies or lots of extras (approximately eight hours of HD material, or an equivalent 48 hours of SD material, depending on bit rate). See Figure 12.13.

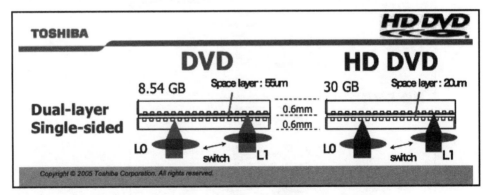

Figure 12.13 *Single-sided, dual-layer HD–DVD. (Courtesy of Toshiba)*

◆ **Single-sided, triple-layer**—These 45GB discs offer plenty of space for multiple movies, TV programs, and archival material, which is perfect for "boxed sets" and entire seasons of your favorite shows. See Figure 12.14.

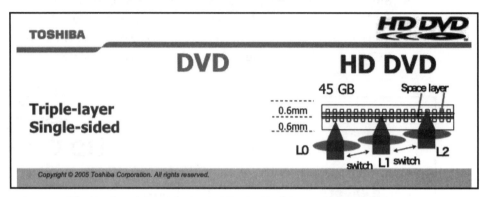

Figure 12.14 *Single-sided, triple-layer HD-DVD. (Courtesy of Toshiba)*

◆ **Double-sided, hybrid disc** (HD DVD-ROM and DVD-ROM)—A long playing, high-definition 30GB HD-DVD disc on one side and an 8.5GB (same as a "DVD-9") on the other for an equivalent standard definition version of the movie. These discs are poised to ease the transition for consumers from SD to HD discs without requiring collectors to purchase two versions of the same film (a reason for some consumers to balk at buying either version right away). Hopefully, these discs will be embraced by movie studios, which are notorious for releasing multiple versions of the same film. See Figure 12.15.

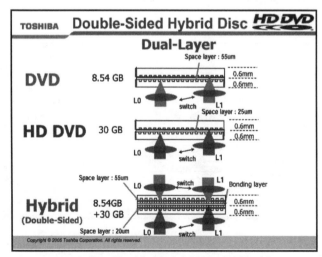

Figure 12.15 *Double-sided hybrid HD-DVD. (Courtesy of Toshiba)*

Blu-ray Disc

Sony's disc-based format for the delivery of HD content is called *Blu-ray*, a competitor to HD-DVD. Blu-ray, which is similar in many ways to HD-DVD, including their use of a blue laser and support for all current HD codecs (MPEG-4, MPEG-2, VC-1), provides higher storage capacities than HD-DVD, as well as a different approach to disc production. The primary difference lies in the Blu-ray disc's structure, which uses a single layer that is 0.1mm deep, with a reflective layer attached to the bottom of the disc (as opposed to HD-DVD's 0.6mm data depth, and discs that sandwich its reflective layer). Overall disc thickness is still 1.2mm, the same as CD, DVD, and HD-DVD.

A single-layer Blu-ray disc has a storage capacity of 25GB (substantially more than a single-layer HD-DVD at 15GB), while its dual-layer discs have a capacity of 50GB (again, more than a dual-layer HD-DVD at 30GB, but closer to a triple-layer HD-DVD at 45GB). Although the current storage limits for Blu-ray video discs are 50GB, there are 100GB and even 200GB versions in development (with four layers and eight layers, respectively). The potential for storing large amounts of data, particularly on recordable Blu-ray media (or BD-R and BD-RE), makes this format a real threat to HD-DVD. Even if HD-DVD discs see widespread adoption for the release of feature films, Blu-ray still looks like the superior choice for a recordable storage medium (although the cost of discs and recorders, as well as the availability of media for each format remains to be seen). It should be noted that recordable Blu-ray discs may offer slightly different capacities than their ROM counterparts. Currently, Sony Pictures Entertainment (including Columbia Pictures), MGM (also owned by Sony), as well as The Walt Disney Company, Apple Computer, and others plan on releasing movies and offering support for the Blu-ray format. In addition, the release of the Playstation 3, the latest version of Sony's flagship video gaming console uses Blu-ray, should give the format a boost.

Some advantages to using Blu-ray Discs, also called BD-ROMs, include a potential for 67 percent more capacity than HD-DVD, in addition to recordable discs (BD-R and BD-RE) that provide 150 percent more recording capacity than comparable HD-DVD media. Most of these statistics are according to Sony's own literature, and are based on predictions of the format's future potential, so information may change over time. Some of the percentages and comparisons to HD-DVD may change in relation to announcements of newer, larger capacity discs from both parties. Additionally, Blu-ray discs include a special hard-coat technology, which makes them more resistant to fingerprints and scratches, which results in (potentially) longer lasting discs, particularly when subjected to frequent use. You may remember the original Blu-ray prototypes that included a protective case (similar to DVD-ROM), although current versions have done away with the casing to become more user friendly.

An exciting possibility for consumers is a special three-layer combo disc, which would preserve two layers for HD content (like a 50GB dual-layer BD-ROM), along with a special third layer that holds ordinary DVD data, for playing back current, standard definition DVDs from the same disc. If you purchased one of these discs (currently developed by JVC), you could place it in a standard definition DVD player today and, later on, when you have purchased an HDTV and special Blu-ray player, access the HD content "hidden" on the disc. This dual functionality is made possible by the different depths at which a red laser and blue laser on a Blu-ray disc would read (although this is not possible with HD-DVDs, since they read at the same depths).

Figure 12.16 *Philips' prototype all-in-one PC writer reads and writes CD, DVD, and Blu-ray Discs.*

For producers of content for Blu-ray discs (particularly Hollywood studios, or others hoping to be onboard the format's release of discs and players), check out Sonic Solutions Blu-ray Creator software. With this application, you can create discs that conform to Blu-ray specifications, as well as taking advantage of some of the format's "expanded" interactivity, including pop-up menus and full-color subpictures (overlays). Apple's DVD Studio Pro 4 can also produce content that can be recorded to Blu-ray discs when they become available. At the beginning of 2005, Philips demonstrated a PC drive with an "all-in-one" Blu-ray recorder, which includes a special triple-laser optical pick-up unit that separates infra-red, red, and blue lasers for maximum compatibility with Blu-ray discs, as well as DVDs and CDs (see Figure 12.16). In the coming year, there are certain to be more announcements about drives and recorders that offer a similar degree of support.

♦ **Single-sided, single-layer**—25GB 0.6mm discs are the smallest Blu-ray discs, yet provide enough space to hold a few HD movies (when recorded with H.264 or VC-1), in addition to bonus material—significantly more than a single-layer HD-DVD's 15GB. See Figure 12.17. The 25GB capacity would also allow for an average movie recorded in MPEG-2 HD (as well as HDV files) to be stored, although MPEG-4 will be more practical for full-length HD movies and extras.

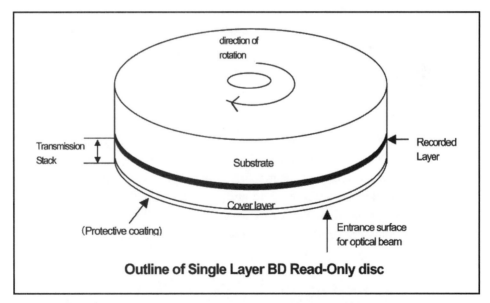

Figure 12.17 *Single-sided, single-layer BD-ROM. (Courtesy of Blu-ray Disc Association)*

◆ **Single-sided, dual-layer**—50GB 0.6mm discs (25 per layer), provide more than enough space for several HD-DVD movies and lots of extras. See Figure 12.18. In fact, there is perhaps so much space on these discs (at least for current storage needs) that it may be difficult to convince some companies of their immediate usefulness, as compared with lower-capacity, and slightly cheaper HD-DVDs.

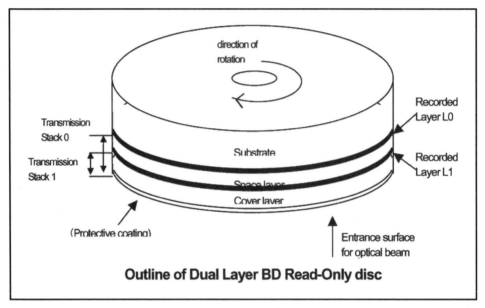

Figure 12.18 *Single-sided, dual-layer BD-ROM. (Courtesy of Blu-ray Disc Association)*

The following chart provides a brief summary of a few of the main differences and similarities between HD-DVD and Blu-ray Discs. For the latest information about new formats, visit the manufacturer's Web sites, particularly if you are interested in information about read and write speeds, which (as of this writing) are still being solidified. You can also check out the HD-DVD Promotion Group (www.hddvdprg.com) or the Blu-ray Disc Association (www.blu-raydisc.com).

Table 12.1 DVD, HD-DVD, and Blu-ray

	DVD	HD-DVD (HD DVD-ROM)	Blu-ray Discs (BD-ROM)
Single Layer Capacity	4.7GB	15GB	25GB
Double Layer Capacity	8.54GB	30GB	50GB
Triple Layer Capacity +	NA	45GB (3-layer)	100GB (4-layer) / 200 (8-layer)
Laser	Red (650nm)	Blue (405nm)	Blue (405nm)
Disc Size (Full Size)	12cm	12cm	12cm
Compression	MPEG-2/ MPEG-1	MPEG-4/ MPEG-2/VC-1	MPEG-4/MPEG-2/VC-1
Maximum Bit Rate (Video and Audio)	9.8Mbps	36Mbps	36Mbps
Approximate Playback Time (H.264 Encoding or Equivalent for HD-DVD and Blu-ray Discs, Depending on Bit Rate)	2+ Hours, SD Resolution (single-layer) 4 Hours, SD Resolution	4+ Hours, HD Resolution (single-layer) 8+ Hours, HD Resolution (dual-layer)	5 1/2 + Hours HD Resolution (single-layer) 11+ Hours, HD Resolution (dual-layer)

HOLOGRAPHIC VERSATILE DISC

You may have heard recently about a new type of media called *HVD* (not *HDV*), or Holographic Versatile Disc. These discs (which are not yet released) record data onto holographic layers in an incredibly small amount of space, allowing for 1TB to (eventually) 3.9TB of data to be stored on a disc equivalent in size to current CDs and DVDs (12cm in diameter). Eventually, these discs, with their greatly increased capacity, could replace current HD-DVD and Blu-ray technology. Imagine, an entire DVD collection that fits on a single disc. The implications for inexpensive storage of computer data on recordable discs would also be significant, especially for video professionals who need to back up large projects. Interestingly, a version of HVD has been developed for a small, plastic card (think of it as a P2 card, but thinner and transparent), which is projected to cost about a dollar apiece with a capacity of 30GB. These cards would be a great alternative to the very expensive P2 cards produced by Panasonic. For example, the ability to record HDV onto one of these cards (either directly from the camera, or as a backup) would be simply amazing, and could transform the way everyone uses digital video, whether consumers or professionals. At this point, it is simply speculation, but exciting to consider.

Overview of DVD Authoring

The process of authoring a DVD has become simpler over the years, although there are still many things to understand about the general workflow and options that are available to the professional user. (The term "author" is used to indicate the process of creating a DVD or other multimedia project.) In this section, a general overview of creating a DVD is discussed, particularly in relation to standard definition DVDs, a format which (until recordable HD-DVD and Blu-ray discs and recorders become available) is the most frequently used way to output any professional video project for viewing and distributing video to a wide audience. Most of the same methodology and techniques for creating an SD-DVD apply to the HD formats, although the newer HD formats will offer the possibility for additional interactivity and storage capacity. For those of you already familiar with the creation of DVDs, the discussion below includes some advanced suggestions, although those who are new to DVD authoring should consider picking up a book or completing tutorials for their particular software of choice (see Figure 12.19), since the coverage included here is not intended to be all-encompassing—the variety of available software and the scope of this book limit it.

Figure 12.19 *Adobe Encore is a DVD authoring application for PCs, which offers excellent integration with Photoshop, After Effects, and Premiere Pro.*

Preparing Your DVD Assets

The first step in the creation of any DVD project is the preparation of assets. This includes the editing and subsequent encoding of your video into the appropriate format, which is most often MPEG-2 for standard definition DVDs (and some HD projects), or H.264 and VC-1 for HD-DVD projects. In addition, your audio may need to be encoded and compressed into AC-3 (also called *Dolby Digital*) or DTS to make it fit better on your disc, or to add surround sound streams. Menu graphics also need to be created, including any still or motion backgrounds, and slideshow images should be reformatted to fit into the correct TV screen dimensions and aspect ratios, unless your authoring software does the conversion for you. It is at this stage that you should also do some arithmetic to budget for the maximum allowed table space on your discs (as discussed later in this chapter). If creating a dual layer project (or DVD-9), you have more space to work with than with a single layer (DVD-5), although it is still important to check whether the bit rates you encoded with fit with the number of other audio, video, and subtitle streams that you want to add. Later in this chapter, methods for encoding video for a DVD are discussed in greater detail.

Still Menu or Motion Menu Creation

Once your assets are collected and imported into your DVD authoring software, you can begin assembling your disc. One of the first steps is the creation of menus, which are used to link to your video assets through the use of buttons and "jump to" commands. Buttons most often utilize a special "highlight" or "overlay" layer, which provides visible feedback when making a selection. Usually, highlights appear over the top of text or underlining a menu choice. Currently, button highlights are capable of a maximum of four colors, as determined by the subtitle feature that they belong to (four colors are considered "advanced" overlays, although most discs use single color "simple" overlays), while the newer HD-DVD specifications allow for full color highlights and interactive designs. Current DVDs limit the number of buttons to 36 for 4:3 aspect ratio menus, and 18 for 16:9 menus (HD-DVD specs currently list 48 as the maximum per menu page).

The menu's background may consist of a still image or a full-motion animation or video piece on a loop. Using video as a background allows for interesting transitions from one menu to the next. For example, you can click on a button and watch a short piece of video or 3D animation (created as another menu item or track), which brings you smoothly to the next menu. In addition to the main menu page, additional submenus can be created to organize your DVD project better (similar to a Web page), including the ever-popular "chapter list" or "scene selection" menu, for navigating better to portions of a movie, and pages that allow you to set up your DVD for a particular language (including audio streams and subtitles) or audio preferences (such as stereo or surround). Like any other designs for video and broadcast formats, creating an attractive DVD menu design is most often a result of a designer's talent, not a secret formula for instantly producing attractive layouts. Just about every DVD authoring package includes some templates to get you started, although customizing the designs to suit your individual project is usually necessary (see Figure 12.20).

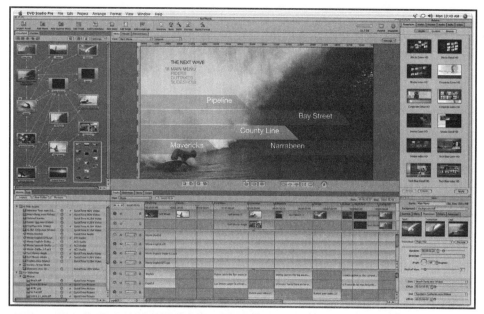

Figure 12.20 *DVD menus in DVD Studio Pro can be created by the user, or customized from existing menu templates, which provide buttons, backgrounds, and motion video elements. (Courtesy of Apple)*

CREATING MENUS FOR DVD WITH PHOTOSHOP

When designing for DVD, just remember that you are dealing with square versus non-square pixels. (Non-square pixels are used for standard definition NTSC and PAL, as well as HDV; however, ordinary HD is square, since it is always used with digital televisions.) If you are creating a standard 4:3 aspect ratio menu, you should set up your document as 720×534 pixels (NTSC) or 768×576 (PAL) in Photoshop and then resize it to 720×480 (NTSC) or 720×576 (PAL) when you are finished creating your designs—just make sure to uncheck the Constrain Proportions option (see Figure 12.21). Although it will appear squashed when viewed in Photoshop, it will appear correctly as viewed by a DVD player, once it has been added to your DVD project. In addition to the consideration of image sizes and pixel aspect ratios, all other principles of broadcast design apply, such as title safe and action safe areas, minimum size for lines in graphics (at least three pixels high, to avoid flickering from interlacing), as well as readable text (roughly 24 pt and up) and "broadcast safe" colors.

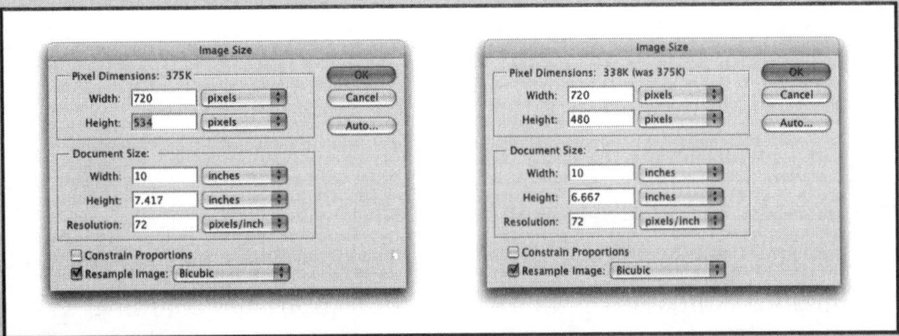

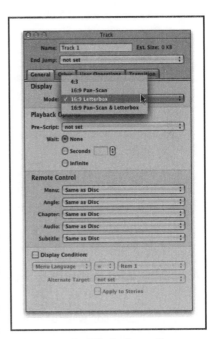

Figure 12.21 *Resizing a Photoshop document (NTSC) for use in a DVD menu.*

Tracks and Slideshows

Tracks are simply the disc items that contain the video for your movies. You can create up to 99 tracks for a DVD project (which includes slideshows, mentioned below), and tracks can be flagged as either 4:3 or anamorphic 16:9 (see Figure 12.22). You can mix the aspect ratios of video on a disc, although you should always remember to flag your tracks correctly and set the display method, such as whether you want a widescreen track to be displayed as letterboxed or pan-and-scan. Markers can be added to tracks to make navigating them easier (a maximum of 99 per track, although one marker is already created for the beginning of a track), and you can enable or disable a user's ability to fast-forward or rewind through a track (playback options are sometimes locked in the "first play" features on a DVD, such as the FBI warning or commercials that are added by movie studios). In addition to tracks, a disc can use slideshows, which are simply collections of photos that play back with or without music. Slideshows operate similarly to a track, and may even be turned into a track in some software to work

Figure 12.22 *Tracks (as well as menus) on a DVD can have a 4:3 or 16:9 aspect ratio, and widescreen images may be viewed as letterboxed or pan-and-scan on a 4:3 television.*

better with them—for example, in case you wanted to mix still images with video content. Once your tracks and slideshows are created, they can be jumped to by clicking the button on a DVD's menu, or by linking one track (or slideshow, or menu) to another, through the use of an "end jump" option.

Using Scripts for Advanced Interactivity

Scripts can be used to create advanced interactivity and to circumvent many of the limitations imposed by the DVD specifications and consumer DVD authoring software. Most users will never use scripts, since the majority of what you need to accomplish is already built into the menu options of your DVD authoring software. However, if you are an advanced user, and if you have a DVD authoring application such as DVD Studio Pro or Sonic Scenarist, you can use scripts to accomplish many tasks, including setting up simple loop scripts (to tell a menu how many times to loop before playing the next item) or for automatically detecting information about a user's player setup to deliver relevant content (such as checking a player's language settings to determine what content to show them).

The number of uses for scripts is endless, although you have a maximum of 16GPRMs to work with in the current DVD specifications (General Parameter Register Memory, or locations to store variables at any given time), although 8GRPMs are more common in software like DVD Studio Pro (however, new features include the ability to split up a single GPRM into 16 bit registers for more complex tasks, such as storing a specific player value with several digits). Curiously, it appears that at least some DVD-ROMs created with Windows Media Video 9 content do not permit the use of GPRMs, although it is uncertain how scripting may be implemented on future HD-DVD formats (interactivity will be enhanced for HD-DVD and Blu-ray discs, as compared with current technology, although its implementation is still a little uncertain as of this writing).

Finishing and Burning a Disc

When a DVD has been assembled, and you are finished testing using the built-in simulator software of your authoring application, you have a couple of choices for finishing the project, including burning the project directly to a DVD and building the project to your hard drive for testing and playback off a computer. The simple "burn" option is available in most DVD software and is the quickest method for outputting a finished disc. Software like iDVD might include a single button at the top of its interface for this purpose. For projects that require a great deal of testing and quality assurance before sending out to a client, it is sometimes best to "build" a project first to your hard drive, test it thoroughly, and then burn the disc (see Figure 12.23). This saves the time and money it takes to burn a disc before finding out that it does not work properly and you need to go back to the project and fix it. The term "build" refers to the encoding and multiplexing (or muxing, which is the interleaving of audio, video, etc.), while "format" refers to the actual writing to a disc or drive. Although DVD-R and DVD+R media is relatively inexpensive, the first batch of HD-DVD recordable discs will make expensive coasters if your project is not set up properly. Once a disc resides on your hard drive, you can then make multiple copies of the project without keeping the original media, as well as needing to reopen a DVD project and multiplex everything a second time.

Figure 12.23 *Roxio's Toast, and similar DVD and CD burning software, such as Easy CD Creator, can be used to copy a DVD project from your hard drive onto a disc, or to create an instant DVD-Video disc from a QuickTime or AVI file on your computer.*

In the end of the process, when a DVD project is built to disc, hard drive, or other media, two folders are created —a "VIDEO_TS" folder, which contains your DVD project, and an empty "AUDIO_TS" folder (see Figure 12.24). You can think of your DVD-Video project as literally being a "VIDEO_TS" folder, which contains all of the files that make up your disc, whether stored on a DVD or your hard drive.

When burning manually to a DVD, both the VIDEO_TS and AUDIO_TS folders should be included, since the DVD player looks for the AUDIO_TS folder, even if it is not used. (The main drawback is that it can slow down the initial player startup a little if it is not found.) For the new HD-DVD formats (both HD-DVD and Blu-ray), the folder that is created is called HVDVD_TS.

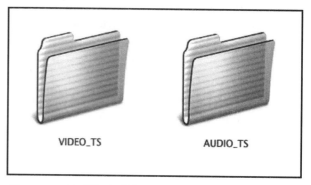

VIDEO_TS   AUDIO_TS

Figure 12.24 *The building of a DVD project results in a VIDEO_TS and AUDIO_TS folder on a standard definition DVD project (HD-DVD projects use HVDVD_TS folders), although the VIDEO_TS is most important, since it contains all of the files for your DVD-Video disc.*

UNIVERSAL DISC FORMAT (UDF)

UDF, or Universal Disc Format, is the type of disc volume used by DVDs to store and play back a DVD-Video Project. In addition to UDF, a DVD is able to store ROM content using the ISO 9660 system (originally designed for CD-ROM), which is the generic file system that allows both Mac and PC users to read data files. A special UDF "bridge" is used on current DVDs to link the two formats and make it possible to include both UDF and ISO 9660 systems on a single disc. When you put the disc in a DVD player, it recognizes the VIDEO_TS folder and plays your DVD-Video project, while inserting into the DVD-ROM drive on a computer permits access to both DVD-Video and data files on a disc, such as DVD-ROM content for bonus files, text documents, images, or Web-ready content. The new HD-DVD standards have done away with ISO 9660 and the need for a UDF bridge. In its place is a new UDF file system, UDF 2.5 (instead of the previous UDF 1.0X specification), which has built-in support for video and data.

Encoding Video for DVD

Before you are able to deliver video on a DVD, you need to prepare your clips and export them to a compatible format, which is almost always MPEG-2 for standard definition DVDs. Although MPEG-1 may be used for DVDs, it is of a lower quality that is not usually associated with DVD-quality video, and it also happens not to be supported by HD-DVD discs. The creation of DVD compliant files can be accomplished in different ways, sometimes depending on the particular platform and software you are using to build your project (see Figure 12.25).

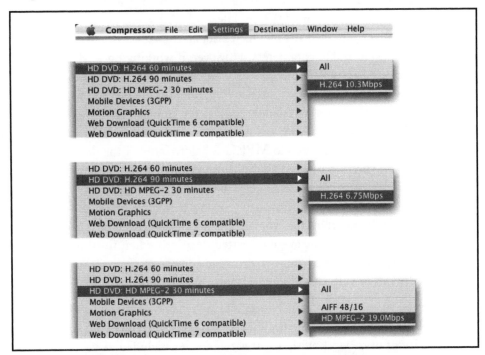

Figure 12.25 *Although the creation of standard definition DVDs is here today and remains the most popular choice for outputting a project, the number of options for encoding video for the HD-DVD format is increasing, including HD MPEG-2 and H.264, such as these presets in Compressor (suitable for current HD DVD-ROM discs that play back on a computer).*

Like any other compression technology, the methods behind MPEG are two-fold. First, there is the software aspect that encodes the video for delivery on a DVD disc. This involves the use of special algorithms to reduce the amount of necessary information in a file. Secondly, there is the hardware aspect, which decompresses the information and plays it back. Actually, the reading of information may be accomplished through software players as well as traditional set-top DVD players. However, software players are still restricted by many of the same limitations, such as bit-rates, copy protection, and region coding. Perhaps the main advantage to playing DVDs on a computer is the ability to use special interactive and online features included as part of the DVD-ROM portion of the disc. An example of this functionality includes features provided by the InterActual Player (visit www.interactual.com for more information).

Windows users have access to software such as Adobe's Encore or Premiere Pro, in addition to Sonic Solutions DVDit!, Ulead's DVD Workshop, Easy CD Creator, Nero, and many others, many of which offer an encoder with several advanced features and customizable parameters. However, if working on a Mac, your options are generally iDVD, DVD Studio Pro, Compressor, QuickTime Pro, or (one of the few non-Apple options) Roxio's Toast. Regardless of the method you are using, the creation of MPEG files is generally simple, and in many cases transparent. When using software like iDVD, for example, you can create a DVD project that automatically encodes your video to MPEG-2 before burning the disc. Simply import the DV or QuickTime video you've captured with your camera or created with your NLE, choose a menu design, and burn your disc. Although creating a DVD can be a simple process, at least when using templates or consumer DVD programs, it is still important that you understand the operation of your DVD creation software, so that you can make educated decisions when finishing your project. This is particularly important if you want to adjust encoding options in "advanced" menu options or with professional authoring applications.

Once you have finalized your project and are ready to export, it is time to consider the best options for creating the format and level of quality that you require. The majority of users work with a software encoder included as part of their DVD authoring application, although you may choose to expand your system based on the type of project and budget you are working with by adding a hardware encoder. Typically, the quality you can expect from today's software encoders rivals anything you see with a dedicated hardware encoder (and are much less expensive), although software encoders take more time to encode, and usually do not encode video in real time. The following sections provide a quick review of the basic options you have for encoding video for use on a standard definition DVD. Eventually, similar options may become available for HDV and HD projects, either as firmware updates or completely new products, to assist in reducing the substantial encoding times for long projects.

Software Encoding

As mentioned, the most basic and inexpensive method for creating an MPEG file is using a software encoder (see Figure 12.26). In fact, the encoder that ships with professional NLEs is software based, and does not require additional hardware (aside from your computer) to create good quality MPEGs. Software encoders are versatile and easy to update. They offer a wide range of choices for creating MPEG video in varying degrees of quality, ranging from great on the high end, to truly terrible when lower bit rates are utilized.

Figure 12.26 *MainConcept provides several different software encoders (primarily for PCs, although some are available for Mac), including an H.264 Encoder.*

Although software encoders are ideal for the majority of users, they are notoriously slow at cranking out long files. Without any hardware to assist them, software encoders must rely on the resources provided by your computer and its processor. Encoding times continue to improve as processor speeds increase and software becomes more efficient. As long as you budget the processing time, you should do fine with one of these encoders. For instance, you might set your machine to encode overnight, or you can let the encoder work in the background as you perform other tasks (if you are using a system like OS X on Mac that supports enhanced multitasking).

Hardware Encoding

If you run a professional studio that requires quick turnaround on high-quality DVD projects, you might also consider purchasing a hardware MPEG encoder. Not only do these devices work more quickly and efficiently than software-only encoders, but they also can increase the quality of material that you create. Although some software encoders are actually better than hardware encoders, especially compared with the low-end hardware cards, they can take a long time to encode at the highest settings. The issue of quality is particularly important if you need to use lower bit rates to fit material on a disc or to create titles that are universally compatible with slower computer-based playback systems. Most hardware encoders work at real-time speeds, even when encoding complex projects. Also, since the best hardware encoders have chips dedicated to specific compression tasks, they can produce great looking encodes more readily. In addition, some encoders offer multipass options for pre-processing of material, which yields superior results (a feature that is also found in software encoders).

Figure 12.27 *The Matrox RT.x100 Xtreme Pro is one example of an inexpensive, real-time hardware encoder (including analog inputs), which also provides other editing and effects features, primarily for SD footage.*

Even though hardware encoders can offer many great features, you should be aware of the limitations they might impose on your budget and the equipment you work with every day. For example, there are several professional hardware encoders that only accept material captured from professional decks. This is the case with several of the Sonic Solutions encoders, such as the SD-1000 and SD-2000, which require a Digital Betacam deck (or similarly equipped device) with serial digital interface (SDI) to encode the video as it is sent through the card. Sonic's SD-500 and inexpensive cards provided by companies like Matrox (see Figure 12.27), Pinnacle, Canopus, and others allow for component, composite, and FireWire input of video. You might use one of these cards in conjunction with downconverted HDV sent through the FireWire output on your camera or deck, in order to reduce the encoding times for long projects, or to make digital "dailies" of your shoots on the universally playable DVD format. This can be a great way to give copies to review footage and make notes before going into the editorial process, while reducing the damage that can occur to tape and camera by playing, fast-forwarding, and rewinding. If you decide to purchase a hardware encoder (particularly if real-time encoding is a necessity), make certain that you have the proper setup to utilize it. Additionally, a cheaper encoder can be great if you have a lot of material on tape that you need to encode, yet do not want to pay for an expensive, professional encoder.

Set-top DVD Recorders

An alternate to using software or hardware connected to your computer is a dedicated, set-top DVD recorder. You can find a DVD recorder at almost any television and video store. These recorders offer a great way to back up analog video (like converting your collection of VHS and Hi8mm tapes to DVD), and some models offer FireWire inputs that accept video from DV camcorders. If your HDV camera is able to output a downconverted DV signal through FireWire (such as the Sony FX-1 and Z1U), then you can quickly and easily back up your video to a standard definition DVD format. You may also use this feature to encode your video in real time (just press play and record), producing a DVD with MPEG-2 files you can later rip onto your computer and reuse in a DVD project with Apple's DVD Studio Pro or Adobe Encore (along with most other "professional" applications). This greatly reduces the time it might take to encode your video using a software encoder (particularly for short films and feature length videos), while bypassing the need to purchase expensive cards for your computer.

If the video that you encode comes directly from a camera or deck, is not for professional delivery, or you simply want a way to quickly back up your video, then this is definitely the easiest and most convenient method for MPEG-2 encoding.

Bit-Budgeting

With any encoder (whether software or hardware), you should consider the amount of space and bandwidth that you have available before encoding material for use on a DVD or any other digital medium. A DVD-5, which holds approximately 4.7GB of material, can fit about two hours of MPEG-2 video with a low bit rate and about one hour of MPEG-2 video with a high bit rate. If you have a lot of material to fit on a disc, this means that you may need to budget the amount of material that you want to include on it before you begin the encoding process. This is particularly important when using a software encoder like Compressor or the Adobe MPEG Encoder, which allow you to choose from a wide range of encoding options.

Generally, calculations are best done in bits or megabits. You can find calculators and spreadsheets online to help you with this process, which will usually tell you what bit rate you need to encode at in order to fit all of your assets onto a disc. A simple calculation for figuring out the bit rate to use on a standard definition DVD-5 (the most common, single layer DVDs in use) is 560/x, where "x" is the length of the video (in minutes) you want to encode. (This calculation assumes that you are using compressed audio, such as AC-3 files, instead of PCM audio.) Using this calculation, a 120-minute file would yield a result of 4.67Mbps, or 560 divided by 120. If you are using uncompressed PCM audio, subtract an additional 1.3Mbps from this total, for a result of 3.37Mbps. Remember, any additional streams of audio, video, or subtitles must be accounted for as well, in addition to menu items, such as the video files used in a motion menu.

BITS AND BYTES

A bit corresponds to either a "1" or a "0" and is the smallest unit of measure in the digital or "binary" world (indicating an "on" or "off" state). Since bits are so small, they are usually measured in groups of a thousand (kilo), million (mega), billion (giga), or trillion (tera). A group of 8 bits is called a byte, such as a megabyte or a gigabyte, which is probably the unit of measure you are most accustomed to seeing. Usually (at least for DVD), bits are used to measure speed, while bytes are used to measure size. For example, the bit rate of a DVD refers to the speed of data transfer, such as 5Mbps (megabits per second), and the capacity of the disc is measured in bytes, such as 4.7GB (gigabytes). This is where it becomes confusing to measure the amount of space on a disc, whether a DVD-R or a hard disk, since bits are the most technically precise measurement (although bytes are still technically "accurate"). In fact, a 1MB file is actually 1,024 kilobytes, not 1,000 as you might think.

To calculate the number of bits in a byte, simply multiply by 8 (remember, 8 bits in a byte) to arrive at a megabit value instead of a megabyte measurement (assuming you are starting with a value such as 5MB), and then multiply by 1,024 to get the kilobit value. After multiplying by 1,024 one more time (or two more times if you started at a gigabyte value), you should have the bit value for your file. For example, the available bits in a 4.7GB DVD can be found by multiplying $4.7 \times 8 \times 1,024 \times 1,024 \times 1,024$, which equals 40372692582.4 bits, or approximately 4.37GB. For a comparison of the discrepancy between bits and bytes, consider that a 4.7GB DVD (DVD-5) is actually comprised of 4.37GB of binary information and an 8.54GB DVD (DVD-9) of 7.95 binary gigabytes. By converting the measurements of all your files into bits, you can calculate more precisely the amount of space required for your DVD assets when space is at a premium. You may have noticed this difference as well when looking at the available capacity on a new hard drive that you have purchased compared with the advertised size on the box.

Encoding Clips and Sequences

Most DVD encoding software offers many presets for making the creation of files for DVDs (and other formats, including the Web) relatively simple. They also offer a great deal of in-depth choices for those brave enough to look a little deeper. Even though you may want to take some time to experiment with different options, it is important that you have a basic understanding of what's involved before attempting to modify unfamiliar parameters. Sticking with the presets is generally safer for new users and even many professionals. However, when you do decide to take the plunge, it's good to know that these options are there. It is only after you have produced several projects that you might wonder if there are ways to adjust settings to get better results. Presets are great for making settings quickly, such as selecting a high bit rate NTSC DVD as the output type, while you still have the option to adjust settings manually by choosing a specific bit rate or encoder quality. If you have the time, and your encoding software offers batch processing of files, it is usually a good idea to encode your video with several different settings and then pick the file with the best quality results. In this section, we discuss a typical method to prepare clips and sequences for export using a popular software application and its subsequent encoding. Although there are many DVD encoders, which differ depending on your choice of operating system and video editing software, many of the options discussed here are relevant no matter which tool you are using.

The creation of MPEG-2 video files for DVD begins by identifying the portions of your program first that you want to export, whether part of a clip or a sequence. The following steps demonstrate generally how to export clips and sequences from an NLE and to compress the video using a software encoder (such as Final Cut Pro for editing and the Compressor application to encode the video for delivery on DVD). Export and encoding options depend on the software you are using, although the steps here simply provide the opportunity to discuss some common parameters you might modify.

1. Open a clip in the Source Monitor or a sequence in the Timeline window that you want to export. If you are working with a sequence, make sure that all of your video, audio, transitions, and effects have been rendered before attempting to export.

2. Navigate to the spot in your clip or sequence where you want the encoding process to begin and place an "in" point by clicking the Mark In button or by pressing "i" on the keyboard. You can usually export everything in the entire Timeline window or clip without placing in and out points. However, in order to make sure you do not include any extraneous information, it is often best to mark points in your Timeline or clip. It is also a good idea to include at least 15 frames of black (for NTSC, 12 frames for PAL) at the beginning and end of your video, in order to avoid odd freeze frames that can result from the MPEG-2's GOP structure (freezing at the end of a fade out, for example, before the screen is completely black).

3. Locate the point where you want the encoding process to end and place an "out" point by clicking the Mark Out button or by pressing "o" on the keyboard.

4. Now that the material that you want to encode has been identified, select File@→Export@→Using Compressor. You may also choose to export using a standard QuickTime exporter (File@→Export@→Using QuickTime Conversion), Adobe MPEG Encoder, or similar export module, which launches another export window from your NLE. If exporting directly using the QuickTime Pro MPEG2 Encoder (for example), adjust the settings for your MPEG file and then save it to your hard drive (see Figure 12.28). Choose the appropriate video standard, aspect ratio, and field dominance for your video. Also, adjust the bit rate to an appropriate value, balancing the need for quality with the amount of space you have on a disc. With the QuickTime MPEG Encoder, 5 to 6Mbps is usually about as low as you want to put the bit rate for SD video without a noticeable loss in quality (although it is getting much better at lower bit rates). Of course, a higher bit rate (such as 7 or 8) yields better looking video while sacrificing disc space and compatibility with some slower computer players.

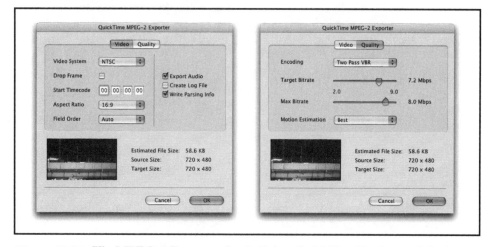

Figure 12.28 *The MPEG–2 Export option built into QuickTime Pro is one of the simplest and most direct options for encoding a file while still allowing for a degree of control over options such as bit rate.*

5. Click the Presets tab or activate the Presets window and select the appropriate setting from the Presets dropdown. For widescreen, anamorphic DVDs with a 16:9 aspect ratio (the usual setting for video that originated on HDV, which is a widescreen format), the default might look like "MPEG-2 60 minute High Quality Encode Widescreen," although you

may want to change this to a lower bit rate setting, depending on the amount of space you have for video on the DVD. Most users will find that the presets work just fine and eliminate the complexity of adjusting settings manually. You can usually double-click or open a preset to view its properties for finer control, as we discuss here. If you decide to stick with your preset (which most often has all the correct settings for filed order, frame rate, etc., as determined by your source file), you can skip the next several steps for modifying settings.

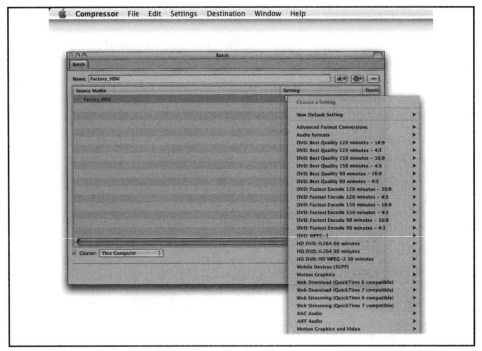

Figure 12.29 *The presets in Compressor 2 offer a wide range of options, many of which should work fine for most users with little, if any, modification.*

6. Open your selected preset to view its properties. Make certain that the correct Video Standard (NTSC or PAL) is selected to match the format of your source material, if it is not already set. This option usually does not allow you to change from one standard to another (although Apple's Compressor 2 and a few other applications now allow you do this); there-fore the Video Standard selected should match your original material. As mentioned, most encoders do not convert from one format to another,

although Compressor 2 for the Mac now includes an excellent format converter, particularly when the high-quality, yet very slow, "optical flow" technology is used to track individual pictures from one frame to the next. For all other standards conversions, you might consider third-party software, such as a Nattress plug-in (for Final Cut Pro), or using a special deck to do the conversion before bringing the video into your computer to be encoded for a DVD. NTSC is the standard for countries like the U.S. and Japan, while PAL is used around the world in places like the U.K. and much of Europe. Also, choose an aspect ratio that matches your video (4:3 or 16:9).

7. Next, choose lower field first from the Fields dropdown if you are work-ing with DV footage, or upper field first if working with HDV. Fields refers to the order in which interlaced images are drawn. If you choose the incorrect field order (or none), your video may appear jittery. The field order is sometimes dependent on the particular card you used to capture your video, although DV is generally lower field (or odd), while HDV is upper field (or even). If your MPEG video appears jittery after encoding, try using a different field order. Usually, automatic field domi-nance does a decent job of detecting the order of your lines.

8. Open the audio tab of your encoder or click an options button to access its audio features. The audio settings area of your export module sets the audio rate and audio type for the sound that is associated with your video file. If you are creating a DVD, particularly if you are only working with NTSC or PAL video, you will most often use PCM audio, although AC-3 (Dolby Digital) is highly recommended for saving space on a disc and allowing more bandwidth for higher video bit rates. In some cases, you will need a separate application to compress your audio files to AC-3 (see Figure 12.30), although you can find applications like Compressor 2 that include the ability to produce AC-3 files from the same encoder that you use for your video files. Additionally, some software allows you to choose MPEG Layer 1 or MPEG Layer 2 from the Audio type dropdown. However, it is important to consider the compatibility issues when using MPEG audio, since many systems are unable to play it.

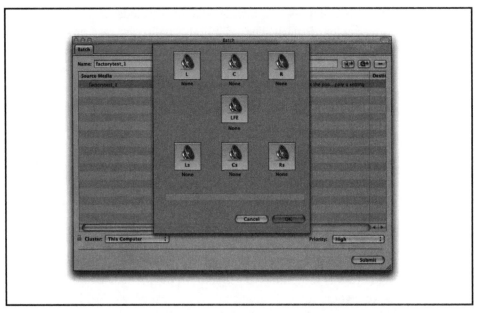

Figure 12.30 *AC-3 files on a DVD offer extremely high-quality, compressed audio files with the capability of up to 5.1 discrete channels of surround sound audio. (DTS is an even higher quality alternative, although encoders and support by players are less common.)*

9. Next, open the multiplexer tab of your encoder if it has one. Although the multiplexer settings, included in some encoding software (such as the Adobe, or Main Concept, Encoder), offer several obscure choices, you may find the option to create a muxed MPEG that combines audio and video into a single file useful. Ordinarily, when you create an MPEG-2 for DVD the multiplexing type is set to None. This produces a separate video and audio file for the clip you encode, which are also called "elementary streams." However, you can also select the option to create a single file that can play audio and video simultaneously. Some DVD authoring systems, like DVDit!, can read these muxed files, although they can require authoring software more time to process. They can be easier to read as a single file when playing back on a computer that reads these streams (assuming you have a player, such as QuickTime with the MPEG-2 option). In general, when manually encoding files, it is usually best (and recommended) that you create elementary streams for your DVD, which include the separate video and audio files for use in assembling in your DVD authoring software. These types of files are more universally compatible with authoring software, and allow you to make changes more easily (such as converting AIFF or WAV files to AC3, or Dolby Digital) or to swap files later on.

10. If you have not done so already, adjust the bit rate to a level that provides an appropriate quality and file size for your project as already mentioned. Notice that the "estimated file size" often displays in an information window as you make changes to the bit rate. (This same "estimated file size" or "disc size" indicator can be seen in your DVD authoring software as well.) Although the estimated file or disk size is only an estimate, it is important that you watch it carefully, particularly for large projects. It is vitally important that you do not exceed the maximum amount of space on a disc, so remember to consider the sizes of any other files that you might eventually add to your disc, such as DVD-ROM content, as well as alternate video, audio, and sub-title streams. In addition to selecting a bit rate to determine the quality of your video, there is often a separate "quality" dropdown or slider in an MPEG encoder. Set this to the best setting possible if you have the time to wait a little longer for the encode. Quality usually refers to the amount of analysis and care that is given to processing the motion in each frame (resulting in longer encoding times), although the results are worth the wait.

11. Take a look at the special processing, filters, or geometry options that are available in the encoder. You might consider the use of special processing for cropping the image area of your video or eliminating potential problems through the use of tools, like noise reduction. Adjustments might include an overall color correction, brightness or contrast, as well as de-interlacing to remove motion artifacts (see Figure 12.31).

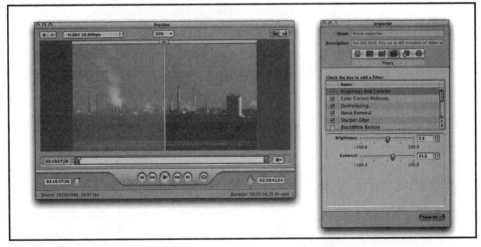

Figure 12.31 *You can apply filters in the MPEG encoder to adjust a video image prior to outputting, such as this example where several filters, including color correction, are used to improve the picture (as seen in the Compressor 2 Preview window).*

12. Click OK when you are finished making changes in your Encoder window. Look at your information in the summary tab or Inspector window to check the changes you have made before proceeding.

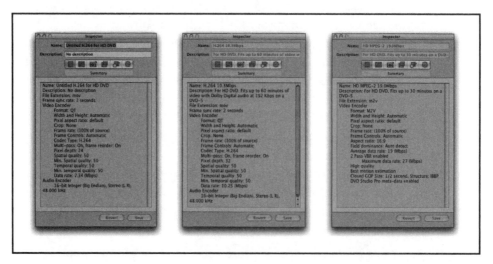

Figure 12.32 *The details about your encoding choices are usually displayed in an Inspector window or information and summary tabs, such as these few windows displaying information about alternate HD encoding options in Compressor 2. (Close inspection of these windows may yield some details about the formats and their limitations or capabilities.)*

13. In the Output section of the Encoder window, type a new filename for the MPEG you are about to create. Make sure to leave the ".m2v" extension (if creating an MPEG-2 for DVD) at the end to identify the file as MPEG-2. Select a location to place the file on your hard drive.

14. When you are finished making all of your settings, click the Export or Submit button to start the encoding process.

BYPASSING COMPRESSING

Although Compressor has many powerful, customizable settings, and it can yield some truly excellent looking video, it does suffer from a few speed issues, as well as some peculiarities when it comes to working directly with Final Cut Pro. Currently, exporting using Compressor 2 out of Final Cut Pro is actually slower than first exporting a QuickTime movie (*not* using QuickTime Conversion, but selecting "QuickTime Movie") and then importing that file into Compressor. Working in this way (creating a QuickTime Movie first, rather than exporting out of Final Cut Pro through

Compressor) also allows you the flexibility of having a QuickTime file that can be encoded using alternate compression software. Also, you cannot currently create a 24fps DVD when exporting via Compressor out of Final Cut Pro (24fps video files can be encoded to MPEG-2 on a DVD, which actually saves space on a disc—fewer frames to compress—and preserves the original film better).

Additionally, encoding out of Final Cut Pro using Compressor (particularly for long files) increases the risk of crashing your computer, and also ties up Final Cut Pro from doing other work (since the Final Cut Pro project you are exporting must remain open and untouched while Compressor reads frames out of your sequence). As an added note, standards conversions may also be faster in other software (converting NTSC to PAL, for example), such as plug-ins provided by Nattress. In fact, as a comparison, standards conversion with Compressor 2 is 35 times slower than the Nattress plug-in (that means a one-minute clip could take 4 hours and 30 minutes to convert), while not offering a significant difference in quality. Even using a lower setting in Compressor 2 may yield poorer quality in comparison, especially if de-interlacing is not full quality.

Creating Chapter Points with Markers

Almost any DVD project, whether professionally produced or created for personal use, includes chapter points to make skipping from one point in the video to the next easier, particularly for longer video programs like movies, or when a single video file is used in place of several shorter clips. By pressing the "next" and "previous" keys on a DVD player's remote control, these chapter points can be accessed quickly. The majority of DVD authoring software (and many NLEs, such as Final Cut Pro and Premiere Pro) allows you to create these markers directly in the Timeline, eliminating the steps required to make markers in a separate DVD authoring application.

Chapter points created in an NLE, such as Final Cut Pro or Premiere, can be imported into most "professional" DVD authoring systems, whether on a Mac or a PC. This makes the task of manually creating markers much easier, since editing software is better equipped to place points easily and precisely on a timeline. The placement of chapter points on an MPEG-2 stream in current DVD applications is often cumbersome and imprecise to use. This is true for most authoring applications, whose simple interface is better suited to the creation of chapter points with clearly defined inter-titles or spaces between chapters rather than frame accurate editing. Unfortunately, markers for MPEG-2 DVDs must occur at the beginning of a GOP, since they require the use of an I-frame. DVDs created with Windows Media Video 9, VC-1, and H.264 can use markers placed anywhere in the video, which is a unique advantage of some HD formats.

The following steps demonstrate how to create chapter points by using the marker feature in Final Cut Pro, which can then be imported into DVD Studio Pro. Adobe's Premiere Pro also works closely with Encore to transmit information about markers, as do other similar "suites" of applications.

1. With your project open, locate a point in the Timeline window to place your first chapter marker. If you were creating markers after your video was encoded to MPEG-2, you would only be able to place a marker on an I-frame, or every half second.

2. Select Mark@→Markers@→Add or press the "m" key to automatically place a marker at the playhead location.

3. Press the "m" key again to open the Marker Editor window (while still on the current frame containing your marker), or choose Mark@→Makers@→Edit. In some software, you can also locate a marker in the timeline and double-click it to launch the marker dialog box.

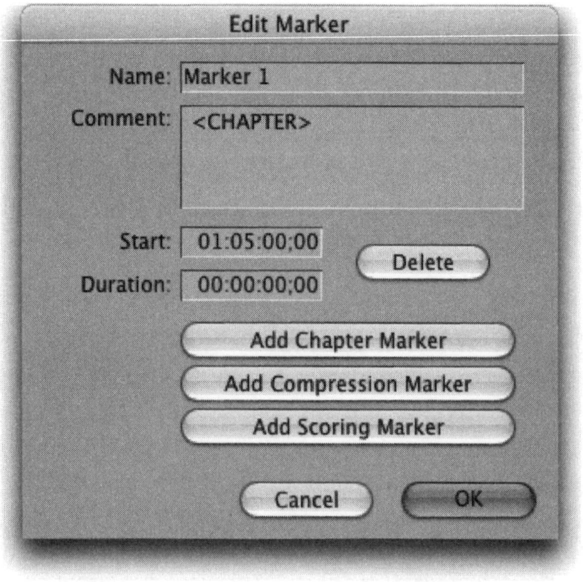

Figure 12.33 *The Marker Editor window in Final Cut Pro.*

4. Type a name for your marker at the top of the Marker window. The name that you choose for your markers should display in your DVD authoring software if exported correctly from your NLE (see Figure 12.34). Using specific names helps you to identify portions of your video to link to using buttons and other features in your DVD authoring software. The names that you assign are not readable on the finished DVD, and only appear if you use them in a "chapter list" or "scene selection" type of menu as determined by your authoring software.

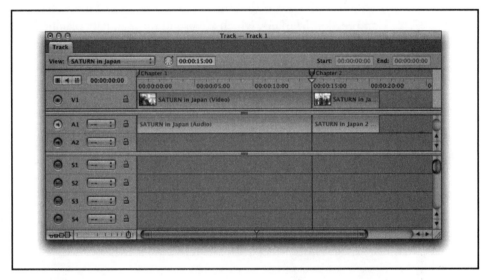

Figure 12.34 *Chapter markers as they appear in a DVD authoring application.*

5. Choose Chapter Marker to identify the type of marker you are creating. In Final Cut Pro, you have the option of creating a few different types of markers, depending on what application you are exporting your video to (such as SoundTrack Pro for audio, or LiveType for the addition of text and titles).

6. Click OK to accept the settings for the current marker.

7. Continue placing markers in the Timeline by repeating the steps above. Although you may create several hundred markers in your NLE (if not more), you are only able to use 99 markers for each video file on a DVD.

8. Export your video file and import it to the DVD authoring application of your choice, making certain to "check" or select the option to include the markers you created in the QuickTime video or project file that you create (see Figure 12.35). In Final Cut Pro, there are export options when outputting a "QuickTime Movie" that specify the type of marker you want to export with your video. In this instance, the "All Markers," "Chapter Markers," or "DVD Studio Pro Markers" option must be selected. The difference between using Chapter Markers and DVD Studio Pro Markers is that the DVD Studio Pro Markers also include Compression Markers, which are useful for manually placing I-frames to improve encoding results where necessary.

Figure 12.35 *Make certain to include your markers in the final QuickTime or other file that you export from your NLE.*

Additional Output Options

As discussed, the final step in any video project is the outputting of your program to the appropriate format. The number of options to choose from is large enough to satisfy just about any distribution needs you might have. Of course, since you have all these choices, deciding on the best format is made more difficult. In addition to HD options like HD-DVD and Blue-Ray, or standard definition DVDs, this may include video for use on the Web, CD-ROM, DVD-ROM, VCD, SVCD, or even VHS. Mobile devices, like a PDA, cell phone, or Sony PSP present additional options.

In general, when you export video out of your editing software (assuming your project originates in Final Cut Pro, Premiere, Avid, or any number of other applications), you can either choose to export a clip or export an entire Timeline. If you want to export only a portion of your program, make sure to set the proper in and out points first. You may also choose "Print to Video," in which case you should have a deck or camera attached to your computer that is ready to record. In most instances, you are probably going to export the entire Timeline, which is your complete sequence as it appears in the Program or Canvas window. Make certain that all your video, audio, and effects are rendered before outputting. Also, make sure to preview your program one last time prior to export.

After you decide which piece of video or sequence of clips you want to output, your software presents options that include exporting your program as a movie, a single frame (still image), audio file, or using one of several possible export engines, including QuickTime, Windows Media, Real Video, and others. Most of these export modules include an "Option" or "Advanced" button that accesses more features. At this point, you should choose a frame rate and compression quality that suits your output type. Usually, your choice of output type automatically limits the available settings or presents new ones. If your video is intended for the Web, then a greater amount of compression is required, as well as a slower frame rate, such as 7, 15, or 24 frames per second (in many cases). However, if the video is destined for a disc-based medium like DVD, or if it is being rendered out at "archival" quality for storing on a hard disk, then a lesser amount of compression needs to be applied. For projects that are destined for backup to tape or hard disk, a suitable QuickTime or AVI codec is necessary to generate and play back the file. Apple developed the QuickTime standard, and its use has spread to PCs as well. In terms of output options, it offers many choices, including high quality presentations for computers, disc-based formats, the Web, and any other delivery option you can imagine. In fact, on Macs, virtually every input, output, and playback option for video is based on QuickTime, since it forms the core of the operating system's multimedia capabilities and offers a great amount of customizable options. AVI is the default format for PCs, just as QuickTime is the default video format for Macs. Both are extremely versatile and can deliver high quality video in a variety of forms.

The following is a list of a few common export options for outputting video files to formats other than HD and SD-DVDs.

◆ **Movie to AVI**—A starting point for creating PC-compliant video files and accessing other compatible codecs for (generally) large, high-quality files.

◆ **Movie to QuickTime Movie**—Another starting point for accessing all of the compatible QuickTime codecs on your computer, and originator of just about every other format on a Mac.

◆ **Movie to Windows Media**—Permits the creation of Windows Media Video 9 (and later) files, including those used for the Web and HD-DVD compliant files, as well as red-laser, Windows Media Video 9 HD DVD-ROMS.

◆ **Movie to FLC**— A Flash file format that is sometimes for animation files played back on computers (Autodesk's animation format).

◆ **Movie to Macromedia Flash Video (FLV)**—A video format specifically designed for use in Macromedia Flash applications (now owned by Adobe).

◆ **Movie to DV Stream**—Creating video that is compatible with DV editing applications and copying to DV tape.

◆ **Movie to Picture**—Outputting the current frame to a still image format, such as BMP, TIFF, JPEG, PNG, or TARGA, and others.

◆ **Movie to Image Sequence**—Outputs a movie as a series of frames, which is useful for some effects work, 3D animations, and other post processing tasks.

◆ **3 G**—3GPP and 3GPP2, a form of MPEG-4 for mobile phones, including third-generation mobile communications and other portable devices (see Figure 12.36).

◆ **VCD and SVCD**—Although used less today than in previous years, a VCD (using MPEG-1) or a SVCD (which uses a smaller form of MPEG-2) can be used to deliver videos on recordable CD media, for inexpensive, lower-quality (as compared with DVD) playback on DVD players that support the format.

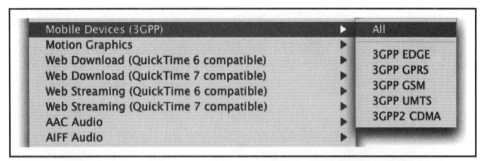

Figure 12.36 *In addition to export options for SD and HD-DVDs, applications such as Compressor and Cleaner include options for creating video files for the Web and mobile devices, such as 3GPP video, which is also a form of MPEG-4— a surprisingly versatile format.*

CREATING VIDEO FOR PORTABLE DEVICES

In recent years, the ability to create video for mobile devices has grown considerably, such as a PDA (personal digital assistant), mobile phone, or personal digital media player (including the Sony PSP). Each device may have its own requirements for image size and video/audio codecs. MPEG-4, in a variety of forms, has become a popular choice for this purpose, since it is high-quality, scalable for different resolutions, and produces small file sizes. In the mobile world, 3GPP (and 3GPP 2) is a worldwide standard for the creation, delivery, and playback of video over 3G (third generation) wireless networks that support high-speed communications. It is basically another form of MPEG-4, and you can create these files on your own computer by exporting them out of QuickTime Pro or a similar application, and then placing them on your phone or PDA by using Blue Tooth, a USB cable, or another means of connecting with your computer. Recently, the Sony PSP (Playstation Portable) has made it fun to carry video with you on a memory stick, which can be an interesting way to show off your demo reel while walking the floor of a trade show, all on a bright, 4.3" widescreen LCD display. Check out www.portablepop.com (also accessible through this book's Web site, www.hdvfilmmaking.com) for more information on creating video for these devices.

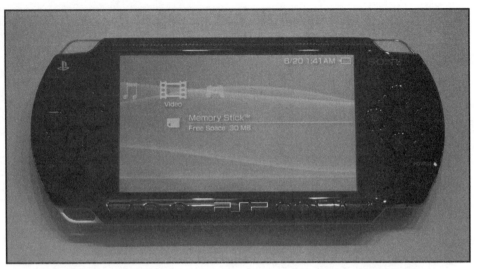

Figure 12.37 *Sony's PSP (Playstation Portable) can play back special MPEG-4 video files, and is a fun choice for sharing demo reels, training materials, or short films.*

HDTV Displays

Although we mentioned in Chapter 3 that an HD monitor or LCD screen is ideal for previewing your video as you shoot, it is also important to have a way to view your finished HDV project on an ordinary television in your home. After all, what use is HD video if you cannot view it and share it with others? Soon, HD-DVD players will be in many homes, and it is important to know a little about the difference between the many so-called "HDTV" and digital TV options available at your local Best Buy, Circuit City, or online retailer. The best advice is to simply do your research. You can find most of a manufacturer's specifications on the Internet, as well as sites that compare prices and features of different models. Newer, less expensive models, along with better HD technology are making their way to stores every day, so keep an eye out for the latest trends in consumer HD devices. Even if you are a content producer without the desire for an HDTV in your own living room, it is helpful to understand how consumers are viewing your projects.

First, not all HDTVs are created equal. Many times, terms like "HDTV ready," "HDTV capable," and "Enhanced Definition" or "Extended Definition" (EDTV) are used to confuse buyers, and they may mean different things. Make certain that you check first to see what resolution the television actually is capable of producing, whether 720p or 1080i. A digital television may still be standard definition, although HDTV ready, in the sense that it can accept an HD signal and down-convert it to SD resolution. Additionally, an EDTV (as they are sometimes called) is actually a standard definition TV that offers a 16:9 aspect ratio image (stretched horizontally), which is progressive scan (as virtually any Digital TV is capable of). The difference between an EDTV and an ordinary SDTV is noticeable, due to the progressive scanning. Although they are widescreen (as many televisions are today, both SD and HD), they bear no relation to true HDTVs. Even authentic HDTVs are not created equally. At this point in time, the majority of HDTVs are 720p. Although these TVs indicate that they can accept a 1080i signal, that 1080-line signal is downconverted to 720 lines. Additionally, the majority of HDTVs with resolutions higher than 720p compromise on the full 1080 line image, with sizes that are closer to 1024 lines. (There are an entire range of resolutions between 720 and 1080 lines.) More than likely, if you are looking at a plasma or LCD HDTV, it is the 720p variety, which is fine for most viewers (it is a vast improvement over standard definition), even though it is not capable of 1080 lines. LCDs for computers are still the best place to find 1920×1080 or higher resolutions, although they are becoming more common as the technology (including chip production and manufacturing techniques) becomes cheaper and more reliable. You can find CRT HDTV sets as well, although they are usually very heavy (you will want to have this delivered), are limited to about 40 inches in size, and tend to warp images around the edges of the frame (depending on the model and price). Currently, it is not feasible to create a full 1920×1080 resolution CRT, since the shadow mask cannot be made fine enough (even on professional broadcast monitors).

DVI AND HDMI

The majority of new digital monitors for computers include a DVI (Digital Visual Interface) or HDMI (High-Definition Multimedia Interface) connection, which keeps the video signal purely digital, without the usual analog to digital conversion. (This is often a good thing, although upconverting and downconverting may be better in some instances with analog component connections.) This is generally the preferred way to view HD (or even SD) digital video, since there is generally little or no image loss, and sync, color, and image resolutions are usually of the highest quality, particularly when the display at least matches the resolution of the input source.

(continued on next page)

(continued from previous page)

One of the main differences between DVI and HMI is that DVI connections can only carry video, while HDMI can include video and audio in the same cable, which is generally more convenient for home theater usage, since it eliminates some of the clutter and complexity of setting up a system. This is one of the reasons why most new HDTVs include HDMI instead of DVI, while computers tend to stick with DVI, since synchronized audio is not as much of an issue (as well as its similarity to the older VGA standard for monitors, which allows for both analog and digital signals to pass through).

If you have an HDMI device that you want to play on an LCD computer monitor with a DVI input (or vice versa), you may be able to connect it by using an inexpensive HDMI-to-DVI converter, like those sold by Gefen (www.gefen.com). One of the drawbacks of these types of digital signals is that you cannot connect them over long distances, at least not without the use of a special "repeater" box connected along the chain that boosts the signal for transmitting over extended cable lengths. DVI for digital devices is often referred to as DVI-D, indicating its digital-only usage (no support for analog computer signals). In addition, a form of digital copy protection is being included with both DVI and HDMI connection on HD devices, such as D-VHS players and HD-DVD players. The HDCP protocol (High Bandwidth Digital Content Protection) encrypts a signal and makes it impossible to record or play back video without a compatible, licensed device. Check to see if your display and playback devices contain HDCP and if they are compatible.

Projecting HDV

For presenting your work in a public venue, or even for noncritical monitoring applications, you might consider one of a number of video projectors. The majority of affordable, consumer/professional projectors support 720p resolutions (only the most expensive, cinema-style projectors currently support 1080i resolutions, see Figure 12.38). One example of an affordable (under $4,000), high-resolution projector would be the Realis SX50 from Canon, which provides SXGA+ resolutions (approximately 1400×1050 lines of resolution), 2500 ANSI lumens (for display in brighter conditions, or at longer distances), and a 1000:1 contrast ratio. For high definition (720p) playback, you need at least SXGA resolution, which displays 1280×1024 lines in 4:3 mode or 1280×720 lines with a 16:9 aspect ratio (also referred to as WXGA for 16:9, although most models allow both 4:3 and 16:9 viewing). When evaluating pixel resolutions for a projector, make sure you are looking at the true or "native" resolution, which is the maximum number of individual pixels that the projector actually displays. Most projectors also accept a signal that is larger than its native resolution and downsample or compress it to fit into a fewer number of pixels. The quality of scaling on a projector often differs by manufacturer and price.

Figure 12.38 *JVC's DLA-HD2K-SYS is an example of a high-end HD projector with full 1920×1080 resolution and 3-chip D-ILA, for uncompromised HD images.*

A few of the commonly cited features for a video projector are lumens and contrast ratio, along with a variety of resolution classifications (SVGA, XGA, etc.), the most pertinent of which were discussed in this chapter. Lumens refers to the brightness, or amount, of light produced by the projector (the amount of light that falls at a distance from its source). Thus a more powerful projector capable of "throwing" light a long distance or for viewing under bright conditions should have a high lumens rating. Most cheaper projectors are best used under dark conditions, or at least away from windows, overhead lighting, or other bright sources that can flood the image. A projector with a rating of at least 1200 lumens is probably what you should be looking at on the low end (particularly if you just need it for your living room or for darker situations and short distances), if not 2000 lumens or higher.

Contrast ratio simply complements the brightness of your image. A high contrast ratio means that you get whiter whites and blacker blacks, preventing a washed-out look. You can often get contrast ratios in the 1,000:1 or 2,000:1 range (the higher number being the best). Another feature that is common to almost all projectors is keystone correction. This feature is the automatic alignment of an image against a flat wall or screen, which eliminates the distortion, determined by projection angle, that would make square pixels appear rectangular. Last, take a manufacturer's ratings with a grain of salt. Most of the specifications claimed by a company are difficult to reproduce, or are only relevant under the best possible conditions. In fact, contrast ratios are one measurement that could be considered a complete invention, created by manufacturers and marketing people, who could not tell you how they are actually achieved in practice (making it difficult, if not impossible, to reproduce). After classifying it generally, a projector (like any monitor, camera, or visual device) is best evaluated by testing under conditions that most closely match the real-world environments you need them to work in. In this case, it is generally best to reference a good *Home Cinema* magazine where projectors are measured using a standard test.

In addition to deciding on the resolution and brightness of a projector (or some television monitors), it is important to consider the display technology that is used. One of the biggest decisions at the moment is between LCD and DLP (as well as LCOS). Each technology has its own quirks and can create different results. LCD, or Liquid Crystal Display, is the traditional choice, while DLP, or Digital Light Processing, and LCOS, or Liquid Crystal on Silicon, are the relative newcomers that have seen success in the home theater market. In this section, some of the advantages and disadvantages of each are discussed, although they represent generalizations about each type. Individual projectors and monitors should be evaluated on their own merits, as each may include improved technology and special features, particularly at different price points. A $2,000 LCD unit may not be directly comparable to a $10,000 DLP projector, so compare wisely. Also, take into account that new variations on projection technology are being developed every day, many times by competing manufacturers.

LCDs function by using three, separate glass panels, one for each of the image's color components (red, green, and blue). Light passes through each of these panels, where individual pixels can be opened or closed to let light through or prevent it from passing, thereby controlling the type and amount of light that makes up the projected image. LCDs generally treat light more "efficiently" than DLP, creating a brighter image at lower wattage. Also, individual pixels tend to be more noticeable, which might be alright for computer images, but not always good for video (may produce a "screen door" effect, which may be softened by defocusing slightly). Images may also appear more saturated with LCD than DLP (although less so for video than computer images), creating a false sense of brightness, but pleasing color (a matter of preference and accuracy —DLP produces good color depth as well). The image pixellation mentioned is probably one of the biggest disadvantages of an ordinary LCD, as are the "dead pixels" that can occur when a pixel on one of the panels becomes permanently stuck in the on or off position.

DLP (developed by Texas Instruments) works by using a chip made up of tiny mirrors (one for each pixel), a spinning color wheel, and a lamp, which passes light through the spinning disc onto the chip to produce color images. The color wheel, which is most often divided up into segments for each color component (red, green, and blue), spins rapidly in sync with the chips, which moves to let light through to the lens. The faster the rotation of the color wheel (number of rotations per frame), the better the color results will be. Probably the biggest potential disadvantage is a certain "rainbow" effect, caused by the perceived separation of color components created by the spinning color wheel. While it is not noticeable to every viewer (some people are more sensitive to it than others), it can be distracting, particularly on older, cheaper units. Newer DLP projectors tend to use discs that spin faster and include more segments to overcome the rainbow effects and produce more saturated colors in the process. Professional, three-chip DLP projectors eliminate the rainbow effect altogether, since they utilize a separate chip for each color, and they also create much better color reproduction. In general, DLP projectors are often preferred for viewing video. The apparent proximity of pixels to each other smoothes out the image a bit and removes much of the pixellation common with LCD projectors, particularly for video images (fewer gaps between mirrors than there are between pixels in an LCD). Higher contrast is also a characteristic of DLP, although color can appear less saturated when compared with an LCD. In addition, DLP projectors may be more portable than LCDs, since they require fewer parts to operate. In fact, Mitsubishi recently released a tiny projector that can fit in the palm of your hand.

LCOS is considered an alternative to DLP, and is based on a similar technology (JVC's version of LCOS is called *D-ILA*). LCOS images are created by using stationary mirrors, instead of moving mirrors (in the case of DLP), and liquid crystals on the chip's surface that open or close to regulate the passage of light. The mirrors are very close together, and they yield an excellent image (surprisingly smooth and sharp), which may surpass both LCD and DLP as the preferred technology for HDTV display devices.

CHOOSING A VIDEO PROJECTOR

When asked what he would look for when purchasing a video projector, **Brian Dressel** (VJ, video performance pioneer, and cofounder of OVT Visuals—www.ovtvisuals.com) had the following recommendations. Brian has designed graphics and projected video for acts such as Paul Oakenfold, FischerSpooner, Motley Crue, Ministry, Jay-Z, the MTV Music Video Awards, and countless others.

Brian Dressel:

I am asked quite often what to look for in a video projector. There are hundreds of choices on the market, from low-end sub $1,000 consumer models to high-end large venue $100K 17,000 lumen monsters. When I got into the business of concert and event projections, we were using 16MM & 35MM film loop, as the projectors were cheap and bright. Plus, we were actually projecting FILM! Those days are long gone now, as you can find high quality video projectors, which are cheap, small, lightweight and extremely high resolution.

There are many things to look for when considering a video projector. I'll break down the most common things to look for:

◆ **Brightness (lumen rating)**—This is dependent on your viewing area and projected image size. Are there windows? You will want to have control over the ambient light level in the room. If you are in a dark room, you can get by with a 1500 lumen projector. If you have ambient or uncontrolled light levels, you'll need to punch it up to a 2200–3500 lumen projector to get a decent image.

◆ **Contrast Ratio**—The higher the contrast ratio, the more detail you will see in brighter scenes and in shadows.

◆ **LCD or DLP**—The verdict is still out on this one. Advances in both technologies give them each advantages. The disadvantages of both technologies are changing quickly. LCD projectors usually have better color saturation, but lower contrast ratios and black levels than DLP projectors. DLP projectors are usually smaller and eliminate the screen-door pixellation look of LCD projectors. Currently, DLP projectors look better than most LCD projectors in the same price range. There is a new projection technology emerging called *LCOS*. It is capable of surpassing both LCD and DLP in the coming years.

◆ **Resolution:** Match the resolution of your image source to your projector, to avoid any image scaling. That gets a little confusing when using HDTV as a source. There are two common HDTV formats, 1080i and 720p. The numbers refer to the vertical resolution and the letters refer to interlaced or progressive. Both formats look equally good, as both have the same effective resolution. Almost all projectors nowadays can project either 1080i or 720p resolutions. But not all projectors do it well. The thing to look for is the native resolution of the projector. The higher the resolution, the better. If you want your HDTV footage to look really good, get a projector with a 1280×720 resolution. If you are a purist and want it to look *great*, then get a projector with a 1920×1080 native resolution. You will pay for it, but projectors are getting cheaper all the time.

◆ **Inputs:** To get HDTV or progressive scan capability, your projector must have component video, DVI, or HDMI connections. You will notice a great difference in quality and features when compared to composite or S-video connections. The cheapest consumer projectors on the market usually have composite or S-video only and are usually of 800×600 resolution or lower.

◆ **Lens:** Zoom ratio and lens shift capabilities are features to look for if you will be traveling with the projector. Sometimes, the projector will be close to the screen, sometimes far away. If you are installing it for permanent use, match the zoom range to your viewing area. For example, if the lens has a 2.0–2.5 zoom range, and your screen size is 8 feet, your projector needs to be 16 to 20 feet from the screen. The formula for this is: screen(width) × lens(throw ratio) = Distance. Vertical and horizontal lens shift is a very nice feature to help with installation. You can basically plunk your projector down, aim it in the general direction of your screen, and use the lens shift feature to point the image at the screen quite easily. It also uses the entire display, unlike keystone correction.

◆ **Keystone Correction:** It's a great feature to have when needed, but avoid using it if possible. When you use keystone correction, you are scaling your image and losing a big percentage of the display. At a 40-degree keystone correction, you have just lost 1/3 of your resolution and light output. There is new technology that is making its way into current projectors, which will eventually correct this problem.

It is also important to choose the proper type of screen for your application. Determine the screen size based on room dimensions and number of people in your audience. Da-Lite, a projection screen manufacturer, recommends the following formula: "Screen height should be approximately 1/6 the distance from the screen to the last row of seats, allowing text to be read and detail to be seen in the projected image." There are many choices for screen surfaces—check out some manufacturers of projection screens to see what suits your needs. If you are using your projector for home use and are on a budget, you can use a white painted wall, provided that the wall is painted with *flat* paint—any gloss at all in the paint will cause weird diffractions, which will detract from your image.

HDV VIDEO MIXER

Currently, most options for live mixing HD video formats like HDV are extremely limited and expensive. However, Edirol's new V-440 video mixer is capable of mixing several HD/HDV signals, as well as SD and computer inputs, which can be controlled from the mixer or through the use of any Roland/Edirol instrument via MIDI, as well as RS-232C control. This is an excellent option for presenters or VJs who want to take advantage of high-resolution projectors and HDV source material. See Figure 12.39 and Figure 12.40 for a look at the mixer's controls and inputs. For links to information on the subject of video mixing, visit www.hdvfilmmaking.com.

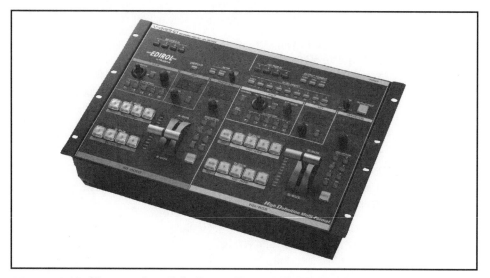

Figure 12.39 *The controls on Edirol's new V-440 HD/HDV video mixer.*

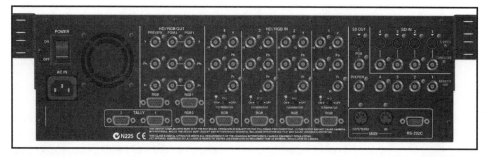

Figure 12.40 *Input and output options on the back of Edirol's new V-440 HD/HDV video mixer.*

Transferring HDV to Film

Although there are now options to screen a film digitally (however rare), the vast majority of theaters can only show 35mm prints, and will probably only be showing film for some time to come. What does this mean for HDV filmmakers? Simply that, in most cases, digital filmmakers who want to see their movies in a theatrical setting must transfer their video to film. Of course, realistically speaking, most video filmmakers will never see their movie transferred to celluloid, simply because of the costs involved, and the slim chance of acquiring a theatrical distribution deal. Certainly, if you want to screen your movie at a festival that only accepts entries on 35mm or 16mm, then you must decide on whether the benefits outweigh the costs.

Most filmmakers wait until they have secured an agreement to buy their movie, at which point the film studio handles the costs involved with video-to-film transfers. Even if you are uncertain about an eventual film-out process, you can do a few things to prepare while shooting (in case the opportunity arises). It should be noted that different video-to-film transfer companies often have their own processes and set of equipment, which may influence the way you prepare your video for transfer. For example, some companies prefer working from NTSC (60i) originated material, while others prefer PAL (50i). In general, PAL is often cited as the preferred method for interlaced video that is transferred to film because its frame rate of 25fps most closely matches film's 24fps. This does not mean that you cannot get a good transfer from an NTSC master. There are even applications, such as Magic Bullet Suite or the Nattress Standards Conversion plug-in, that may do the conversion for you, in preparation for transfer (producing a digital master file). If you think you will be transferring to film at some point, make sure to talk with someone at the company where you intend to transfer it before you begin filming. In most cases, it is best to leave the video as 60i or 50i and let the specialists handle it their own way. There are several companies that specialize in transfers, including Technicolor, EFilm, and Swiss Effects.

RECOMMENDATIONS FOR VIDEO-TO-FILM TRANSFER

When asked about a set of recommendations for shooting and preparing HDV for transfer to film, **David Pfluger** at Swiss Effects in Zurich (www.swisseffects.ch) provided all of the advice that follows. Swiss Effects is a company responsible for past transfers of such movies as *Waking Life, The Kid Stays in the Picture, Center of the World, Pieces of April, Everything Put Together*, and *Gunner Palace*, to name just a few.

General remarks about new video formats:

Many new video formats have been issued recently, due to technical progress in the field of resolution, compression technology, and the introduction of progressive scan video. Under pressure from the market, companies are trying to quickly put out new products to establish a standard before their competitors can follow up. As a consequence, the software for post is, at first, often missing or incomplete, and the documentation of the product is sometimes quite modest. Consumers, on the other hand, are eager to get the latest products to give their projects the best possible quality, in order to stand out in the vast landscape of filmmakers. This often leads to confusion, misinformation, and false rumors. It is important to give yourself and the market time to understand what a new technology is able to accomplish, and for what field of use it's best suited.

Filming on HD:

The option to record in HD resolution with small and cheap cameras is a great possibility for filmmakers around the world. As a consequence, more and more DOPs with experience only in standard definition video filmmaking are pushing into the field of HD. Due to financial restrictions, up to now this domain has mainly been reserved for filmmakers coming from the motion picture film sector. It is a fact that HD filmmaking demands much "film" knowledge and technical care on the set to achieve a result that can compete with a motion picture film image. Still, video has a smaller variation of apertures compared to film and is susceptible to problems such as white clipping. It is a harsh misunderstanding to think that because video is generally stronger under low light conditions, it is easier to receive a good, or even beautiful, image by using it. It is a necessity, especially for DOPs with no motion picture film experience, to educate themselves to be ready for HD filmmaking.

Basic settings for the Sony HDV cameras in favor of transfer to 35mm:

There are many providers of film-out services today and many different types of film recorders. We at Swiss Effects consider it most important to choose the workflow, technique, and film stock, according to the type and quality of footage given to us, and to know what the filmmaker has in mind for the look of his project.

There are only a few basic settings that may be considered essential for the quality of a transfer to 35mm or 16mm film. Most of the settings and choices reflect the taste of the filmmaker and need to be respected individually.

Here are the basic settings for the HDV HVR-Z1U and the HDR-FX1, which we consider to be optimum for our film-out facilities:

Sharpness: There is a range of values 1 to 15 for detail enhancement. The camera should be set to a value between 8 and 12. You can go to the higher end for wide shots and lower for close ups.

Skintone Detail: Off

Black Stretch: On (not available for the FX1)

But as mentioned, there is more to the process than just these settings.

NTSC/PAL and HD 60i/50i issues:

For standard definition, Swiss Effects has always recommended to record in PAL format for two reasons: PAL has a better resolution and the image frequency of 50i can be used for frame by frame film recording without any pulldown procedure. The new HDV cameras by Sony offer interlaced recording in 50i or 60i. In both recording modes, the resolution is the same 1920×1080 pixels (actually squeezed as 144×1080 pixels). The "PAL frequency" offers no additional resolution advantage anymore.

Still, the issue of the image frequency remains. 60i needs to be converted into 24p by a pulldown procedure. This image processing is available in different qualities by different providers. As usual, better quality is usually more expensive and requires longer rendering times. In spite of that, a processed image can never be as good as an untouched image. A pulldown will always leave its traces on the result, be it a reduced sharpness or a shuttering effect in motion. Additionally, the better resolved HD image will show these artifacts more clearly. Our recommendation remains to shoot in 50i. For a video version in NTSC or HD 60i, a telecine can be made off the 35mm negative, which will even give some of the film look to the video master.

Cine Frame modes and true progressive scan:

Do not use the cine frame mode, since it is not a true progressive recording mode (the camera does an internal deinterlace). De-interlacing is not out of the question, though. It can improve the motion reproduction to make it more film-like, but this can be done in post with a tool superior to what the camera does under time constraints. Generally, de-interlacing will slightly reduce sharpness.

(continued on next page)

(continued from previous page)

Low light/gain:

The HVR-Z1U and the HDR-FX1 are not as strong as other video cameras under low light conditions. Still, using the gain should be avoided whenever possible. Gain does introduce video noise, which tends to be even more visible on film. This noise, unlike film grain, has an artificial character.

Compression and color, sharpness and movement:

Even though the resolution of an HDV image is basically the same as HDCAM, it does not have the same sharpness. This is due to the very strong compression used on the image. The colors are not as brilliant as in professional HD cameras, which may also be attributed somewhat to compression. Generally, HDV has its own look and it's easy to distinguish between HDV and HD material. Matching the two types of footage for intercutting takes a great deal of skill in color grading. More than that, when using HDV as a second unit (for example), a lot of matching work can be avoided by using the camera properly. In close-ups, the difference in resolution will not be as obvious as in wide shots. Using HDV for more close-up shots will already help a lot to avoid mismatching.

The compression of HDV works in a way that a whole image is recorded every few frames and, in the frames in-between, only the difference between images will be processed. In a stable image shot from a tripod, this method works very successfully and good quality images can be fit into the relatively limited data stream. As soon as there is a lot of motion (i.e., a lot of change in the image content), the compression needs to be increased while maintaining the data limit. Worst cases are pans, as the whole image content changes from frame to frame. Here the compression artifacts are worst and most likely to be visible. In a fast pan, the image is blurred and details cannot be recognized; in slower pans, image sharpness can be reduced due to this fact.

Some words on "film look:"

There are many cameras that offer a "film look" gamma setting. With most cameras, this setting is meant to produce a "film look" on video. This does not mean that it will be equally in favor of a transfer to film. It can even have an unwanted effect. Only very few cameras offer gamma settings that are actually meant for tape to film transfer. What makes a "film look" is not easy to define technically, and it is an often-misused term. "Film look", and the general quality of a transfer to film, starts on the set and is affected by every step in production and post-production. If one decides to film in "dogma" style, the result will never have the classic "film look," no matter what technical wizardry is used to make it look like film in post. The style of camera work and the (absent) lighting gives it the typical video look.

Run a test!

No matter what format you choose and what look you are aiming for, it is always wise to run a film-out test. The best technician will not be able to describe accurately how the result of a transfer will look, nor does he really know what you have in mind. Testing is cheap and makes you aware of what to pay attention to, as well as potentially saving you much trouble and money.

David Pfluger

Swiss Effects

www.swisseffects.ch

Index

Numbers

2D animations
  3D comparison, 172-173
  keyframes, 352-354
  overview, 352
  plug-ins, 355-357
  simulations, 374
  software, 355-357
  speed, 354-355

2D particles (3D animations), 372-373, 378

3D animations
  2D comparison, 172-173
  animating, 367
  backgrounds, 374-375
  Booleans, 363
  compositing, 369-374
  curves, 363
  Dames, John, 376-378
  deformers, 363
  designing, 377
  environments, 369-372
  HDRI, 366
  image-based modeling, 371-372
  lights/lighting, 365-366
  matchmoving, 370-371, 376
  materials, 364-365
  matte paintings, 374-375
  metaballs, 364
  modeling, 362-364
  motion tracking, 370-371, 376
  NURBS, 363
  overview, 360-361
  particles, 372-373, 377-378
  polygons, 362
  post-production, 377
  proxies, 377
  rendering, 367-368
  simulations, 374

  techniques, 369-374, 377
  textures, 364-365
  video, 369-372

180 degree rule, 176-177, 202

A

AAF (Advanced Authoring Format), 234
achromatic diopter lenses, 135
acquiring. *See* shooting
adapters
  connections/cables, 41-42
  lenses, 133
Add composite mode, 346-347
additive/subtractive color, 271-272
Adobe Premiere Pro, 214-216
Advanced Authoring Format (AAF), 234
Advanced HAD (Hole Accumulation Diode), 32, 35
Advanced Metal Evaporated (AME II), 45
Advanced Technology Attachment (ATA), 74
Advanced Television Systems Committee (ATSC), 6-8
Advanced Video Coding (AVC), 381-382
After Effects, 331
AJA Kona 2 capture cards, 97-98
AJA Kona 2 Web site, 98
alignment, 197-198
alpha channels, 336-337
Alpha composite mode, 351-352
ambient noise (microphones), 141
AME II (Advance Metal Evaporated), 45
analog video, 12-13
Andersson Technologies Web site, 370
angles
  LCD viewscreens, 38
  shooting, 181-182, 201-202
animatics
  editing, 242
  storyboards, 168, 170
animating 3D animations, 367

animations
  2D animations
    3D comparison, 172-173
    keyframes, 352-354
    overview, 352
    plug-ins, 355-357
    simulations, 374
    software, 355-357
    speed, 354-355
  3D animations
    2D comparison, 172-173
    animating, 367
    backgrounds, 374-375
    Booleans, 363
    compositing, 369-374
    curves, 363
    Dames, John, 376-378
    deformers, 363
    designing, 377
    environments, 369-372
    HDRI, 366
    image-based modeling, 371-372
    lights/lighting, 365-366
    matchmoving, 370-371, 376
    materials, 364-365
    matte paintings, 374-375
    metaballs, 364
    modeling, 362-364
    motion tracking, 370-371, 376
    NURBS, 363
    overview, 360-361
    particles, 372-373, 377-378
    polygons, 362
    post-production, 377
    proxies, 377
    rendering, 367-368
    simulations, 374
    techniques, 369-374, 377
    textures, 364-365
    video, 369-372
aperture/iris
  correction (sharpness), 125
  exposure controls, 120-123
  focus controls, 114-115
appearing point (compositions), 191-192
artifacts

DVD encoding, 419
  shooting, 187
aspect ratios. *See also* resolution
  graphics (text), 332-333
  HD, 27-28
  HDTV (ATSC), 6-8
  HDV, 14-15, 330-331
  LCD viewscreens, 175
  rule of thirds, 175
  shooting (compositions), 173-175
  viewfinders, 175
asset preparation (DVD authoring), 400-401
ATA (Advanced Technology Attachment), 74
ATSC (Advanced Television Systems Committee), 6-8
attaching cameras
  lights/lighting, 155-156
  microphones, 39
audio
  capturing, 288-289
  connections/cables, 40-44
    adapters, 41-42
    balanced, 42-43
    I/O, 44
    ports, 44
    RCA, 40-44
    unbalanced, 42-43
    XLR, 40-44
  dialogue, 314-315, 321
  DVD encoding, 417-418
  editing
    clipping, 295
    cutting/pasting tracks, 321
    Emrich, Brian, 305-311
    Hill, Robert, 313-318
    humming, 313-314, 318-320
    mixers, 294-297
    multiple tracks, 290-296, 320
    noise, 313-314, 318-320
    organizing tracks, 315, 321
    synchronizing, 292-293
    techniques, 320-321
    timelines, 291-293
    tracks, 291-292
    transitions, 294, 320
    volume, 294
    VU meters, 295

filters. *See* special effects
HDV, 18-19
microphones
    ambient noise, 141
    attaching, 39
    audio, 39-40
    background noise, 138, 141
    boom microphones, 138-139
    controls, 137-141
    headphones, 138
    orientation, 138
    room tone, 141
    shoes, 39
    wind, 138, 141
    wireless microphones, 139-140
music. *See* music
naming, 315
noise
    ambient noise, 141
    background noise, 138, 141
    editing, 313-314, 318-320
    room tone, 141
    zoom controls, 108
organic, 316-317
overview, 38-39, 288
sample rates, 289-290
special effects, 314-315
    bandpass, 301
    compressor/limiter, 301-302
    delay, 300-302
    echo, 300-301
    EQ, 302-303, 314
    High Pass Filter, 303
    High Shelf Filter, 303
    Low Pass Filter, 303
    Low Shelf Filter, 303
    Notch, 304, 318-319
    overview, 297-298
    Peak Limiter, 304
    reverb, 299-300
    Vocal DeEsser, 304
    Vocal DePopper, 304
stereo, 317-318
takes, stacking, 316-317
techniques, 305-311

authoring DVDs
    building, 404-406
    burning, 404-406
    DVD-ROMs, 406
    formatting, 404-406
    menus, 401-403
    overview, 400
    preparing assets, 400-401
    scripts, 404
    slideshows, 403-404
    testing, 404-406
    tracks, 403-404
    UDF, 406
automatic focus controls, 110-111
AVC (Advanced Video Coding), 381-382
Avid Xpress Pro, 211-214

B

back lights, 124, 157
background noise, 138, 141
backgrounds
    3D animations, 374-375
    back lights, 124, 157
    lights/lighting, 157
balanced connections/cables, 42-43
bandpass (audio special effects), 301
barn doors (lights/lighting), 160-161
batches, capturing, 237
batteries (cameras), 103
BeachTek Web site, 41
benefits, HDV, 7, 19
B-frames (bidirectional frames), 230-231
bit rates
    calculating (DVD encoding), 412-413
    constant bit rates, 386-387
    DVD encoding, 419
    HDV output, 386-388, 419
    variable bit rates, 386-387
black and code timecodes, 235
black-and-white viewfinders, 114
black stretch, 126
Blackmagic Design DeckLink HD capture cards, 95-97
Blackmagic Design DeckLink HD Web site, 96
blend modes. *See* composite modes
blocking storyboards, 171

blow outs, 124

blue only color correction, 275-276

blue/green screens

    compositing, 338-344

        color keying, 339-343

        techniques, 342-343

    lights/lighting, 162-164, 280-281, 340-341

    vectorscopes, 280-281

Blu-ray discs, 395-399

Bluth, Don, 170-173

Booleans (modeling 3D animations), 363

boom microphones, 138-139

bouncing lights/lighting, 162

breaks (timecodes), 235

brightness

    color correction, 264-265, 267-269, 275-279, 281

    DVD encoding, 419

    exposure controls

        aperture/iris, 120-123

        back lights, 124

        black stretch, 126

        brightness, 126

        cameras, 115-127

        CineFrame, 126-127

        CinemaTone, 126

        color phase, 125

        contrast, 125-126

        gain, 122

        gamma, 125-126

        monitors, 119

        overexposure, 124

        shadows, 126

        sharpness, 125

        shutter speed, 117-123

        skin tone, 125-126

        spot light, 124

        television, 119

        zebra stripes, 116-117

    lights/lighting, 157

    luma, 264-265, 267-269, 275-279, 281

broadcast safe color correction, 277, 279

Brown, Garrett

    stabilization interview, 188-195

    Web site, 189

building (DVD authoring), 404-406

burning (DVD authoring), 404-406

buying editing systems, 69-70

C

cables. *See* connections/cables

calculating bits, 412-413

calibrating color correction, 263-264, 274-277

camcorders. *See* cameras

cameras

    audio. *See* audio

    batteries, 103

    charging, 103

    comparison, 48

    connections/cables. *See* connections/cables

    controls. *See* controls

    decks

        connections/cables, 89-93

        Sony HVR-M10U, 58-59

    disks, loading, 103-104

    ergonomics, 46-47

    exposure controls. *See also* brightness

        aperture/iris, 120-123

        back lights, 124

        black stretch, 126

        brightness, 126

        cameras, 115-127

        CineFrame, 126-127

        CinemaTone, 126

        color phase, 125

        contrast, 125-126

        gain, 122

        gamma, 125-126

        monitors, 119

        overexposure, 124

        shadows, 126

        sharpness, 125

        shutter speed, 117-123

        skin tone, 125-126

        spot light, 124

        television, 119

        zebra stripes, 116-117

    filters, 151

    FireWire connections/cables, 90-92

    focus. *See* focus

    holding, 103

JVC, 59-60
LCD viewscreens , 37-38
   angles, 38
   aspect ratios, 175
   lights/lighting, 38
lenses, 35-37
   adapters, 133
   close-ups, 135
   controls, 131-137
   converters, 133
   fish eye, 133-134
   telephoto, 134-135
   wide-angle, 132-134, 190-191
   zoom, 134-135
lights/lighting. *See* lights/lighting
media, loading, 103-104
menus, navigating, 104
microphones
   ambient noise, 141
   attaching, 39
   audio, 39-40
   background noise, 138, 141
   boom microphones, 138-139
   controls, 137-141
   headphones, 138
   orientation, 138
   room tone, 141
   shoes, 39
   wind, 138, 141
   wireless microphones, 139-140
monitors, 105
multiple, 136-137
operating overview, 102-103
Panasonic HVX-200 DVCPRO HD, 64
power, 103
SDI connections/cables, 92-93
sensors, 31-35
   Advanced HAD, 32, 35
   CCDs, 31-35
   CMOSs, 31-34
shooting. *See* shooting
shots. *See* shots
Sony
   HDR-FX1, 48-53
   HDR-HC1, 54-58

   HVR-A1U, 54-58
   HVR-Z1U, 48-53, 62-63
stabilization, 37, 187-196
tapes, loading, 103-104
timecodes (free run), 136-137
types, 30-31
viewfinders, 37-38
   aspect ratios, 175
   black-and-white focus controls, 114
white balance controls, 130-131
zoom controls, 106-110
   controls, 109
   digital/optical comparison, 110
   focus. *See* focus
   lenses, 134-135
   noise, 108
   shot transitions, 129-130
   speed, 109
Canopus Edius, 222-224
capture cards, 95-97, 239
capturing
   audio, 288-289
   editing
      batches, 237
      cards, 239
      drivers, 239
      dropped frames, 239
      frame handles, 238
      memory, 239
      scene breaks, 237
      settings, 238
      troubleshooting, 238-239
   HDV, 9-11
cards
   capture cards, 95-97, 239
   graphics cards, 74-76
CCDs (charge-coupled devices), 31-35
Century Optics Web site, 131
Chaimson, Dave, 217-218
chapter points, 421-424
charge-coupled devices (CCDs), 31-35
charging cameras, 103
choosing
   cameras, 48
   editing systems, 69-70

choreography
  editing, 241-242
  storyboards, 171
chroma (color correction), 264, 266, 270-271, 276, 279-281
CineFrame, 126-127
CineLook. *See* DigiEffects
Cinema 4D Web site, 360
CinemaTone, 126
clipping audio, 295
clips
  DVD encoding, 413-421
  in/out points, 245-246
  nesting, 250
  Timelines
    editing, 245-247, 250-253
    Pen tool, 253
    razor blade, 252
    rippling edits, 252
    rolling edits, 252
    sliding, 252
    slipping, 252
    time remapping, 252
  tracks/layers, 248-250
  transitions, 256-257
close-ups
  lenses, 135
  shooting compositions, 179-180
CMOSs (Complementary Metal Oxide Semiconductors), 31-34
coding method, 386-387
color
  color correction. *See* color correction
  color keying (blue/green screens), 339-343
  color phase (exposure controls), 125
  color samples, 27-28
  color temperature (lights/lighting), 145-147
  DVD encoding, 419
  graphics (text), 334
  lights/lighting, 145-147, 162
  white balance
    camera controls, 130-131
    color correction, 266
    lights/lighting, 145-147
color bars (color correction), 263-264, 274-277

color correction
  additive/subtractive color, 271-272
  blue only, 275-276
  brightness, 264-265, 267-269, 275-279, 281
  broadcast safe, 277, 279
  calibrating, 263-264, 274-277
  chroma, 264, 266, 270-271, 276, 279-281
  color bars, 263-264, 274-277
  color space, 272-274
  contrast, 276
  DVD encoding, 419
  hue/saturation, 264, 266, 270-271, 276, 279-281
  ITU-BR standards, 273
  luma, 264-265, 267-269, 275-279, 281
  monitors, 263-264, 274-277
  oscilloscopes, 277-281
  overview, 260-262
  principles, 266-272
  RGB color, 271-273
  samples, 274
  secondary, 282
  simulations film, 282-286
  SMPTE, 275
  software, 283-286
    DigiEffects CineLook, 285
    Magic Bullet, 283-285
    Nattress Film Effects, 286
  tape to tape, 263
  vectorscopes, 279-281
  video scopes, 264-265, 277-281
  waveforms, 264, 277-279
  white balance, 266
  workflow, 262-266
  Y'CbCr color, 273
  zebra stripes, 281
color keying (blue/green screens), 339-343
color phase (exposure controls), 125
color samples, 27-28
color space (color correction), 272-274
color temperature (lights/lighting), 145-147
comparisons
  cameras, 48
  editing systems, 69-70
Complementary Metal Oxide Semiconductors (CMOSs), 31-34

components, connections/cables, 106

composing music, 311-312

composite modes, 344-352

   Add, 346-347

   Alpha, 351-352

   Darken, 350-351

   Difference, 347-348

   Hard Light, 349-350

   Lighten, 351

   Luma, 352

   Multiply, 348

   Normal, 346

   Overlay, 349

   Screen, 348-349

   Soft Light, 350

   Subtract, 347

compositing

   3D animations, 369-374

   alpha channels, 336-337

   blue/green screens, 338-344

      color keying, 339-343

      techniques, 342-343

   composite modes, 344-352

      Add, 346-347

      Alpha, 351-352

      Darken, 350-351

      Difference, 347-348

      Hard Light, 349-350

      Lighten, 351

      Luma, 352

      Multiply, 348

      Normal, 346

      Overlay, 349

      Screen, 348-349

      Soft Light, 350

      Subtract, 347

   overview, 336-338

   rotoscoping, 338

compositions

   180 degree rule, 176-177, 202

   alignment, 197-198

   animatics, 168, 170

   appearing point, 191-192

   aspect ratios, 173-175

   blocking, 171

Bluth, Don, 170-173

camera placement, 178-180

choreography, 171

close-ups, 179-180

edges, 196-197

field of vision, 173

film comparison, 171

full screen video, 174

Goldman, Gary, 170-173

live action comparison, 171

medium shots, 179

music, 172

negative space, 197

number of shots, 168

overview, 166

pan and scan, 174

panels, 168

people, 196-202

places, 196-200

PoV, 199

previsualization, 168-170

reverse shots, 198-199

rule of thirds, 175-176

software, 168-170

storyboards, 166-173, 180

thumbnails, 168

time-lapse, 199-200

timing, 172

wide shots, 178

widescreen, 173-175

compression

   data streams, 17

   DVD

      DVD recorders, 411-412

      encoding, 415-416, 420-421

      hardware, 410-411

      overview, 407-408

      software, 409-410

   editing, 69, , 229-230

   error correction, 18

   generation loss, 12-13

   HD, 27-28

   HDV

      output, 386-387

      schemes, 16-20

interframe editing systems, 69
interframe/spatial, 229-230
intraframe editing systems, 69
intraframe/temporal, 229-230
RAIDs, 80
    controls, 81-82
    FireWire comparison, 80
    hardware, 82
    JBOD, 87
    mirroring, 81
    overview, 80-82
    RAID 0, 82-83, 88
    RAID 1, 83-84, 88
    RAID 10, 89
    RAID 3, 84-85, 88
    RAID 30, 89
    RAID 5, 85-86, 88
    RAID 50, 86-87, 89
    software, 82
    uncompressed editing, 247-248
compressor/limiter audio special effects, 301-302
Congress, 7
connections/cables. *See also* output
    audio, 40-44
        adapters, 41-42
        balanced, 42-43
        I/O, 44
        ports, 44
        RCA, 40-44
        unbalanced, 42-43
        XLR, 40-44
    cameras
        audio, 40-44
        components, 106
        decks, 89-93
        FireWire, 90-92
        SDI, 92-93
consortium (HDV), 13-14
constant bit rates, 386-387
contrast
    color correction, 276
    DVD encoding, 419
    exposure controls, 125-126
controls
    cameras

        playback, 104-105
        profiles, 127-129
        recording, 104
        shot transitions, 129-130
        white balance, 130-131
    exposure
        aperture/iris, 120-123
        back lights, 124
        black stretch, 126
        brightness, 126
        cameras, 115-127
        CineFrame, 126-127
        CinemaTone, 126
        color phase, 125
        contrast, 125-126
        gain, 122
        gamma, 125-126
        monitors, 119
        overexposure, 124
        shadows, 126
        sharpness, 125
        shutter speed, 117-123
        skin tone, 125-126
        spot light, 124
        television, 119
        zebra stripes, 116-117
    focus
        aperture/iris, 114-115
        automatic, 110-111
        black-and-white viewfinders, 114
        cameras, 110-115
        deep, 115
        depth of field, 114-115
        expanded, 113
        manual, 111-115
        peaking, 113
        selective, 114-115
    lenses
        adapters, 133
        cameras, 131-137
        close-ups, 135
        converters, 133
        fish eye, 133-134
        telephoto, 134-135
        wide-angle, 132-134, 190-191

zoom, 134-135
microphones
boom microphones, 138-139
cameras, 137-141
wireless microphones, 139-140
RAIDs, 81-82
zoom
cameras, 106-110
controls, 109
digital/optical comparison, 110
noise, 108
speed, 109
converters (lenses), 133
copying (generation loss), 12-13
Coreaudiovisual Web site, 376
correcting color. *See* color correction
Creative Cow Web site, 374
credits. *See* text
curves (3D animations), 363
cutting/pasting audio tracks, 321
Cycore FX Web site, 357

D

D5-HD, 26
D7-HD, 23-24
Dames, John, 376-378
Darken composite mode, 350-351
data rates (HD formats), 27-28
data streams, 17
Debevec, Paul, Web site, 366
DeckLink HD capture cards, 95-97
decks
cameras, connections/cables, 89-93
Sony HVR-M10U, 58-59
deep focus controls, 115
deformers (modeling 3D animations), 363
degradation (generation loss), 12-13
degrees (Kelvin scale), 145-147
de-interlacing video, 327-330
delay (audio special effects), 300-302
depth of field
focus controls, 114-115
lights/lighting, 162
designing
3D animations, 377

compositions. *See* compositions
dialogue (audio), 314-315, 321
Difference composite mode, 347-348
diffusion (lights/lighting), 156
DigiEffects
CineLook, 285
Web site, 329
digital video (DV)
analog video comparison, 12-13
generation loss, 12-13
HDV comparison, 20
Digital Visual Interface (DVI), 429-430
digital/optical comparison (zoom controls), 110
disks
cameras, loading, 103-104
RAIDs, 80
controls, 81-82
FireWire comparison, 80
hardware, 82
JBOD, 87
mirroring, 81
overview, 80-82
RAID 0, 82-83, 88
RAID 1, 83-84, 88
RAID 10, 89
RAID 3, 84-85, 88
RAID 30, 89
RAID 5, 85-86, 88
RAID 50, 86-87, 89
software, 82
DivX, 390
dolly shots, 184-185
drivers, capturing, 239
drop frame rates, 8, 235-236
dropped frames
capturing, 239
drop frame rates, 8, 235-236
D-Theater, 22
dutch shots, 182
DV (digital video)
analog video comparison, 12-13
generation loss, 12-13
HDV comparison, 20
DV100, 23-24
DVCPRO HD, 23-24

DVD
  authoring
    building, 404-406
    burning, 404-406
    DVD-ROMs, 406
    formatting, 404-406
    menus, 401-403
    overview, 400
    preparing assets, 400-401
    scripts, 404
    slideshows, 403-404
    testing, 404-406
    tracks, 403-404
    UDF, 406
  chapter points, 421-424
  compression
    DVD recorders, 411-412
    hardware, 410-411
    overview, 407-408
    software, 409-410
  encoding
    artifacts, 419
    audio, 417-418
    bit calculations, 412-413
    bit rates, 419
    brightness, 419
    clips, 413-421
    color, 419
    color correction, 419
    compression, 415-416, 420-421
    contrast, 419
    DVD recorders, 411-412
    fields, 417
    file size, 412, 419
    filters, 419
    hardware, 410-411
    interlaced video, 417
    multiplexing, 418
    muxing, 418
    naming, 420
    noise reduction, 419
    overview, 407-408
    quality, 419
    sequences, 413-421
    settings, 413-421
    software, 409-410
    standards, 416-417
  markers, 421-424
  output
    formats, 424-428
    mobile phones, 427
    PDAs, 427
    portable devices, 427-428
DVD recorders, 411-412
DVD-ROMs
  DVD authoring, 406
  HDV output, 383-384
*DV*Film Web site, 329
D-VHS, 21-22
DVI (Digital Visual Interface), 429-430

E

echo audio special effects, 300-301
edges
  compositions, 196-197
  sharpness, 125
Edit Decision Lists (EDLs), 234
editing
  animatics, 242
  audio
    clipping, 295
    cutting/pasting tracks, 321
    Emrich, Brian, 305-311
    Hill, Robert, 313-318
    humming, 313-314, 318-320
    mixers, 294-297
    multiple tracks, 290-296, 320
    noise, 313-314, 318-320
    organizing tracks, 315, 321
    synchronizing, 292-293
    techniques, 320-321
    timelines, 291-293
    tracks, 291-292
    transitions, 294, 320
    volume, 294
    VU meters, 295
  capturing
    batches, 237
    cards, 239
    drivers, 239

dropped frames, 239
frame handles, 238
memory, 239
scene breaks, 237
settings, 238
troubleshooting, 238-239
choreography, 241-242
clips
    in/out points, 245-246
    nesting, 250
    Pen tool, 253
    razor blade, 252
    rippling edits, 252
    rolling edits, 252
    sliding, 252
    slipping, 252
    time remapping, 252
    timelines, 245-247, 250-253
    tracks/layers, 248-250
    transitions, 256-257
color correction. *See* color correction
compression, 229-230
editing systems. *See* editing systems
GOP, 230-231
HDV, 9-11, 231-233
    error correction, 18
    native, 10, 232-233
logging, 233-234
    AAF, 234
    EDLs, 234
    scene breaks, 237
    XML, 234
MPEG, 228-232
music
    Gonzales, Steve, 254
    Hill, Robert, 313-318
    Hirsch, Paul, 241
offline, 239-241
online, 239-241
overview, 206
shooting, 201-202
software
    Adobe Premiere Pro, 214-216
    Avid Xpress Pro, 211-214
    Canopus Edius, 222-224

Chaimson, Dave, 217-218
Final Cut Express HD, 210-211
Final Cut Pro, 207-210
Haubrich, Frederic, 208-210
Hirsch, Paul, 243
Holland, Carter, 212-214
iMovie HD, 210-211
Lumiere HD, 208-210
Matrox, 224-227
overview, 207
Pinnacle Liquid Edition, 228
Sony Vegas, 216-218
Townhill, Richard, 215-216
Ulead Media Studio Pro, 219-221
special effects, 241-242
storyboards, 242
structure
    Gonzales, Steve, 253
    Hirsch, Paul, 243
techniques, 244-248, 253-256
    Gonzales, Steve, 253-256
    Hirsch, Paul, 244
technology, 242-243
timelines
    clips, 245-247, 250-253
    in/out points, 245-246
    navigating, 245
    Pen tool, 253
    razor blade, 252
    rippling edits, 252
    rolling edits, 252
    sliding, 252
    slipping, 252
    time remapping, 252
    tools, 250-253
timing, 254
tools
    Pen tool, 253
    razor blade, 252
    rippling edits, 252
    rolling edits, 252
    sliding, 252
    slipping, 252
    time remapping, 252
    timelines, 250-253

uncompressed, 247-248

editing systems

  buying, 69-70

  choosing, 69-70

  comparison, 69-70

  compression, 69

  graphics cards, 74-76

  hard drives, 71-74

  Macintosh, 76-80

  overview, 68-69

  PCs, 76-80

  RAIDs

    controls, 81-82

    FireWire comparison, 80

    hardware, 82

    JBOD, 87

    mirroring, 81

    overview, 80-82

    RAID 0, 82-83, 88

    RAID 1, 83-84, 88

    RAID 10, 89

    RAID 3, 84-85, 88

    RAID 30, 89

    RAID 5, 85-86, 88

    RAID 50, 86-87, 89

    software, 82

  RAM, 71

  recommendations, 76-80

Edius, 222-224

EDLs (Edit Decision Lists), 234

Eldred, Jody

  cameras filters, 151

  HDV to film transfer interview, 438-441

  lights/lighting interview, 150-152

  projectors interview, 434-435

elementary streams, 17

Emrich, Brian, 305-311

encoding DVD

  artifacts, 419

  audio, 417-418

  bit calculations, 412-413

  bit rates, 419

  brightness, 419

  clips, 413-421

  color, 419

color correction, 419

compression, 415-416, 420-421

contrast, 419

DVD recorders, 411-412

fields, 417

file size, 412, 419

filters, 419

hardware, 410-411

interlaced video, 417

multiplexing, 418

muxing, 418

naming, 420

noise reduction, 419

overview, 407-408

quality, 419

sequences, 413-421

settings, 413-421

software, 409-410

standards, 416-417

environments (3D animations), 369-372

EQ audio special effects, 302-303, 314

ergonomics (cameras), 46-47

error correction, 18

expanded focus controls, 113

exporting HDV output, 386

exposure controls. *See also* brightness

  aperture/iris, 120-123

  back lights, 124

  black stretch, 126

  brightness, 126

  cameras, 115-127

  CineFrame, 126-127

  CinemaTone, 126

  color phase, 125

  contrast, 125-126

  gain, 122

  gamma, 125-126

  monitors, 119

  overexposure, 124

  shadows, 126

  sharpness, 125

  shutter speed, 117-123

  skin tone, 125-126

  spot light, 124

  television, 119

zebra stripes, 116-117
Extensible Markup Language (XML), 234
eye lines, shooting, 202

F

faces (lights/lighting), 149
Fahs, Chad, Web site, 5
field of vision, 173
fields
    DVD encoding, 417
    interlaced video, 324-330
file size (DVD encoding), 412, 419
fill lights, 156-157
film
    HDV transfer, 437-441
    simulations (color correction), 282-286
    storyboards comparison, 171
filters
    audio. *See* special effects
    cameras, 151
    DVD encoding, 419
Final Cut Express HD, 210-211
Final Cut Pro, 207-210
FireWire
    connections/cables, 90-92
    RAIDs comparison, 80
fish eye lenses, 133-134
flicker, shooting, 187
Flip4Mac, 385-390
fluorescent lights, 160
focus
    controls
        aperture/iris, 114-115
        automatic, 110-111
        black-and-white viewfinders, 114
        cameras, 110-115
        deep, 115
        depth of field, 114-115
        expanded, 113
        manual, 111-115
        peaking, 113
        selective, 114-115
    shot transitions, 129-130
    zoom controls, 106-110
        controls, 109

    digital/optical comparison, 110
    lenses, 134-135
    noise, 108
    speed, 109
Focus Enhancements Web site, 103
fonts, 332
formats
    DVD output, 424-428
    HD
        aspect ratios, 27-28
        color samples, 27-28
        comparison, 26-28
        compression, 27-28
        D5-HD, 26
        data rates, 27-28
        DVCPRO HD, 23-24
        D-VHS, 21-22
        frame rates, 27-28
        HDCAM, 24-26
        HDV. *See* HDV
formatting (DVD authoring), 404-406
fps. *See* frame rates
frame rates
    HD formats, 27-28
    HDTV (ATSC), 7-8
    HDV, 15-16, 331, 389
    timecodes
        black and code, 235
        breaks, 235
        drop frame rates, 8, 235-236
        free run, 136-137, 236
        non-drop frame rates, 8, 235-236
        NTSC, 235-236
        record run, 236
        SMPTE, 235
frames
    B-frames (bidirectional frames), 230-231
    dropped
        capturing, 239
        drop frame rates, 8, 235-236
    editing, 230-231
    frame rates. *See* frame rates
    GOP, 230-231
    graphics (text), 335
    handles, capturing, 238

HDV output, 388-389

interlaced video, 324-330, 389

I-frames (intraframes), 230-231

    intraframe compression, 69

    intraframe/temporal compression, 229-230

keyframes (2D animations), 352-354

P-frames (predicted frames), 230-231

progressive scan video, 389

size, 389

free run timecodes, 236, 136-137

fresnel lights, 159

F-stops (aperture/iris)

    correction (sharpness), 125

    exposure controls, 120-123

    focus controls, 114-115

full screen video, 174

full shots (wide shots), 178

G

gain (exposure controls), 122

gamma. *See* contrast

generation loss, 12-13

Goldman, Gary, 170-173

Gonzales, Steve

    music, 254

    structure, 253

    techniques, 253-256

    timing, 254

GOP (editing), 230-231

graphics

    2D animations

        3D comparison, 172-173

        keyframes, 352-354

        overview, 352

        plug-ins, 355-357

        simulations, 374

        software, 355-357

        speed, 354-355

    3D animations. *See* 3D animations

    graphics cards, 74-76

    menus (DVD authoring), 401-403

    overview, 324

    text, 332-335

        aspect ratios, 332-333

        color, 334

        fonts, 332

        frames, 335

        importing, 333-334

        resolution, 332

        safe areas, 335

        software, 333

        tracks/layers, 248-250

    video. *See* compositing

graphics cards, 74-76

green screens. *See* blue/green screens

GR-HD1 JVC camera, 59-60

Grizzly Pro Web site, 136-137

GY-HD100U JVC camera, 60-63

H

H.264 HDV output standard, 381-382

HAD (Hole Accumulation Diode), 32, 35

halogen lights, 159

handles (frames), 238

hard drives

    editing systems, 71-74

    RAIDs, 80

        controls, 81-82

        FireWire comparison, 80

        hardware, 82

        JBOD, 87

        mirroring, 81

        overview, 80-82

        RAID 0, 82-83, 88

        RAID 1, 83-84, 88

        RAID 10, 89

        RAID 3, 84-85, 88

        RAID 30, 89

        RAID 5, 85-86, 88

        RAID 50, 86-87, 89

        software, 82

hard light, 148

Hard Light composite mode, 349-350

hardware

    DVD compression/encoding, 410-411

    lights/lighting, 158-161

    RAIDs, 82

hardware capture cards, 95-97, 239

Haubrich, Frederic, 208-210

HD (high-definition video), 4

defined, 4, 6
formats
  aspect ratios, 27-28
  color samples, 27-28
  comparison, 26-28
  compression, 27-28
  D5-HD, 26
  data rates, 27-28
  DVCPRO HD, 23-24
  D-VHS, 21-22
  frame rates, 27-28
  HDCAM, 24-26
  HDV. *See* HDV
  HDV relationship, 7-8
  overview, 4-9
HDCAM, 24-26
HD-DVD, 390-394, 399
HDMI (High-Definition Multimedia Interface), 429-430
HDR Shop Web site, 366
HDR-FX1 Sony camera, 48-53
HDR-HC1 Sony camera, 54-58
HDRI (High Dynamic Range Images), 366
HD-SDI (Serial Digital Interface), 92-93
HDTV (high-definition television), 5
  aspect ratios, 6-8
  ATSC Web site, 6
  Congress, 7
  DV (digital video)
    analog video comparison, 12-13
    generation loss, 12-13
    HDV comparison, 20
  frame rates, 7-8
  Japan, 7
  output, 428-430
  overview, 5-8
  resolution, 6-8
  scan modes, 7-8
  standards, 6-8
HDV
  After Effects, 331
  aspect ratios, 14-15, 330-331
  audio, 18-19
  benefits, 7, 19
  capturing, 9-11
  compression schemes, 16-20

consortium, 13-14
data streams, 17
defined, 4, 6
DV (digital video)
  analog video comparison, 12-13
  comparison, 20
  generation loss, 12-13
editing, 9-11, 231-233
  error correction, 18
  native, 10, 232-233
film transfer, 437-441
frame rates, 15-16, 331
HD relationship, 7-8
mixers, 436
output, 11-13
  AVC, 381-382
  bit rates, 386-388, 419
  coding method, 386-387
  compression, 386-387
  constant bit rates, 386-387
  DivX, 390
  DVD-ROMs, 383-384
  exporting, 386
  Flip4Mac, 385-390
  frame rates, 389
  frame size, 389
  frame types, 389
  frames, 388-389
  H.264, 381-382
  input frames, 388
  interlaced video, 389
  keyframes, 388
  MPEG-2, 382-383
  MPEG-4, 381-382
  output frames, 388-389
  overview, 380-381
  progressive scan video, 389
  quality, 387, 419
  standards, 381-383
  variable bit rates, 386-387
  VC-1, 383-384
  Windows Media Video 9, 384-390
  Windows Video tab, 386
overview, 13-14
post-production, 9-13

production, 9-13
projectors, 430-436
resolution, 14-15
scan modes, 14-15
shooting, 9
tapes
    AME II, 45
    lubricants, 45-46
    stocks, 44-46
    super oxidation, 45
Web site, 14
HDV Film Making Web site, 5
headphones, 138
heads/tails (pre-roll/post-roll shooting), 201
height, shooting, 182
High Dynamic Range Images (HDRI), 366
high hat shots, 181
High Pass Filter audio special effects, 303
High Shelf Filter audio special effects, 303
High-Definition Multimedia Interface (HDMI), 429-430
high-definition television. *See* HDTV
high-definition video. *See* HD
Hill, Robert, 313-318
Hirsch, Paul
    animatics, 242
    choreography, 241-242
    editing software, 243
    music, 241
    special effects, 241-242
    storyboards, 242
    structure, 243
    techniques, 244
    technology, 242-243
holding cameras, 103
Hole Accumulation Diode (HAD), 32, 35
Holland, Carter, 212-214
Holographic Versatile Disc (HVD), 399
Hoodman Web site, 38
hue/saturation (color correction), 264, 266, 270-271, 276, 279-281
humming audio, 313-314, 318-320
HVD (Holographic Versatile Disc), 399
HVR-A1U Sony camera, 54-58
HVR-M10U Sony deck, 58-59
HVR-Z1U Sony camera, 48-53, 62-63

HVX-200 DVCPRO HD Panasonic camera, 64

I

i.Link. *See* FireWire
I/O. *See* connections/cables; output
I-frames (intraframes), 230-231
    intraframe compression, 69
    intraframe/temporal compression, 229-230
image sensors, 31-35
    Advanced HAD, 32, 35
    CCDs, 31-35
    CMOSs, 31-34
image stabilization, 37, 187-196
image-based modeling (3D animations), 371-372
iMovie HD, 210-211
importing
    text, 333-334
    video resolution, 358
in/out points, 245-246
incandescent lights, 159
input frames (HDV output), 388
interframe compression, 69
    interframe/spatial compression, 229-230
interlaced video, 324-330
    DVD encoding, 417
    HDV output (frames), 389
intervalometer shooting, 199-200
interviews
    Bluth, Don (storyboards), 170-173
    Brown, Garrett (stabilization), 188-195
    Canopus Edius (editing software), 222-224
    Chaimson, Dave (editing software), 217-218
    Dames, John (3D animations), 376-378
    Eldred, Jody
        camera filters, 151
        HDV to film transfer, 438-441
        lights/lighting, 150-152
        projectors, 434-435
    Emrich, Brian (audio)
        editing, 305-311
        techniques, 305-311
    Goldman, Gary (storyboards), 170-173
    Gonzales, Steve (editing)
        music, 254
        structure, 253

techniques, 253-256

timing, 254

Haubrich, Frederic (editing software), 208-210

Hill, Robert (editing audio), 313-318

Hirsch, Paul (editing)

animatics, 242

choreography, 241-242

music, 241

software, 243

special effects, 241-242

storyboards, 242

structure, 243

techniques, 244

technology, 242-243

Holland, Carter (editing software), 212-214

Matrox (editing software), 225-227

Townhill, Richard (editing software), 215-216

Ulead Media Studio Pro (editing software), 219-221

intraframes (I-frames), 230-231

intraframe compression, 69

intraframe/temporal compression, 229-230

iris/aperture

correction (sharpness), 125

exposure controls, 120-123

focus controls, 114-115

ITU-BR standards (color correction), 273

J

jacks. *See* connections/cables; output

Japan, 7

JBOD (Just a Bunch of Disks), 87

jitter, troubleshooting, 325

JVC cameras

GR-HD1, 59-60

GY-HD100U, 60-63

JY-HD10U, 59-60

JY-HD10U JVC camera, 59-60

K

Kelvin scale, 145-147

key lights, 155-157

keyframes

2D animations, 352-354

HDV output, 388

keying color (blue/green screens), 339-343

Kona 2 capture cards, 97-98

L

layers. *See* tracks/layers

LCD (Liquid Crystal Display) viewscreens , 37-38

angles, 38

aspect ratios, 175

lights/lighting, 38

lenses, 35-37

adapters, 133

close-ups, 135

controls, 131-137

converters, 133

fish eye, 133-134

telephoto, 134-135

wide-angle, 132-134, 190-191

zoom, 134-135

Lighten composite mode, 351

lights/lighting

3D animations, 365-366

back lights, 124, 157

backgrounds, 157

barn doors, 160-161

blue/green screens, 162-164, 280-281, 340-341

bouncing, 162

brightness, 157

cameras

attaching, 155-156

diffusion, 156

exposure, 115-127

white balance, 130-131

color, 146-147, 162

color correction. *See* color correction

color temperature, 145-147

depth, 162

Eldred, Jody, 150-152

exposure controls. *See also* brightness

aperture/iris, 120-123

back lights, 124

black stretch, 126

brightness, 126

cameras, 115-127

CineFrame, 126-127

CinemaTone, 126
color phase, 125
contrast, 125-126
gain, 122
gamma, 125-126
monitors, 119
overexposure, 124
shadows, 126
sharpness, 125
shutter speed, 117-123
skin tone, 125-126
spot light, 124
television, 119
zebra stripes, 116-117
faces, 149
fill lights, 156-157
fluorescent, 160
fresnel, 159
gain, 122
halogen, 159
hard light, 148
hardware, 158-161
incandescent, 159
Kelvin scale, 145-147
key lights, 155-157
LCD viewscreens, 38
overexposure, 124
overview, 144
reflectors, 162
rim lights, 124, 157
safety, 164
setup, 152-157
shadows, 126, 149
size, 157
soft light, 148-149
spot light, 124
stands, 160-161
techniques, 161-164
three-point, 154-157
vectorscopes, 280-281
white balance, 145-147
    camera controls, 130-131
    color correction, 266
Liquid Crystal Display (LCD) viewscreens , 37-38
    angles, 38

aspect ratios, 175
    lights/lighting, 38
Liquid Edition, 228
live action/storyboards comparison, 171
loading cameras, 103-104
logging (editing), 233-234
    AAF, 234
    EDLs, 234
    scene breaks, 237
    XML, 234
long shots (wide shots), 178
loops, 312-313, 315
Low Pass Filter audio special effects, 303
Low Shelf Filter audio special effects, 303
lubricants (tapes), 45-46
luma, 264-265, 267-269, 275-279, 281. *See also* brightness
Luma composite mode, 352
Lumiere HD
    editing overview, 208-210
    Web site, 210

M

Macintosh, 76-80
macro lenses, 135
Magic Bullet, 283-285, 329
Manfrotto Web site, 183
manual focus controls, 111-115
markers (DVD), 421-424
matchmoving (3D animations), 370-371, 376
materials (3D animations), 364-365
Matrox, 224-227
matte paintings (3D animations), 374-375
Maxon Cinema 4D Web site, 360
media, loading, 103-104
Media Studio Pro
    editing overview, 219-221
    Web site, 220
medium shots, 179
memory
    capturing, 239
    RAM, 71
menus
    cameras, navigating, 104
    DVD authoring, 401-403
metaballs, 364

microphones
    ambient noise, 141
    attaching, 39
    audio, 39-40
    background noise, 138, 141
    boom microphones, 138-139
    controls, 137-141
    headphones, 138
    orientation, 138
    room tone, 141
    shoes, 39
    wind, 138, 141
    wireless microphones, 139-140
mirroring RAIDs, 81
mixers
    audio, 294-297
    HDV, 436
mobile phones (DVD output), 427
modeling 3D animations, 362-364
    Booleans, 363
    curves, 363
    deformers, 363
    image-based modeling, 371-372
    metaballs, 364
    NURBS, 363
    polygons, 362
monitors
    cameras, 105
    color (lights/lighting), 146-147
    color correction, 263-264, 274-277
    exposure, 119
    overview, 93-94
motion tracking (3D animations), 370-371, 376
moving, shooting, 184-196
MPEG
    editing, 228-232
    GOP (editing), 230-231
    HDV output standards, 381-383
    MPEG-2, 382-383
    MPEG-4, 381-382
MPEG-2, 382-383
MPEG-4, 381-382
multiple cameras, 136-137
multiple tracks (audio), 290-296, 320
multiplexing (DVD encoding), 418

Multiply composite mode, 348
music
    composing, 311-312
    editing
        Gonzales, Steve, 254
        Hill, Robert, 313-318
        Hirsch, Paul, 241
    loops, 312-313, 315
    samples, 313
    storyboard compositions, 172
muxing, 418

N
naming
    audio, 315
    DVD encoding, 420
native editing, 10, 232-233
Nattress Film Effects, 286
navigating
    camera menus, 104
    timelines, 245
negative space (compositions), 197
nesting clips, 250
noise (audio)
    ambient noise, 141
    background noise, 138, 141
    editing, 313-314, 318-320
    room tone, 141
    zoom controls, 108
noise reduction (DVD encoding), 419
non-drop frame rates, 8, 235-236
Normal composite mode, 346
Notch audio special effects, 304, 318-319
NTSC timecodes, 235-236
number of shots
    shooting, 202
    storyboards, 168
NURBS modeling, 363

O
oblique shots, 182
offline editing, 239-241
online editing, 239-241
Open HD Web site, 70
operating cameras, 102-103

optical/digital comparison (zoom controls), 110

organic audio, 316-317

organizing tracks (audio), 315, 321

orientation (microphones), 138

Orphanage, Magic Bullet, 283-285, 329

oscilloscopes (color correction), 277-281

output. *See also* connections/cables

    Blu-ray discs, 395-399

    DVD

        encoding. *See* encoding DVD

        formats, 424-428

        mobile phones, 427

        PDAs, 427

        portable devices, 427-428

    DVI, 429-430

    encoding DVD

        artifacts, 419

        audio, 417-418

        bit calculations, 412-413

        bit rates, 419

        brightness, 419

        clips, 413-421

        color, 419

        color correction, 419

        compression, 415-416, 420-421

        contrast, 419

        DVD recorders, 411-412

        fields, 417

        file size, 412, 419

        filters, 419

        hardware, 410-411

        interlaced video, 417

        multiplexing, 418

        muxing, 418

        naming, 420

        noise reduction, 419

        overview, 407-408

        quality, 419

        sequences, 413-421

        settings, 413-421

        software, 409-410

        standards, 416-417

    HD-DVD, 390-394, 399

    HDMI, 429-430

    HDTV, 428-430

    HDV, 11-13

        AVC, 381-382

        bit rates, 386-388, 419

        coding method, 386-387

        compression, 386-387

        constant bit rates, 386-387

        DivX, 390

        DVD-ROMs, 383-384

        exporting, 386

        Flip4Mac, 385-390

        frame rates, 389

        frame size, 389

        frame types, 389

        frames, 388-389

        H.264, 381-382

        input frames, 388

        interlaced video, 389

        keyframes, 388

        MPEG-2, 382-383

        MPEG-4, 381-382

        output frames, 388-389

        overview, 380-381

        progressive scan video, 389

        quality, 387, 419

        standards, 381-383

        variable bit rates, 386-387

        VC-1, 383-384

        Video tab, 386

        Windows Media Video 9, 384-390

    HVD, 399

output frames (HDV), 388-389

overexposure, 124

Overlay composite mode, 349

P

pan and scan shooting, 174

Panasonic cameras, 64

panels (storyboards), 168

panning, 174, 185-187

Particle Illusion Web site, 372

particles (3D animations), 372-373, 377-378

PCs, 76-80

PDAs (DVD output), 427

Peak Limiter audio special effects, 304

peaking (focus controls), 113

Pen tool, 253

people, shooting, 196-202

performance (RAIDs), 80

   controls, 81-82

   FireWire comparison, 80

   hardware, 82

   JBOD, 87

   mirroring, 81

   overview, 80-82

   RAID 0, 82-83, 88

   RAID 1, 83-84, 88

   RAID 10, 89

   RAID 3, 84-85, 88

   RAID 30, 89

   RAID 5, 85-86, 88

   RAID 50, 86-87, 89

   software, 82

P-frames (predicted frames), 230-231

photogrammetry (3D animations), 371-372

Pinnacle Liquid Edition, 228

pixels. *See* aspect ratios

places, shooting, 196-200

playback controls (cameras), 104-105

plug-ins (2D animations), 355-357

point of view, 199

polygons (3D animations), 362

portable devices (output), 427-428

ports. *See* connections/cables; output

post-production

   3D animations, 377

   process overview, 9-13

PoV, 199

power (cameras), 103

predicted frames (P-frames), 230-231

Premiere Pro, 214-216

preparing assets (DVD authoring), 400-401

pre-roll/post-roll shooting, 201

previsualization (storyboards), 168-170

principles (color correction), 266-272

production process, 9-13

profiles (controls), 127-129

program streams, 17

progressive scan video, 324-330, 389

projectors

   Eldred, Jody, 434-435

   HDV, 430-436

   video, 430-436

proxies (3D animations), 377

Q-R

quality

   DVD encoding, 419

   HDV output, 387, 419

RAID 0, 82-83, 88

RAID 1, 83-84, 88

RAID 10, 89

RAID 3, 84-85, 88

RAID 30, 89

RAID 5, 85-86, 88

RAID 50, 86-87, 89

RAIDs (redundant arrays of independent disks), 80

   controls, 81-82

   FireWire comparison, 80

   hardware, 82

   JBOD, 87

   mirroring, 81

   overview, 80-82

   RAID 0, 82-83, 88

   RAID 1, 83-84, 88

   RAID 10, 89

   RAID 3, 84-85, 88

   RAID 30, 89

   RAID 5, 85-86, 88

   RAID 50, 86-87, 89

   software, 82

RAM (random access memory), 71

razor blade (timelines), 252

RCA connections/cables, 40-44

recommendations, editing systems, 76-80

record run timecodes, 236

recording controls, 104

Red Giant Software, Magic Bullet, 283-285, 329

redundant arrays of independent disks. *See* RAIDs

reflectors (lights/lighting), 162

rendering 3D animations, 367-368

resolution. *See also* aspect ratios

   graphics (text), 332

   HDTV (ATSC), 6-8

   HDV, 14-15

   importing, 358

video, 358
reverb audio special effects, 299-300
reverse shots, 198-199
ReVision FieldsKit, 329
RGB color (color correction), 271-273
rim lights, 124, 157
rippling edits, 252
rolling edits, 252
room tone (microphones), 141
rotoscoping, 338
rule of thirds, 175-176
rules
    180 degree rule, 176-177, 202
    rule of thirds, 175-176

S

safe areas (text), 335
safety (lights/lighting), 164
sample rates (audio), 289-290
samples
    color correction, 274
    color samples, 27-28
    music, 313
    sample rates (audio), 289-290
SATA (Serial Advanced Technology Attachment), 74
scan modes
    HDTV (ATSC), 7-8
    HDV, 14-15
scene breaks, 237
schemes (compression), 16-20
scores. *See* music
Screen composite mode, 348-349
screens. *See* aspect ratios; blue/green screens
scripts (DVD authoring), 404
SD (standard definition), 5
SDI (Serial Digital Interface), 92-93
secondary color correction, 282
selective focus controls, 114-115
sensors, 31-35
    Advanced HAD, 32, 35
    CCDs, 31-35
    CMOSs, 31-34
sequences (DVD encoding), 413-421
Serial Advanced Technology Attachment (SATA), 74
Serial Digital Interface (SDI), 92-93

settings
    capturing, 238
    DVD encoding, 413-421
setup (lights/lighting), 152-157
shadows
    exposure controls, 126
    lights/lighting, 149
sharpness, 125
shoes (cameras), 39
shooting
    cameras
        alignment, 197-198
        angles, 181-182, 201-202
        artifacts, 187
        Brown, Garrett, 188-195
        close-ups, 179-180
        dolly shots, 184-185
        dutch shots, 182
        editing, 201-202
        eye lines, 202
        flicker, 187
        height, 182
        high hat shots, 181
        medium shots, 179
        moving, 184-196
        multiple shoots, 136-137
        number of shots, 202
        panning, 174, 185-187
        people, 196-202
        placement, 178-180
        places, 196-200
        pre-roll/post-roll, 201
        shot length, 201
        speed, 187
        stabilization, 37, 187-196
        techniques, 201-202
        tilting, 185-187
        tripods, 182-184, 196
        wide shots, 178
    compositions
        180 degree rule, 176-177, 202
        alignment, 197-198
        animatics, 168, 170
        appearing point, 191-192
        aspect ratios, 173-175

blocking, 171
Bluth, Don, 170-173
camera placement, 178-180
choreography, 171
close-ups, 179-180
edges, 196-197
field of vision, 173
film comparison, 171
full screen video, 174
Goldman, Gary, 170-173
live action comparison, 171
medium shots, 179
music, 172
negative space, 197
number of shots, 168
overview, 166
pan and scan, 174
panels, 168
people, 196-202
places, 196-200
PoV, 199
previsualization, 168-170
reverse shots, 198-199
rule of thirds, 175-176
software, 168-170
storyboards, 166-173, 180
thumbnails, 168
time-lapse, 199-200
timing, 172
wide shots, 178
widescreen, 173-175
HDV, 9
shots. *See* shots
shot length, 201
shot transitions, 129-130
shots
artifacts, 187
close-ups, 179-180
dolly shots, 184-185
dutch shots, 182
flicker, 187
full shots (wide shots), 178
high hat shots, 181
length, 201
long shots (wide shots), 178

medium shots, 179
number of
shooting, 202
storyboards, 168
oblique, 182
panning, 174, 185-187
PoV, 199
reverse shots, 198-199
shooting. *See* shooting
speed, 187
stabilization, 37, 187-196
tilting, 185-187
time-lapse, 199-200
transitions, 129-130
wide shots (wide shots), 178
shutter speed, 117-123
simulations
2D animations, 374
3D animations, 374
film color correction, 282-286
size
files (DVD encoding), 412, 419
frames (HDV output), 389
lights/lighting, 157
screens. *See* aspect ratios
skin tone, 125-126
slideshows (DVD authoring), 403-404
sliding (timelines), 252
slipping (timelines), 252
SMPTE
color correction, 275
timecodes, 235
Web site, 275
soft light, 148-149
Soft Light composite mode, 350
software
2D animations, 355-357
color correction, 283-286
DigiEffects CineLook, 285
Magic Bullet, 283-285
Natress Film Effects, 286
composite modes, 344-352
Add, 346-347
Alpha, 351-352
Darken, 350-351

Difference, 347-348
Hard Light, 349-350
Lighten, 351
Luma, 352
Multiply, 348
Normal, 346
Overlay, 349
Screen, 348-349
Soft Light, 350
Subtract, 347
DVD compression, encoding, 409-410
editing
Adobe Premiere Pro, 214-216
Avid Xpress Pro, 211-214
Canopus Edius, 222-224
Canopus Edius interview, 222-224
Chaimson, Dave, 217-218
Final Cut Express HD, 210-211
Final Cut Pro, 207-210
Haubrich, Frederic, 208-210
Hirsch, Paul, 243
Holland, Carter, 212-214
iMovie HD, 210-211
Lumiere HD, 208-210
Matrox, 224-227
Matrox interview, 225-227
overview, 207
Pinnacle Liquid Edition, 228
Sony Vegas, 216-218
Townhill, Richard, 215-216
Ulead Media Studio Pro, 219-221
graphics (text), 333
RAIDs, 82
storyboards, 168-170
video, de-interlacing, 329-330
Sony
cameras
HDR-FX1, 48-53
HDR-HC1, 54-58
HVR-A1U, 54-58
HVR-Z1U, 48-53, 62-63
decks (HVR-M10U), 58-59
i.Link. *See* FireWire
Vegas, 216-218
sound. *See* audio

soundtracks. *See* music
spatial compression, 229-230
special effects
audio, 314-315
bandpass, 301
compressor/limiter, 301-302
delay, 300-302
echo, 300-301
EQ, 302-303, 314
High Pass Filter, 303
High Shelf Filter, 303
Low Pass Filter, 303
Low Shelf Filter, 303
Notch, 304, 318-319
overview, 297-298
Peak Limiter, 304
reverb, 299-300
Vocal DeEsser, 304
Vocal DePopper, 304
editing (Hirsch, Paul), 241-242
overview, 324
speed
2D animations, 354-355
frame rates. *See* frame rates
RAIDs, 80
controls, 81-82
FireWire comparison, 80
hardware, 82
JBOD, 87
mirroring, 81
overview, 80-82
RAID 0, 82-83, 88
RAID 1, 83-84, 88
RAID 10, 89
RAID 3, 84-85, 88
RAID 30, 89
RAID 5, 85-86, 88
RAID 50, 86-87, 89
software, 82
shooting, 187
zoom controls, 109
spot light, 124
stabilization, 37, 187-196
stacking audio takes, 316-317
standard definition (SD), 5

standards
  DVD encoding, 416-417
  HDTV
    ATSC, 6-8
    Web site, 6
  HDV output, 381-383
    AVC, 381-382
    H.264, 381-382
    MPEG-2, 382-383
    MPEG-4, 381-382
    VC-1, 383-384
  ITU-BR (color correction), 273
stands (lights/lighting), 160-161
stereo, 317-318
stocks (tapes), 44-46
storyboards
  compositions
    animatics, 168, 170
    blocking, 171
    Bluth, Don, 170-173
    choreography, 171
    film comparison, 171
    Goldman, Gary, 170-173
    live action comparison, 171
    music, 172
    number of shots, 168
    panels, 168
    previsualization, 168-170
    shooting, 166-173, 180
    software, 168-170
    thumbnails, 168
    timing, 172
  editing (Hirsch, Paul), 242
streaming data, 17
structure, editing
  Gonzales, Steve, 253
  Hirsch, Paul, 243
Studio Artist Web site, 358
Subtract composite mode, 347
subtractive color, 271-272
super oxidation (tapes), 45
synchronizing
  audio, 292-293
  multiple cameras, 136-137
Synthetik Studio Artist Web site, 358

SynthEyes Web site, 370
systems. *See* editing systems

T

tails (pre-roll/post-roll shooting), 201
takes (stacking audio), 316-317
tape to tape color correction, 263
tapes
  cameras, loading, 103-104
  stocks
    AME II, 45
    HDV, 44-46
    lubricants, 45-46
    super oxidation, 45
  tape to tape color correction, 263
techniques
  3D animations, 369-374, 377
  audio
    editing, 320-321
    Emrich, Brian, 305-311
  compositing (blue/green screens), 342-343
  editing, 244-248, 253-256
    audio, 320-321
    Gonzales, Steve, 253-256
    Hirsch, Paul, 244
  lights/lighting, 161-164
  shooting, 201-202
technology, editing, 242-243
telephoto lenses, 134-135
television
  exposure controls, 119
  HDTV. *See* HDTV
temperature
  color temperature. *See* color temperature
  Kelvin scale, 145-147
temporal compression, 229-230
testing (DVD authoring), 404-406
text (graphics), 332-335
  aspect ratios, 332-333
  color, 334
  fonts, 332
  frames, 335
  importing, 333-334
  resolution, 332
  safe areas, 335

software, 333
tracks/layers, 333-334
textures (3D animations), 364-365
three-point light, 154-157
thumbnails (storyboards), 168
tilting cameras, 185-187
time remapping (timelines), 252
timecodes
    black and code, 235
    breaks, 235
    drop frame rates, 8, 235-236
    free run, 136-137, 236
    non-drop frame rates, 8, 235-236
    NTSC, 235-236
    record run, 236
    SMPTE, 235
time-lapse shooting, 199-200
Timelines
    audio, 291-293
    clips
        editing, 245-247, 250-253
        Pen tool, 253
        razor blade, 252
        rippling edits, 252
        rolling edits, 252
        sliding, 252
        slipping, 252
        time remapping, 252
    in/out points, 245-246
    navigating, 245
    tools, 250-253
timing
    editing, 254
    storyboards, 172
titles. *See* text
tools (timelines), 250-253
Townhill, Richard, 215-216
tracking
    3D animations, 370-371, 376
    panning, 174, 185-187
tracks/layers
    audio editing, 291-292
        cutting/pasting, 321
        multiple, 320
        organizing, 315, 321

clips, 248-250
compositing. *See* compositing
DVD authoring, 403-404
graphics (text), 333-334
transfer modes. *See* composite modes
transferring HDV to film, 437-441
transitions
    audio, 294, 320
    clips, 256-257
    shots, 129-130
transport streams, 17
Trapcode Web site, 356, 372
tripods, 182-184, 196
troubleshooting
    capturing, 238-239
    video jitter, 325
Turbo Squid Web site, 365
tutorials, Web sites, 5
types, cameras, 30-31

U
UDF (Universal Disc Format), 406
Ulead Media Studio Pro
    editing overview, 219-221
    editing software interview, 219-221
    Web site, 220
unbalanced connections/cables, 42-43
uncompressed editing, 247-248
updates, Web sites, 5

V
variable bit rates, 386-387
Varizoom Web site, 109
VC-1 HDV output standard, 383-384
vectorscopes, 279-281
Vegas, 216-218
video
    3D animations, 369-372
    analog video, 12-13
    de-interlacing, 327-330
    DV (digital video)
        analog video comparison, 12-13
        generation loss, 12-13
        HDV comparison, 20
    full screen video, 174

graphics cards, 74-76
HD. *See* HD
interlaced, 324-330
   DVD encoding, 417
   HDV output (frames), 389
jitter, 325
progressive scan, 324-330
projectors, 430-436
widescreen compositions
   aspect ratios, 173-175
   field of vision, 173
   full screen video, 174
   pan and scan, 174
   shooting, 173-175
video scopes (color correction), 264-265, 277-281
Video tab, 386
viewfinders, 37-38
   aspect ratios, 175
   black-and-white focus controls, 114
viewscreens (LCD), 37-38
   angles, 38
   aspect ratios, 175
   lights/lighting, 38
Vocal DeEsser, 304
Vocal DePopper, 304
volume, 294
VU meters, 295

W

waveforms (color correction), 264, 277-279
Web sites
   AJA Kona 2, 98
   Andersson Technologies, 370
   ATSC, 6
   BeachTek, 41
   Blackmagic Design DeckLink HD, 96
   Brown, Garrett, 189
   Century Optics, 131
   Coreaudiovisual, 376
   Creative Cow, 374
   Cycore FX, 357
   Debevec, Paul, 366
   DigiEffects, 329
   DVFilm Maker, 329
   Fahs, Chad, 5

Focus Enhancements, 103
Grizzly Pro, 136-137
HDR Shop, 366
HDTV standards, 6
HDV, 14
HDV Film Making, 5
Hoodman, 38
Lumiere HD, 210
Magic Bullet, 329
Manfrotto, 183
Maxon Cinema 4D, 360
Nattress, 286
Open HD, 70
Particle Illusion, 372
ReVision FieldsKit, 329
SMPTE, 275
Synthetik Studio Artist, 358
SynthEyes, 370
Trapcode, 356, 372
Turbo Squid, 365
tutorials, 5
Ulead Media Studio Pro, 220
updates, 5
Varizoom, 109
Wondertouch, 372
white balance
   camera controls, 130-131
   color correction, 266
   lights/lighting, 145-147
whiteness, 124
wide-angle lenses, 132-134, 190-191
wide shots, 178
widescreen compositions
   aspect ratios, 173-175
   field of vision, 173
   full screen video, 174
   pan and scan, 174
   shooting, 173-175
wind, microphones, 138, 141
Windows Media Video (WMV) 9, 384-390
wireless microphones, 139-140
Wondertouch Web site, 372
workflow (color correction), 262-266

X-Z

XLR connections/cables, 40-44

XML (Extensible Markup Language), 234

Xpress Pro, 211-214

Y'CbCr color, 273

zebra stripes

    color correction, 281

    exposure controls, 116-117

zoom controls, 106-110

    controls, 109

    digital/optical comparison, 110

    focus. *See* focus

    lenses, 134-135

    noise, 108

    shot transitions, 129-130

    speed, 109